CHAN INSIGHTS AND OVERSIGHTS

CHAN INSIGHTS AND OVERSIGHTS

AN EPISTEMOLOGICAL CRITIQUE
OF THE CHAN TRADITION

BERNARD FAURE

PRINCETON UNIVERSITY PRESS

PRINCETON, NEW JERSEY

Copyright © 1993 by Princeton University Press
Published by Princeton University Press, 41 William Street,
Princeton, New Jersey 08540
In the United Kingdom: Princeton University Press, Chichester, West Sussex

Library of Congress Cataloging-in-Publication Data
Faure, Bernard.
Chan insights and oversights: an epistemological critique of the Chan tradition /
Bernard Faure.
p.   cm.
ISBN 0-691-06948-4
ISBN 0-691-02902-4 (pbk.)
1. Knowledge, Theory of (Buddhism).   2. Hermeneutics—Religious aspects—Zen
Buddhism.   3. Zen Buddhism—Study and teaching.   4. Zen Buddhism—Doctrines.
I. Title.

BQ4440.F38   1993   294.3—dc20   92-37150

This book has been composed in Linotron Sabon

Princeton University Press books are printed
on acid-free paper, and meet the guidelines for
permanence and durability of the Committee on
Production Guidelines for Book Longevity
of the Council on Library Resources

Second printing, and first paperback printing, 1996

Printed in the United States of America by Princeton Academic Press

10   9   8   7   6   5   4   3   2

For Anna Seidel

CONTENTS

ACKNOWLEDGMENTS

THE PRESENT BOOK was originally conceived as a companion volume to *The Rhetoric of Immediacy* (Princeton, 1991). Research was permitted by grants from the Japan Foundation, the Social Science Research Council, the Society for the Humanities at Cornell, and the Center for East Asian Studies at Stanford.

Among friends who have read the manuscript and offered corrections and suggestions, special thanks go to Wendi Adamek, Neil McMullin, John Kieschnick, and Kuo Li-ying. Carl Bielefeldt has helped me in countless other ways. I also received invaluable stimulation from graduate students at Cornell and Stanford. Louis Frédéric helped me solve the technical problems at the time of printing out the manuscript. Finally, I have greatly benefited from the help of Margaret Case and Molan Chun Goldstein at Princeton University Press, and my copyeditor, Lisa Nowak Jerry.

A portion of chapter 4 appeared under the title "Bodhidharma as Textual and Religious Paradigm" in *History of Religions* 25, no. 3 (1986): 187–198. (© 1986 by The University of Chicago. All rights reserved.) An earlier version of chapter 5 appeared under the title "Space and Place in Chinese Religions" in the same journal, 26, no. 4 (1987): 337–356. (© 1987 by The University of Chicago. All rights reserved.)

Being in France during the final revision of the manuscript, I was unable to check the English translations of a number of the works quoted. I have therefore given in the bibliography both the French and the English editions, and, depending on circumstances, referred to the former or the latter in the text and footnotes.

ABBREVIATIONS

BEFEO   *Bulletin de l'Ecole Française d'Extrême-Orient*. Paris: Ecole
          Française d'Extrême-Orient.

DNBZ   *Dai Nihon bukkyō zensho*. Takakusu Junjirō et al. , eds.
          Tokyo: Yūseidō, 1913–1922. Reprint Suzuki gakujutsu
          zaidan, ed. Tokyo: Kōdansha, 1970–1973. 100 vols.

DZ   *Daozang [Zhengtong daozang*, 1445]. Including the *Wanli xu*
          daozang [1607]. 1,120 vols. Shanghai: Commercial Press,
          1923–1926. Reprint Taibei: Yiwen yinshuguan, 1962. 60
          vols.

EOEO   *Extrême-Orient, Extrême-Occident.*

HJAS   *Harvard Journal of Asiatic Studies.*

IBK   *Indogaku bukkyōgaku kenkyū* [Journal of Indian and Bud-
          dhist Studies].

JAOS   *Journal of the American Oriental Society.*

QTW   *Qinding Quan Tang wen* [1814]. Dong Gao (1740–1818) et
          al., eds. Taibei: Huaiwen shuju, 1961.

SKSLHB   *Shike shiliao xinbian*. 30 vols. Taibei: Xinwen feng.

SZ   *Sōtōshū zensho*. Sōtōshū zensho kankōkai, ed. , 1229–1935.
          Reedition Tokyo: Sōtōshū shūmuchō, 1970–1973. 18 vols.

T.   Taishō shinshū daizōkyō. Takakusu Junjirō and Watanabe
          Kaigyoku, eds. Tokyo: Taishō issaikyō kankōkai, 1924–
          1932. 100 vols.

ZZ   *Dai Nihon zokuzōkyō*. Nakano Tatsue, ed. Kyoto: Zōkyō
          shoin, 1905–1912. 150 vols. Reprint Taibei: Xinwenfeng,
          1968–1970.

CHAN INSIGHTS AND OVERSIGHTS

INTRODUCTION

> You will find contradictions here. Since no thinking can take
> place without them, and we are not in geometry,
> their statistical presence is almost *de rigueur*.
> (Paul Valéry, *Tel Quel*)

M UCH HAS BEEN written about Zen Buddhism over the past
decades. The present book, however, does not belong to the
plethoric genre of "Zen mysticism." It is an analysis of the
conditions of possibility of a certain type of discourse labeled Chan/Zen
and of the various constraints that have informed it. Its main purposes are
to present a "topology" of Chan—that is, an analysis of Chan *topoi* and
categories—and to open the field of Chan/Zen studies to the questions
raised in other academic disciplines in the hope of bringing Chan/Zen
closer to the mainstream of Western thought. I am primarily interested in
Chan/Zen ideologies; the term *ideology* is understood both in the general
sense of a system of representations and in the Althusserian sense of a
teaching that presents an inverted image of its relationships with reality.[1]

Why use two names—Chan and Zen—when one would seem to suffice?
As it is well known, Zen is the Japanese pronunciation of the Chinese
character Chan (itself the transcription of the Sanskrit *dhyāna*), and Japanese Zen developed out of the Chinese tradition known as Chan Buddhism. There is undeniably a continuity between Chan and Zen, and most
scholars consider the two terms interchangeable. However, there are many
historical, cultural, and doctrinal differences as well, and these differences
are not merely superficial: they would surely affect the "essence" of Zen, if
this term had any referent. Two basic assumptions of this book are that
there is no such "essence" and that discontinuities are, when one focuses
on them, at least as obvious as continuity. True, Zen *succeeded* historically
to Chan, but what did it actually *inherit* from it? Has it not, rather, thrived
in areas left uncharted by "early" and "classical" Chan? Chan and Zen are
not monolithic entities, but fluid, ever-changing networks; or perhaps one
might compare them to those "duck-rabbit" images analyzed by Ludwig
Wittgenstein, in which, depending on one's viewpoint, a certain pattern

---

[1] Georges Duby (quoting Louis Althusser) defines ideology as "a system (possessing its
own logic and rigor) of representations (images, myths, ideas or concepts depending on the
cases) endowed with an existence and a historical role within a given society" (Duby 1974,
149). For Althusser, however, ideology also refers to "the imaginary representation of the
subject's relationship to his or her real conditions of existence" (Althusser 1972, 162)

(duck) emerges at the detriment of the other (rabbit) (Wittgenstein 1958, 194e). Therefore, if I chose to lay emphasis on certain aspects of the Chan tradition to the detriment of others, it is not to deny the importance of the latter, but to counterbalance the dominant "spiritual" and philosophical interpretations of Zen.

The Chan tradition first acquired its legitimacy as a narrative about patriarchs, and, although some points of the narrative have been questioned by historians, the ideological function of the narrative itself has rarely been scrutinized. There is no point in repeating this process and trying to turn Chan history into a "seamless stūpa" (J. *muhōtō*)—a symbol of death and perfection often used in Chan/Zen literature. The homogeneity of the Zen tradition cannot be taken at face value. The terms Chan and Zen themselves cover at times vastly different religious or intellectual trends, some of which appear and reappear under various guises, behind entirely different sectarian affiliations. This alone should alert us to the fact that the sectarian categories used and abused by most Chan/Zen scholars may not be the most appropriate means to understand the actual evolution (and devolution) of these trends.

The field of Chan and Zen studies has been particularly thriving in Japan since the war, and the area seems to be gaining some recognition in Western scholarship too, despite the lingering associations of Zen with the counterculture pervasive during the 1960's. The main factors for this development have been the discovery of the Dunhuang library at the turn of the century and its gradual exploitation. The pionneering contributions of Asian scholars such as Hu Shih and Yanagida Seizan, based on the discovery of new Chan manuscripts, has permitted a drastic rewriting of early Chan history. Now that the initial rush has come to an end and that a new Chan corpus has emerged, the time has come to reconsider the various presuppositions that have accompanied the constitution of Chan/Zen as sectarian tradition(s) and as object(s) of study.

The first task is to question the validity of the traditional (Chan and scholarly) debates. This may enable us to shift our focus from areas where there is already a proliferation of discourse to areas that have remained for various reasons relatively neglected by traditional scholarship. In this process, the historical approach needs to be supplemented by other methodologies such as sociology, anthropology, or literary criticism. It is clear, however, that each methodological approach creates its own object and must in turn be questioned, on not only methodological grounds but also hermeneutical and epistemological grounds. Above all, we must always keep in mind that each approach, however "objective" it claims to be, has certain ideological implications and fulfills specific functions within the academic field. Even if Pierre Bourdieu rightly urges us to "objectify the objectification itself" and to clarify the position of the writer (Bourdieu

1980, 51–70), this does not entail, as he seems to believe, that doing so will secure a much vaunted "scientificity." Most social scientists remain dependent on a "communicative model" of scholarship when they believe that, by reintegrating the subjectivity of the observer as a parameter in the analysis, they will eventually reach objectivity. More generally, social scientists tend to forget the compulsive nature of their search for "scientificity"; thus, they downplay the performative or rhetorical nature of their discourse and the semiotic function of their scientific apparatus. The most reflexive and "dialogical" account can be just as staged and performative as traditional "objective" scholarship (see Rabinow 1986, 246).

However that may be, Chan scholarship, despite its high level of philological expertise, has not yet reached the level of methodological sophistication of disciplines such as anthropology or literary criticism and remains in most cases narrowly historical or hermeneutical. Before examining in chapter 3 the main characteristics and limitations of Sino-Japanese Chan historiography, I want to focus here on the various epistemological and hermeneutical issues that face us when we deal with religious and intellectual traditions like Chan/Zen. One starting point is the acknowledgment of the so-called hermeneutic circle and the realization that we are living in what Hans-Georg Gadamer has labeled "effective history" (see Heidegger 1962, 194–195; Gadamer 1982, 267–274). Thus, our understanding of Chan and Zen is informed by not only Sino-Japanese historiography (to the extent that we continue to rely on it), but also the entire Orientalist tradition that gave rise to the various disciplines that define the space of Chan/Zen studies in our culture—and in particular by the circumstances of the Western reception of Buddhism. For this reason, the general questions raised by Edward Said in his ground-breaking work, *Orientalism*, are especially relevant for the field of Chan/Zen studies (see Said 1979).

CHAN AS SECONDARY ORIENTALISM

Said's denunciation of the universalist tendencies of Orientalism is an attempt to reveal the contradictions of any discourse that represses its own historicity. However, his criticism cannot avoid the same pitfalls—nor can any criticism for that matter. For example, while Said sees Western culture as an undifferentiated whole, a negative "essence" that cannot possibly be redeemed, he conspicuously downplays, and sometimes simply forgets, the recurrence of similar negative features in non-Western discourses.

Although Said is interested primarily in the Orientalist discourse on the Near East and Islam, his argument remains valid in the case of the "Far East": India and China in particular had become the objects of a similar

Orientalist discourse—a discourse to which we return in chapter 1, perhaps best summarized in Hegel's judgment that China and India are not in full possession of what they say. (Hegel 1953, 23, 86–87). These Orientalist assumptions are still common, even in the more nuanced thinking of those who, like Maurice Merleau-Ponty, believe that "Western philosophy can learn [from India and China] to rediscover the relationship to being and the initial option that gave it birth, and to estimate the possibilities we have shut ourselves off from in becoming 'Westerners' and perhaps to reopen them" (Merleau-Ponty 1964b, 139).

While Merleau-Ponty envisions a larger rationality that might encompass East and West, most people who look toward Eastern religions (and Zen in particular) are convinced of the failure of rationality and are searching for an "authenticity" that the West has supposedly lost. For them, Asia has become the source of all wisdom, and Europe has lost possession of its own language. This inversion of the signs of traditional Orientalist discourse, which characterizes the changes in the Western perception of Zen, also characterizes some trends of anthropological discourse. However, it would be an error to believe that much has changed: in all cases, whether the Oriental or primitive Other is caricatured or idealized, the ethnocentric and Orientalist premises of Western discourse are similar.

Although Said's criticism of Orientalism was long overdue, its radicalism is not only in some respects a case of reverse ethnocentrism, but it also proves counterproductive by both forgetting that even the most blatantly Orientalist approach might yield some valuable insights and failing to recognize that the post-Orientalist vision has its own blind spots. To paraphrase the Japanese Zen master Dōgen (1200–1253), "When one side is clarified, one side is obscured." Accordingly, one usually privileges a certain vision that remains, just like the opposite vision it condemns, largely ideological. Said is not sufficiently sensitive to the reasons that prevented earlier scholars, who were not always simply agents of Western imperialism, from escaping the trap of Orientalist categories. He therefore fails to question the sociohistorical and epistemological changes that have allowed him (and us, dwarves sitting on the shoulders of Orientalist giants) to perceive this trap. By denying all earlier attempts, within the framework of Orientalism, to question Orientalist values, Said forgets to acknowledge his own indebtedness to this tradition and the epistemological privilege that made his own vision possible. In other words, Said paradoxically shows us how easy it is to fall into methodological scapegoatism:[2] in condemning individuals for failures that are ultimately owing to

[2] I borrow this term from Dominick LaCapra, who defines it as "the self-purifying projection of everything one opposes (but surreptitiously shares) onto an out-group that is perceived in excessively homogeneous and self-serving terms" (LaCapra 1988, 681)

epistemological constraints,[3] we tend to forget, just as the Orientalists did, that our vision is not entirely our own, that it is grounded in a specific time and space. Now, from any given vantage point there may be varying degrees of perceptiveness. Thus, some Orientalisms are definitely better than others, as may also be the case with some "post-Orientalisms." As Arthur Lovejoy said, "the adequate record of even the confusions of our forebears may help, not only to clarify those confusions, but to engender a salutary doubt whether we are wholly immune from different but equally great confusions" (quoted in Boon 1982, 27). There is no pure and definitive epistemological break in the field of Chan studies, and the Chan tradition is a good example of the way epistemological awareness can be reappropriated for rhetorical and ideological purposes. Despite stylistic changes, the cluster of oppositions characteristic of classical Orientalism can be found at work in recent Western writings on Chan/Zen. It may well be that one cannot leave frontally the Orientalist discourse, any more than the closure of Western metaphysics from which it derives.[4] Orientalism cannot simply be rejected once and for all, for such a denial would merely replicate it. We admit the premises of ethnocentrism and the prevalence of Western rationality even when we denounce their imperialism. Let us keep in mind that, to quote Jacques Derrida, "each time that ethnocentrism is precipitately and ostentatiously reversed, some effort silently hides behind all the spectacular effects to consolidate an inside and to draw from it some domestic benefit" (Derrida 1974, 80). Perhaps we cannot entirely escape this predicament, or this temptation, any more than we can transcend the limits of our discourse; but we can at least take into account these performative and transferential elements of any scholarship, including ours.

One might also argue that the "genealogical flaw" denounced by Said—that is, the historical connection between the emergence of Orientalism as a discipline and the rise of Western imperialism—is not irremediable. After all, the Orientalist's predicament is merely an exotic variant of the hermeneutic circle, and we know since Heidegger that this "circle" is a prerequisite of understanding, rather than its denial.[5] Any attempt to understand another person or tradition offers a similar challenge. Elaborating on

[3] Although I (naturally and rhetorically) include myself in this collective pronoun, I want to emphasize that I am not concerned here with Said *as an individual*, but rather with the discursive position he represents.

[4] On the impossibility of frontally exiting the closure of metaphysical discourse, see Derrida 1972b. The collusion between Western metaphysics and Orientalism may be illustrated by the fact that a paradigmatic Orientalist like Jules Barthélémy Saint-Hilaire, a disciple of Eugène Burnouf and the author of a book that was to influence heavily the Western interpretation of *nirvāṇa*, was considered by his contemporaries to be one of the finest specialists on Aristotle (Barthélémy Saint-Hilaire 1862).

[5] According to Heidegger, "What is decisive is not to get out of the circle but to come into it the right way" (Heidegger 1962, 194–195).

Heidegger's insight, Hans-Georg Gadamer has for instance explored the positive aspects of prejudice (Gadamer 1982, 238–253). Whereas Said tends to find his models of "post-Orientalism" among non-Western scholars, I would like on the contrary to advocate the need of a specifically Western approach to Chan/Zen—one that would try to avoid the traps of both Orientalism and "post-Orientalism," while preserving their insights. Despite (or because of) its attempt to remain faithful to an "original" tradition, the narrowly hermeneutical approach is likely to fail given its cultural, spatial, and epistemological gaps. An alternative is the performative approach, which, while remaining aware that it reinterprets a given text in the light of its own limited, "localized," understanding, is not afraid to use it rhetorically to produce a new discourse. This approach may paradoxically remain more faithful to a tradition like Chan, characterized among other things by a shift away from scholastic commentary toward a kind of rhetoric—illustrated for instance in the "Recorded Sayings" genre (Ch. *yulu*). This is not to say that all interpretations or applications are possible or equally correct, as the most radical interpreters of "deconstruction"—against Derrida himself—would have us believe (see Staten 1984, 122). The rhetorical freedom that allows us to take some liberties with a textual tradition must derive from a long acquaintance with it, from having gone many times around the hermeneutic circle.

Intended for a Western audience, Said's discourse has to acknowledge in fact what it denies in theory: the prevalence of Western categories, deriving from the necessity to translate everything into the language of Western philosophy. Because of this, his criticism of Orientalism remains a product of Western discourse, and we still need to think in which kind of space this discourse is possible. There is probably no way for Westerners to understand Asian religions from a purely traditional Indian, Chinese, or Japanese perspective, but perhaps is there no need either to do so. As Mikhail Bakhtin argued, "exotopy," or more simply outsideness, is a powerful factor in understanding another culture, as long as it does not claim any transcendental privilege (see Todorov 1984, 109; Bakhtin 1986, 7).

It is precisely this privilege that Christian missionaries in China and Japan failed to relinquish when they spoke about Buddhism; but the same failure is found in such "na(t)ive" exponents of Zen as D. T. Suzuki, and it would perhaps be hard to decide which version of Zen, the negative or the idealized, is most misleading. Even if the degree of reductionism is not quite the same in both cases, both interpretations share responsibility for the strange predicament in which Westerners who approach Chan/Zen find themselves: they are unable to consider it a serious intellectual system, for the constraints of Western discourse on Zen cause them to either devaluate it as an Eastern form of either "natural mysticism" or "quietism" or to idealize it as a wonderfully exotic Dharma. In this sense, Zen can be seen as a typical example of "secondary Orientalism," a stereotype concocted as much by the Japanese themselves as by Westerners.

THE CULTURAL "ENCOUNTER DIALOGUE"

Orientalism is but one historical variety of larger epistemological issues, that of the West's encounter with other cultures and of its tendency to disparage and/or idealize them. In Marc Augé's words: "What appears to be an anti-ethnocentrism is in fact a constant of our literary and philosophical tradition, and turns out to be, in the last analysis, one of the most imperialist of ethnocentrisms" (Augé 1982, 11). Both the ethnocentric and anti-ethnocentric extremes arise from the same root, the tendency to make absolute the differences among cultures and traditions.

Although the racial and sociopolitical distinctions, denounced by Said, to the mutual understanding of cultures, are the most damaging, cultural differences also derive from deeper epistemological choices made by various cultures in regard to either writing and literacy or their formulation of the notions time and of self. Much work has been done recently in anthropology on these epistemological issues: Walter Ong and Jack Goody, among others, have described the epistemological divide created by the technology of writing; Johannes Fabian has explored the implications of the time models used by the anthropologists and how they affect our understanding of other cultures; Louis Dumont has questioned the validity of Western individualistic categories for attempting to understand holistic, hierarchical societies. I address these epistemological questions in the second part of the book and consider in some detail the impact of language, writing, space, time, and subjectivity on the perception (or construction) of Chan.

This perception has also been informed by various notions or "white metaphors" such as "tradition." The term itself implies that there are things to be transmitted, *tradita*, that there is a continuity, an orthodoxy, and that departures from it lead to heterodoxy, or even worse, heresy. Admittedly, one can find within Chan a tradition to which these notions may apply. But what about this other "tradition" whose representatives claim that, because there is no possible representation of truth, there is nothing to transmit, no *traditum*; in other words, that there is paradoxically no Chan tradition, only departures from it? How are we to do justice to such "heterology" and to make room for this nomadic or "interstitial" thinking within our historical or philosophical discourse, a discourse whose terminology, while raising a host of purely academic questions, already negates this heterology by reducing it to the homology of an unchanging tradition?

As Michel Foucault has shown, tradition plays the role of a master narrative that controls the proliferation of discourse (see Foucault 1972). The historical narrative tends to reproduce the homogenizing effects of the traditional account by reinforcing its linearity even when it would seem to question its content. As a result, the heterogeneity or multivocality of the tradition—its tensions and divergences—is silenced. Even when they claim to be critical, scholarly writings about tradition turn out to be in league with the tradition they describe. To avoid condoning this ideological connivance, and to allow the repressed areas of Chan discourse to re-emerge, these writings must themselves become multivocal and nonlinear, aware of the powerful effects of their own rhetoricity.

In their manifesto against another orthodoxy, psychoanalysis, Gilles Deleuze and Félix Guattari argue that one should try to avoid organizing, stabilizing, and neutralizing multiplicities according to one's own axes of meaning (Deleuze and Guattari 1983, 40). Although the approach they advocate is a powerful instrument for deconstructing or driving a critical wedge into an ideological discourse like that of Chan, the utterly decentered and noninterpretive writing that it calls for would perhaps prove unreadable. I want to retain their metaphorical use of the *rhizome*, a metaphor particularly helpful to deconstruct the treelike structure of Chan genealogies and the traditional model of textual influences—and one that may enable us to unsettle the structure of a text or of a tradition without passing entirely beyond textuality.[6] Nevertheless, if we want to keep in mind the relationship—and also the tension—between the levels of practice and of representation, we cannot simply dismiss the traditional view as purely ideological; on the contrary we need to take seriously into account the tradition's attempts to structure its own multiplicity.

Comparison, Counterpoint, Intertwining

One stylistic effect of the rhizome model on my own writing may be the intrusion of a Western terminology in the midst of Chan discourse, and conversely. Although I often refer to Western thinkers in this study of Chan/Zen, my purpose is not to engage in a style exercise in comparative philosophy. My task remains comparative insofar as I believe, with

[6] Orientalist models can be found even in Deleuze/Guattari's text, for example, when they rhetorically ask: "Isn't there in the East . . . a kind of rhizomatic model that contrasts in every respect with the Western model of the tree?" (Deleuze and Guattari 1983, 41). Despite a quick disclaimer ("Of course it's too easy to present the Orient as rhizome and immanence") (ibid., 44), they go on to affirm that "the tree of Buddha itself becomes a rhizome" (ibid.). This may be true at the level of practice, where rhizomatic influences flourished, but certainly not at the level of representations, where treelike genealogies dominated the Buddhist (and particularly the Chan) tradition.

Jonathan Z. Smith, that "the findings in one field should be of some relevance to scholars in other fields" (Smith 1982, 19–52). My aim, however, is not to compare the ideas of Western philosophers with those of Chinese or Japanese Buddhists on the basis of superficial terminological resemblances; it is rather to intertwine and cross-graft these various types of discourse, in the hope that they might enhance each other. I try to point out the recurrence of similar discursive strategies in various traditions, echoes, and counterpoints that come less from a doctrinal similitude than from their rhetorical function. The obvious problem here is that of the translation, or perhaps better the hybridization, of discourses based on different linguistic protocols: the so-called "theory," produced by modern and mainly Western scholars, remains prevalent in the humanities and the social sciences, and philologically minded history is still the dominant methodology in traditional Buddhology, Sinology, and Japanology. My attempt to mediate between these discourses is somewhat of a Buddhist *upāya*, a kind of (un)skillful means to encourage both Western adepts of theory to read Buddhist texts and Orientalists to reflect on the relevance of theory for their fields. Obviously, the position espoused here involves the risk of attracting crossfire criticism from both orthodoxies, but this risk may be compensated by the advantages (or simply the pleasure) of blurring the genres.

The book is divided into two parts. The first part (chapters 1 to 4), deals with methodological issues, the second (chapters 5 to 9) with epistemological issues. Chapter 1 retraces the history of the reception of Chan/Zen in the West through Christian missionaries and the emergence of notions like mysticism and quietism, which came to characterize Zen. Chapter 2 examines what we could call the "Suzuki effect," that is, the influence exerted by D. T. Suzuki and his epigones on the Western understanding of Zen. Chapter 3 critically examines the models that have dominated Chinese and Japanese historiography. Chapter 4 deals with alternative methodologies, namely structuralism and hermeneutics, and argues for a performative approach that takes into account the rhetoricity of Chan. Chapter 5 describes the emergence of Chan as a processus of "spatialization of thought" and examines the different spatial conceptions that coexisted within Chan and within other religious trends. Chapter 6 applies a similar approach to the Chan/Zen notion(s) of time. Chapter 7 returns to the question of performativity through a study of Chan conceptions of language. Chapter 8 tries to read Chan alternatively as oral and written discourse and to see how these heuristic "readings" affect our interpretation of Chan "recorded sayings." Chapter 9 takes up the question of Chan individualism and examines how Western categories of subjectivity have informed or deformed our understanding of the Chan/Zen tradition.

PART ONE

Chapter One

CHAN/ZEN IN THE WESTERN IMAGINATION

> "But China obscures the issue," you say. And I reply: "China
> obscures the issue but there is light to be found. Look for it."
> (Pascal, *Pensées*)

WESTERN attitudes toward Chinese and Japanese religions were formed largely from the descriptions given by Christian missionaries to those countries. Earlier accounts provided by travelers, such as Marco Polo, John of Montecorvino, Odoric of Pordenone, and others, were too vague and never mentioned the Buddhist sects as such (Demiéville 1964). So misleading, for instance, was Marco Polo's description of Cathay that it took some fifteen years for the Jesuit missionary Matteo Ricci (1552–1610) to realize that this empire was none other than China.

MISSIONARY ACCOUNTS

The first mention of Chan appears in Ricci's journals, while Japanese Zen is discussed in the letters of Francis Xavier (1506–1552). The images one gets from these accounts are strikingly different; they reflect not only the idiosyncrasies of the two Jesuits but also the different roles played by Buddhism in Chinese and Japanese societies. Whereas the Buddhist tradition in China, and Chan in particular, had been largely assimilated by popular religion, the Zen sect in Japan, under the system of the so-called Five Mountains, remained associated with the ruling class and dominated intellectual discourse. As another Jesuit, Alessandro Valignano (1539–1606), wrote in 1583, whereas in Japan "bonzes are of the first rank," in China "they are cudgeled at every step" (quoted in Demiéville 1967, 95).

The Zen sect had been favored by the Ashikaga shogunate and had, during the Ashikaga (Muromachi) and the earlier Kamakura periods, supervised commercial and cultural relations with China through the famous *Tenryūbune* (Tenryūji ships) sponsored by the Tenryūji branch of the Rinzai school in Kyoto. Zen temples played an important cultural role with their schools, the so-called *terakoya*, and they controlled the celebrated Ashikaga College (referred to by Xavier as the "University of Bando"), a major center for classical Chinese learning. At the beginning of the

Tokugawa period, the temples still had important administrative and diplomatic privileges, for instance in the issuing of passports (Boxer 1951, 262). Only later in that period did Zen suffer a setback owing to the rising tide of Confucian orthodoxy. Nevertheless, the generally accepted theory of a decline of Buddhism under the Tokugawa must be revised, for it is the result of an unquestioned teleological scheme that flies in the face of fact.

The Jesuits in Japan

The first encounter with Chan/Zen took place in Japan, where Francis Xavier arrived in August 1549. Xavier's stay in Japan was relatively short, and he had to rely in the beginning on the poor information provided by the Japanese convert Yajirō, who spoke some Portuguese.[1] In contrast to Ricci's, Xavier's judgment reflects the sociopolitical importance of Buddhism in Japanese society prior to the anti-Buddhist repression of 1571, as well as the strong impressions left by his first encounters with Zen masters. Although Xavier and his confreres were puzzled by the many similarities between Buddhism and Christianity and first interpreted them as proof of a past knowledge, obscured in time, of Christian teachings, they eventually attributed them to the work of the devil (Schurhammer 1982, 224).

Xavier had mixed feelings for Zen. His first reaction was negative: "Among the nine sects, there is one which maintains that the souls of men are mortal like that of beasts. . . . The followers of this sect are evil. They were impatient when they heard us say that there is a hell."[2] However, Xavier's respect for Zen increased after his encounter with the abbot of the Fukushōji, "Ninxit" (Ninjitsu, d.1556), whom he described:

> I spoke many times with some of the most learned of these, especially with one to whom all in these parts are greatly attached, both because of his learning, life,

[1] This is how, for example, kōan practice was described to Xavier by Yajirō: "Pablo de Santa Fee, the Japanese, our companion, told me one thing which consoled me much; and what he told me is that in that monastery of his land [the Fukushōji, a Sōtō Zen monastery in Kagoshima], where there are many fradres and a school, they have among them a practice of meditating which is as follows: He who has charge of the house, their superior, who is the most learned, calls them all together and addresses them in the manner of a sermon; and then he says to each one of them that they should meditate for the space of an hour on the following: When a man is dying and cannot speak, since the soul is being separated from the body, if it could speak in such a separation and withdrawal of the soul, what things would the soul say to the body? And also, of those who are in hell or purgatory, if they would return to this life, what would they say? And after the hour has passed, the superior of the house examines each one of them on what he experienced during that hour when he meditated; and if he says something good, he praises him; and, on the other hand, he reproaches him when he says things which are not worth remembering" (Schurhammer 1982, 68–69).

[2] See *Epistolae S. Francisci Xaverii*, Rome, 1944–1945, 2: 265–266; quoted in Schurhammer 1982, n. 66, p. 283.

and the dignity which he has, and also because of his great age, since he is eighty years old; and he is called Ninxit, which means "Heart of Truth" in the language of Japan. He is like a bishop among them, and if he were conformed to his name, he would be blessed. In the many conversations which we had, I found him doubtful and unable to decide whether our soul is immortal or whether it dies together with the body; sometimes he agreed with me, and at other times he did not. I am afraid that the other scholars are of the same mind. This Ninxit is such a great friend of mine that he is amazing. (Schurhammer 1982, 85)

Xavier recounts how on one occasion Ninjitsu brought him into the Meditation Hall (*zendō*), and, when asked what the monks sitting in *zazen* were doing, he ironically replied: "Some of them are counting up how much they received during the past months from their faithful; others are thinking about where they can obtain better clothes and treatment for their persons; others are thinking about their recreations and their amusements; in short, none of them are thinking about anything that has any meaning at all" (Schurhammer 1982, 74). Perhaps Ninjitsu's irony was lost on Xavier, who soon became convinced of the corruption of the Buddhist monks.[3] The depravity of the Buddhists is a recurring theme in Xavier's descriptions of Japan, and he boldly attempted to amend the ways of the monks he met. More than his criticism of monastic immorality, his growing awareness of the fundamental differences between Buddhist and Christian dogmas led him to foresee future troubles. He was actually ready for this, even hoping that God would bestow on him the grace of martyrdom in Japan (see Schurhammer 1982, 92–93).

Although Xavier eventually met with strong opposition in Kagoshima on the part of Shingon and perhaps Jishū monks, he always remained on friendly terms with Zen monks (Schurhammer 1982, 125). As noted earlier, his attitude toward them was rather ambivalent, a mixture of fascination and contempt: he was amazed in particular by the fact "that the laity live better in their state than the *bonzos* live in theirs; and, though this is manifest, the esteem which they have for them is amazing. There are many errors among these *bonzos*, and the worst of these are found among those who have the greatest knowledge (Schurhammer 1982, 85).

Xavier therefore resolved to defeat these bonzos (a term deriving from the Japanese *bōzu*, monk) with their own weapons, and, while in Yamaguchi, he started to collect the teachings of the various Buddhist sects. According to Schurhammer, "every day during the course of the disputations he posed questions to them about their teachings, and he employed

---

[3] Although Ninjitsu never converted to Christianity, he remained Xavier's friend. Frois wrote of him: "This old man lived on [after Xavier's departure] for some years; but, so as not to lose the position which he had and the credit and reputation which he had with the people and the revenues which he possessed, he haplessly and wretchedly preferred to land in hell."

arguments against them which the bonzes, *bikunis*, magicians and other adversaries were unable to answer" (Schurhammer 1982, 227). The Zen monks, however, gave him some hard times. Cosme de Torres reports: "Among them came some of shorn nobility, whom we could not have defeated without special help from our Lord. For since they are people who are accustomed to practice great meditations, they asked questions to which neither St. Thomas nor Scotus could have given answers that would have satisfied them, since they were men without faith. From this it became evident that it was not we who spoke" (quoted in Schurhammer 1982, 272). In a letter to Loyola, in which Xavier asked that new missionaries be sent to Japanese universities to dispute with skeptical scholars there, he added that even the two Fathers he had left behind in Yamaguchi were not "fitted to be sent to the Japanese universities" (Lach 1965, 671). Similarly, a letter written by Torres urges that "those who are to come to these regions must be very learned in order to answer the very deep and difficult questions which they pose from morning to night" (Schurhammer 1982, 270). The impression that the Zen monks made on Torres was indeed very deep, as can be seen from his description of them: "There are others who are called *Jenxus* (i.e., *Zenshū*), and there are . . . two kinds of them. One group says that there is no soul, and that when a man dies, everything dies, since they say that what has been created out of nothing returns into nothing. These are men of great meditation, and it is difficult to make them understand the law of God. It takes great effort to refute them" (Schurhammer 1982, 268). A similar description is given by Luis de Guzman (1544–1605): "The sects which deny eternal life are known as *Xenxi* [*sic*]. They appeal to those who want to sin freely. Their bonzes have a certain way of meditation, as they seek to find peace from their sins. The teachers of Zen each day assign their disciples some points on which to meditate. In their rich temples the followers of Zen worship idols who represent great warriors from the past" (quoted in Lach 1965, 715). In his protocol to Torres's "Disputations," Fernandez states: "First came many *Jenxus*, priests and laymen. We asked them what they were doing to become Saints. They laughed and replied that there are no Saints, and that there is consequently no need to look for one's way; since that which was nothing has come into being, it cannot help being reduced again into nothing" (Schurhammer 1982, 282). Louis Frois (1528–1563) describes Zen meditation in the following terms: "For those *Jenxus*, to be born and to die is everything. There is no other life. Neither punishment for the bad nor reward for the good. No creator, no Providence. . . . A hundred times a year they devote themselves to the exercise of *Zagen* [i.e., *zazen*], a kind of meditation of one hour and a half. They reflect on this axiom: there is nothing. . . . Why such an exercise? Obviously, to stifle the remorse of their conscience" (see Cros 1900, 2: 77).

Thus, despite their strong reservations concerning the morality of Zen monks, Xavier and his successors held their intellectual achievements in high esteem. They attempted to learn from their teachings, although they became convinced of their diabolic inspiration.[4] They even tried to imitate their organization in order to supplant them. Having realized that it was "absolutely necessary" to adapt to the Japanese way of life, Valignano decided in his *Advertimentos* that the missionaries were to abandon the status of laymen, which they had adopted thus far, and to borrow instead the ceremonial rankings of the monks of the Rinzai branch of Zen (Elison 1973, 62). This was, Valignano thought, the best way to rapidly gain recognition and to achieve "conversion from above." This is also the tack his confrere Ricci was to attempt in China, with regard to Confucianism. Although, conscious of the similarities they shared with Zen, Jesuits in Japan stressed the differences. Typical in this respect is the way in which Frois, in his "Cultural Contrasts between Europe and Japan" (1585), juxtaposes Christian and Buddhist monasticism to the detriment of the latter (Frois 1955, 147; see also Boxer 1951, 70).

From this period dates the first systematic effort to describe Japanese religions, the anonymous *Summary of Errors* (see Lach 1965, 681). After Valignano, at the turn of the seventeenth century, a special course in Buddhist doctrine was established in the Jesuit college of Nagasaki, "to confute the bonzes with their own texts" (Boxer 1951, 221) Buddhists, however, did not remain inactive in this duel and refuted, in turn, the Christian teachings. The most famous were several Zen monks, notably Sessō (d.u.), a monk of Nanzenji, and Suzuki Shōsan (1579–1655), a layman who wrote a tract entitled *Ha-Kirishitan* (Refutation of Christianity).[5]

The Jesuits in China

The outstanding achievements of Matteo Ricci, the man whom Demiéville called the "founding father of Western Sinology" (Demiéville 1966, 38), had a high cost: in particular, his prejudices against Buddhism and Chinese religion have had enduring consequences; he circumscribed the field of Sinology by excluding entire areas of the Chinese intellectual and religious life.[6] We may therefore wonder to what extent "every Western Sinologist

---

[4] See Charlevoix 1828, 1: 26. Valignano recognizes more precisely in Amidism the demoniac Protestant heresy, declaring that Amidists "hold precisely the doctrine which the devil, father of both, taught to Luther" (Valignano 1990, 88; Elison 1973, 43).

[5] See Anesaki 1930 and Elison 1973. On Suzuki Shōsan, see Tyler 1977 and Ooms 1985, 122–143. Ironically, Suzuki compared the Christian belief in a soul to the Sāṃkhya philosophy, prefiguring later Christian missionaries in their attempt to reduce Chan/Zen to Vedantism.

[6] On Ricci's attitude toward Chinese religion, see also Rule 1968; Brandauer 1968; Kern 1984–1985; Aubin 1987.

should recognize his forebearer in him [Ricci]" (Demiéville 1967, 88). Certainly, this genealogy has lost some of its legitimizing power and needs to be questioned if it cannot be transcended.[7] The interest in Confucianism that Western Sinology inherited from Ricci and the Jesuit missionaries in China still dominates the field. Marcel Granet, for instance, downplayed the role of Daoism and Buddhism in his picture of Chinese religion (Granet 1927), and Max Weber, although not himself a Sinologist, reflected the same premises in his sociological work on China (Weber 1951). Even the "militantly anti-clerical ex-Catholic" J.J.M. de Groot (1854–1921), while focussing on popular Chinese religion, betrays a Confucian prejudice, at least in his early work.[8] With a few exceptions,[9] recent American scholarship– continues to concentrate its energy on the "great tradition" of Confucianism.

Ricci and his confreres were at first considered by Chinese authorities to be a new brand of Buddhist missionaries from the West (India). They reinforced this initial misperception by calling themselves *osciano*, a transcription of the Chinese *heshang*, the term most commonly used for Chan priests. Ricci encountered Chan soon after his arrival in China, and it is worth quoting at some length what he wrote concerning Chan Buddhists:

> The sacrificing priests of this cult are called *Osciami* [sic]. Their faces and their heads are kept clean shaven, contrary to the custom of the country. Some of them are on continual pilgrimage; others lead a very trying life in caves in the mountains. The greater part of them, numbering as one might figure about two or three millions, live in the numerous cloisters of the temples. These latter are supported by alms and by revenues formerly established for that purpose, though they also provide for their keep by personal labor. This special class of temple servants is considered to be, and in reality is, the lowest and most despised caste in the whole kingdom. They come from the very dregs of the populace, and in their youth are sold into slavery to the *Osciami*. From being servants they become disciples and afterward succeed to the positions and to the emoluments of their masters. This method of succession is accepted in order to preserve the office. Not a single one of them could ever have elected of his own

[7] Incidentally, Demiéville himself, together with his masters Chavannes and Maspero, were exceptional Sinologists in this respect as well, the latter by their interest in Daoist religion, the former by his ground-breaking work on the history of Chan. See Chavannes, 1919; Maspero 1981.

[8] After 1886–1891, perhaps owing to his disappointment when confronted with the Chinese social reality, de Groot's sinophilia gave way to a global rejection of Confucian intolerance, and he went as far as to dedicate his *Sectarianism and Religious Persecution in China* (1974) to "all missionaries of all Christian denominations laboring in China." See Werblowsky 1986, 119; and Freedman 1974.

[9] See, for example, Raymond Dawson's criticism of the anti-Buddhist bias of Western Sinology in *The Chinese Chameleon* (1967), 64; (see also Girardot 1979, 83–111).

will to join this vile class of cenobites as a means to leading a holy life. Being like unto their masters as to ignorance and inexperience, and with no inclination toward learning and good manners, their natural bent to evil becomes worse with the lapse of time. There may be some exceptions to this way of life but, if so, they constitute the very few among them who have a liking for learning and accomplish something by their own industry. Though not a marrying class, they are so given to sexual indulgence that only the heaviest penalties can deter them from promiscuous living. (Gallagher 1953, 100–101, 223)

It was not until 1595, however, that Ricci changed the title of *osciano* to that of *predicatore letterato*, a translation of the Chinese term used for *literati* (Demiéville 1966, 89). This renaming was accompanied by a drastic change in apparel, from the robe of the Buddhist monks to the silk garments of the followers of Kongfuzi—the so-called *Sinarum philosophus*, whose name Ricci latinized for posterity as Confucius.[10] According to Henry Bernard, "this change [from Buddhist to Confucian robes] made the proselytizing of women, whom custom authorized to go to pagodas, a little more difficult, but in due time one would find a remedy for it. On the other hand, it introduced him [Ricci] right in the midst of what one may call without too much exaggeration the world of the 'true gods' of China" (Bernard 1937, 207). Ricci's decision is justified by Bernard as follows: "We have said what Chinese religion was: a heterogeneous helter-skelter [*sic*] of deities worshipped according to the changing and blind whim of the crowd. Finding nothing clear in the minds of the people, missionaries turned toward cultured minds" (Bernard 1935, 98). A more likely motivation was suggested by Jean-Jacques Ampère: "Jesuit missionaries . . . were naturally attracted toward dominant and, as we say today, governmental doctrines. . . . They felt, on the contrary, very little esteem for the forty or fifty systems that, like Jansenism or Calvinism, were good only to trouble the obedience and submission of minds: this is what led them to neglect what one could call the heterodox philosophy of China" (Ampère 1833, 361–362). Although one can readily identify in Ricci and his colleagues a "religious" prejudice, their bias against Buddhism and local religions may also result, paradoxically, from a certain secularism that led them to feel more at home with Confucianism. This secularist tendency, paving the way to the "accommodation" theory, was also one cause of the Jesuits' controversy with Jansenism.

At the beginning of his eighteen-year stay in southern China, Ricci received hospitality in a famous Chan monastery, the Nanhua si of Caoxi (in Northern Guangdong), where the mummy of the Sixth Patriarch Huineng (d. 713) was preserved. This hospitality was interpreted by Ricci's transla-

---

[10] See *Confucius Sinarum Philosophus* (Paris, 1683), "a kind of encyclopedia of Chinese thought," compiled by the Belgian Jesuit Philippe Couplet and a group of colleagues.

tor, Nicholas Trigault (1576–1628), as pure machiavellianism on the part of Chan monks: "In their very politest way, they offered him the whole temple and assured him that everything connected with it was at his disposal." However, adds Trigault, they had agreed among themselves not to show him any place suitable for lodging (Gallagher 1953, 223; Bernard 1937, 146–148). According to Ricci's account, revised by Trigault:[11]

> The temple itself, magnificent in its grandeur, is built upon the most beautiful of all the hills and is copiously supplied with fresh water from a large mountain, graciously designed and wonderfully built. On the plateau and contiguous to the temple is the cloister, the dwelling, as they say, of a thousand priests of the idols. They are the lords of this demesne, inherited as a benefice from the impious piety of their ancestors. This institution had its origin with a man named Lusu [*Luzu*, the "Sixth Patriarch" Huineng], some eight hundred years ago. They say that he lived on this very spot and that he acquired a great reputation for sanctity because of his unusually austere manner of living. He wore iron chains against his flesh, and he was continually sifting rice and lightly pounding it, the way they do. In a single day he would prepare enough of it for a thousand temple dwellers, or conventuals. His flesh became so torn and mutilated by the iron chains that it was actually putrefied and running with maggots, and if one of them fell he would replace it and say, "Can you find nothing to gnaw? Why are you thinking of deserting me?" His body is enshrined in this magnificent temple, which was built in his honor, and the people, who venerate his memory and whatever belonged to him, come here on pilgrimage from all corners of the realm. (Gallagher 1953, 222; Bernard 1937, 1: 146)

A little further, Ricci describes the famous Hall of the Five Hundred Arhats (*Luohan*) and Huineng's "flesh-body":

> This whole edifice was practically filled with idols fashioned from copper and other metals or from wood enriched with gilded decorations. There were more than five hundred of these idols in a single hall. . . . The temple ministers also showed them the body of *Lusu*, enveloped in that peculiar shiny bituminous substance, known only to the Chinese. Many say it is not his body, but the people believe that it is and they hold it in great veneration. (ibid., 223)

Ricci and his companions showed nothing but contempt for their hosts, and, uncompromising in their Christian faith, they refused to pay homage to the "idols" worshiped in the monastery. Ricci left the monastery, "ac-

---

[11] In a general way, Trigault's "translation" of Ricci's work is not very faithful, being full of distortions and interpolations "amounting, at times, to cumulative fraud" (Rule 1968). As far as Buddhism is concerned, however, Ricci and his "interpreter" essentially agree. Furthermore, we are not so much concerned here with Ricci himself as with the Jesuit attitude toward Buddhism, and because in this sense Trigault is also representative, there is no need to cling to an "original" text of Ricci's journals.

companied by the Grand master of the temple and two of his companions," to ask for an audience with the lieutenant governor, to whom he complained that the temple "was too far from the town and too far away from the educated classes and the Magistrates, among whom, as among their equals, they were accustomed to live. He explained that these temple dwellers had an unsavory reputation, that one could not live with them in safety, and that his law and the books pertaining to it were altogether different from theirs" (ibid.). To convince the confused magistrate that he did not worship idols, Ricci drew his breviary from his sleeve. "The Grand Master of the Temple was looking on at all this and said it was all very true, because, only the other day, Ricci had visited the shrines of the idols and had paid no homage to any of them, even to Lusu himself" (ibid.). In a spirit of compromise, the Chan priest went on to explain that "idols as such were not worthy of any honor, but the wise men of the past, realizing that religion could not be preserved among the ordinary people without some kind of images, invented these figures for that very purpose" (see Ricci 1942–1949; 1: 283–284; Gallagher 1953, 224–225). Such unbearable proof of Buddhist hypocrisy gave Ricci his final argument, and the Nanhua si was definitively discarded as a possible place to stay.

However, the controversy did not end there, for after moving from Caoxi to Shaozhou, Ricci established his mission on the land of the "Quam hiao Temple" (the Guangxiao si in Canton), a temple belonging to the same branch of Chan as the monks he had just so deliberately provoked. This marked the beginning of a long polemic between the Jesuits and the Buddhists. After the departure of Ricci for Beijing, the situation in Shaozhou itself was aggravated by the active iconoclasm of his successor, Longobardo. Longobardo's life was even endangered at one point, after a long drought that had heated the tempers of the inhabitants. "So they gave up hope in the city gods, and for the occasion they brought in a celebrated monster from the country. Its name was *Locu* [read *Luzu*, Huineng again!]. They paraded it about, bowed before it and made offerings to it, but like its counterparts it remained deaf to their pleading. It was this occasion that gave rise to the saying, Locu is growing old." The cause of the drought was disclosed by an oracle, according to which "the goddess Quomyn [Guanyin] is angry, because every day she is having her back burned. . . . The reference was to the burning of the statue idols of this goddess by the [Christian] neophytes. . . . Some of the malcontents conspired to do away with Father Longobardo as the author of the public calamity, if he dared to return to their village" (Gallagher 1953, 425). Fortunately, a heavy rain brought some appeasement. Brought before the magistrate of Shaozhou, Longobardo admitted that he had burnt idols, but was acquitted after pleading very cleverly that "he thought that the whole class of the literati were in favor of blotting out old laws pertaining to the protection of idols" (see Ricci 19422–1949, 2: 328; Gallagher 1953, 462; and Rule 1968, 116).

Although Ricci's tactical alliance with Confucianists against Buddhism helped him to gain recognition from the ruling classes, eventually it became counterproductive. Ricci's attitude toward Buddhism must be placed in its religious context—that of aggressive Counter-Reformation Catholicism engaged in a spiritual battle to win over Chinese society to Christianity. It is perhaps inappropriate to condemn him retrospectively for his lack of tolerance, when the very notion of tolerance would have seemed perfectly irrelevant to him. This virtue was associated with atheists like Voltaire and with whorehouses (*maisons de tolérance*), as in Claudel's witty remark: "Tolerance? Tolerance? There are houses for that" (Etiemble 1964, 50).

Nevertheless, Ricci could not have failed to realize that some criticisms he leveled at Buddhism applied equally well to him and the religion he represented. For example, when he argued that, "if there were so many errors in [Buddhist teachings] about natural things and things of this life, all the less reason to believe their teaching on supernatural things and those of the other world" (Rule 1968, 110). Likewise, when he declared: "The eagle flies, and so does the bat. . . . The Law of the true God is an ancient Law, and Buddha, born in the Orient, has by chance heard of it. Every party leader who wants to dogmatize must cover his lies with a few truths, otherwise who would follow him?" (Bernard 1933, 110). The most damning counter-truths, however, recorded by his successors in a work written after his death, are his attribution of the rapid downfall of Chinese dynasties to the baneful influence of Buddhism and his claim that: "In the main it is manifestly evident—I would not dare to exaggerate [!]—that in the one thousand six hundred years since our countries became Christian, . . . there has not been a single change of dynasty, not a single war and not the least dispute."[12] Admittedly, it would be naive to expect a sixteenth-century Jesuit, a "warrior" for Christ, to apologize for or to compromise his faith, and to that extent Ricci's rejection of Buddhism is consistent. Ricci, however, did compromise with Confucianism, and his justification of his faith was not free of cunning and deception.

For instance, we have seen that Ricci condemned Huineng for adapting his teaching to meet the needs of the common believers, in other words, he used "skillful means" (*upāya*) like the iconic representations of the divine ("idols"). Such a condemnation is rather paradoxical on the part of a sixteenth-century Italian, particularly when one considers how far, in his

[12] *Bianxue yidu*, in *Tianxue chuhan* 2: 647; quoted in Gernet 1982, 150. The same argument was used by the Japanese convert and later apostate Fabian Fucan in his *Myōtei mondō*. Contrary to a Japan plagued with civil wars, said he, "in the Kirishitan countries there is no Buddha's Law; but the Royal Sway flourishes there and its virtue abounds and fills the Four Seas" (Elison 1973, 53)

attempt to emphasize the compatibility between the teachings of Confucius and those of Christ, Ricci went to adapt Christianity to China and
himself to Confucianism.[13] As Spence points out, "to get this message
across, every means that skills, artifice, training and memory could provide
had to be called into play" (Spence 1984, 258). This appeared necessary,
because, as Trigault remarked; "Whoever may think that ethics, physics
and mathematics are not important in the work of the Church is unac-
quainted with the taste of the Chinese, who are slow to take a salutary
spiritual potion unless it be seasoned with an intellectual flavoring" (Gallagher 1953, 325). Ricci was careful to downplay the central Christian
mystery of the crucifixion, aware as he was that, in the eyes of a Chinese,
such an infamous end was proof that Christ was not divine.[14] According to
one of Ricci's companions, "Father Matteo, for his part, did not want to
say that this was our God, considering the difficulty in declaring so high a
mystery before such ignorant people and at such a time" (Ricci 1942–
1949, 2: 115; Rule 1968, 112). In this respect, Ricci was closer to the
Buddhist notion of the "Two Truths" than to the Christian teaching.[15]
Even his rejection of Buddhism and Daoism may be considered as "skillful
means" (upāya), a way to reaffirm his orthodoxy, not only to Confucianists, but also to Christians in Europe, who had been shocked by his enthusiasm for Confucius. By deliberately misinterpreting the ambiguous
passages in Confucius's works, Ricci was trying to prove that early Confucianism was theistic; he claimed with some reason that neo-Confucianism

[13] In particular, the strange allegories that Ricci used to illustrate his *Memory Palace* could
have prepared him to understand as allegorical and mnemonic representations the Buddhist
iconography of the *maṇḍalas*. When Le Comte, in his *Nouveaux Mémoires* (Paris, 1965), 1:
18–19, waxes ironical on such Chinese superstitions as throwing spirit money into the water
to pacify the ocean, he could also refer to the passage in Ricci's biography where Ricci and his
friends "tossed talismans made of the wax from the paschal candles of Rome into the stormy
seas as they rounded the Cape of Good Hope in 1578"; see Spence 1986, 19. See also Gernet's
review, in *T'oung Pao* 72, 2–5 (1986): 333, and *TLS* (27 September 1985), 1059–1060.

[14] See, for example, the pamphlet entitled *Huihe xiedang hou gaoshi*: "These Barbarians
have published an *Epitome of the Doctrine of the Lord of Heaven* where it is written in full
that the Lord of Heaven was born in such and such a year of the reign of the Han Emperor Ai,
that his name was Yesu and that his mother was called Yalima [Maliya]. Then he is only a
Barbarian of the Western seas. They also say that he died nailed by evil officials on a scaffolding
shaped like the character ten. Then he is only a barbarian sentenced to death. How could one
call Lord of Heaven a tortured barbarian?" (quoted in Gernet 1982, 80).

[15] See Valignano's criticism of Buddhist *upāya*: "It is morally reprehensible to urge a
person to what is not permissible, for example to idolatry. On the other hand, the avowal that
this 'inner' doctrine is true only for themselves and insufficient for guiding the people is a
striking witness against themselves. For if the laws of the 'interior' teaching were correct, they
should suffice to keep the people from evil and lead them to good. . . . The conclusion is . . .
that in spreading such doctrines they are in fact seeking something else than the people's good,
namely, wealth and esteem. . . . By these arts and deceptions they deceive men, knowing that
unless they employ these methods they will trap no fish" (Schütte 1980, 2: 80–81).

had been "perverted" by Buddhist influence.[16] In the process, however, he compromised some of his Christian beliefs, and it is not entirely clear who was being converted by whom. Owing to his mnemotechnical skills, Ricci was perceived by the Chinese as a thaumaturge, and, like his Buddhist counterparts, he was quite willing to play the role of an exorcist.[17] Eventually worshiped as a god, he is still known in China today under the name of Li Madou.

As is well known, the "accommodative method" and the "conversion from above" policy that Ricci had borrowed from the Father Visitor Valignano, and, more precisely, Ricci's adoption of Confucian rites, found many opponents, even within the Jesuit society.[18] It was primarily Ricci's disagreement with his successor, the Sicilian Niccolo Longobardo (1559–1654), that triggered the so-called "Chinese Rites controversy."[19] This controversy, which began just after Ricci's death, ran well into the seventeenth century. Reactivated at the end of the century by the *Nouveaux mémoires* (1696) of Louis Le Comte (1655–1728), it deeply agitated French intellectuals at the beginning of the eighteenth century and ended with the defeat of the Jesuits: "Chinese rites" were definitively condemned by the Papal Bull *Ex quo singulari* in 1742; the Jesuits were forbidden in France in 1764, and the Society of Jesus was suppressed in 1773.

This explosion of sectarian polemics around an apparently trifling matter can be traced back to many causes, the most fundamental of which may have been the clash between the two antagonistic worldviews advocated by the Jesuits and the Jansenists. Opposed to the uncompromising, wrathful, and omnipotent ancient God of Pascal and the Jansenists was the new, benevolent God of the Jesuits. Jansenists were quick to condemn those who, "in order to reconcile the hearts of men with religion, conceal the hardship of the latter, and merely hint at things" (Groethuysen 1927, 125). Pascal hated the Jesuits, and, in his fifth "Provincial Letter" (1576), criticized them severely for suppressing "the scandal of the Cross" and allowing their Chinese converts to practice idolatry by applying mentally to

---

[16] Buddhist influence (Chan) is evident in the writings of Zhu Xi (1130–1200), despite or because of the anti-Buddhist bias of the latter, but above all in those of Wang Yangming. On Zhu Xi and Buddhism, see Sargent 1957.

[17] On the development of Christian exorcism in China, see Zürcher 1985.

[18] Ricci was even criticized as someone in whom the Devil had found "a faithful servant, who far from destroying, established his reign among the heathen, and even extended it to the Christians." See S. Wells Williams, *The Middle Kingdom* (New York: Scribner's Sons, 1899), 2: 293 (quoted in Harris 1966, 124).

[19] Longobardo is considered to be the author of a remarkable tract, *Traité sur quelques points de la religion des Chinois*, in which he attacks Ricci's theses. The book was burnt by the Jesuits, but a Spanish version was printed in Madrid in 1676 by Dominicans, and a French translation was eventually published in Paris in 1701, at a time when the "Rites controversy" was raging. See Longobardo 1701.

Christ "the worship paid publicly to the idol Chacim-Choan and their Keum-fucum [Confucius]" (Pascal 1967, 76).

The Jansenists also condemned Pelagianism, which they recognized as a view that people are inclined by nature to embrace: like Pelagius, a fifth-century heretic who was defeated by Augustine, people are naturally inclined to believe in free will and in the goodness of human nature and to forget about original sin and predestination. Whereas the Catholic tradition saw only sins and good works, the Jesuits (and in a different way the Protestants), distant heirs of Pelagius, emptied the doctrine of original sin of its meaning and introduced a variety of methods for salvation and new interpretations of human actions (Groethuysen 1927, 153). They eluded the problem of evil, in a way not too different from Chan (which, in certain respects, shows affinities with the Pelagian doctrine), and were, paradoxically, supported by the "philosophers" and by rationalists such as Voltaire. As the last of their representatives in Beijing, Father Amiot, was to complain, "We had to suffer the pain of seeing ourselves quoted in works of darkness destined to fight against the religion that we preach at the risk of our lives" (Pfister 1932–1934, 1: 839).

Another distant offshoot of Pelagianism was the Quietism of Miguel Molinos, and, as we will see, Chan has often, if only superficially, been labeled a quietist teaching owing to its antinomian tendency. In a sense, the Jesuits had more in common with Buddhist intellectuals than with Confucianists, and this resemblance may explain the hostility of the former osciano Ricci toward his Chan counterparts, and his eagerness to distance himself from them.[20] As a perceptive Chinese opponent to Ricci remarked: "This is why I say that apparently you criticize Buddhism, but you secretly steal its conceptions. You pretend to respect Confucianism, but in reality you destroy it."[21] It is significant that Buddhism as a whole was first rejected by Ricci as a demoniacal parody of Christianity. Ricci's attitude in this regard was dictated in part by his cultural prejudices and his moral contempt for the unhappy state of affairs in the Buddhist monasteries that he visited and in part also by an intuitive "mimetic rivalry" (Girard 1965). Although Ricci probably never had enough knowledge of the teachings he disparaged to appreciate their potential threat to his own conceptions, he knew that a religion of universal salvation such as Buddhism was a strong

[20] However, one may argue, like Kern, that the philosophical tradition from which Ricci stemmed was much more distant from Buddhism than were other Christian trends that were influenced by neo-Platonism, such as those of Saint Victor and the Rhenan mystics (Kern 1984–1985, 124).

[21] A similar point had been made in Japan by a Zen monk of the Rinzai sect, Sessō, in his pamphlet against Christians, the *Taiji jashūron* (On Quelling the Pernicious Faith, 1648): "They attacked Confucianism and Shintō, but were most intent on countering Buddhism because of its great similarity to their own religion" (quoted in Elison 1973, 231).

opponent and was aware of its enduring popularity, a popularity "that seems impossible to extinguish" (Gallagher 1953, 100). As he lamented, "This second sect is acquiring a new impetus, even now in our own times, building many temples and restoring others" (ibid., 101).

One might wonder how Ricci's opinion of Chan would have evolved had he been able to debate with such worthy opponents as Zhuhong (1535–1615), whose criticism of his *True Meaning of the Lord of Heaven* (De Deo vera ratio) remained unknown to him?[22] The controversy in which Ricci became embroiled on a few occasions with Buddhist monks like "Sanhoai (Huang Sanhui)" merely confirmed his prejudice against Buddhism (See Bernard 1933, 338–342). The political power of the Buddhist clergy had declined sharply after the execution of a monk named "Thacon" (Daguan), who had been accused of sedition.[23] Ricci welcomed this event, which he attributed to the will of God. On that occasion he described Buddhism: "Condemned as it was by increasing prejudice, discredited by so much ignominy, and deprived of so many protectors, it became so weak and lifeless that it failed to overshadow Christianity, as it had hoped to. On the contrary, having lost the flower of its honor, . . . it had to give way to a new and a growing enlightenment" (Gallagher 1953, 405; see also Bernard 1937, 2: 93–97).

Ricci's knowledge of the Buddhist doctrine remained extremely limited and rather fanciful. He claimed for instance that the "sect of idols" had invented nothing: it merely borrowed from Daoism its belief in nothingness, from Christianity its conceptions of a trinity and of heaven and hell, from Democritus its belief in a multiplicity of worlds, and from Pythagoras its notion of the "transmigration of souls" (See Gallagher 1953, 99, 590). Ricci's misinterpretation of the Buddhist notion of emptiness (*śūnyata*) and the subsequent Western identification of Buddhism with nihilism and atheism were accentuated and disseminated by Trigault (Gallagher 1953), and they exerted an enduring influence in the West.[24] To a Chinese opponent who reproached him for attacking Buddhism without having read its canonical scriptures, Ricci replied that there was no need to read the entire Buddhist canon to realize that Buddhists were placing Buddha above God,

[22] On Zhuhong, see Yü 1981. Concerning his and other Buddhists' criticisms of Ricci, see Lancashire 1968–69, 82–103; and Gernet 1985, 216–217. Ricci never met Hanshan Deqing, another famous Chan monk who arrived in Shaozhou in 1595, after Ricci's departure for Beijing, but he mentions in his *Memoirs* (*Storia*) the encounter between Hanshan and Longobardo in 1604. On Hanshan, see Hsu 1979.

[23] Daguan had, on one occasion, expressed a desire to meet Ricci, who replied that "he had no desire to learn anything from him," and commented: "The pride of this particular impostor was simply unbearable. What else could he have learned in the school of Satan?" (Gallagher 1953, 402).

[24] It must be remembered that these terms, like quietism, were primarily polemical: Pascal and the Jansenists were atheists for the Jesuits, and conversely.

thereby transgressing the First Commandment. As to the canon itself, "the very number and variety of its writings has resulted in such a complicated mixture of doctrine and of nonsensical trifles that even those who profess to believe in it cannot riddle it out" (Gallagher 1953, 99). Even if, toward the end of his life, Ricci seems to have moderated his judgment, he still believed that "whatever ray of truth there may be in this doctrine is, however, unfortunately obscured by clouds of noisome mendacity" (Gallagher 1953, 100). In the long run, Ricci's unfair criticism of Buddhism was detrimental to Christianity and was objected to even by those Confucianists who, as he had himself remarked, borrowed many ideas from the "sect of the Idols," for instance the "pantheist" notion that the world is of a single substance (see Demiéville 1967, 90).

Yet, Ricci's antagonism toward Buddhism was relatively mild compared to the active iconoclasm and aggressive evangelism of his successor Longobardo (see Harris 1966, 133). This agonistic attitude found its definitive expression in the writings of the French Jesuits of the Mission of Peking, which was founded in 1685, among whom where such figures as Charles Le Gobien (1653–1708), Louis Le Comte (Lecomte), and Joachim Bouvet (1665–1730), a correspondent of Leibniz and an advocate of "figurism." The English translation of Le Comte's *Nouveaux mémoires sur l'état présent de la Chine* (1696) had gone through several reeditions by the mid-eighteenth century, and it exerted a great influence on all later Western descriptions of Buddhist monasticism (see Almond 1988, 119). It is on Le Comte that du Halde (1674–1743), who had never been to China, relied to describe in *The General History of China* (1741) the teachings of the "Idolaters" as "nothing but a Heap of Fables and Superstitions brought from the *Indies* into China, and maintained by the bonzes, who deceive the People under the Appearances of false Piety; they have introduced the Belief of the Transmigration of Souls, and promise more or less Happiness in proportion to the Liberality that is shewn to them" (du Halde 1741, 8: 15). The Jesuits had an enormous influence on the "philosophers" (Montesquieu, Voltaire, etc.), with the notable exception of the freethinker La Mothe Le Vayer, who rejected Trigault's disparaging portrayal of Buddhism, a teaching in which he discerned a "sublime philosophy." But, even for him, as later for Max Weber, the rationalist tendency was strongest in Confucianists, who were "even more distant from the crime of idolatry than Buddhists (see Etiemble 1964, 47–48).

BUDDHISM AND QUIETISM

Although the eighteenth-century European rationalists attacked the Society of Jesus and its proselytism in China, they remained entirely dependent on the Jesuits' information on China, mainly through the collection of *Lettres édifiantes et curieuses* (published until 1818) and through Jean-Baptiste du Halde's *Description géographique* (1735).[25] In many ways, the Jesuits paved the way for the philosophers' description of China as a "paradisiacal universe," a model of rational government, and Chinese religion as a "heap of superstitions." The humanist tendency of the Jesuits backfired onto Christianity when Voltaire began advocating to "crush the infamous" (*Ecrasez l'infâme*), that is, superstition, hence Catholicism, "under the weight of China and the virtue of the Chinese."[26]

Because Jesuits had tried to establish the supremacy of Christianity through the use of reason and logic, they partly deprived themselves of their transcendental privilege and were exasperated when Buddhists resorted to the hermeneutical device of the Two Truths, ultimate and conventional, and the subsequent distinction between esoteric and exoteric Buddhism (see Lecomte 1990, 369). Whereas Western reason could not pretend to transcend the framework of conventional truth, Chan Buddhists claimed to have access to the ultimate truth of esoteric Buddhism.

According to du Halde, the "inner doctrine" advocated by Chinese Buddhists (and more specifically by Chan monks) taught that "a *vacuum* or Nothing is the Principle of all Things, that from this our first Parents had their Origin, and to this they returned after their Death" (ibid., 51). Du Halde goes on to explain how this ontological conception leads to a kind of "quietism":

> To live happily we must continually strive by Meditation, and frequent Victories over ourselves, to become like this *Principium*, and to this end accustom ourselves to do nothing, to desire nothing, to perceive nothing, to think on nothing; there is no Dispute about Vices or Virtues, Rewards or Punishments, Providence and the Immortality of the Soul; all Holiness consists in ceasing to be, and to be swallowed up by Nothing; the nearer we approach to the nature of a Stone, or the Trunk of a Tree, the more perfect we are; in short it is in Indolence and Inactivity, in a Privation of every Motion of the Body, in an Annihilation of all the Faculties of the Soul, and in the general Suspension of all Thought, that Virtue and Happiness consist; when a Man has once attained this happy State he will then meet with no further Vicissitudes and Transmigrations, he has nothing to fear for the Future, because properly speaking he is Nothing; or if he is any thing he is happy, and to say every thing in one word he is perfectly like the God Fo. (du Halde 1741)

Du Halde relied on Le Gobien's description, which compares Buddhist meditation to Stoicist apathy or indifference (an idea taken up by Scho-

[25] These works were supplanted after 1776 by the sixteen volumes of the *Mémoires concernant l'histoire, les sciences, les arts, les moeurs, les usages, etc. des Chinois* (see Cibot 1776–1814).

[26] See, for instance, Voltaire, *Correspondance*, 112, letter of 28 November, 1762.

penhauer). As he points out, the Christian missionaries, in their denunciation of quietism, found powerful allies in Confucianists:

> However, the greatest part of the Learned have opposed this Sect . . . ; they attack'd it with all their might, proving that this Apathy, or rather this monstrous Stupidity, overturned all Morality and Civil Society; that Man is raised only above other Beings by his thinking and reasoning Faculties, and by his Application to the Knowledge and Practice of Virtue; that to aspire after this foolish Inactivity is renouncing the most essential Duties, abolishing the necessary Relation of Father and Son, Husband and Wife, Prince and Subject, and that if this Doctrine was follow'd it would reduce all the Members of a State to a Condition much inferior to that of Beasts. (ibid., 50–52)

After characterizing as quietistic the teaching of Bodhidharma, du Halde reiterates his argument: "Suppose, after this example, every Private Person should take it in their Heads to imitate this kind of Life, what would become of the most necessary Professions? Who would take care of cultivating the Fields, and make the useful Products of the Loom? Whence would they have garments, and Food to support Life? Can it be imagined that a Doctrine, whose Practice, if it were universal, would put the Empire in Confusion should be the true Doctrine?" (ibid., 277).

Like his predecessors, du Halde seems oblivious to the fact that the same criticism could be addressed to Christian monasticism. Indeed, du Halde's apocalyptic description bears an uncanny resemblance to the eighteenth-century "capitalist" critique of Christian eremitism, as summarized in the following passage: "What a strange fanaticism it is to want to convert cities into cloisters, and the palaces of princes into places of retirement for recluses? Let us blush for all eternity at these excesses, and let us not impute to religion, but to the spirit of domination by which most of these extravagant doctors are possessed, these maxims that lead only to the destruction of society" (quoted in Groethuysen 1927, 234) The lesson was not lost on some of du Halde's readers, such as Voltaire or the Protestant La Croze (or Lacroze). Commenting in his *Histoire du christianisme des Indes* on the account given by the Jesuit Philippe Marini—who argued that the "sect of Xaca [Śākyamuni]" blended "the hypocrisy of the Pharisees, the temerity of the Atheists blasphemies, and the filth of the heresies of the Novators, principally of Luther and of Calvin"—La Croze wrote ironically: "If this judicious missionary had looked closely, he would have found in what his confreres have told us about the Bonzes of Japan, who are devotees of Xaca, important places by which they quite resemble the Jesuits" (La Croze 1724, 509–510).

In his preface to Miguel Molinos's *Spiritual Guide*, La Croze also quotes the description of the "Buddhist doctrine," "Foe Kiao" (*fojiao*), given by the Jesuit Philippe Couplet (1622–1693) in the preface to his translation of Confucius. Buddhism is presented there, in terms similar to those of du

Halde, as a form of ataraxy deriving from the imitation of the "first principle." La Croze criticized Couplet's comparison between Buddhism and
Quietism, arguing that, unlike Buddhists, Quietists aim at emptying themselves not to dwell in emptiness, but to be filled by God's Love.[27] Despite
these isolated criticisms, the association of Buddhism (and more particularly Chan) with Quietism has persisted until the present day.[28] When
applied to Buddhism by eighteenth-century writers, the term quietist was
fraught with connotations that can be properly understood only when
placed in their Western context. In most cases, the criticism of Buddhism
was actually aimed at enemies back home. In the article "Brahman" of his
Dictionnaire historique et critique (1697), for instance, the French Protestant Pierre Bayle (1647–1706) amalgamated Buddhism with Quietism,
noting that it was criticized by Confucianists in the same way that
Fénelon's quietism was criticized by La Bruyère. Bayle compared the "extravagant" style of the Western mystics to that of the "speculative Chinese"
and equated Chan quietism with the doctrine of Spinoza. The writings of
Spinoza were the actual target of much criticism leveled at Chinese philosophy and religion, and Confucius himself became the "Spinoza of the Far
East." According to Longobardo, "Chinese religion was an absolute materialism which smelled highly of Spinozism and excluded all those ideas
adopted by the Jesuits for the defense of its pretended spirituality" (Guy
1963, 75). Diderot declares that "the frightening language of our modern
atheist [Spinoza] is precisely the one that [the Chinese] spoke in their
schools" (ibid., 336) Likewise, after describing the teachings of Japanese
Zen, Bayle compared them to those of Spinoza: "It is quite certain that we
have here several things that Spinoza did not teach; but, on the other hand,
it is absolutely certain that he taught, like these Japanese priests, that the
first principle of all things, and all beings that make up the universe, are of
one and the same substance, that all things are God, and God all things, so
that God and all things are one and the same being. One cannot wonder
enough that an idea so extravagant and so fraught with absurd contradic-

[27] Incidentally, the French translation of the *Spiritual Guide* was prefaced by Albert
Camus's mentor, the French philosopher Jean Grenier, who had also introduced the *Daode
jing* to a French audience (see Molinos 1970). Grenier had been influenced by the Jesuit Léon
Wieger's translations, which may explain Bernard-Maître's praise: "Like many of our Western contemporaries, Mr. Jean Grenier has experienced the seduction of Far-Eastern thought;
however, unlike most of them, he returned from it with a clearer vision of the values of
Christianity" (quoted in Etiemble 1964, 106).
[28] For example, in a little book on quietism by J. R. Armogathe, the second part discusses
quietism in non-Christian religions and makes mention of the so-called Council of Tibet at the
end of the eight century, where Indian and Chinese Buddhists debated on the respective value
of *gradualism* and *subitism*. (Armogathe 1973). This controversy, which arose in China from
the sectarian fight between the Northern and Southern schools of Chan, has been masterfully
studied by Demiéville in a book subtitled "A Controversy on Quietism" (Demiéville 1952).
The vagueness of the term *quietism* when applied to Chan is evidenced by the fact that,

tions could ever have hidden itself in the souls of so many people so distant from each other, and so different from each other in temper, education, custom and genius" (Bayle 1983, 125–126). In another passage, Bayle writes: "If we did not know the folly of our quietists, we would believe that the writers who tell us about these speculative Chinese have neither understood things nor related them very well; but considering what happens among Christians, it would be out of place to be incredulous concerning the folly of the *Foe Kiao* [*fojiao*] or *Vu guei Kiao* [*wuwei jiao*] sect" (Bayle 1983, 41).

Nevertheless, Bayle was among the first to raise some doubts concerning the "nihilism" of the Buddhists. He argued that the term *Cum hiu* (*kongxu*) should not be interpreted in the philosophical sense of "nothingness," but simply in the ordinary sense of "emptiness": "At this rate, the disciple of Confucius would be guilty of the sophism called *ignoratio elenchi* because he would have meant by *nihil* that which has no existence whatsoever, whereas his opponents would have meant with this same word that which does not have the qualities of matter. I believe they meant roughly by this word what the moderns mean by the word 'space'" (Bayle 1983, 42). In his article "Japan," Bayle refers, without naming them, to Zen adepts: "They neglect the externals, apply themselves exclusively to meditation, reject any discipline that has to do with words, and apply themselves only to the exercise they call *Soquxin Soqueut* [J. *sokushin sokubutsu*, "This very mind is the Buddha"], that is to say, the *heart*" (Bayle 1983, 125).

Chan meditation was generally characterized as a kind of mysticism, leading to what the Dutch Protestant Engelbert Kaempfer, who visited Japan as "physician to the Dutch embassy" called in his *History of Japan* (1690–1692) "Enthusiastic Speculation," his rendition of the Japanese term *satori* (awakening). Kaempfer also describes "*sasen*" (J. *zazen*) as "a profound meditation of divine mysterious and holy things; which so entirely takes up a man's mind, that his body lies, as it were, destitute of all sense and life, unmoved by any external object whatsoever" (Kaempfer 1732, 2: 61). On the whole, however, Westerners were more interested in Asian variants of prefigurations of rationalism and humanism, which were found mainly in Confucianism, and Buddhism—at least in its Chinese version—was dismissed as irrational and magical.[29] With the emergence of

---

whereas in the Armogathe book the "gradual teaching" is labeled "quietist"—a gradualism that the author, following tradition, sees as characteristic of a Northern school supposedly dedicated to meditation and quietude; for Demiéville, it is precisely the "sudden" teaching, with its trust in the perfection of human (or rather Buddha) nature and the resulting antinomianism, that merits the quietist label.

[29] This point of view still finds supporters. In his praise of the Jesuit Antoine Possovino (born 1553), the free-thinker Etiemble, for example, writes: "He understood very well . . . that Buddhism . . . is a religion based on a mysticism; that this mysticism, as it often, if not

Romanticism, mysticism became more fashionable, but this did not suffice to modify the negative perception of Buddhism inherited from the Jesuits.

CHAN AND INDIAN MYSTICISM

Although the discussions of quietism and nihilism conveyed by the Jesuits during the seventeenth and eighteenth centuries paved the way for Western characterizations of Buddhism, only during the nineteenth century was Buddhism definitively constituted as an object of discourse and "reified as a textual object" (Almond 1988, 139). This textualization permitted the emergence of the "historical" Buddha and the convenient opposition between a pure, canonical, early Buddhism and the degenerate Buddhist religion of contemporary Asia (Almond 1988, 25, 37–40). The first part of the nineteenth century was marked by the "Oriental Renaissance," a phenomenon masterfully described by Raymond Schwab (1984). The discourse initiated by the Jesuits survived their temporary suppression, but some of its themes were eclipsed at the time of the French Revolution, when "Indian mysticism ousted Chinese illumination" (Reichwein 1925; 153). Sinology was reorganized on a new basis in France in 1814, with the creation at the Collège de France of a chair first occupied by the young and brilliant Jean-Pierre Abel Rémusat (1788–1838). In that same year, the last volume of the *Mémoires concernant les Chinois* was published by the founder of French Orientalism, Sylvestre de Sacy (1758–1838). Whereas the Enlightenment had found its model in China, Romanticism turned to India, the source of all mysticism (Schwab 1984; Halbfass 1988). The notion of an "originary mysticism" was itself a very recent idea.[30] The knowledge, however, of East Asian Buddhism was not advanced much at first by this proclivity because Indian Buddhism had not yet been rediscovered, despite ample evidence provided by the Jesuits that Chinese and Japanese Buddhism found their origins in India.[31] In the *Encyclopédie*, Diderot complained that, whereas the "dreamings of a Xekia [i.e.,

---

always, happens, incites man to a kind of quietism; lastly, that Buddhism could well constitute one of the metamorphoses, one of the avatars, of atheism" (Etiemble 1964, 45)

[30] Concerning the emergence of mysticism in the seventeenth century, see Certeau 1982. For a critique of the notion of "originary mysticism" as a mythical object and an analysis of its ideological function, see Isambert 1982.

[31] Antoine Gaubil wrote from Beijing in 1729 that "everything [the Chinese] have has come from the Indies, and you can easily be instructed from the Indies, unless that, everything having been lost in the Indies, one want to find again in China what cannot be found in the Indies." See Gaubil, *Correspondance de Pékin, 1722–1759* (Geneva: Droz, 1970), 233. Likewise, Engelbert Kaempfer wrote in his *Histoire naturelle* that Japanese Buddhism could be traced back to the Indian Buddha (Kaempfer 1732, 2: 59). See also Bernard 1941; and Glüer 1968.

Śākyamuni]" could "spread in India, China and Japan and become the law of hundred of millions of men," in the West, "a man is sometimes born among us with the most sublime talents, writes the wisest things, yet does not change the slightest custom, lives in obscurity, and dies ignored" (1875, 8: 456). Only toward the middle of the nineteenth century did Indian Buddhism suddenly come to the forefront, with the discovery of the *Lotus Sūtra* in Nepal by Hodgson and its ground-breaking translation by Eugène Burnouf, a French scholar whom Max Müller called "the true founder of a scientific study of Buddhism" (Welbon 1968, 109). The romantic search for origins gave way, however, to cultural versions of evolutionism in which Buddhism, like Hinduism, was reduced to one early stage of mankind.[32]

A variant of the evolutionist schema was applied by Hegel, who considered Asia as a metaphysical "Orient" and Buddhism as the "religion of substantiality" or of "being in itself" (*Insichsein*) (see Halbfass 1984; Dumoulin 1981). Hegel remained very dependent on Jesuit accounts, from which he inherited the conception of the Buddhist principle (*li*) as the "matter of all things" (*Grundstoff*).[33] From the outset, Hegel was convinced that "world history moves from East to West, Europe being the end of world history." He inherited the view that Buddhist meditation was a type of quietism, but judged it "a definite and necessary step of religious representation" (Dumoulin 1981, 462). Despite his misunderstanding of the Buddhist "principle," Hegel was able to distinguish between Buddhist emptiness and nothingness: "This does not mean that God is nothing, but that He is Indeterminate and that this Indeterminateness is God," or "the Being which is without further determination." Consequently, even if he thought to the end of his life that Eastern thought was *aufgehoben*, superseded by Western thought, he must have felt that the "teaching of Fo" was not pure Nihilism.

Owing to the lingering Jesuit influence, the study of Confucianism continued to prevail in Western Sinology, while Chinese Buddhism and Chan came to be considered mere offshoots of Indian mysticism. According to Norman Girardot, Western scholarship, in its emulation of Confucianism, "has on the whole remained a philologically oriented exegetical tradition based on the classical texts. The mesmerizing quality of this is shown by the fact that even after Western scholarship had recognized the less than objective and historical basis for this approach, the 'great tradition' of Confucianism continued to consume most of the efforts of the Chinese specialists.

---

[32] This conception was summarized by Goethe, in a discussion with Eckermann about Hindu philosophy (see Goethe 1949, 224).

[33] Longobardo (1701) first misinterpreted the Confucian *li* or "universal substance of all things" as being of a material nature, in his effort to prove that early Confucianism was materialist and therefore irreconcilable with Christianity.

The 'little traditions' of Taoism and Buddhism were simply ignored or, as an afterthought, fitted into the preexisting scheme established as the 'great tradition'" (Girardot 1979, 94).

The Jesuits returned to China in 1840, but they did not recuperate their mission in Beijing, where they had been supplanted by the Lazarists of St. Vincent de Paul. Although some among them, like Séraphin Couvreur (1835–1919) and Léon Wieger (1856–1933), did achieve significant sinological work, they never reached their former level of influence. With the overall shift from Jesuits to Protestant missionaries, the attitude toward Chinese Buddhism changed from one of relative disinterest or rivalry to one of active contempt for what was considered mere atheism and paganism. The optimism of the Jesuits was a thing of the past: even Confucianism could no longer redeem the "heathen Chinese" and their "false sects." Here is how Comte d'Escayrac de Lauture, in his *Mémoires sur la Chine*, attempts to justify his loquacious ignorance of Chinese religion: "I walk here in the dark, on paths that were never illuminated by the true light and are not worth being illuminated more completely" (d'Escayrac de Lauture 1865, 66).

As colonialism expanded over Asia, the image of China evolved from that of a model of enlightened government to that of a decadent, apathetic, and racially inferior country. In his *Christianisme en Chine, en Tartarie et au Tibet*, Father Huc declared: "Europe . . . is destined by Providence to regenerate the Asians, whose intellectual and moral vigour seems exhausted" (Huc 1857, 1: iv–v). In the view of Huc and his contemporaries, this degeneration was primarily owing to the influence of Buddhism.

Fostered by the development of scholarly Orientalism, the conjunction of pseudo-erudition, Christian intolerance, and colonialist self-importance reached one of its summits in a work of Jules Barthélémy Saint-Hilaire entitled *The Buddha and His Religion*. Well-known for his work on Aristotle and Western philosophy, this disciple of Eugène Burnouf was convinced that "Buddhism has nothing in common with Christianity, which stands as high above it as European societies stand above Asian societies" (*Trois lettres à M. l'abbé Deschamps* 1880, 2; quoted in Lubac 1952, 158). Barthélémy Saint-Hilaire's misguided conceptions, unfortunately, had a great influence on Friedrich Max Müller (1823–1900) and many other writers of the second half of the nineteenth century (see Neufeldt 1983). At any rate, if Barthélémy Saint-Hilaire devoted a whole book to refuting what he considered an inferior teaching, it is because Buddhism provided him with an ideological foil, a convenient way to extol the virtues of positivism and Western democracy:

> I believe that the study of Buddhism, in its more general outlines, will . . . show
> how a religion which has at the present day more adherents than any other on the

surface of the globe, has contributed so little to the happiness of mankind; and we shall find in the strange and deplorable doctrines which it professes, the explanation of its powerlessness for good. By a simple retrospection we shall be able to more thoroughly appreciate the moral inheritance which has been transmitted to us since the time of Socrates and Plato, and to guard it with all the more care and gratitude. (Barthélémy Saint-Hilaire 1895, 12)

To reassert the intellectual superiority of the West, Barthélémy Saint-Hilaire borrows from Voltaire an often-quoted passage: "To claim that these [Asian] peoples are atheistic is the same imputation as if we said that they are anti-Cartesian; they are neither for nor against Descartes: they are true children. A child is neither an atheist nor a deist; he is nothing" (Barthélémy Saint-Hilaire 1895, 176; see also d'Escayrac de Lauture 1865, 64). He ends, however, by defining Buddhism as a pure atheism, and denying it even the label of "mysticism":

> On the course that Indian philosophers pursued, two ways only were open, each as unfortunate as the other: either to stand still for ever in the immobility of Brahmanism, or to pursue with Buddhism the desperate courses of self-ignoring atheism and utter nihilism. The Buddha stopped at nothing, and his blind courage is one of the most striking qualities of his great spirit. In the present day, however, and after the teaching of Descartes, it seems difficult to understand and impossible to excuse such errors and such weaknesses. (ibid., 28)

Barthélémy Saint-Hilaire not only justified European colonialism by the moral decadence of Buddhism, but he also saw in the teaching of the Buddha a potential threat against democratic values at home:

> In the teaching of the Buddha, and in the wretched governments it has contributed to form, there is no place for liberty or for God. . . . Liberty cannot exist in human societies unless it is first received and enshrined in the soul of man; it is of spiritual birth. . . . Asia can, as it appears, dispense with liberty, but to us liberty is life itself, and philosophers must beware of furnishing arguments, even unintentionally, to those who contend against liberty, and would be glad to destroy it by invoking in defence of their arguments what they believe to be the teachings of science" (ibid., 29–30)

Saint-Hilaire's caricatural paternalistic tone makes us realize how much the assumptions of readership have changed since the time when these lines were written. Ironically, Saint-Hilaire's argument, and the smile of the implied reader, have in the meantime turned against him:

> The reader may smile as he glances over these legends; he may more probably feel impatient of their folly and absurdity. However, these extravagances form a part of the history of the human mind, and ought not to be contemptuously set

aside, even when they stray into the wildest superstitions. Moreover, a careful study will enable us the better to appreciate the intelligence of the peoples to whom the Buddha addressed himself, and whom he was destined to reform. (ibid., 67–68)

Obsessed as he was by the question of Nirvāṇa, Barthélémy Saint-Hilaire failed to distinguish properly between Indian and Chinese Buddhism. The closest he came to Chan was in his interpretation of meditation as a form of quietism, that is, as a forerunner of annihilation: "The doctrine of Dhyāna may therefore be considered a decisive commentary on that of Nirvāṇa; for, as by this transitory ecstatic state a transitory annihilation is already sought, so an eternal and definite annihilation may be sought in Nirvāṇa" (ibid., 144). Barthélémy Saint-Hilaire saw it his duty to describe this "hideous faith," which "shed such light on the destinies of the Asiatic world" (ibid., 144–145); he went as far as to paradoxically question, in the very name of the Enlightenment, the universality of reason: "In presence of such a curious and deplorable phenomenon, [the fact that the Chinese lack a word for God], confirmed moreover by their religion, it may be doubted if the intelligence of these nations is made of the same order as our own; and if in those climates, where life is held in abhorrence and where nothingness takes the place of God, human nature is the same as with us" (ibid., 177).

Barthélémy Saint-Hilaire's feeling of cultural superiority was not entirely innocent, for he also foresaw the potential appeal of the Buddha's message in the West, appeal that became manifest with Edwin Arnold's *The Light of the East*. To neutralize this influence he warned his readers:

> Buddhism can teach us nothing, and to follow its teaching would be disastrous to us. Notwithstanding its specious appearance, it is but a tissue of contradictions, and it is no calumny to say that, looked at closely, it is spiritualism without soul, virtue without duty, morality without liberty, charity without love, a world without nature and without God. What lesson can we draw from such teachings? And how much we should have to forget to become its disciples! How much lower we should have to descend in the scale of civilization! (ibid., 178–179)

One may reproach Barthélémy Saint-Hilaire for hiding his polemical tactics behind the scholarly erudition borrowed from his master Burnouf and understand Schwab's irritation with a man who, in his eyes, "ha[d] a great number of *prud'hommeries* on his mind" (Schwab 1950, 130; see also Welbon 1968, 75). However, Richard Welbon is justified to warn us that "to be righteously indignant *or* condescending in response to Barthélémy Saint-Hilaire's comments on Buddhism would be to miss the point entirely. That different stylistic and rhetorical conventions control the formal presentation of scholarly studies fifty or a hundred years later should not suggest to the sensitive reader that there are corresponding differences of sophistication with regard to insight into the subject matter" (Welbon 1968, 76). Indeed, it is because nineteenth-century Orientalists believed themselves more sophisticated than their Christian predecessors that they were so long in rediscovering what the Jesuits had already found, the Indian origins of Mahāyāna Buddhism. Nevertheless, Barthélémy Saint-Hilaire should not be entirely absolved on epistemological grounds: whatever his other philosophical achievements may have been, he was a rather mediocre Orientalist who did not compare with his master Burnouf. Yet Burnouf himself, who dismissed the miracles told in the *Lotus sūtra* as "incredible nonsense" (Burnouf 1973, 1: 417) was certainly not free from prejudice and condescendence. Barthélémy Saint-Hilaire was a mediocre mind, but a very successful vulgarizer, who merely amplified Burnouf's positivistic misinterpretation of Buddhism and Nirvāṇa.[34]

Similar epistemological limitations did not prevent a few of Burnouf's and Barthélémy Saint-Hilaire's contemporaries from reaching more accurate conclusions about Buddhism. As one of them, Ad. Franck, said after hearing Barthélémy Saint-Hilaire's lecture on Buddhist Nirvāṇa (1862), "In sum, and again confessing my ignorance of Sanskrit, I believe that our learned colleague has forced the sense of the texts he has translated. I believe that historical analogies, or the similarity of expressions employed by most of the pantheistic or mystical systems do not allow us to understand nirvana as absolute nothingness and to consider Buddhism to be an atheistic religion."[35]

Barthélémy Saint-Hilaire would have been well advised to read more carefully Rémusat's "Observations sur la religion samanéenne," an essay published posthumously in 1843, almost twenty years before *Le Buddha et*

[34] The influence of Burnouf on his contemporaries cannot be overestimated. Jules Michelet, for instance, wrote: "A great genius has revealed to us the Indian Christianity. . . . Burnouf has unveiled Buddhism, that distant Gospel, a second Christ at the end of the world. . . .Touching identity! . . . Unique miracle of two Gospels!" (Michelet, *Histoire des Français*, [1876] 10: 31). Gustave Flaubert, in his *Bouvart et Pécuchet*, shows the penetration of Buddhism in provincial bourgeoisie: " 'Do you know about it?' Pécuchet said to Monsieur Jeufroy, who was confused. 'Very well, listen to this. Buddhism recognized the vanity of earthly things better and earlier than Christianity. Its practices are austere, its faithful are more numerous than all Christians put together, and as for the Incarnation, Vishnu did not have one but nine! So, judge from that!' " (Flaubert 1976, 251). Pécuchet refers here to the Hindu belief that Buddha was the ninth (and penultimate) avatar of the god Viṣṇu. In *The Temptation of St. Antony*, first written in 1848 and revised until 1874, the Buddha appears just after Vishnu to St. Antony and Hilarion and tells them his life, whose episodes are compared by Hilarion to the prophecies concerning the Messiah, while Antony compares Buddha's temptation by Māra to his own. When he disappears, Hilarion comments: "You have just witnessed the belief of several hundred million men!" (Flaubert 1980, 167–171).

[35] Ad. Franck, *Séances et Travaux de l'Académie des sciences morales et politiques de l'Institut Impérial de France* (1862), 345; quoted in Welbon 1968, 77.

sa religion. In this work, Rémusat refuted the many errors of his predecessor, Joseph de Guignes, and denounced in particular the interpretation of Buddhism as a form of nihilism advocating the "law of Vou goei [*wuwei*, nonaction, term used to translate Nirvāṇa] or nothingness." According to Rémusat, "*Wou'weï* means the absolute, pure being, without attributes, without relations, without actions, perfection, mind, emptiness, nothingness, *non-being*, as opposed to what is contained in the entire visible and invisible nature" (see Rémusat 1843, 46–47).

In another essay on Chinese philosophy, "De la littérature chinoise," Rémusat stressed the need for a careful hermeneutics of Hindu and Buddhist concepts (ibid., 183). Against the accusations of nihilism leveled at Buddhism, he argued that "all these objections are a truly overweening verbosity from which one could have been defended had one given it some thought." That the alleged nihilism of the Buddha resulted from a blatant misinterpretation, "this is," claimed Rémusat, "what the slightest inspection of a Buddhist text on this topic would have revealed to less prejudiced judges" (ibid., 184–185). Rémusat concluded: "One could reproach [the Buddhists] for their abuse of contemplative subtleties and their excess of mysticism; but this excess and this abuse are diametrically opposed to the gross ineptitude for which they are blamed" (ibid., 186).

Although he was not entirely free himself from the flaws he denounced, Rémusat gave with his main work, an unfinished translation of the *Foe Koue ki ou Relation des royaumes bouddhiques de Fa-hien* published posthumously in 1836, the first relatively accurate account of the religion so despised by the Jesuits before him and by Barthélémy Saint-Hilaire and cohorts after him. The "annihilation" thesis, which was spread after Barthélémy Saint-Hilaire by people such as Ernest Renan, Hypolyte Taine, and Joseph-Arthur de Gobineau, became the established view among Europeans. It was slightly nuanced on philosophical grounds by Friedrich Max Müller, who suggested that it was a deviation from the original teachings of the historical Buddha.

After examining the intellectual background against which the study of Buddhism developed, I return to Chan "mysticism" because this aspect of Chan is what attracted the Westerners' attention. James Livingstone Stewart, for instance, in his *Chinese Culture and Christianity*, declares that those Buddhists he calls "the Mystics" are the more consistent descendants of Ta-mo and Buddha (Stewart 1926, 253). The alleged affinities between Buddhism and Christian mysticism were pointed out by Karl Neumann, who published side by side two Buddhist sūtras and a tract by Meister Eckhart, to show "their identity at their highest point" (Neumann 1891; quoted in Lubac 1952, 206). The vexing question of the possible influences of Buddhism on Christianity, which was raised in reaction to the earlier missionary attempt to interpret Buddhism as a degenerate Christianity, need not be explored here, but it is important to consider a theory that was to influence considerably the development of comparative religion, namely the description of Chan/Zen and Christian mysticism as two specific cases of a more fundamental religious phenomenon, a kind of "perennial mysticism." Take for instance the following comments, offered by Joseph Edkins after his relation of the legendary encounter of the Indian monk Bodhidharma with emperor Liang Wudi:

> This extract exhibits Buddhism very distinctly in its mystic phase. Mysticism can attach itself to the most abstract philosophical dogmas, just as well as to those of a properly religious kind. This state of mind, allying itself indifferently to error and to truth, is thus shown to be of purely subjective origin. The objective doctrines that call it into existence may be of the most opposite kind. It grows, therefore, out of the mind itself. Its appearance may be more naturally expected in the history of a religion like Christianity, which awakens the human emotions to their intensest exercise, while, in many ways, it favours the extended use of the contemplative faculties, and hence the numerous mystic sects of Church history. Its occurrence in Buddhism, and its kindred systems, might with more reason occasion surprise, founded as they are on philosophical meditations eminently abstract. It was reserved to the fantastic genius of India to construct a religion out of three such elements as atheism, annihilation, and the non-reality of the material world; and, by the encouragement of mysticism and the monastic life, to make these most ultimate of negations palatable and popular. The subsequent addition of a mythology suited to the taste of the common people was, it should be remembered, another powerful cause, contributing, in conjunction with these quietist and ascetic tendencies, to spread Buddhism through so great a mass of humankind. In carrying out his mystic views, Ta-mo [Bodhidharma] discouraged the use of the sacred books. He represented the attainment of the Buddhist's aim as being entirely the work of the heart. (Edkins 1890, 101–102)

Insofar as Chan was perceived as a kind of mysticism, it was considered typically un-Chinese; in other words, it was seen as profoundly Indian, even more so than Buddhism itself. Consequently, the origins of Chan were sought in various Indian teachings outside Buddhism. For the Jesuit Léon Wieger, a Protestant converted to Catholicism, who showed a basic contempt for Chinese "paganism," Chan was merely an offshoot of Vedantism.[36] In his premature synthesis, *A History of the Religious Beliefs and Philosophical Opinions in China*, Wieger writes:

> What is this doctrine, this system? . . . Has Bodhidharma invented a new thing, for which a special pigeon-hole must be appropriated in the collection of

---

[36] The same prejudice toward "pagan" superstitions appears in the work of another Jesuit, Henri Doré (1859–1931), whose famous *Recherches sur les superstitions en Chine* (5 volumes, 1914–1929) in fact plagiarized a Chinese work, the *Ji shuo quanzhen*, a work compiled in 1878 by a Chinese Jesuit, Father Hoang (see Demiéville 1966, 90). Despite its various shortcomings, Doré's work provides useful information on popular legends related to Chan.

the aberrations of the human mind? . . . No! I have already insinuated this above; Bodhidharma invented nothing. He merely imported into China the Indian Vedantism. . . . In the discourse of Bodhidharma, if one were to put *Brahman* in place of Buddha, of *bodhi*, and of the mystic body, one would have a perfect Vedantist *sutra*. It is useless to demonstrate that by reasoning. It will suffice to cite the principal points of the *Vedanta* . . . to render the identity obvious. (Wieger 1927, 528)

Concerning the characteristic use of *kōan* in Chan maieutics, Wieger noted:

> Hence the immense literature of the *Yü-lu*, written words, of the *Ch'an* school; a quantity of folios filled with incoherent, meaningless answers, made to any kind of questions, and carefully registered, without any commentary or explanation. These are not, as has been supposed, allusions to interior affairs of the convent, unknown to us. They are exclamations which escaped from the stultified ones, momentarily drawn from their coma. Oracles of *Brahman* which the other monks scrutinize to occupy themselves. (ibid., 530)

The conclusion of Wieger's text could have been written by Barthélémy Saint-Hilaire himself: "Let us sum up briefly. The *Ch'an*, still numerous in China and Japan, are Vedantists. They are not Buddhists. They do not observe any Buddhist practice. At present, the best among them are idle quietists, or stupid dreamers. The others amuse themselves by proposing or solving enigmas and charades, in prose or verse. It is better not to speak of their morals" (ibid., 532). In the end, however, he has to admit that the use of kōan was specific to Chan: "I do not know if the Indian Vedantists ever used similar processes to those which I have just enumerated. If they did not, the honor of their invention is to be attributed to the Chinese" (ibid., 532–533).

A slightly more positive (and somewhat positivist) account of the Linji school of Chan, which he calls the esoteric school, is given by E. Lamairesse, who interprets Bodhidharma's antinomianism as a kind of "Protestant" reaction against the increasing ritualism of Chinese Buddhism and an interiorization of morality (Lamairesse 1893, 84). Contrary to Ricci's view, Lamairesse approves the fact that "Chinese thinkers hold this system in great esteem, because they despise the adoration of images" (ibid., 86), and he notes that in the Tiantai school "the assistance of the senses was added to the mental abstraction of Bodhidharma" (ibid., 93). Nevertheless, Lamairesse compares the Chan teaching, according to which "the heart (mind) must keep itself in a state of perfection by rejecting everything that is exterior and by locking itself up in an existence as unconscious as sleep" (ibid., 63), to the "Sankya of the Patanjalis" [*sic*]. He remarks in another passage that Nirvāṇa is not annihilation, but beatitude through science (*gnosis*): "Nirvāṇa is the most perfect science, the broadest sight that can be conceived" (ibid., 68–69).

Wieger's assimilation of Chan with Vedantism has been uncritically accepted by many Western scholars. Henri Doré defines Chan as "the School of contemplation or of Chinese Vedantism (Dhyana)," and he adds: "It is the doctrine of *farniente* that fits so well the bonzes: 'To dream idly and do nothing.'" (Doré 1914–1929, 16: 263). This conception was spread until recently by the Jesuit Henri Bernard. For instance, after relating Ricci's story, quoted earlier, about how the sixth Chan patriarch Huineng used to feed maggots on his putrefied body, Bernard comments: "In Buddhist garb, it was the same Chan Vedantism that had been imported to China by Bodhidharma and that still flourishes in the Far East."[37] According to Bernard, that same metaphysical system was transplanted to Japan under the name of "Chinese wisdom," a mixture of neo-Confucian morality and Buddhist/Vedantist metaphysics" (Bernard 1935, 95). Bernard attributes to this crypto-Vedantism the failure of Christianity in Japan: "In reality, the Christian philosophy of the sixteenth century was not sufficiently armed to deeply penetrate the mentality of Japanese Vedantism, which was sustained by a tradition, a literature and an organized cult" (ibid., 96).

Other Western scholars, such as Edkins, also believed firmly that Chan was a Jain outgrowth:

> The word Ch'an . . . , originally signifying 'resign,' had not the meaning 'to contemplate' (now its commonest sense), before the Buddhists adopted it to represent the Sanscrit Dhyana. The word in Chinese books is spelt in full *jan-na*, and is explained, 'to reform one's self by contemplation or quiet thought.' Perhaps an Eastern extension of the Jaina, or some lost sect, still existing in India, took place thus early. The marked difference between the Buddhism of Bodhidharma, and that already existing in China, requires some such opposition." (Edkins 1890, 129)

In a later passage, Edkins resorts to a different argument, the resemblance between the patriarchal lineages of Jainism and Chan: "In seeking the best explanation of the Chinese and Japanese narrative of the patriarchs, and the seven Buddhas terminating in Gautama or Shakyamuni, it

---

[37] See Bernard 1937, 145; 1935, 66. See also Blyth 1960–1964, 1: 28. Interestingly, this idea has resurfaced recently, although for radically different ideological motivations, in the writings of Japanese scholars such as Hakamaya Noriaki (1986) and Matsumoto Shirō (1986). Elaborating on Takasaki Jikidō's work on the *Tathāgatagarbha* tradition, Hakamaya argues that the Tathāgatagarbha theory, which paved the way for the development of Chinese and Japanese Buddhism and constitutes an essential element of Chan/Zen teachings, is a radical departure from Buddhism and in fact a resurgence of Vedantism. One might rather argue with Paul Mus that both Indian Buddhism and Vedantism were antiritualist and "philosophical" reactions against, as well as offshoots of, Brahmanism (See Mus 1935, 127–210). Structural affinities do not always imply doctrinal influences.

is important to know the Jain tradition as they were early in the sixth century of our era, when the patriarch Bodhidharma removed to China" (ibid., 157).

Not surprisingly, various authors have also traced Chan back to Hīnayāna/Theravāda Buddhism. For instance, James L. Stewart, focusing on the Hīnayāna-influenced Buddhists who had made their way into China, writes: "Prominent among these new teachers was no less a personage than the twenty-eighth patriarch or pope of Buddhism [Bodhidharma]. . . . He disbelieved in all outward forms and images, even in the use of sacred books, and taught the abstraction of the mind from all objects of sense and its own thoughts. In this the smaller vehicle of the south held closer to the Buddha's Law" (Stewart 1926, 251). Despite this rather sympathetic presentation of Bodhidharma, Stewart finds accents that recall the style of Wieger to describe what he calls "Mystic" meditation: "One has but to look at the faces of these misguided seekers of the Way, to believe that the process in many cases is too sadly true and that they become half comatose creatures devoid of the glow and splendor of the Divine image within. Others, doubtless, find, as has been demonstrated in many another monkish system, that this way of meditation, far from bringing the destruction of the desires, brings through inactivity but greater incitement, and makes baser thoughts more dominant" (ibid., 254). Apparently, this characterization of Buddhist meditation had become a cliché among Christian missionaries by the end of the nineteenth century,[38] and mysticism and contemplation were seen as mere spiritual counterparts to (and alibis for) indolence and laziness (Almond 1988, 50).

Scholarly efforts to trace Chan and Zen back to their Indian sources have not been abandoned. A relatively recent example is provided by Shanta Ratnayaka's "Zen is the Theravāda Branch of Buddhism in Mahāyāna Countries."[39] The author first attempts to demonstrate how Zen differs from Mahāyāna, and then, resorting to available "historical evidence"

[38] Similar accounts in Philosinensis [!] 1834, 214–225; Culbertson 1857, 79; and Davis 1857, 2: 48. See Almond 1988, 120. To give just one example: "They have, nearly all of them [Buddhist monks], an expression approaching to idiotcy [sic], which is probably acquired by that dreamy state in which one of their most famous professors is said to have passed nine years with his eyes fixed upon a wall" (Davis, ibid.).

[39] See Ratnayaka 1980. Practically all references are to Suzuki and the "essence of Zen." See also Winston King, "A Comparison of Theravāda and Zen Buddhist Methods of Meditation and Goals": "My basic assumption is that the two types of meditation are fundamentally similar in function and experience, although certain features of technique, mode of expression, and emotional flavour vary with their respective cultural context" (1970, 305). Although King argues convincingly for some methodological affinities between Theravāda and Chan forms of meditation, he does not seek to reduce one to the other. Nevertheless, his assumption of an experiential similarity tends to reinforce claims that Theravāda and Zen are the earliest, that is, the purest, forms of Buddhism—by opposition to the "degenerate" forms of Mahāyāna.

concerning the South Indian monk Bodhidharma, he concludes that the latter was probably influenced by Theravāda. The alleged similarities between Bodhidharma's teaching and Theravāda are the "independence of the Scriptures" (hardly a typical feature of Theravāda!), the emphasis on an "inner experience acquired through meditation," the importance of "sudden awakening," and the use of paradoxical or cryptic expressions (kōan), not to mention the uncannily similar monastic life-styles. Thus, concludes Ratnayaka, what Bodhidharma brought to China was the contemplative technique known as *vipaśyanā*, and not the dhyāna from which Chan falsely derives its name. However, this type of comparison is so obviously flawed by its shallow understanding of crucial Chan notions such as "sudden awakening," its overall reductionism, and its ideological stakes, that it hardly needs to be discussed here. In a more sophisticated essay, "Reflections on the Relation between Early Buddhism and Zen," David Kalupahana, after correctly noting that Chan was as much a result as a rejection of the Madhyamika-Yogācara syncretism, suggested that Chan masters were influenced by another Buddhist tradition, probably the tradition stemming from the Chinese translation of the *Āgamas*, the earliest discourses of the Buddha (Kalupahana 1976, 171). Kalupahana attempts to explain the absence of any reference to the *Āgamas* in Chan literature by suggesting that these texts were too well-known as representative of the Hīnayāna viewpoint; thus, they would have been improper for Mahayanists to quote. However, it is well known that Chan monks did use some clearly Hinayanistic Scriptures, like the *Sūtra in Forty-two Sections (Si shi erzhang jing*, T. 17, 784), which they simply rewrote in Mahayanistic fashion. Because he relies too heavily on the problematic notion of textual influence, in what may appear an attempt to downplay Chan's novelty, Kalupahana fails to make a convincing case. This is not to say that no comparison between Chan/Zen and Indian Buddhism or Indian religion is possible or useful. Many ritual aspects of Chan, for instance, find clear antecedents in Buddhist (and even pre-Buddhist) India. However, instead of dwelling on hypothetical doctrinal influences between one "mysticism" and another, it would be more rewarding to point out structural affinities between advocates of the "Supreme Vehicle" like Chan and Vajrayāna (see Hoffman 1971).

THE APOSTLE BODHIDHARMA

I have examined some "philosophical" arguments that structured the Orientalist discourse about Chan Buddhism. Another principle of organization was biographical (or better, hagiographical). After the eviction of the Jesuits from China, and until the early twentieth century, most information available in the West on Chan and Zen was provided casually, as part of material on China or Buddhism. In that period little attention was paid to Chan/Zen doctrine as such, for Chinese Buddhism, unlike Indian Buddhism, was not considered worthy of serious study. At least one topic related to Chan, however, was consistently taken up; the topic had been first stressed by Jesuit missionaries: it is the life of Bodhidharma, the founder of the school of "mystic contemplation," and, according to Edkins, "an ascetic of the first water" (Edkins 1890, 86), whose followers had "extended themselves on every hand, and gained an almost complete victory over steady orthodoxy" (ibid., 157).

The interest in Bodhidharma resulted from a rather curious error, typical of the early missionary zeal to attempt to prove that Buddhism was a degenerate form of Christianity. Struck by the similarities between Christian and Buddhist monks, Francis Xavier had already suggested this possibility. Ricci, when he visited the Nanhua monastery in Southern China, also noticed these similarities and suggested two possible Christian sources:

> It is historically clear that this doctrine was brought into China at the identical period in which the Apostles were preaching the doctrine of Christ. Bartholomew was preaching in upper India, namely in Hindustan and the surrounding countries, when Thomas was spreading the Gospel in lower India, to the South. It is not beyond the realm of possibility, therefore, that the Chinese, moved and interested by reports of the truths contained in the Christian Gospel, sought to contact it and to learn it from the West. Instead, however, . . . the Chinese received a false importation in place of the truth they were seeking." (Gallagher 1953, 98)

Whereas Ricci's successors attributed this Christian influence to the apostle Thomas, Ricci denied that the Chinese ever received directly the teaching of an apostle and suggested that they only had a vague taste of the Gospels through the indirect influence of another apostle, Bartholomew: "This [Buddhist] philosophy seems not only to have borrowed from the West [i.e., from Democritus and Pythagoras] but to have actually caught a glimpse of light from the Christian Gospels. . . . In reciting prayers they frequently repeat a certain name, which they pronounce Tolome [Bodhidharma?] but which they themselves do not understand. Again, it might possibly be that in doing this they wish to honor their cult with the authority of the Apostle Bartholomew" (Gallagher 1953, 99).

More than a century later, Gabriel de Magaillans had forgotten Ricci's caution and gave a detailed account of the preaching of the Gospels in China:

> These *Lamas* are ordinarily dressed with red and yellow robes . . . ; somewhat in the way in which the Apostles are represented, and as if they had imitated in

this the Apostle St. Thomas, who, to all appearances, came to China and stayed there for some time. For the Histories and Chronicles of China record that, during the reign of the *Han* family, at the time in which our Lord Jesus-Christ was born, there came from the Indies to this Empire a Holy Man called *Tamo*, who preached and taught a Holy Law; that the bonzes opposed it and persecuted the Saint in such a way that, seeing that he was making no progress, he returned to the Indies; that he carried a staff in his hand and was bareheaded; and that one day, as he desired to cross that large River called *Kiam*, or "Son of the Sea," by the Chinese, and no one wanted to ferry him across because they had been prejudiced against him by the Bonzes, he crossed that river dry-shod. One reads about many other miracles and wonderful actions of this Saint. One should not raise objections because the Chinese call him *Tamo* instead of Thomas:[40] for as we corrupt Chinese names, they too corrupt those of other Nations, so that it is often impossible to recognize them." (Magaillans 1688, 347–348)

In his *Histoire du Christianisme des Indes* (1724), La Croze, quoting a letter written from Fuzhou by Father Maigrot in 1699, already pointed out the error of Magaillans and Le Comte: "[These] missionaries have confused the Apostle St. Thomas with a certain *Tamo*, . . . one of the most unworthy frauds that ever entered China" (La Croze 1724, 43). In another passage, he refers to "the idol *Tamo*, which some imbecile or deceitful missionaries have dared to pass as the Apostle Saint Thomas," and who "descends from Xaca through hundred twenty-eight [*sic*] degrees of succession" (ibid., 506). One century later, Rémusat denounced together the absurdities found in the Chan notion of a lineage of twenty-eight Indian patriarchs spanning from Buddha to Bodhidharma, (Rémusat 1825– 1826, 127) and in the Jesuit amalgamation of *Damo* with Thomas:

> The name of Bodhidharma . . . gave rise to curious errors. Old missionaries have taken him for Saint Thomas. Father Couplet believed that he was the twenty-eighth descendant of the Buddha; and Georgi, by adopting this erroneous supposition, and moreover committing an error of hundred generations, or about three thousand years, makes *Ta-mo* the one hundred and twentieth descendant of Chakia [Śākyamuni], and thinks that he is the same as a certain Thomas, a disciple of Manes. It is superfluous to point out the absurd character of such comparisons. (ibid., 126)

Yet, Rémusat himself failed to distinguish Bodhidharma from the "historical" Buddha: "In the fifth century of our era, Buddha, then born as the son of a king of Mabar, in Southern India, judged it opportune to leave Hindustan never to return there, and went to stay in China. . . . This god was then called *Bodhidharma*; in China, where it is usual to disfigure

---

[40] Incidentally, according to Voragine's *Golden Legend*, "Thomas" is etymologically derived from "abyss," "twin," or *thomos*, "division," "sharing." Small wonder then that Thomas found in *Damo* an *alter ego* and that the Christians were divided on this question.

foreign words, he was called *Tamo*, and several missionaries, who had heard about him under this name, believed that the person in question could only be Saint Thomas" (ibid., 135).

At the turn of the century. J.J.M. de Groot mentions the existence in eighteenth century Jiangsu of a sect founded by a certain Zhang Baotai, who claimed to be the physical descendant of Bodhidharma in the forty-eighth generation (de Groot 1901, 278–279). According to de Groot, the followers of this sect, apparently influenced by Lamaism, believed in successive reincarnations of their Indian patriarch: "Bodhidharma was supposed to have reincarnated himself in each patriarchal generation. . . . Each living abbot is not only Bodhidharma's lawful successor for the maintenance of Buddha's doctrine of Salvation, but also an incarnation of his spirit. It is generally admitted that the soul of the great Patriarch lives in him. So every new abbot means a re-incarnation of the Saint" (ibid.).

When it became clear from the Bodhidharma legend that he could not have been one of the Christian apostles, Jesuit missionaries, trying to hide their earlier enthusiasm for this solitary figure, sharply criticized his quietistic meditation.[41] As noted earlier, du Halde, emulating the Confucian critics of Chan, had already complained about this aspect of Bodhidharma's teaching:

> This *Tamo*, the Person so cried up, who is come out of the West into China, passed as they say nine years in the Mountain Tsong [Song shan] in continual contemplation; he continued immoveable with his Eyes fixed upon the Wall, without changing his situation, and yet this contemplative Sluggard wanted none of the Necessaries of Life, but had a plentiful Supply of all sorts of Provisions and Clothes: Suppose, after his Example, every private Person should take it in their Heads to imitate this kind of Life, what would become of the most necessary Professions? Who could take care of cultivating the Fields, and make the useful Products of the Loom? Whence would they have Garments, and Food to support Life? Can it be imagin'd that a Doctrine whose Practice, if it were universal, would put the Empire in Confusion should be the true Doctrine?" (du Halde 1741, 3:277)

Here again, the Jesuits were quick to find the beam in their neighbor's eye. Almost two centuries later, Léon Wieger was still writing in the same vein about the Chan patriarch: "The truth is that Bodhidharma was rejected by

---

[41] Concerning this point, Reginald F. Johnston, writing in 1913, says: "It is distressing to find that the ridiculous theory, first put forward by Catholic missionaries, that Bodhidharma was the Apostle St. Thomas, is for ever rising phoenix-like from the flames of destructive criticism" (375). This theory was apparently still accepted by some Christian missionaries. Even when it was debunked, other, even more absurd, theories were put forward. For example, Louis Gaillard, in his *Croix and Svastika*, suggests that the mention "religion of Ta-mo" (reading Damas for Ta-mo) might refer to the Nestorians (Gaillard 1987, 77).

the monks of India as an unbeliever, and repulsed by those of China on the same ground. Bodhidharma was not a Buddhist. After his death, his doctrine spread in China, and his disciples formed a sect, falsely classed among the Buddhist sect" (Wieger 1927, 523).

According to Wieger, not only was Bodhidharma's doctrine rejected by the Buddhist monks, he himself was not even a Buddhist, and the type of meditation he advocated was proved a mere fraud leading to moral corruption:

> Now Bodhidharma rejected the recitations also, which were useless according to his opinion. Prohibiting all the books and all study, he set up the sole principle, of personal and individual *buddhification*, by a kind of contemplation of his interior, which I will call *endovision*. . . . That contemplation without theme, without process, not methodical like that of the Mahayanist . . . , but purely intuitive, ought to form the only preoccupation of the aspirant to perfection. It was to that, that Bodhidharma applied himself uninterruptedly during his last years. It was in practicing it that he died. Now, such contemplation cannot be sustained, as an intellectual act. The only result that it can produce, if it is practiced seriously, is idiocy. And if it is not practiced seriously, that mental idleness leads fatally to immorality. (ibid., 254)

The vehemence of Wieger's criticism of Chan is strangely reminiscent of the attacks on Chan "quietism" made by Chan monks like Shenhui, and his judgment on Bodhidharma himself calls to mind that of the Tokugawa historian Tominaga Nakamoto.[42] Significantly, Wieger showed a greater tolerance toward Pure Land Buddhism, which seems to have appealed to him with its notion of a savior. A more understanding account of Bodhidharma's teaching was given by Reginald F. Johnston: "It is this Indian sage, this searcher of hearts and scorner of books, who is regarded as the founder, in China, of the Ch'an or Contemplative school of Buddhism. 'You will not find Buddha in images or books,' was the teaching of the venerable Tamo. 'Look into your own heart: that is where you will find Buddha'" (Johnston 1913, 83). According to Johnston, "Tamo's system has been described as 'the Buddhist counterpart of the Spiritual Exercises of St. Ignatius of Loyola'; but there are other Christian saints and mystics with whom he may be compared even more fittingly." The examples given by Johnston are St. Francis of Assisi, St. Paul, St. Augustine, Richard and Hugo of St. Victor, and of course Meister Eckhart (ibid., 84–85). Nevertheless, Johnston believed that the results of Buddhist "mysticism" are

[42] See the following passage in Tominaga's *Shutsujō kōgo*: "Ah, Bodhidharma! He went to such a distant land for the sake of his Dharma-way, desiring to spread it, but his words were so lofty that no one could believe or receive it, and he died at the hand of a wicked, miserable unbeliever. I regard Bodhidharma as the man most to be pitied in the whole earth, past and present" (Tominaga 1990, 152).

mixed, and that "there is reason to suspect that some monks who believed themselves to have attained the exalted state of mystical union were apt to confuse that state with the less honourable condition of physical somnolence" (ibid., 86). Contrary to Wieger, however, Johnston preferred Chan to Amidism: "Ch'an doctrines are to the educated Buddhist what the Amidist doctrines are to the ignorant" (ibid., 93).

CLAUDEL AND BUDDHISM

Let us close this survey of the Orientalist misrepresentations of Chan/Zen Buddhism with a more ambivalent case, that of the French poet Paul Claudel, who was a diplomat in China and Japan. Although nuanced by his poetical genius, Claudel's attitude toward Buddhism was at first typically negative. In a text written in 1898, deploring the alleged atheism of the Buddha, to whom "it was given to perfect pagan blasphemy" and to achieve the "monstrous communion" with nothingness, Claudel glosses the term Nirvāṇa as follows: "People have been surprised by this word. As for me, I see in it the idea of *pleasure* added to that of Nothingness. And here is the last and Satanic mystery, the silence of the creature entrenched in its integral denial, the incestuous quietude of the soul resting on its essential difference."[43]

Claudel was touched, however, by the simplicity of the Chinese and Japanese monasteries. Visiting a Chinese Buddhist temple in 1896, he described meditating monks in the following terms: "Four bonzes, perched on wooden stools, meditate inside the gate. Their shoes remain on the ground in front of them, and, without feet, detached, imponderable, they are seated over their own thought. They do not move at all. . . . The consciousness of their inertia suffices to the digestion of their intelligence."[44]

In that same year, while visiting another temple, the "Temple of Consciousness," Claudel wrote: "Shall I not compare this vast landscape that opens before me, up to the double enclosure of mountains and clouds, to a flower whose mystical heart is that seat? Is it not the point where the place, composing itself in its harmony, takes as it were existence and conscience of

---

[43] "Les gens se sont étonnés de ce mot. Pour moi, j'y trouve à l'idée de Néant ajoutée celle de *jouissance*. Et c'est là le mystère dernier et Satanique, le silence de la créature retranchée dans son refus intégral, la quiétude incestueuse de l'âme assise sur sa différence essentielle" (Claudel 1974, 105).

[44] "Quatre bonzes, juchés sur des escabeaux, méditent à l'intérieur de la porte. Leurs chaussures sont restées à terre devant eux, et, détachés, impondérables, ils siègent sur leur propre pensée. Ils ne font pas un mouvement. . . . La conscience de leur inertie suffit à la digestion de leur intelligence" (Claudel 1974, 32).

itself, and whose occupant unites in the contemplation of his mind one line and the other?"[45]

After 1906, having read Léon Wieger's "translation" of Laozi and Zhuangzi, Claudel became attracted to Daoism, interpreting *wuwei* or "non-action" as man's receptiveness to God and apparently identifying the Dao with divine grace (Etiemble 1964, 99). A later text of his, dated January 1925 and addressed to a Japanese painter, begins with an elogious reference to Chan: "One of the cardinal tenets of the Chan sect is that the great Truths are ineffable. They cannot be taught, they communicate themselves to the soul through a kind of contagion. A reasoning will always be neutralized by another reasoning, but the tumult at the bottom of our soul will not be able to resist very long against silence, nor the water against the reflection."[46]

Significantly, Claudel wrote these lines a few years before D. T. Suzuki published his famous *Essays on Zen Buddhism*. The transition in Claudel's writings about Buddhism and Zen, from the "monstrous communion" with nothingness to the peaceful harmony with the Dao, seems to prefigure the reversal of signs that took place in the Western perception of Zen since the 1930s.

As noted earlier, this reversal should not be interpreted too quickly as a proof that we have transcended the limits of our predecessors; the contrary prevails. Perhaps the impossibility in which we are to rid ourselves of cultural and epistemological constraints does not prevent us from understanding other cultures, as long as we remain conscious of these constraints and consider them as providing the necessary perspective for any "thick description." Inasmuch as the Chan/Zen tradition is alive and does not simply seduce us with the "beauty of the dead" (Certeau 1986) that characterizes "scientific" objects, it is constantly reinvented and its rhetorical tactics subvert the patronizing discourse of orthodox scholars. Thus, Western scholarship, despite or because of its assumed prejudices, and in particular because it is less constrained by the dominant discourse of later Zen orthodoxy, might be able to contribute significantly to this "reinvention of the tradition."

[45] "Ne comparerai-je pas ce vaste paysage qui s'ouvre devant moi jusqu'à la double enceinte des monts et des nuages à une fleur dont ce siège est le coeur mystique? N'est-il pas le point géométrique où le lieu, se composant dans son harmonie, prend, pour ainsi dire, existence et comme conscience de lui-même, et dont l'occupant unit dans la contemplation de son esprit une ligne et l'autre?" (Claudel 1974, 59–60).

[46] "Un des principes de la secte Zen est que les grandes Vérités sont ineffables. Elles ne peuvent pas être enseignées, elles se communiquent à l'âme par une espèce de contagion. Un raisonnement toujours va être neutralisé par un autre raisonnement, mais le tumulte au fond de notre âme ne pourra se déprendre longtemps contre le silence, ni l'eau contre le reflet" (Claudel 1974, 219).

Chapter Two

THE RISE OF ZEN ORIENTALISM

WE HAVE REACHED the point where Zen emerged as an epistemological object, a unit of discourse in Western Orientalism.
As we saw in the previous chapter, this emergence was prepared by a long history of (failed) encounters between the West and Buddhism. However, through the work of a single individual—the Japanese
scholar Suzuki Daisetsu, better known in the West as D. T. (Daisetz
Teitarō) Suzuki—Zen suddenly acceded to full visibility. Suzuki took on
the task of transmitting Zen to, and interpreting it for, the West in terms
that made it a topic of interest to Western scholars of religion and not just a
scapegoat for missionary-influenced "great tradition" Sinologists. His first
endeavor was to provide a doctrinal basis for a unified and universal Buddhism with his discussion and English translation of the *Awakening of
Faith in Mahāyāna* (see Ketelaar 1990, 187–191). He also contributed to
the formation of a "minimal" canon of Zen.[1]

Suzuki was preceded in the West by his master Shaku Sōen, who first
came to the United States in 1893 to participate in the World Parliament of
Religions. Sōen's addresses to the Parliament relied heavily on Suzuki's
translations. The World Parliament revealed the cultural misunderstandings still at work behind an apparent religious pluralism (see Ketelaar
1990). These misunderstandings surfaced, for example, in the "controversy on Buddhism" that opposed Sōen (and later the Ceylonese monk
Dharmapāla) to the theologians John Barrows and F. F. Ellingwood, who
drew their arguments from Western scholars such as Burnouf, Barthélémy
Saint-Hilaire, and Max Müller.[2] Sōen's acquaintance with Paul Carus led
the latter to invite Suzuki in 1897 to work as an assistant in translating *The
Gospel of the Buddha* and other Asian texts. Sōen returned to the United
States in 1905–1906 and toured the country in the company of Suzuki.
Two other early exponents of Zen were Nukariya Kaiten, author of *The
Religion of the Samurai* (London 1913), and Anesaki Masaharu, who

---

[1] This "canon" included works such as the *Green Cliff Record* (Ch. *Biyanlu*, J.
Hekiganroku), the *Ten Oxherding Pictures* (Ch. *Shiniu tu*, J. *Jūgyūzu*), the *Platform Sūtra of
the Sixth Patriarch* (Ch. *Liuzu tanjing*, J. *Rokuso dangyō*), the *Song on the Realization of the
Way* (Ch. *Zhengdao ge*, J. *Shōdōka*), or Hakuin's *Orategama*. Later, it came to include the
works of Shenhui and the Japanese master Bankei.

[2] See Shaku Soyen, John Barrows, and F. F. Ellingwood, "A Controversy on Buddhism,"
The Open Court 11 (1897): 43; quoted in Fader 1982.

represented the modernizing trend in Zen and who lectured on Zen at the Collège de France in Paris (Anesaki 1921). None of them, however, had Suzuki's fluency in a Western language, and their influence was short-lived. Another significant contribution to the emergence of Zen "Orientalism" was Okakura Kakuzō's *The Book of Tea*, which, together with Suzuki's *Zen and Japanese Culture*, turned Zen into an aesthetic teaching that formed the quintessence of the Japanese spirit (see Okakura 1964; Suzuki 1970).

Suzuki's Zen

Spanning from the turn of the twentieth century to the mid-1960s, Suzuki's work played a major role in the constitution of a Zen discourse in Japan and the West. In the wake of Suzuki, a significant contribution to the elaboration of a Zen philosophy was made by the so-called Kyōto School, which was founded by Suzuki's friend Nishida Kitarō (1870–1945). Despite their different intellectual itineraries, both Suzuki and Nishida were still speaking from within the discursive arena opened by Western Orientalism. That is to say, their description of Zen is in many respects an inverted image of that given by the Christian missionaries, and they relied on Christian categories even when rejecting them. If the Western standpoint represented an Orientalism "by default," one in which Buddhism was looked down upon, Suzuki and Nishida, among others, represent an Orientalism "by excess," a "secondary" Orientalism that offers an idealized, "nativist" image of a Japanese culture deeply influenced by Zen.

The importance of Suzuki's work has been at times greatly overestimated. According to Lynn White, for example, "it may well be that the publication of D. T. Suzuki's first *Essays in Zen Buddhism* in 1927 will seem in future generations as great an intellectual event as William Moerbeke's Latin translation of Aristotle in the thirteenth century or Marisglio Ficino's of Plato in the fifteenth."[3] Likewise, Arnold Toynbee declared in all seriousness that Suzuki's introduction of Zen to the West would be later compared to the discovery of nuclear energy (Franck 1982, 5). More recently, Gerald Cooke wrote that "no one compares with Suzuki in carrying out this task [of making Zen relevant to the West] in terms of solid scholarly grounding plus personal experience plus productivity in the medium of English. Here was the Commodore Perry of Japan's opening of the West to a first extensive exposure to East—bold, affirmative, persistent" (Cooke 1974, 276).

How, we might ask, could these statements have been uttered at all, and

[3] Lynn White, ed. *Frontiers of Knowledge in the Study of Man* (New York: Harper and Brothers, 1956), 304–305.

why were the obvious shortcomings of Suzuki's Zen apparently invisible to Suzuki himself and to his many Western followers (among whom were such leading figures in the intellectual world as Erich Fromm, Carl Gustav Jung, Thomas Merton, and Aldous Huxley)? In a different way, the over-reaction of some of Suzuki's critics (notably Koestler) betrays a similar fascination with the man. For all its rhetoric, the success of Suzuki's work was not related to its literary or philosophical qualities; it was rather the result of a historical conjuncture that prompted the emergence in the West of a positive modality of Orientalist discourse, which found in the image of Zen fostered by Suzuki a particularly appropriate object.

Suzuki allegedly wanted to construct a bridge between East and West and to provide a Zen response to the modernization of Japan.[4] Whether he achieved this goal or merely established a bridgehead is a moot point. At any rate, his work is located at the crossroad between Western and Japanese cultures. In this chapter, I take up the question of the influence of Suzuki's English writings on Western intellectuals, reserving for later the question of Suzuki's role in Japanese Buddhist scholarship. The English-language works of Suzuki are sufficiently well-known, and in any case too voluminous, to be reviewed here in great detail. Suffice it to consider a few examples taken from his early work, *Essays in Zen Buddhism*, and a few other seminal writings that illustrate certain prevalent tendencies in Suzuki's work.

Suzuki's success had also a lot to do with his undeniable personal charisma. As noted already, he did not leave his interlocutors indifferent, and most judgments on his work are influenced by personal reactions to his personality. It is therefore hard to dissociate the image of the man, with his genuine simplicity, warmth, and his status of enlightened layman, from the impression left by his assertions concerning the Chan/Zen tradition. However, I want to consider here the "Suzuki effect," which requires examining a certain type of discourse, how this discourse was propagated by Suzuki, and conversely how Suzuki himself was the product of it. Suzuki's obvious sincerity and his intense yearning for transcendence did not prevent his thinking from being ideologically flawed, informed as it was by his culture, his social status, and his sectarian affiliations. This, of course, raises the questions of the place whence he spoke and whether an enlightened person can assume any privilege with regard to historical determinations. Suzuki claimed this privilege for Zen masters, and by implication for himself. Leaving this question open, we can still point out some aspects of his description of Zen that bear witness to the ideological effects of this

---

[4] On the role of Suzuki in the modernization of Zen, see Cooke 1974, 275–282.

discourse and discern various contradictions or changes in Suzuki's thought.

The Rinzai Approach

According to one of his Western admirers, the Trappist monk Thomas Merton, Suzuki "was entirely free from the dictates of partisan thought-patterns and academic ritualism," and his work, "one of the unique spiritual and intellectual achievements of our time," is "without question the most complete and most authentic presentation of an Asian tradition and experience by any one man in terms accessible to the West."[5] Likewise, the Japanese Zen scholar and disciple of Suzuki Furuta Shōkin argues that, despite the fact that many of Suzuki's works deal with Rinzai philosophy, "this does not mean it should be taken as Rinzai Zen in the sectarian sense." According to Furuta, Suzuki's ideas "are unrelated to any particular Zen sect." This fact "gives his Zen its unique character, and it will elude any attempt to fit it into a sectarian framework" (Furuta 1967b, 123).

Let us nevertheless try.

Did Suzuki emphasize the Rinzai teaching simply because he was more acquainted with it than with the Sōtō teaching, or did his omission of Sōtō Zen imply a sectarian bias on the part of a man whose pivotal role in the history of Zen was compared by Furuta to that of Dōgen (Furuta 1967b, 116)? Suzuki fully endorsed the Rinzai account of the controversy that opposed the Song Chan masters Dahui Zonggao (1089–1163) and Hongzhi Zhengjue (1091–1157) regarding the respective value of kōan practice (J. kanna zen) and sitting meditation (mokushō zen). Suzuki painstakingly refuted the view of those Sōtō Zen masters who, like Hongzhi and Dōgen, downplay kōan and satori and advocate instead a quietistic form of meditation (shikan taza, "sitting-only") (Suzuki 1949–1953, 2: 22). While he presented Dahui Zonggao as a representative of Zen orthodoxy, he never mentioned the names of Dahui's rivals, nor the strong criticism leveled at Dahui by Dōgen. Tracing the kanna-zen/mokushō-zen controversy back to the paradigmatic "sudden/gradual" controversy, he implicitly misconstrued the Sōtō position as "quietist" and "gradual" by drawing a parallel between it and the traditionally misconstrued gradualism of the Northern school. In fact, the Rinzai position, as Suzuki describes it, is the one that could most aptly be labeled "gradual" and dualistic because it stresses the use of "expedient" means (the kōan) to reach the goal of satori. In a passage that refers explicitly to the Sōtō tradition,

---

[5] Thomas Merton, "D. T. Suzuki: The Man and his Work," *The Eastern Buddhist*, n.s., 2, 1 (1967): 3–9.

Suzuki tries to soften his criticism: "Most Japanese adherents of the Sōtō school of Zen belong to this class of kōan denouncers. This divergence of views as to the kōan exercise and the experience of satori comes rather from the differences of philosophical interpretation given to Zen by the followers of the Sōtō and the Rinzai. As far as the practice is concerned, both the Sōtō and the Rinzai are descendants of Bodhidharma and Hui-neng" (Suzuki 1949–1953, 2: 116). This argument is not convincing, because what is really at issue in Suzuki's criticism of Sōtō Zen is first a question of practice and realization, then only a matter of philosophical interpretation (provided that the two can be thus separated).

In an article that constitutes an isolated attempt to deal with the problems of a heterogeneous, multivocal tradition and where Suzuki acknowledges "three types of [Zen] thought" by contrasting the teachings of Dōgen to those of the Rinzai masters Hakuin and Bankei, his dislike for Dōgen's Zen comes out clearly: "It can be said that '*taza*-ism' places weight on philosophy and overlooks the psychological or practical side. The nonduality of 'practice and realization are nondual' belongs to philosophy. This nonduality alone is not enough. Once we speak of practice and realization, we are compelled to give thought to each of them" (Suzuki 1976, 7).

Intent on criticizing Dōgen's stress on meditation, Suzuki observed how Dōgen, speaking from the ambivalent standpoint of a great thinker and that of a "devout, passionate, solemn, practical, conscientious man of religion and student of Zen" (ibid., 12), "mixes at will in a confusing way the two senses in which he takes zazen, using the word at random to assault just about everything around" (ibid., 7–8). Ironically, the same reproach could be made of Suzuki himself. For him, the fact that Dōgen placed stronger emphasis on zazen than on satori explains why there is in him "a strong tendency to take the standpoint of nonduality as a peak and to see, from there, the myriad different ways leading out" (ibid., 13). Thus, Dōgen's work reveals "a *contemplation* of the Silent Illumination type, and the dynamic aspect of the reciprocal interrelation between one thing and another, the aspect of discrimination in non-discrimination, rather tends to be obscured" (ibid.).

According to Suzuki, "the odor of Silent Illumination" that accompanies Dōgen's kind of sitting is not easily removed. This "faint shadow of stagnation and inactivity" in Dōgen's Zen is, Suzuki argues, what Hakuin described as "sitting still and silent like a withered tree and holding on to the death" (Suzuki 1976, 16) Dōgen's famous description of his own awakening, "body and mind dropping off, dropping off body and mind" (J. *shinjin datsuraku, datsuraku shinjin*) is, in Suzuki's dialectical interpretation, merely negative, and Dōgen "makes no mention of anything emerging beyond this negation" (Suzuki 1976, 4). "In Dōgen's utterance," Suzuki insists, "something is lacking. There is no way that just sitting, if it ends in the experience of body and mind dropping off, can avoid being mere Silent Illumination, taking that designation in a pejorative sense." Suzuki concludes that, "from the standpoint of what Zen calls the Great Function and the Great Activity (J. *daiki, daiyū*), Dōgen's Zen is definitely too passive" (ibid.). However, if indeed Dōgen's assertion of the nonduality of practice and realization "belongs to philosophy," Suzuki's description of satori seems open to the same criticism.

In sum, Suzuki generally misrepresents Dōgen's understanding of Zen practice, and his conspicuous silence about the Sōtō tradition in the rest of his work seems motivated by sectarian prejudice. Even when he talks about Chinese Chan, he reads Japanese Zen back into it. This is because, although "the history of Zen in Japan is far younger than in China, . . . it was so adaptable to the character of the Japanese people, especially in its moral and aesthetic aspects, that it has penetrated far more deeply into Japanese life than into Chinese" (Suzuki 1970, 346). Suzuki also fails to mention Sŏn, the Korean version of Chan, although he knew about it from traveling in Korea during the Japanese occupation. We may assume that he shared Nukariya Kaiten's judgment that Sŏn was a deviation from the authentic tradition and as such unworthy to be compared to "pure" Japanese Zen. Suzuki's notion of Zen as a "pure" and "virile" teaching led him to focus on the Kamakura and Muromachi periods—times when Zen suposedly embodied the highest values of the rising warrior class—and to downplay Heian Buddhism as the product of a "feminine" society.

Paradoxically, we may argue that precisely because of his biases Suzuki can be considered representative of Zen—*as a sectarian* tradition. The appeal to the "pure" tradition, to the "essence" of Zen, is indeed a typical feature of the sectarian attitude. This attitude was already exemplified by Dōgen, for whom true Zen stood above the Zen school. Just as Dōgen refused to call his teaching "Zen," Suzuki claims that Zen is "neither a religion nor a philosophy" or better that it is "the spirit of all religion and philosophy."[6] The assumption that there is an "essence" of Buddhism, a kind of perennial Dharma to which only "authentic" masters would have access, is to be rejected as ideologically suspect. It is interesting to note that, despite its supposedly unconditioned character, the "pure experience" of

---

[6] See the following passage: "If its temples were to be destroyed, its priestly order abolished, and its cardinal sutras and documents taken away, the Zen sect of Buddhism would inevitably die out. Even then, the Zen which I mean would continue to live. By this statement, the difference between Zen and the Zen sect, I believe, is made clearer" (Suzuki 1941, 16); trans. Hiroshi Sakamoto, "A Unique Interpreter of Zen," *The Eastern Buddhist* n.s., 2, 1 (1967): 36.

awakening is said to be inaccessible to the isolated practitioner and can only be triggered with the guidance of a master affiliated to the orthodox tradition (Suzuki 1949–1953, 2: 59).

Suzuki rejected both Northern Chan and Sōtō Zen as "quietist." Unjustifiably conflating "quietism" and "gradualism," he also criticized quietism—that is, Northern Chan—for being too "intellectualist" and implicitly accused Sōtō Zen of the same error.[7] In the strict sense, the word "quietism," if it is to be used at all in a Buddhist context, refers to an antinomian teaching that bears some resemblance to Miguel de Molinos's doctrine. At first glance, and if we are to believe the description given by Suzuki himself, precisely Rinzai Zen could be characterized by its antinomianism. In his earlier work, and more particularly in his *Essays*, Suzuki stressed the "spiritual freedom" that rebelled against all institutional (and therefore stultified) practices in the name of pure spontaneity (Suzuki 1949–1953, 1: 73). Later in his life, Suzuki's attitude seems to have changed drastically, but a certain ambivalence is already perceptible in the *Essays*. At times Suzuki condemns quietism and passivity; at other times he seems to advocate them (ibid., 2: 312). As he became more aware of the dangers of antinomianism, presumably in response to the initial Western understanding of Zen as a kind of libertarianism—as exemplified by the "Beat Zen" of Jack Kerouac, Allen Ginsberg, and Alan Watts—he began to warn against this misinterpretation.[8] Thus, in an article written in 1960, he declared that "Zen is decidely not latitudinarian, nor antinomian. The masters are always very emphatic on this point of self-discipline. . . . What Zen emphasizes most strongly in its disciplinary practice is the attainment of spiritual freedom, not the revolt against conventionalism. . . . So it is that Zen may find more of its great followers among the 'conformists' than among the rebellious and boisterous nonconformists" (Franck 1982, 21). With evident satisfaction Suzuki described the "militaristic severity" of the Meditation Hall (*zendō*): in his opinion, manual work is "what saved Zen from deteriorating into quietism or mere intellectual gymnastics" or "from falling into the pitfalls of antinomianism as well as a hallucinatory mode of mind" (Suzuki 1949–1953, 3: 314–315).

Suzuki's earlier praise of Chan antinomianism and iconoclasm (or bibli-

---

[7] The only Sōtō monk who seems to have found credit with Suzuki was the monk-poet Ryōkan, who was precisely a rather atypical Sōtō monk. See Suzuki 1970, 364.

[8] See for example Suzuki's stern warning against the use of psychedelic drugs in a symposium on "Religion and Drugs," in which he compares the mental states described by Huxley and Watts as *makyō* ("demonic states"). "What is crucial," Suzuki argues, "is not the experiences themselves, but *the one* who does the experiencing, or what Rinzai calls 'the master behind all the experiences.'" See Suzuki, "Religion and Drugs," *The Eastern Buddhist* n.s., 4, 2 (1971): 128–133; Alan Watts, "Ordinary Mind is the Way," ibid., 134–137; and Ueda Shizuteru, "The LSD Experience and Zen," ibid., 149–152.

oclasm) is strongly reminiscent of what Pierre Bourdieu calls a "strategy of condescension," that is, a symbolic transgression that permits to accumulate the profits of conformity to the rule and those of its transgression (see Bourdieu 1982, 131). This research of a symbolic gain may also explain why the spontaneity or freedom of interpretation advocated by Suzuki is reserved for himself and other "masters," while it is denied to Westerners who are not (and will apparently never be) steeped enough in the tradition: "In your drinking [tea] there may be no Zen, while mine is brim full of it" (Suzuki 1949–1953, 3: 161). The apparent contradiction between Suzuki's "conformist" stand and his earlier, more iconoclastic interpretations suggests that his alleged iconoclasm was all along a subtle kind of conformism. It is an interesting feature of the Chan tradition (and of all similar iconoclastic trends) that its radical language, aimed at debunking an orthodoxy, soon becomes the sign or emblem of a new orthodoxy. The change of vocabulary must not hide the underlying continuity.

The ambivalence of the *Essays* with regard to the alleged anti-intellectualism of Zen paved the way for another radical change in Suzuki's late work on that question. As a "popularizer" of Zen, Suzuki was acutely aware that the "sudden teaching" was elitist and had to be adapted if it was to reach a wider audience. The need for "skillful means" (*upāya*) is something that Northern Chan masters had already understood, and despite his sectarian condemnation of the Northern school, Suzuki must at times have felt a certain affinity with it.[9]

According to Suzuki, the Chan need for upāya was finally met with the institutionalization of the kōan system. "Unless the aristocratic nature of Zen was somewhat moderated, so that even men of ordinary capacity could live the life of a Zen master, Zen itself might rapidly disappear from [China]. . . . Zen was to be democratized, that is, systematized. . . . The path must be made walkable, to a certain extent at least; some artificial means must be devised to attract some minds who may one day turn out to be true transmitters of Zen" (Suzuki 1949–1953, 2: 125–126). In a footnote to this citation, Suzuki added that the type of Chan advocated by Bodhidharma and epitomized by the legendary nine-year "wall-contemplation" of the Indian patriarch was clearly "something unapproachable" for ordinary practitioners. Thus, while in theory he remained an uncompromising partisan of the "sudden" teaching, in actual practice, Suzuki was after all advocating a kind of "gradual" Chan. He saw clearly that Huineng, the "founder" of the Southern school, "was a great advocate of absolute idealism," whereas his rival Shenxiu "was a realist and refused to ignore a world of particulars where Time rules over all our doings."

[9] These affinities with Northern Chan are revealed even in Suzuki's paradoxical (but compelling) interest in "Southern" Scriptures such as the *Laṅkāvatāra-sūtra* and the *Avataṃsaka-sūtra*. See for instance Suzuki 1949–1953, 1: 89.

Nevertheless, Suzuki felt compelled to maintain that "all the true 'mystics' are followers of the 'abrupt' school. The flight from the single to the single is not, and cannot be, a gradual process" (Suzuki 1949–1953, 1: 213). Thus, although he was "excellent and full of merit" as a practical guide, Shenxiu (like Suzuki himself?) "missed the ultimate goal of Zen when he emphasized the process to reach the end. . . . When process is emphasized, the end is forgotten, and process itself comes to be identified with end" (ibid. 1: 213–214). The crux of Sudden Chan is precisely its refusal to hold up an end against a means or process, for this dualism is seen as the very source of delusion and gradualism. The major contradiction in Suzuki's position, one of which he was acutely aware, is that he negated in actual practice what he advocated in theory, namely, that Zen "is a direct method, for it refuses to resort to verbal explanation or logical analysis, or to ritualism" (Ibid. 3: 318). This, of course, is the criticism that can be leveled at the kōan practice that constituted the central element of Suzuki's Zen. Conscious of this, Suzuki remained uncertain in his judgment of this practice, arguing at times that kōan are "the utterances of *satori* with no intellectual mediation" (ibid., 2: 101), at other times that they are a mere *upāya*, a sign of degeneracy,[10] and also, paradoxically, an improvement and a mark of authenticity of the Zen tradition (ibid., 2: 112–113).

In his preface to Nishida's *A Study of Good*, Suzuki stressed the importance of Kegon (Ch. Huayan) philosophy in Zen: Kegon and Zen (or rather, the synthesis of both, known as Kegon-Zen) are presented as the climax of Buddhist thought. Not only do we find the classical teleological schema, but also the ideological implications of this philosophical choice are quite obvious. Kegon (Huayan) influenced Chan/Zen by providing it with a theoretical justification for its irenistic detachment from social problems. The Huayan advocacy of the harmonious interpenetration of the principle and phenomena (Ch. *lishi wu'ai*) is the kind of abstract and conservative view that one is more likely to take from a dominant situation, a situation that Chan had just been able to reach by the mid-Tang when Huayan was flourishing at the court.[11]

Suzuki and Mysticism

In the preface to a Kyōto School anthology, *The Buddha Eye*, Frederick Franck refers to Suzuki as the "Francis Xavier of Zen to the Western world" (Franck 1982, 2). Although this was clearly intended as a compliment,

---

[10] See Suzuki 1949–1953, 2:81–87, where the kōan systematization is presented as a necessary evil, a historical development made necessary by the intellectual sclerosis of Chan ritual dialogues (Ch. *wenda*, J. *mondō*).

[11] Compare the role played by the Huayan philosophy in the ideological "revolution" aimed at legitimizing the Empress Wu at the turn of the eighth century and the symbolical role

there is also some unintended truth in Franck's comparison. Suzuki's work is in some ways an attempt at a spiritual *reconquista*, and his "dialogue" with Christians may have the same motivations as Xavier's conversations with Japanese Buddhists. To be sure, Suzuki's understanding of Christianity is at times almost as simplistic and reductionistic, mutatis mutandis, as that of Buddhism in the case of most Jesuit missionaries.

Nevertheless, Suzuki deeply influenced specialists of Christian mysticism such as Rudolf Otto and Thomas Merton. For instance, in an article that he wrote for *The Eastern Buddhist*, Otto commented that, contrary to Shinshū followers, "Zen followers are mystics" and saw in the paintings of Bodhidharma a "reflection of the Numinous" (Otto 1924); whereas Merton likened Suzuki's approach to that of the Church Fathers and considered the cultural trappings of Zen as "accidental" (Merton 1967, 219).

Downplaying sociocultural determinations, Suzuki argued that Zen consciousness and Christian consciousness are the same (Suzuki 1949–1953, 2: 304). In fact, he believed that, although a posteriori interpretations of the mystical experience may differ, all "mysticisms" are fundamentally the same. Using the notion of mysticism as "the common denominator by virtue of which various traditions may be called religious" (Fader 1976, 184), Suzuki was able to compare Zen monks with Meister Eckhart or Zen passivity with Christian quietism: "Eckhart, Zen, and Shin thus can be grouped together as belonging to the great school of mysticism" (Suzuki 1969, xix).

This inclusive comparativism, however, has a hidden agenda—namely to prove that Zen is "mystically" superior to Christianity. Suzuki's point is that Zen, being more affirmative, "more daringly concrete in its paradoxes than other mysticisms," constitutes the highest form of mysticism (Suzuki 1949–1953, 1: 270–272). In an early essay dated 1916, after distinguishing between four types of mysticism—devotional, contemplative, intellectual, and superstitious—Suzuki already concluded that Zen was to be put in a category of its own (Sakamoto 1977, 56). Although he spent his life promoting a highly culturally bound form of Zen, he always claimed that, as the "ultimate fact of all philosophies and religions" (Suzuki 1949–1953, 1: 265), it is a unique phenomenon in the history of mysticism, "whether Eastern or Western, Christian or Buddhist" (ibid., 1: 281).

In contrast to Merton, who hazarded "with diffidence" statements about Buddhism and was acutely aware that, as a Catholic priest and monk, he could not be sure that he had trustworthy insights into the spiritual values of a tradition with which he was not really familiar (Merton 1967, 5), Suzuki was always confident in his own judgment on Chris-

---

of the "Great Buddha" of Tōdaiji, a figure taken from the *Avataṃsaka-sūtra*, in the state ideology during the Nara period.

tianity.[12] However, his interpretation of Christianity remained superficial and polemical. He argued, for example, that Christian tenets such as the crucifixion are merely symbolical, "while Buddhism is . . . free from the historical symbolism of Christianity" (Suzuki 1949–1953, 1: 152). Even in their expression of spiritual "poverty," Zen masters are "more poetic and positive than Christians" like Meister Eckhart.[13] This is because, says Suzuki, "in Christianity *we* [emphasis added] seem too conscious of God . . . , [whereas] Zen wants to have even this last trace of God-consciousness, if possible, obliterated" (ibid., 1: 350). The relation between Christianity and Buddhism is compared by Suzuki to that between wine and tea: whereas tea is tasteless but stimulating, wine "first excitates and then inebriates" (Suzuki 1970, 273). This line of argument led Suzuki to the conclusion that Zen is neither a philosophy nor a metaphysics nor a religion, but it is, rather, "the spirit of all religion or philosophy." Suzuki went so far as to assert that "if there is a God, personal or impersonal, he or it must be with Zen and in Zen" (Suzuki 1969, 347). Implicit in such statements is an almost Protestant view of religion as a reality that has nothing to do with cults, dogmas, or collective beliefs, but rests on the "inner experience" of the individual. However, owing to the atypical character of such "mystical" experiences, their extreme rarity, and the Christian theology they often presuppose, it seems illegitimate to derive from them a general (if not always explicit) theory of religion, as Suzuki and Nishida, following William James, have done.

Because Zen is supposedly free from all ties with any specific religious or philosophical tradition, Suzuki argues, it can be practiced by Christians and Buddhists alike, "in the same way that big and small fishes can live happy together [do they really?] in the same ocean" (Benz 1962, 22). Suzuki's view of Zen's "oceanic nature" reveals the extent of the exorbitant privilege that he confers on his own interpretation. The patent sectarian motivation behind this apparently open-minded "dialogue" between Zen and Christianity allows us to see it as a paradigmatic case of "militant comparativism."

Aware that Zen was not always in good company in "the great school of mysticism," however, Suzuki later came to deny that it was a form of mysticism at all. Criticizing Heinrich Dumoulin's *A History of Zen Buddhism* for presenting Zen as a kind of mysticism, he wrote: "I too used the

---

[12] Here is how Suzuki interpreted Meister Eckhart in Buddhist terms: "This 'little point' [wherein the soul turns back upon itself and finds itself and knows itself to be a creature] is full of significance and I am sure that Eckhart had a *satori*" (Suzuki 1969, 79). On this point, see also Nishitani Keiji, *Kami to zettaimu* (Tokyo: Sōbunsha, 1971), 138–139.

[13] Suzuki 1949–1953, 1: 347. In a "dialogue" between Paul Tillich and Hisamatsu Shin'ichi, Tillich politely disagreed with Hisamatsu's (that is, Suzuki's) interpretation of

term in connection with Zen. I have long since regretted it, as I find it now highly misleading in elucidating Zen thought. Let it suffice to say here that Zen has nothing 'mystical' about it or in it. It is most plain, clear as the daylight, all out in the open with nothing hidden, dark, obscure, secret or mystifying in it" (quoted in Sakamoto 1977, 65–66). Yet, in his book, Dumoulin had himself criticized Suzuki's understanding of mysticism: "In a crass oversimplification, Suzuki considers the essence of Christian mysticism to be 'the personal and frequently sexual feelings' of the mystics" (Dumoulin 1963, 277).

Suzuki also liked to compare Zen to Western philosophy, to Zen's advantage: "The philosopher according to whom *cogito ergo sum* is generally weak-minded. The Zen master has nothing to do with such quibbles" (Suzuki 1970, 408). We may also question the accuracy of his understanding of Western philosophy. If Meister Eckhart, despite (or because of) his undeniable spirituality, cannot be said to represent the entire Christian tradition, neither can the intellectualist strain emphasized by Suzuki be said to represent the entire Western philosophical tradition. From the pre-Socratics, Socrates and the Stoics, all the way to Kierkegaard and Nietzsche, philosophy was a path of self-transformation, not merely the intellectual pastime that Suzuki describes.

Likewise, Suzuki liked to contrast the verbosity of Western literature with the conciseness of Japanese *haiku* inspired from Zen. If he praised writers such as Henri David Thoreau and Ralph Waldo Emerson, it is only because he detected an Oriental influence in their writings: "I am now beginning to understand the meaning of the deep impression made upon me while reading Emerson in my college days. I was not then studying the American philosopher but digging down into the recesses of my own thought, which had been there since the awakening of Oriental consciousness" (Suzuki 1970, 343–344). Not too surprisingly, he was led to conclude that "the American Transcendentalist's attitude toward nature has no doubt a great mystical note, but the Zen masters go far beyond it and are really incomprehensible" (ibid.).

On the one hand, Zen receives in Suzuki's writings a transcendental status, but on the other hand, it is secularized and put into a kind of empirical, psychological framework. Suzuki's psychological interpretation of satori and of mystical experiences in general,[14] for which he was in-

---

Meister Eckhart's notion of *Armut* ("complete poverty") in Zen terms. See Tillich and Hisamatsu 1971–1973, Pt. 1: 98.

[14] Before describing the "psychological antecedents" of satori, Suzuki gives its "chief characteristics": (1) irrationality; (2) intuitive insight; (3) authoritativeness; (4) affirmation; (5) sense of the Beyond; (6) impersonal tone. The last point, seen as a major difference with the Christian mystical experience, makes Suzuki ask himself: "Is this owing to the peculiar

debted to William James,[15] and his unfortunate rendering of the Chinese term *wuxin* (J. *mushin*, no-mind or no-thought) as "Unconscious," have provided a fertile ground for misunderstanding and have attracted to Zen psychologists and psychoanalysts such as C. G. Jung, Erich Fromm, Karen Horney, and Hubert Benoit.[16] Significantly, the psychological interpretation of Zen was criticized by those earlier followers of Suzuki-ism who, like Rudolf Otto and the Jesuit Heinrich Dumoulin, wanted to retain for Zen its status of "natural mysticism" (see Benz 1962, 35). Thus, while Dumoulin complains that "Zen was divested [by Suzuki] of its original religious character, and an effort was made to fit it into a therapeutic system" (Dumoulin 1963, 281), his own approach does not escape reductionism.[17]

Despite his nativist tendency, Suzuki relied heavily on the categories of nineteenth-century Orientalism.[18] He simply inverted the old schemas to serve his own purposes—to present Zen as the source and goal of all mystical experiences. Zen allegedly transcends all religions; it is, however, at the same time presented by Suzuki as a specific product of Chinese culture that was eventually brought to fruition in the context of Japanese culture (Suzuki 1949–1953, 1: 109, 172). For example, the Sudden/ Gradual controversy is said to have helped "the further *progress* of pure Zen by eliminating unessential or rather undigested elements" borrowed from Indian Buddhism (ibid., 1: 203). Yet, despite his evolutionist framework, Suzuki denied any essential historical continuity between Indian religious traditions and Zen, a position hard to reconcile with his desire to prove Zen's historical connection with the original experience and teaching of the Buddha. Suzuki's teleological approach is also reflected in his

---

character of Buddhist philosophy? Does the experience itself take its colour from the philosophy or theology?" He hastens to answer negatively to this—rather rhetorical—question. See Suzuki 1949–1953, 2: 28–34.

[15] See the criticism of James's book by Marcel Mauss—a criticism that seems to foreshadow Hu Shih's objections to Suzuki (Mauss 1968, 1: 58–65).

[16] See Benz 1962, 23–31. In his introduction to the book *Zen Buddhism and Psychoanalysis*, C. G. Jung writes: "The man who has enlightenment, or *alleges* that he has it, thinks in any case that he is enlightened. *Even if he were to lie, his lie would be a spiritual fact.*" See Fromm, Suzuki, and de Martino 1960. This uncritical acceptance of Suzuki's assertions is astonishing, coming from someone who ought to be professionally suspicious. See however Fromm's criticism of Zen; ibid., 116.

[17] See the following passage: "Furthermore, as a mystical phenomenon, the *satori* experience is imperfect. No human effort to attain enlightenment, no matter how honest and self-sacrificing, can ever lead to the perfect truth, but only the eternal Logos, 'who coming in the world enlightens every man' (John 1: 9).'"; Dumoulin 1963, 290.

[18] Suzuki's East-West dichotomy in particular is surprising coming as it did from such a relentless advocate of "non-duality." See, for example, the following passage, which seems directly taken from the *Roget's Thesaurus* of antonyms: "The Western mind is: analytical, discriminative, differential, inductive, individualistic, intellectual, objective, scientific, gener-

criticism of so-called Hīnayāna, for instance when he argues that "all the reconstructions and transformations which the Mahayanists are supposed to have put on the original form of Buddhism are really nothing but an unbroken continuation of one original Buddhist spirit and life," while, paradoxically, "primitive" Buddhism is also "the result of an elaboration on the part of the earlier followers of the Buddha" (ibid., 1: 57).

Suzuki constantly shifts his frame of reference; at times he emphasizes the ahistorical nature of Zen, and at other times he explains the uniqueness of Zen through its historical development. The former standpoint was criticized by the Chinese historian Hu Shih as a form of obscurantism, and this led to the well-known controversy between the two scholars, to which I return in chapter 3. Although Suzuki's apparently free-floating, and certainly contradictory, discourse may be charitably interpreted as reflecting the "unlocalized" mind of the enlightened master, it can also apppear as a situational reflex to "cash in" on both sides of every issue. Characteristically, Suzuki's claim to orthodoxy may be seen as a symptom of the "boundary anxiety" (Berling 1980, 10–11) in someone who was always marginal to the Zen tradition, living as he did on the borderline between lay and clerical life, between the Zen and Pure Land sects, between tradition and modernization, and between Japanese and Western culture.

Suzuki's thought is indeed a kind of nativism, an attempt to deal with the Western challenge that bears similarities to Okakura Kakuzō's praise of "Teaism" (as opposed to Western theism?) and Kamei Katsuichirō's "Return to the East."[19] But, in contrast to most Japanese native thinkers, Suzuki was relatively isolated from his own people. He left Japan and went to live in the United States, and the subsequent evolution of his thought reflects his confrontation with Western values (intellectualism) or trends of thought (Christianity, psychoanalysis, existentialism, antinomianism of the 1960s). After returning to Japan with his American wife, he earned his livelihood as an English teacher and remained on the fringes of the academic world. In other words, his appeal to the Zen tradition and his advocacy of a "return to the sources" of Japanese spirituality may be effects

---

alizing, conceptual, schematic, impersonal, legalistic, organizing, power-wielding, self-assertive, disposed to impose its will upon others, etc. Against these Western traits, those of the East can be characterized as follows: synthetic, totalizing, integrative, nondiscriminative, deductive, nonsystematic, dogmatic, intuitive (rather, affective), nondiscursive, subjective, spiritually individualistic and socially group-minded, etc." (See Fromm, Suzuki, and De Martino 1960, 5).

[19] See, for example, Kamei Katsuichirō's analysis of the way in which the "love of Asia" preached by Okakura Kakuzō and the like led to the invasion of China: "I would as an overlord of Asia preach with equanimity the love of Asia" (Tsunoda, de Bary, and Keene 1964, 397). Kamei argued that we must free ourselves from "any infantile notions such as the simple schematization . . . according to which the East stood for the spirit and the West for material things" (ibid., 399).

of both post-Meiji modernization and his own ambiguous social and intellectual status. A number of contradictions were contrived in his person: he
was an anti-intellectual scholar, a Westernized nativist, an ecumenical sectarian, and an idealist advocate of Zen pragmatism; at times he was
disavowed by the very tradition he claimed to represent for being too
philosophical and/or journalistic; this isolated individual, despite his
many scholarly publications, obtained an academic position fairly late in
his life (he was fifty-one when he entered Ōtani University) and remained a
layman on the threshold between clerical and lay life.

Not surprisingly, the nativist or chauvinistic elements in Suzuki's
thought increased greatly during the war. At that time he also exerted the
greatest influence on Nishida's writings. His two books, *Japanese Spirituality* and *Zen and Japanese Culture*, are roughly contemporary with
Nishida's last writings. Although Suzuki's style does not rival Nishida's,
both writers attempted to extend to Japanese spirituality in general the
ontological privilege initially granted to Zen by Suzuki. For Suzuki, non-
discriminatory wisdom (*prajñā*)—that is, Zen—finds its true expression in
Japanese culture. Consequently, Zen imperialism leaves no aspect of Japanese culture untouched; it annexes even Confucianism and *bushidō*. As
Paul Demiéville, in a sharp review of Suzuki's *Zen and Japanese Culture*,
remarked: "Almost all the culture of that country . . . is interpreted in
relation to Zen, which becomes a master-key giving access not only to
aesthetics (painting, poetry), but also to Japanese militarism."[20] With
Suzuki, the commonsensical approach that would see Zen as a product of
Japanese culture is inverted, and Japanese culture becomes a multifaceted
expression of a unique phenomenon, or rather of a metaphysical principle
named Zen.[21] Not only would such absolutist claims be hard to defend on
rational ground or to privilege over similar claims in other traditions or
cultures, their ideological nature, which becomes plain when they turn into
nativist or nationalist claims, disqualifies them altogether.

For one brief moment toward the end of the war, Suzuki seemed to forget
his triumphalist accents and gave a rather different interpretation of Zen
aestheticism: "The Japanese thinkers so far have not intellectually taken up
foreign stimulations, though there are ample indications now that promise
a fruitful future for rationalist thinking in Japan. Ultra-nationalism has
unfortunately set a check on the growth of vigorous original thought
among the Japanese. . . . The Japanese political system, I think, is to be

[20] Paul Demiéville, review of D. T. Suzuki, *Zen and Japanese Culture*, in *Orientalistische Literaturzeitung* 61, 1/2 (1966): 93.

[21] Take for instance the following statement: "Inbalance, asymmetry, . . . poverty, *sabi* or *wabi*, simplification, aloneness, and cognate ideas make up the most conspicuous and characteristic features of Japanese art culture. All these emanate from one central perception of the truth of Zen, which is 'the One in the Many and the Many in the One'" (Suzuki 1970, 28).

held responsible for the impotence or lame development of the Japanese philosophical genius" (Suzuki 1970, 308). If the Japanese as a people escaped into aestheticism because of an oppressive regime (the feudalistic rule of the Kamakura and Muromachi periods), it may be because of another oppressive regime (Shōwa militarism) that Suzuki as an individual chose the same route. Perhaps we have here the beginning of a sociopolitical explanation, by Suzuki himself, of the "impotence or lame development" of his own philosophical genius. This possibility, however, probably quite disturbing to Suzuki, was precluded by his belief system, and he soon returned to a more orthodox explanation by arguing that Japanese aestheticism is not simply an escape from oppression, but the expression of "an innate desire to transcend ourselves, whether we are living under a feudalistic political system or in a liberal democratic country" (Suzuki 1970, 309).

The Western Critics of Suzuki

Various criticisms have been voiced about Suzuki's writings: logical inconsistencies, ideological flaws, sectarian bias, epistemological problems (having to do with the status of language and the anti-intellectual premises of a scholar), their ambiguity regarding social issues, their rhetorical aspect, the lack of literary and imaginative quality, and the pedestrian character of the work of a reputedly enlightened figure. Among Western intellectuals, some of the most virulent critics have been Alfred Koestler and René Etiemble, and I review their criticisms as examples of the negative responses provoked by Suzuki.

The Koestler/Suzuki Controversy

On the surface, Arthur Koestler's criticism of Suzuki had to do mainly with epistemological and ethical issues. Koestler claimed that Suzuki's views, which he calls Suzuki's "double-think," are not only ambiguous but also logically flawed and fraudulent, leading to ethical relativism. Koestler's description of Zen, as he saw it practiced in Japanese monasteries, is admittedly grim. According to him, "Zen students are taught to put away reason and morality, and to act instead as an automaton, a 'robot'" (Fader 1980, 52). As for the transcendental nature of Zen, so frequently underscored by Suzuki and used as a buttress for his own assertions, Koestler finds nothing unique about it: "Painters paint, dancers dance, musicians make music, instead of explaining that they are practising no-thought in their no-minds. Inarticulateness is not a monopoly of Zen; but it is the only school which made a monopoly out of it" (Koestler 1961, 58). As for Zen spontaneity, it has degenerated into an "automatic" and mechanistic spontaneity that imbued Japanese culture with the "stink of Zen" (see Fader 1980, 56). The Zen teaching of Suzuki must therefore be dismissed by Westerners "as one of the 'sick' jokes, slightly gangrened, which are always fashionable in ages of anxiety" (Koestler 1961, 58).

Suzuki took the trouble to respond to Koestler's criticism and tried to prove that the latter's understanding of Zen had its own stink (see Suzuki 1961). He attempted, in his typical fashion, to show that Zen was neither illogical nor anti-intellectual, but that it had its own type of logic, stemming from "pure experience" and differing from (or indifferent to) the dichotomous logic of Western philosophy. In this sense, Suzuki's Zen recalls Lévy-Bruhl's characterization of the "primitive mind" as illogical (or rather alogical), and the criticisms leveled at Lévy-Bruhl's dichotomization of primitive and civilized thinking might apply to Suzuki's paradoxical dichotomization of nondualistic Zen and dualistic Western thinking (see Lévy-Bruhl 1910).

Suzuki's understanding of Western logic seems rather reductionistic, and, as noted earlier, he underestimated the achievements of Western philosophy at least as much as Koestler underestimated those of Zen. Whereas Suzuki believed that "philosophers and logicians are generally satisfied with the images that symbolize Reality," his appreciation of the "Zen man," by contrast, was very high, although the idealized image he gave of the latter bears little resemblance to the ordinary Zen monk or layman, including Suzuki:

> It is the Zen man who goes around performing deeds in this most original fashion. His creativity oozes out of every pore of his skin. He is "the most honoured individual in the whole world." He follows no pattern of tradition, he is his own master and every behaviour of his is fresh and exhilarating. He is the real "aristocrat" of Meister Eckhart. He is the one who is behind all the stimulating writings produced by "Mr. Arthur Koestler" (who, unfortunately, seems not to be cognizant of "the stink" radiating from his own "Zen").[22]

In his discussion of the Koestler-Suzuki controversy, Larry Fader queries "whether or not Suzuki's response to Koestler is adequate from Koestler's point of view" and concludes, rather quickly, that it is (Fader 1980, 60). Although he admits that there is no criterion to prove that Suzuki is not simply a genial hoaxer, as Koestler would have it, Fader thinks that Suzuki's non-Aristotelian logic is the only correct way to express the

---

[22] Suzuki 1961, 57–58. Suzuki's reply is followed by this ironic (and irenicist) note from the anonymous editor of the journal: "Having presented Mr. Koestler (in his Tyrolean mountain retreat) with a copy of the above and an opportunity to reply, and having received as his final rejoinder a silence too deep for words, we take it in the true spirit of Zen that he has at last achieved *satori*. With this evidently happy outcome, the discussion is now closed" (ibid.).

"pure" and "nonrational" experience of Zen and to lead one back to it. Fader goes one step further, by attempting to show how "Suzuki's position may be used to criticize Koestler, as well" (ibid., 62). He argues that Koestler, although he never withdrew his criticisms, later came to acknowledge the shortcomings of reason, in a way "remarkably similar to Suzuki's own formulation of Zen" (ibid., 63). Unfortunately, Koestler never went beyond that point and failed to accept the "logic of Zen."

Incidentally, C. G. Jung also responded to Koestler's article by stressing the importance of the irrational elements, not only in Zen, but also across cultures. Nevertheless, Jung agreed with Koestler insofar as he recognized that the specific form taken by the collective Unconscious in another culture could be of little help to solve Western problems. In this sense, the Western fascination with Zen appeared to both like an escape; whereas in Koestler's opinion the predicament was created by the abandonment of rationalism, in Jung's opinion it was the result of the Western repression of the Unconscious. Even if it could learn from Zen, psychoanalysis remained, for Jung, the only acceptable solution to the Western predicament (see Fader 1979, 70–72).

On the question of the degeneracy of Zen in Japan, Suzuki seems to agree with Koestler, lamenting the stupidity of the high-ranking abbots who had been "embarrassed" by Koestler's questions. According to Suzuki, those abbots should have silenced Koestler with "Rinzai's *Khatz*! or Tokusan's stick" and chased him out of the temple.[23] Had this been the case, affirms Suzuki, Koestler "would never have written the article in which Zen stinks altogether too much in the wrong way!" (Suzuki 1961, 56). This is most likely wishful thinking, for it is precisely the conformism shown by Zen masters in their use of the shout and the stick that irritated Koestler in the first place. Moreover, Suzuki himself, although he claimed not to be embarrassed by commonsensical questions about Zen, was inclined to give rather convoluted discursive answers to such questions, a far cry from Linji's and Deshan's spontaneous responses. In any case, Suzuki's distinction between an "ideal Zen" and a possibly degenerate "traditional Zen" begs the question of his own situation in the Zen tradition. If, in Suzuki's words, "each Zen teaching must be fully and radically original," then Koestler's criticism of the Zen tradition, and of Suzuki as well, appears justified. At any rate, against those who, like Christmas Humphrey, "quibble" that Zen "has its own life independent of history," Koestler seems entitled to write: "Now that statement is true of any system of ideas, but no longer true when that system becomes embodied in a church, cult, or school; and

---

[23] Linji (J. Rinzai) and Deshan (J. Tokusan) were well-known for their use of shouts and blows in their "dialogues" with their disciples. Parenthetically, the institutionalization and Japanization of the Chan masters' shout is typical of Zen's (and Suzuki's) formalism. The Chinese character *he* (J. *katsu*) means simply "he shouted"—rather than "Khatz!"

the only contemporary embodiment of Zen is Japanese Zen" (Koestler 1960b, 58).

Responding to Koestler's reproach that the amoral nature of Zen leads it to support fascism, Suzuki appealed to the "revolutionary spirit" of Zen, which "proves to be a destructive [i.e., subversive] force" whenever the sociopolitical situation has reached a deadlock. Unfortunately, he did not provide any concrete example and seemed again to have in mind a rather "ideal" type of Zen that has little or nothing to do with Japanese Zen. Although some religious traditions may promote inner detachment vis-à-vis political systems, most religions tend to be politically conservative and nationalistic—and Zen has been no exception in this regard. Suzuki acknowledged this point when he attributed the failure of Zen to its "particularization," its necessary compromise with a given sociopolitical order. However, the same assessment could be made about Zen arts, which are said to be particularized expressions of Zen and as such should have no claim to preserve its "purity."

Although Fader seems willing, on Suzuki's behalf, to take up Koestler's suggestion that Zen might have affinities with fascism, he interprets this to mean Nazism and leaves aside the question of Japanese militarism.[24] He argues rather unconvincingly that, "while Nazism played upon the German people's herd instinct," Zen thought, being "free from particular nationalistic claims," would constitute an antidote to fascism because it "confronts one with the problematic nature of individual, nationalistic and, indeed, every other form of ego-identity," (Fader 1980, 70) and would therefore, as Suzuki argued, be "impervious to [political] manipulations" (Fader 1976, 363). To make such a claim, Fader has apparently never read the abundant Zen literature on the "Protection of the State" (on which, see Demiéville 1957).

Suzuki seemed oblivious to Japan's responsibility for the war. In a footnote to *Zen and Japanese Culture*, he placed all the responsibility on Western intellectualism: "The intellect presses the button, the whole city is destroyed. . . . All is done mechanically, logically, systematically, and the intellect is perfectly satisfied. Is it not time for us all to think of ourselves from another point of view than that of mere intellectuality" (Suzuki 1970, 338). According to Suzuki, all this would not have happened if the Westerners had, like the Japanese, had more respect for nature. In another footnote, he wrote: "I sometimes wonder if any of the Great Western soldiers ever turned into a poet. Can we imagine, for instance, in recent times, that General MacArthur or General Eisenhower would compose a

---

[24] Koestler was quick to point out the Nazi background of another famous advocate of Zen in the West, Eugen Herrigel. In a preface that Suzuki wrote for Herrigel's work, *Zen in the Art of Archery* in 1953, he referred to it as "this wonderful little book by a German philosopher" (Herrigel 1953, 9; Koestler 1960b, 59).

poem upon visiting one of those bomb-torn cities?"[25] Apparently, Suzuki was unaware that perhaps the chief cause of war and its fuel were found in the same warrior mystique that he exalted in several previous chapters of the same book.

At any rate, despite his claims to speak from a position beyond or anterior to the subject/object dichotomy, Suzuki remained at the same level as his critic Koestler and grasped the issue in essentially intellectual terms. Forgetting the Zen saying that "a painted rice-cake does not appease hunger," he failed to realize that talking about originality is not the best proof of originality. He also missed Koestler's point about the irrational and amoral components of Zen and chose instead to answer secondary objections concerning the nature of satori. Why repeat the same worn-out Zen statements if he really wanted to change Koestler's views, when these statements were the very source of Koestler's antipathy toward Zen? The apparent inability to understand an interlocutor's point and to respond adequately to his evident frustration is problematic in the case of a person who claimed to see everything from a superior, unlocalized perspective; all the more so when this position is taken by someone who, like Fader, does not even have a claim to transcendental impartiality and seems to merely imitate his master.

The tone of the above remarks may lead us to discern in the Suzuki-Koestler controversy the contagious effects of the scapegoat mechanism. The question, however, is not to decide who is right and who is wrong, as if truth could be all on one side. Although there may be some right on both sides, from another perspective all protagonists in this controversy are wrong: not only Koestler, with his "jaundiced critical perspectives," but also Humphrey and Fader (and myself, of course, to the extent that I happen to share *some* of Koestler's objections, without endorsing his inflexible rationalism or his condescending attitude), as well as Suzuki who also could not escape unscathed this predicament. But, if by now distancing oneself from this controversy and bracketing the truth claims of its protagonists, one pays more attention to its disturbing polemical tone, it appears that each protagonist expresses a different context and ideology. In this sense, Western humanism, for all its rationalism, is as culturally determined, hence as irrational as Zen "irrationalism."

In a simplified form, Koestler's criticism of Zen in the name of rationality seems to prefigure the current criticism leveled by Habermas at the (mostly) French heirs of Nietzsche's *gaya scienza* (notably Bataille, Foucault, Derrida, and Lyotard).[26] Needless to say, Derrida and Foucault have little in

---

[25] Suzuki 1970, 337; Suzuki implicitly compares General MacArthur to General Tojo, whose poem, written after the destruction of Port-Arthur, he has just cited.

[26] See, for instance, Habermas 1987. The analogy between the two controversies can be seen, for example, in Bataille's text on Nietzsche, where he expresses his affinities with Zen

common with Suzuki, apart from the gut reaction they seem to provoke in their rationalist critics. With respect to this current debate, however, and despite my interest in the type of ideological critique performed by Habermas and the Frankfurt School, I admit to feeling more sympathy for the "Gallic" position, for cultural or karmic reasons. Before elaborating on the question of Zen ideology, it may be useful to examine a Gallic *and* humanist criticism of Suzuki's Zen, that of René Etiemble.

Etiemble and "Zaine"

A well-known French literary critic and a passionate advocate of comparative literature, René Etiemble has consistently denounced the "abusive Eurocentrism" of his colleagues and has fought for the recognition of non-Western literatures. His longtime interest in China led him to express, with the polemical verve that characterizes this distant heir of Voltaire, his opinions on various aspects of Chinese culture (see Etiemble 1964, 1988). These opinions were always motivated by his uncompromising humanist ideals and the contemporary developments on the French intellectual and political scenes. If Etiemble was, despite his strong anticlericalism, attracted to a religious tradition like Chan, it is partly because of the humanistic (and anticlerical) tendencies he discovered in one of its leading representives, Linji Yixuan (d. 867). In Etiemble's view, "No difference, . . . except in the methods, can be discerned between the liberation given by Chan and that given by humanism" (Etiemble 1964, 190). Although he agrees with Giuseppe Tucci's description of an ideal "Buddhist humanism," he concurs with Demiéville in considering Linji "more Chinese than Buddhist." According to Etiemble, Linji's originality as a Buddhist comes, paradoxically, from his Confucian vision of things, and Confucianism, for Etiemble as for the Jesuits, remains the *summum bonum* of Chinese thought. Chan is therefore accepted only to the extent that it comes close to Confucian humanism and rejected insofar as it remains a variant of Buddhist mysticism or quietism. Although Etiemble still relies on the traditional categories of "mysticism" and "quietism" ("providing that this word is cleansed of its bigoted tinge"), to counter what he calls "whining ecumenism" he clearly points out the fundamental differences between Christian and non-Christian mystics.[27] Thus, he denounces those who,

---

and quotes Suzuki at some length, although he still finds Zen (and Suzuki) deadly serious. See Bataille 1973, 6: 79, 91, 401, 404.

[27] Etiemble's position is vividly expressed in his diatribe against Izutsu Toshihiko's *Sufism and Taoism: A Comparative Study of Key Philosophical Concepts* (Berkeley: University of California Press, 1967): "All this stinks of the rottenness that Freud already detected in Jung, and gives a mediocre opinion of 'those beautiful souls in love with comparative mysticism'." See Etiemble's review in *Nouvelle Revue Française* 328 (May 1980): 179.

"due to their abusive ecumenical spirit, confuse the Zen experience with that of Christian or Muslim mystics" (Etiemble 1964, 190), as readily as he imagines a humanist *philosophia perennis* in which Western and Chinese humanisms would unite.[28]

Unfortunately, the "humanist" Linji is a rather isolated figure in the long and complex history of the Chan/Zen tradition, and Etiemble deplores the type of Zen ("something like a Christianity vulgarized by Daniel-Rops") introduced to the West by "the unavoidable and mediocre" Suzuki, and its negative influence on French society: *"Zut à ce Zen-là, et zut au Zen de Suzuki,* because Suzuki is to Zen what Lin Yu-tang is to Confucianism. . . . Never mind, everyone has read Suzuki's *Zen.* That everyone read it, well and good; that everyone reads nothing else, there is the harm, or the peril" (Etiemble 1964, 130). To distinguish this "passive, quietist, nihilist mystique, which aspires only to 'knowledge without differentiation'" from the "original" Chan/Zen humanism, Etiemble uses the depreciatory spelling "Zaine": "Zen is today something so French that I suggest that the Academy, as soon as it will reach the beginning of the letter Z, in two or three centuries, naturalize Zen as *Zaine*" (ibid., 133).

Like Koestler, Etiemble criticizes the "anti-intellectualism" of Zen, its quietism or "will to powerlessness," and its evil social effects; he contrasts them with the active moral and political involvement of the enlightened mind (in the Western sense): "Someone like Voltaire does require answers on the Calas scandal or the Audin scandal. A Zenist, on the other hand, enters into Zen: like some animals that, when frightened, enter into catalepsy, he chooses that happy state in which life can no longer be distinguished from death, nor untruth from truth. What a fine thing Zen is!" (ibid., 133). Etiemble denounces the collusion he sees between Zen and what he calls the "Taoist myth" and the "myth of Rimbaud," as well as a certain "confusedly syncretistic conception of *comparative mysticism,*" arguing that this eventually leads to a resignation in the face of an ever-resurgent fascism: "What does it matter to these irrationalists? Rimbaud, Zen, the Tao, everything is good to them, which puts us defenceless into the hands of the executioners who are watching us" (ibid., 108, 110). Unlike Koestler, Etiemble does not even bother to refute Suzuki: Zen, or rather *Zaine,* plays only a minor role in the "betrayal of the intellectuals" (*trahison des clercs*),[29] or in the larger contest between humanism (Western or Chinese) and the evil forces that threaten it. Our modern Voltaire finds

---

[28] "Etiemble's humanistic optimism is well reflected in the following passage: 'How to avoid the conclusion that a precise knowledge of all humanisms, including that of the execrated—and sometimes truly execrable—Mandarins, could singularly revive the notion of humanism?" See "Littérature comparée," in *Encyclopedia Universalis* (Paris, 1971): 10, 13.

[29] In this expression, which was the title of a famous book by Julien Benda, the French *clercs* has the double-entendre of "clerics" and "intellectuals" (see Benda 1927).

in this Oriental "cult" only "enough to exasperate those who, [like himself,] after having shouted: 'Hurrah for Zen!' must, for that very reason,
shout: 'Down with *zaine*!', that is: down with a Zen degenerated by the
incompetence and the vulgarity of Europe" (Etiemble 1964, 187). And, to
those who want to contrast "Buddhist humanism" with Confucian morality, he replies: "To the caricature of a Confucianism that has fallen to the
status of an ideology, it will always be easy to oppose the ideal of
the Buddha, as to Stalinist practices the generosity of the Sermon on the
Mount; but if, to the stakes of the Inquisition, to the corruption of Chinese
Buddhism, you oppose the view that Marx or Epicure had about humanism, aren't then all religions looking good! They are always wrong, those
who give themselves up to the vain game that consists in opposing an
incarnated religion, that of the others, to the outline of a religion, ours"
(ibid., 139). Ironically enough, it is precisely what Etiemble himself seems
to be doing.

Despite his denunciation of French and Western "provincialisms,"
Etiemble fails to realize that his own brand of humanism may just be
another kind of provincialism. Etiemble does not even consider the possibility that Voltaire's universalism served as the ideological basis on which
colonialism and its evolutionist theory of mankind's spiritual development
could be justified.[30] Despite the generous stance Etiemble takes toward the
cultures of the Third World, in contrast with Koestler's rather narrow
apology of Western culture, both remain heirs of the Enlightenment, and, if
their knowledge of Zen has somewhat improved, their understanding of it
has not advanced much beyond that of the Jesuits and the "Philosophers."[31] Like Suzuki, they remain trapped in Orientalist categories: although discursive strategies differ, the field in which they are inscribed
remains the same, and it is reinforced by these antagonisms.

NISHIDA AND THE KYŌTO SCHOOL

> When all is said, Nishida belongs to the East.
> (Suzuki, Preface to *A Study of Good*)

The so-called Kyōto school was founded by the Japanese philosopher
Nishida Kitarō (1870–1945), and the main themes of the so-called

[30] A striking example of the collusion between the universalist ideal of liberalism and
American cultural/political imperialism may be found in Richard Rorty's thought, as it is
expressed in a debate between Rorty and Jean-François Lyotard in "La traversée de l'Atlantique," *Critique* 456 (1985): 557–584.

[31] Another virulent criticism of Suzuki is that of the German theologian Ernst Benz
(b. 1907). Benz characterizes the contemporary interest in Zen as a form of "Zen snobbism."
He holds Suzuki responsible for this secularization of Zen that has resulted in an *"ersatz-*

"Nishida philosophy" (*Nishida tetsugaku*) served as a rallying point after his death. I do not try to address the strengths of the philosophical ideas of the "most demanding thinker Japan ever produced" (Piovesana 1968, 91), but I merely try to assess the "Nishida effect" on the current "philosophical" discourse about Zen and note the recurrence of a certain Orientalist "esprit simpliste" in the interstices of Nishida's complex thought. Although the question of the ideological elements in this thought leads us to examine briefly Nishida's political positions in a way that cannot do justice to his philosophy, it should be clear that my reading differs from recent political readings of Martin Heidegger, Paul de Man, or Mircea Eliade.[32] Much criticism leveled at Nishida by Japanese and Western historians derives from the same scapegoating mechanisms also at work in the denunciation of Orientalism. Although I am primarily concerned with the Zen rhetoric elements in Nishida's discourse, I do by the same occasion question the readiness with which this rhetoric can lend itself to appropriation by nationalist ideologies. Without falling into sociopolitical reductionism, it remains necessary to protest against the prevailing tendency, among Western scholars, to read the works of Nishida and the Kyōto school as expressions of a "pure philosophy" stemming from a "pure experience."

Despite a number of recent publications, Nishida's thought has not yet had much impact on the West.[33] It is much more complex and rigorous than that of Suzuki, although it has often been presented by exponents of the Kyōto School as paralleling Suzuki's. Not Nishida's philosophy per se, but the extent to which the Kyōto school and D. T. Suzuki have served the "Orientalist" purpose is of interest here. It would probably have been more appropriate to address the work of later thinkers like Nishitani Keiji, a successor of Nishida who coauthored several books on Zen with Suzuki, but limit the examination to Nishida as the founder of the Kyōto School. For present purpose, it can be said that in most cases Nishida's disciples have merely amplified tendencies already present in his work.

It is significant that Nishida and Suzuki were schoolmates and that their friendship lasted until Nishida's death in 1945.[34] Taking their cues from

religion." Although his criticism is in line with Koestler's, he reproaches the latter for his "dogmatic rationalism," while also finding fault with Suzuki's rationalistic and psychological interpretation of Zen irrationalism. See Benz 1962; Fader 1982, 349–370.

[32] Concerning Heidegger, see Victor Farias, *Heidegger et le Nazisme* (Paris: Verdier, 1987); Pierre Bourdieu 1988; Lacoue-Labarthe 1987. Concerning Paul de Man, see Derrida 1986. Mircea Eliade's participation in the Romanian Iron Guard, although well documented, has not been the object of much debate at Chicago and elsewhere.

[33] Western literature on Nishida and the Kyōto school has steadily grown in recent years. On the philosophy of Nishida, see in particular Noda 1955; Dilworth 1969, 1970a, 1970b, 1978; Waldenfels 1966; Maraldo 1989. On the Kyōto School, see also Ogawa 1968; Hans Waldenfels 1966, 372–391; Kasulis 1982; Maraldo 1989.

[34] See Abe Masao, ed., *A Zen Life: D. T. Suzuki Remembered* (New York: Weatherhill, 1986), 3–26.

Zen, the two men offered opposite responses to the challenge of Western philosophy. Whereas Suzuki underscored the antisystematic nature of Zen and relentlessly expressed his contempt for Western philosophy, Nishida attempted to systematize Zen insights in a way compatible with Western philosophy. Thus, *Nishida philosophy* has sometimes been read as a "Zen philosophy" based on the notion of "pure experience" (*junsui keiken*).

Nishida's search for harmony through philosophy appears to be an attempt to come to terms with his existential problems. At least at the beginning of his philosophical career, Nishida was too aware of Suzuki's example to feel satisfied with his own meditative practice or intellectual achievements.[35] He eventually managed to gain some degree of spiritual realization, but shortly before his "insight" (*kenshō*), he noted that he had been "mistaken to use Zen for the sake of scholarship" (Knauth 1965, 342). Although the fact that he chose to have his grave in a Zen monastery in Kyoto does not in itself imply a deep faith in Zen, it was read as a significant symbol of the connection between the Kyōto school and Zen.

Nishida has been sharply criticized after the war for lending his support to the imperial(ist) ideology of the Japanese government, but these criticisms have not led—as in Heidegger's case—to a thorough questioning of his philosophy. The Marxist characterization of Nishida's conservatism as belonging to the "cringing harmony type" (*jidaiteki chōwa kei*) did not prevent "Nishida philosophy" from knowing a growing success in recent years.[36] One might argue that this judgment reflects a sociopolitical conception of philosophy that fails to do justice to Nishida's philosophical position. Lothar Knauth, for example, feels that Nishida "responded totally to an intellectual and historical challenge" and that, unlike his friend Suzuki, he "tried to do away with the simplistic counterposing of tradition and modernization" (Knauth 1965, 358). David Dilworth also thinks that "Nishida's thought as a whole remained remarkably free of those currents [i.e., ultranationalist ideologies] despite the attempt to coopt his name on occasion. If anything, Nishida's text may be rather atypical in that respect." However, Dilworth adds: "Nevertheless, a comparatively mild strain of chauvinistic definition does appear in Nishida's writings during those years. It is only [*sic*] a *leitmotiv* in the overall corpus of his writings" (Nishida 1987, 129).

[35] In his diary, Nishida appears as a rather unsatisfied and almost culturally alienated individual, obsessed with his smoking habit and writing to himself in snatches of German and various other Western languages. On Nishida's diaries, see Knauth 1965 and Shibata 1981.

[36] See Miyajima Hajime, *Meijiteki shisōzō no keisei* (Tokyo, 1960), 376–382; quoted in Knauth 1965, 357. On the ideological elements in Nishida's thought, see Pierre Lavelle, "The Political Thought of Nishida Kitarō" (ms.) and *La pensée politique du Japon contemporain* (Paris: Presses Universitaires de France, 1990), 78–81. On Nishida's political ideas, see also Yamada Munemutsu, *Nishida Kitarō no tetsugaku: Nihonkei shisō no genzō* (Tokyo: San'ichi shobō, 1978); and Nakamura Yūjirō, *Nishida tetsugaku no datsu kōchiku* (Tokyo: Iwanami, 1987).

Nishida did write some fairly ambiguous pages on the condition of the "national polity" (*kokutai*), and he lectured in 1941 to the emperor on the philosophy of history. *The Problem of Japanese Culture* (*Nihon bunka no mondai*) was originally delivered in 1938 as a series of lectures at Kyōto University; this attempt to emphasize the affinities between Japan and the West caused him to be attacked as pro-Western during the war. In particular, his reservations concerning the adventurism of the Land Army made him the subject of criticism from the extremist faction, which succeeded in censoring several of his writings before publication (Knauth 1965, 348). Although Nishida asserted that, "underlying the Oriental view of the world and humanity, there has been something equal, if not superior, to Occidental conceptions" (Tsunoda, de Bary, and Keene 1964, 2: 352), he asserted, against the nationalists, that "we cannot take any culture and call it *the* culture" (ibid., 353). Against Orientalism, he argued that "the Orient, though it is spoken of as one, cannot be regarded as one in the sense that the European countries constitute one world" (ibid., 354). Yet, he set out to discover the logic underlying Oriental culture. Although he did not, like Suzuki, reject Western logic in the name of Oriental intuition, he contrasted Occidental logic—a logic that takes things as its objects—with Oriental logic—a logic that takes the mind as its object (ibid., 356).

Nishida's ideal of harmony, however, derived from the Kegon-Zen philosophy, and the accompanying tendency to shun all conflict could all too easily have perverse effects. Western readers may be attracted by his conception that individuals are "creative elements of a creative world" (Tsunoda, and de Bary, and Keene 1964, 2: 359), a world in which "each of us, as the individuated manyness of a world of absolutely contradictory self-identity lives with free will" (ibid., 361). However, the ideological effect of Nishida's conception becomes disturbingly clear when his theoretical individualism eventually turns into an apology for the imperial system: as a solution to the conflict between individualism and holism, Nishida suggested that, in the particular case of Japanese history, which is centered on the imperial household, both the individual and the whole "mutually negate themselves" for the emperor (Arima 1969, 11). Nishida's lectures to the emperor in 1941 on the philosophy of history were taken by his followers as a testimony of his denial of Japan's "divine mission" and of his courageous stress on individualism at a time when the individual was being sacrificed on the altar of patriotism. This interpretation, however, is bluntly contradicted by Nishida's assertion of *kokutai* (national polity) ideology, according to which there is an essential identity between the divine realm of the *kami*, the divine emperor, and Japan, the "divine land" (*shinkoku*). These ideas find their most complete expression in two specific essays, *The Problem of Japanese Culture* (*Nihon bunka no mondai*, 1940) and *The National Polity* (*Kokutai*, 1944) (see Tsunoda, de Bary, and Keene 1964, 2: 350–365).

A variety of readings of Nishida continue to confront the modern reader. For someone who is fortunate enough to have direct access to the realm of "pure experience," the point of view of ultimate truth in which the subject/object dichotomy does not obtain, historical values of the conventional level must appear rather meaningless. Even if one remains at the level of conventional truth, to interpret the truth-claim of philosophy in terms of sociopolitical determinism is perhaps unfair. Nishida would probably have argued, as he did about earlier (philosophical) criticism: "It has not been a criticism from within my own standpoint. A criticism from a different standpoint which does not truly understand what it is criticizing cannot be said to be a true criticism" (Nishida 1987, 128). Of course, the same standard could be applied to Nishida himself, for example, in his criticism of the Western religious tradition. In such a conflict, or rather *différend*, of interpretations," no single interpretive approach can pretend to defeat the others definitively. The fact remains that, once a philosophical discourse becomes the sign of some orthodoxy, it lends itself to ideological appropriation. Was Nishida an "accomplice of silence," or even an active supporter of the *Dai Nippon* ideology, or was he merely an ardent defender of Japanese culture? Although it is too early to pass judgment on the actual state of the documentation, we should be aware that Nishida's statements, whatever their extenuating circumstances, are highly problematic and have grave consequences for his philosophy. The ideological component of Nishida's philosophy is so explicit that philosophers can no longer overlook it.

Pure Experience

Because it is not my purpose to focus on moral and political issues, I turn to the epistemological elements of the so-called Nishida philosophy and note some of its problematic aspects. First, a brief discussion of the notion of *pure experience* is in order. One claim of the Kyōto school is that the pure experience, being like Suzuki's prajñā the realization of "absolute nothingness," is independent of any sociocultural context. The negative terms in which it is described, however, are reminiscent of the description of Awakening in the Mahāyāna tradition—and also, of the neo-Platonic tradition of Meister Eckhart to which Nishida constantly referred. This leads us to suspect that the pure experience itself, not only his a posteriori description, is from the outset informed by expectations specific to Buddhism. According to Steven Katz, "there are *no* pure (i.e., unmediated) experiences. . . . That is, *all* experience is processed through, organized by, and makes itself available to us in extremely complex epistemological ways" (Katz 1978, 26). In other words, even nothingnesses "are texts" (Boon 1982, 234). The term *pure experience* also recalls Christian mysticism and Protestant theology. Religious experience was first and foremost "an event of the soul" for Nishida, who writes: "Just as color appears to the eye as color, . . . so too God appears to the religious self as an event of one's own soul" (Nishida 1987: 48). One might argue, however, as Marcel Mauss did in his critique of William James, that "this theory of religious experience, as source of religion, considers only states rarely given, exceptional, that is, in last analysis, it rests on a pathological religious psychology" (Mauss 1968, 1: 59).

Formulated in terms influenced by William James's philosophy, as well as Fichte's notion of "absolute will" and by the Greek "logic of place," Nishida's notion of "pure" or "immediate" experience" seems to derive from an experience that he had as a high school student in Kanazawa. The role played by memory in this case brings to mind Freud's concept of *Nachträglichkeit* (*après-coup*, "differed action"): that is, the retrospective manipulation of "memory traces" (*Erinnerungsspuren*), the active reconstruction of the meaning of the past in function of new situations, and ultimately the possibility to remember an event that may have never been experienced as such and yet exerts potent psychological effects.[37] One consequence of Freud's hypothesis is that there is no pure present in which such an experience could take place, because the present, or the full presence to things, is always derived, reconstituted (see Derrida 1967, 314).

At any rate, the main influence on Nishida's formulation of pure experience is clearly that of Zen. It is well known that Nishida, following Suzuki's example, practiced Zen for about a decade, beginning in 1897, at various monasteries in Kamakura and Kyoto, eventually achieving some insight at Daitokuji in the summer of 1903. In a short piece, "How to Read Nishida," Suzuki claimed that

> Nishida's philosophy of absolute nothingness or his logic of the self-identity of absolute contradictions is difficult to understand, I believe, unless one is passably acquainted with Zen experience. Nishida himself was a good student of Zen. He thought it was his mission to make Zen intelligible to the West. . . . [He] experienced [the] Ultimate and then, desiring to give it an intellectual analysis to his own satisfaction, reflected on the experience so as to make it intelligible to the sophisticated mentality as well as to himself, and the result was "Nishida philosophy." (Nishida 1960, iii–vi)

Suzuki apparently toned down his anti-intellectualism to introduce his intellectual friend's first book. Although Nishida himself never felt the urge to respond to the claim made by Suzuki on his behalf, Suzuki's statement, despite its problematic aspects, became the basis for the later readings of Nishida's philosophy in the Kyōto school.

If there is some truth in the Zen dictum that the finger pointing at the

---

[37] See Jean Laplanche and J.-B. Pontalis, *Vocabulaire de la psychanalyse* (Paris: Presses Universitaires de France, 1967), 33.

moon is not the moon, then it follows that the notion of pure experience is by no means the pure experience itself. Assuming that such an experience can be found, any attempt to characterize it, even the least reifying one, will betray it. Thus, as a philosophical category used by the early Nishida and his disciples in various discursive contexts, pure experience came to function performatively and to produce specific effects outside the field of philosophy. According to the Marxist critic Arima Tatsuo, for instance, "with all its logical embellishments, [it] was used to preach social resignation as a means of achieving individual enlightenment" (Arima 1969, 13).

Thus, assuming that pure experience itself is ontologically "pre-critical"—that is, anterior to any discrimination between subject and object—Nishida's *philosophy* of pure experience remains nevertheless ideologically uncritical. As Nishida's former disciple, Tanabe Hajime, pointed out, Nishida "evidently draws illegitimate conclusions from premises taken from the field of religion and tranferred to the field of philosophy, thereby transgressing the bounds of philosophy" (Waldenfels 1966, 372). For Tanabe, "the religious experience of absolute nothingness cannot become the principle of a philosophical system," and therefore the combination of Eastern "mystical" experience with Western logical thought was bound to be a failure (ibid., 373).

Such need not always be the case, provided that the religious commitment be clearly spelled out and that the categories in use be carefully chosen. To be sure, the categories used by Nishida were not sufficiently elaborated to avoid Tanabe's criticism, and it was necessary to point out their epistemological limitations; but this does not mean that a larger rationality cannot include the religious dimensions of human experience. Just as there is, since Kant, an "analytic of finitude" according to which "the limits of knowledge provide a positive foundation for the possibility of knowing" (Dreyfus and Rabinow 1983, 30), might there be someday an "analytic of infinitude"?

The East-West "Dialogue"

Because Nishida's borrowings from the languages of Zen and of the Western mystical tradition were not sufficiently qualified, they generated semantic difficulties that became more obvious in the writings of his successors—for instance Nishitani Keiji and Ueda Shizuteru. Inasmuch as meaning is contextual, it is highly problematic to translate the Japanese term *mu* as "Nothingness" and to equate it with the *Nichts* of the German mystics or conversely to confuse the Western connotations of "Being" with those of the Japanese term *yū* ("to have," "there is"). This "linguistic-cum-ontological confusion," which led Nishida to contrast "Oriental Nothingness" with Western "Being," has also prompted comparativists to compare

Heidegger's *Being and Time* with Dōgen's conception of *uji* (usually "translated" as "being/time").

The problem arises as to whether Nishida actually set out to "explain Zen to the West" and compare it with Western spirituality or whether he was merely perceived as doing so. It is clear from Nishida's diary and other writings that his understanding of the Zen and Christian traditions remained relatively superficial. His interpretation of Buddhism is idiosyncratic, and he himself admitted that his Zen was rather different from the teaching of the Zen tradition. His quotations from Chan/Zen texts such as *The Platform Sūtra* (*Tan jing*), *The Emerald Cliff Record* (*Biyan lu*), *The Essentials of Mind Transmission* (*Chuanxin fayao*), *The Record of Linji* (*Linji lu*), *The Record of National Master Daitō* (*Daitō kokushi goroku*), and Dōgen's *Shōbōgenzō*, are indeed free and eclectic, as are his quotations from Christian mystics and theologians such as Scotus Erigena, Meister Eckhart, Jacob Boehme, Nicholas Cusanos, Martin Luther and Søren Kierkegaard. Nishida, however, never seems to question his "performative" use of Western and Buddhist sources to illustrate his theses. Although Nishida illustrates his conception of the nondual identity of the absolute with quotations of these (mostly neo-Platonist) Christians, I strongly doubt that, as Dilworth claims, "if anything, these cross-cultural analyses are one of the strengths of Nishida's text" (Nishida 1987, 130).

Only late in his life did Nishida explicitly identify his standpoint with Zen (and Pure Land). In his last work, Nishida even attempted to correct popular misunderstandings about Zen: thus, for him, Zen has nothing to do with mysticism (ibid., 108)—although mysticism is something extremely close to Zen [!] (ibid., 109). He contended that, despite the closeness of Zen and of what has been called mysticism in Western philosophy since the time of Plotinus, Western mysticism was never able to transcend the standpoint of "object logic": "Indeed, the One of Plotinus stands at an opposite pole to the Zen experience of nothingness. Neo-Platonism did not in fact attain to a religious celebration of the ordinary and the everyday as we find it in the Zen tradition" (Ibid., 109).

Significantly, also toward this time Nishida took his most nationalist stand in essays such as "The Problem of Japanese Culture" (Nihon bunka no mondai) and "The Logic of Place and the Religious Worldview" (Bashōteki ronri to shūkyōteki sekaikan) (see Nishida 1987; Yuasa 1986, 1987). He was perhaps influenced on this point too by Suzuki, who wrote his nativist books on *Japanese Spirituality* and *Zen and Japanese Culture* in the mid-1940s. As noted earlier, Nishida eventually placed the formulas borrowed from Western philosophy and Buddhism in the service of nationalism, apparently espousing the *kokutai* ideology. He interpreted for instance the cardinal Zen notion of "no-mind" (Ch. *wuxin*, J. *mushin*) and the Pure Land notion of *jinen hōni* (natural spontaneity in accordance to the Dharma) as the purest manifestations of the Japanese spirit. He identified this Japanese spirit, "which goes to the truth of things as an identity between actuality and reality," that is, "the realization of this absolute at the bottom of ourselves" (Tsunoda, de Bary, and Keene 1964, 2: 364), with not only Mahāyāna Buddhism, and more precisely with its Japanese variants Zen and Amidism,[38] but also Shintō ideology, the so-called Way of the Gods (*kannagara no michi*). The following passage is worth quoting at some length in this respect:

> As for the characteristics of Japanese culture, it seems to me to lie in moving from subject to object (environment), ever thoroughly negating the self and becoming the thing itself, becoming the thing itself to see, becoming the thing itself to act. To empty the self and see things, for the self to be immersed in things, "no-mindedness" (*mushin*) or effortless acceptance of the grace of Amida (*jinen hōni*)—these, I believe, are the states we Japanese strongly yearn for. . . . The essence of the Japanese spirit must be to become one in things and in events. It is to become one at that primal point in which there is neither self nor others."[39]

Without blaming Nishida for what he could not possibly have foreseen at the time, can one forget that this "point of high fusion" found its ultimate expression in Hiroshima? Interestingly, the translator of this excerpt, Abe Masao, the main representative of the Kyōto school in the West, has omitted the following sentence: "This [process] seems to have as its center this contradictory auto-identity that is the Imperial Household" (Nishida 1965, 6: 104; see also Nishida 1991, 74).

The expression "to empty the self and see things, for the self to be immersed in things" (*Onore o kū shite mono o miru, jiko wa mono no naka ni bossuru*) is a reminiscence of Dōgen's *Shōbōgenzō Genjō kōan* (*T. 52*, 2582: 23c; see also Faure 1987, 114). Nishida frequently quotes Dōgen in this nationalist and expansionist context. For example,

---

[38] Nishida was strongly influenced by Amidism, as can be seen in this excerpt: "Even Mahāyāna did not truly attain to the world-creatively real in the sense that I have just indicated. I think that it was perhaps only in Japanese Buddhism that the absolute identity of negation and affirmation was realized, in the sense of the identity of the actual and the absolute that is peculiar to the Japanese spirit. Examples of this realization are found in such ideas of Shinran as 'in calling on the name of Buddha non-reason is reason' and 'effortless acceptance of the grace of Amida.' But even in Japan, it has not been positively grasped. It has only been understood as an absolute passivity to Amida, or as some non-discriminating wisdom in a merely irrational, mystical sense" (Nishida 1987, 102). Shinran's notion of "natural conformity with the Dharma" (*jinen hōni*, a term rendered by Dilworth as "effortless acceptance of the grace of Amida") recurs often in *The Problem of Japanese Culture*, and Nishida points out that this notion has nothing to do with the Western concept of nature (Nishida 1965, *bekkan* 6: 127–129).

[39] Nishida 1965, *bekkan* 6: 104; Tsunoda, de Bary, and Keene 1964, 2: 362; see also Nishida 1987, 102; Nishida 1991, 73–74.

Today, the problem of our national culture can only be considered as that of its broadening to an horizontal "universality," while retaining of the vertical "universality" that has characterized it for millennia. This amounts necessarily to promoting a culture of flexibility of mind (*jūnanshin*), a culture of dropping off body and mind (*shinjin datsuraku*). . . . And it is necessarily to establish in a contradictorily self-identical way one single world entrusted to things. It is this, I believe, in which resides the Japanese mission, that is, to construct the Eastern mind." (Nishida 1965, 6: 107; 1991, 76–77)

Nishida, however, nuances this statement by what sounds like a critique of Japanese imperialism: "If, as subject, we assimilate the other by negating it, this is no other than imperialism, this is not the Japanese spirit" (ibid.).

Despite Nishida's fondness for Dōgen, his understanding of Zen, like Suzuki's, may be considered biased or reductionistic in several respects. Apart from references to Dōgen, Nishida was greatly indebted to Suzuki, particularly in his later writings. Although Nishida desired to elaborate a philosophy of the "concrete," his concepts of "pure experience," "absolute nothingness," and so on, remained fundamentally abstract and dualistic. If applied thoroughly, the Mahāyāna logic of nonduality would deny the possibility of "pure experience" or even the linguistic pertinence of the expression because the very distinction between pure experience and the "impure" ordinary experience, or between philosophical/metaphysical language and ordinary language, remains, not only dualistic, but also utopian. There is no metaphysical or metalinguistic position available to the philosopher, only values that become ideological when they are denied as such. Even the "concrete world" of which Nishida speaks so often is an abstraction, an idealistic product without much resemblance to any sociocultural reality. Perhaps this impossibility to return to the "real thing" is the price that Nishida, like most philosophers, had to pay to establish the philosophical authority of his discourse. Ironically, when he tried to apply the Buddhist notion of the "actual *qua* absolute," Nishida ended up equating the "actual" with the kokutai and the Imperial House. Although Nishida was a product of Japanese modernity, he was unable to accept this fact and overcome his nostalgia for Japanese and Western orthodoxies. His philosophy appears more like an exorcism than a set of operative notions enabling him (and us) to understand and act upon reality. Although he was more influenced by Bergson, by certain aspects Nishida resembles Durkheim, whom he mentions only in passing when arguing, in his last writings, that "every historically crystallized society begins from a religious ground—from what Durkheim has called *le sacré*" (Nishida 1987, 116). In his case too, the individualism of the beginning gave way to a mystical conception of society (or nation). According to Nishida, "Each nation is a world that contains the self-expression of the absolute within itself" (ibid., 122). After a final quotation from Suzuki, he closes his book with the following statement: "The nation is the mirror image of the Pure Land in this world" (ibid., 123).

Already in the preface to *From Acting to Seeing* (*Hataraku mono kara miru mono e*, 1927), Nishida stated his desire to "supply philosophical foundations" for traditional Oriental culture. In this work, he refers to "the form of the formless, the voice of the voiceless which lies at the basis of Eastern culture, transmitted from our ancestors for thousand of years" (ibid., 127). Their common interest in Western mystics like Meister Eckhart led both Nishida and Suzuki to misrepresent Christianity as some kind of inferior version of Mahāyāna Buddhism, thus reversing the old schemas applied to the East by Westerners. Like Suzuki's work, Nishida's entire attempt to elaborate a "logic of the East" based on the notion of "contradictory identity" (*mujunteki dōitsu*), the so-called logic of *sokuhi* ("is" and "is not") is governed by Orientalist categories and reveals a "nativist" bias.[40] Nishida was indebted to Suzuki for his discovery of the logic of sokuhi in the *Diamond Sūtra* (Nishida 1987, 70). In his final essay in particular, he repeatedly quoted Suzuki and used Zen anecdotes in the style of Suzuki—a style that became characteristic of much of the later Kyōto school's production. Suzuki is invoked in particular to support the contrast drawn by Nishida between East and West: "If the concept of compassion has not been foundational for Western culture (as Suzuki Daisetsu maintains), then I think there is a basic difference between Eastern and Western culture in this regard."[41] Although many important philosophical insights remain, the ideological function of such simplistic assumptions undermines the validity of the "Nishida philosophy" (*Nishida tetsugaku*). As David Dilworth remarks, "The danger of confusing the socio-historical and metaphysical spheres when defining things 'Eastern' and 'Western' potentially remains, I think, in some aspects of *Nishida tetsugaku*" (Dilworth 1970c, 212). Because he is more nuanced and subtle than other nativist thinkers, including Suzuki, Nishida has exerted and continues to exert a greater seduction on intellectuals, a dangerous power that has allowed him to rally a number of them to the nationalist ideology (see Nishida 1991, 14–15).

[40] See for example, the notion of "self-identity of absolute contradictories" (*zettai mujunteki jiko doitsu*), Nishida's version of the Buddhist logic of dialectical identity (*sokuhi*), in *On the Philosophy of Descartes* (*Dekaruto no tetsugaku ni tsuite*, 1943) in Nishida 1965, 11: 189. See also *Zen bunka no mondai* in Nishida 1965, *bekkan* 6: 104.

[41] See Nishida 1987, 107–108. Already in *Fundamental Problems of Philosophy*, in "The Forms of Culture of the Classical Periods of East and West Seen from a Metaphysical Perspective," Nishida had determined that, whereas the ground of reality was Being for Western philosophy, it was Nothingness for the East.

The Postwar Kyōto School

The dichotomic framework established by Nishida's (and Suzuki's) logic of contradictory identity and its use of "Oriental Nothingness" (J. *mu*) as an ideological weapon paved the way for the kind of theological/ philosophical confrontation of "East" and "West" that has occupied much of the "philosophical" activity of the postwar Kyōto school and resulted in a rather sterile "dialogue" between Zen and Western philosophy, or Zen and Christianity.[42] A recent example of the Kyōto school's monological "dialogue" can be found in Abe Masao's *Zen and Western Thought* (1985), one of "those prominent Japanese philosophers [who] confuse metaphysical and cultural predicates to some degree in their works" (Nishida 1987, 146). This state of affairs, however, owes as much to Suzuki's as to Nishida's influence on the Kyōto school.

As noted earlier, the development of the nationalist tendencies in Nishida's thought can be seen in the work of his disciples. It reached its full expression in the symposia organized in 1942 by the group on the philosophy of world history, the so-called right wing of the Kyōto school composed of Kōsaka Masaaki (1900–1965), Nishitani Keiji (1900–1991), Kōyama Iwao (b. 1905), and Suzuki Shigetaka. These symposia advocated total war as the unification of all dimensions of human life. In the January 1942 symposium, "Sekaishiteki tachiba to Nihon" (The Standpoint of World History and Japan; see Kosaka, et al. 1942), Nishitani, an authority on Zen who later coedited several books with D. T. Suzuki and is perceived as the main representative of the Kyōto school today, made the following comments: "Is it not that the political consciousness of the Germans is more advanced? I believe too that in people such as Hitler the consciousness of the necessity to restore an interior order is clearer than in Japanese rulers. . . . Although today the various peoples of the East have no national consciousness in the European way, this is perhaps a chance for the construction of the Coprosperity sphere . . . , because it means that they are being constituted as people of the Coprosperity sphere from a Japanese point of view."[43] As far as I know, Nishitani has never manifested any regret for such youthful errors, nor has this aspect of his work ever been

---

[42] On this "irenically polemic" dialogue, as Cooke calls it (1974, 276), see Takeuchi Yoshinori, "Buddhism and Existentialism: The Dialogue between Oriental and Occidental Thought," in *Religion and Culture: Essays in Honor of Paul Tillich,* ed. W. Leibrecht (New York: Harper & Row, 1959), 291–365. For a more open "dialogue," see Waldenfels 1980; for a critique of the concept of "Oriental Nothingness," see Wargo 1972.

[43] Kōsaka, et al. 1942, 201. Likewise, in the April 1942 symposium "Tōa kyōeiken no rinrisei to rekishisei" (Ethics and Historicality of the Great Asian Coprosperity Sphere"), Kōsaka Masaaki declared: "The Sino-Japanese war is also a war of morality. Now that we have entered the Great Asian War, the war is much larger in scale now, namely, a war between

discussed among his disciples. Unfortunately, the irony in the title of Notto Thelle's "profile" of Nishitani, "The Flower Blooms at the Cliff's Edge," is purely inadvertent (see Thelle 1984).

Although not directly related to Nishida, Umehara Takeshi's School of Japanese Studies, also known as the New Kyōto school, has contributed to the expansion of a discourse initiated by Suzuki with his *Zen and Japanese Culture*. The ideological agenda of this school was advanced with the nomination of Umehara as director of the International Center for Japanese Culture (*Kokusai Nihon bunka sentaa*) in Kyoto, a center created in 1986 by the Nakasone government.[44] More than ever, Zen appears as an ideological instrument to promote a cultural image of Japan in the West and as an essential component of the so-called "cultural exceptionalism" (*Nihonjinron*, lit. "Treatises on the Japanese") (see Harootunian 1988b, 473).

To repeat, I am not concerned here with "Nishida philosophy" as such, but, as in the case of Suzuki, with the "Nishida effects" on the constitution of an authorized discourse on Zen, a discourse monopolized by the later Kyōto school and advanced by journals such as *The Eastern Buddhist* or *Philosophy East and West* and by institutions such as the F.A.S. ("For All Mankind Society"!), an idealistic and rather grandiloquent lay movement founded in 1958 by Hisamatsu Shin'ichi (1889–1980) and dedicated to "universalism, individual self-awareness, critical spirit and a will to reformation."[45] My main purpose in this chapter was not to criticize philosophical or political ideas but to analyze a certain rhetorical style that, like Suzuki's and the Kyōto school's, remains trapped in Orientalist and nativist structures. I ended, however, by raising two different sets of questions concerning the ideological role of "Zen philosophy" and the epistemological status of Zen Orientalism.

---

the Oriental morality and the Occidental morality. Let me put it differently, the question is which morality will play a more important role in the World History in the future" (*Chūōkōron*, April 1942, 120–121; quoted in Sakai 1988, 492–493).

[44] The nativist thinking of Umehara appears openly in a dialogue he had with Prime Minister Nakasone in 1986. In this dialogue, published in *Bungei shunjū*, both interlocutors marvel at the pantheistic love of nature and other perennial characteristics of the Japanese. In response to Nakasone's assertion that Japanese culture is the oldest in the world, Umehara explains that he has never regretted abandoning the study of Western philosophy to return to that of Japanese thought. See Nakasone Yasuhiro and Umehara Takeshi, "Shōwa rokujūichinen o mukaete: Sekai bunmei no nagare to Nihon no yakuwari," *Bungei shunjū* (1986): 297–300.

[45] According to Hisamatsu, "F" also stands for *formless* self, "A" for the stand of *all* mankind, while "S" points to the obligation to create a *suprahistorical* history. Therefore, these three letters symbolize the three dimensions of human life: self, world, and history. See Cooke 1974, 303.

Admittedly, only a discourse blind to its own conditions of production could blame Nishida (or Suzuki) for using Orientalist categories and chauvinist rhetoric at the time he wrote—a time when the opposition of East and West had become an all powerful collective representation—in the Durkheimian sense. An ideological critique remains necessary, however, if only because these categories and the underlying rhetoric are still active, despite a radically different historical context, in the thought of contemporary Kyōto school philosophers (see Asada 1988, 633–634). Furthermore, as in the case of Heidegger, we cannot help asking to what extent the "philosophical text" is affected in its content by the ideological and political "context." In other words, we must wonder how essential these Orientalist and nationalist stigmata are—to not only Nishida philosophy but also Zen philosophy as championed by the Kyōto school and its Western admirers.

Like the New Kyōto school of Umehara Takeshi, Nishida and the Kyōto school have provided arguments to the *Nihonjinron* ideology. Paradoxically, even recent critics of these trends end up contributing in a strange way to this ideology—not unlike Nishida himself when he thought that "a point of union between Eastern and Western culture could be sought in Japan." Karatani Kōjin (b. 1941), for example, argues that Japanese thought, as exemplified by Motoori Norinaga, was postmodern and poststructuralist *avant la lettre* (or *avant la Grammatologie*), or rather he asserts that it does not need poststructuralism and postmodernity, because it has never known a "rationalist" phase (with the benign exception of *karagokoro*, "Chinese mind," term under which Motoori Norinaga includes Buddhist philosophy) against which to react.[46] This again warns us against the temptation to localize the effects of ideology in a specific discourse, in contrast to which our own discourse could claim to be ideologically neutral.

With Suzuki, Zen coopted the whole field of Japanese culture and, imposing on Japanese ideology the myth of transparency, claimed the status of a transcendental spirituality. With Nishida and the Kyōto school, Zen acquired a crosscultural philosophical status. Thus, through the work of Suzuki, Nishida and their successors, a new field of discourse was created—one that differs markedly from the earlier Chan/Zen discourse(s) it claimed to replicate or interpret. Although the leitmotives of transparency and purity are not mere alibis, they are the products of what one

[46] On the other hand, critics of the *Nihonjinron* like the Buddhist scholars Matsumoto Shirō and Hakamaya Noriaki adopt reverse ethnocentrism that denies the authenticity of Japanese Buddhism (and most of Chinese Buddhism). Their criticism of the *Tathāgatagarba* theory and of its Japanese variant, the *hongaku* ("innate awakening") theory, is made in the name of "pure Buddhism"—a conception as essentialist and ideological as the nativism they denounce. See Matsumoto 1986 and Hakamaya 1986.

might, using Bourdieu's terminology, call a Zen *habitus*—that is, the perfect adequation to values that seem "transparent" only because their conditions of production have been occulted (Bourdieu 1980, 88). For those who enter this field, everything may appear spontaneous or natural. The success of this discourse is proved by the fact that, for Suzuki's critics as well as his followers, the existence of something called Zen is always taken for granted.

Chapter Three

RETHINKING CHAN HISTORIOGRAPHY

> You, while projecting your own faults on us, are like a person
> who, having mounted his horse, forgets his horse.
> (Nāgārjuna, *Mūlamadhyamikakārikā*)

A S IT IS KNOWN to us through East Asian sources, Chan/Zen is
the product of two traditions that sometimes overlap, sometimes
contradict or ignore each other: namely, the Buddhist orthodoxy
and the Sino-Japanese historiographical tradition. The paradigmatic example of contradiction between these two currents is provided by the
debate that opposed D. T. Suzuki and the Chinese historian Hu Shih in the
columns of the journal *Philosophy East and West* in 1953. Perhaps one
should speak rather of a dialogue of the deaf or even of what Jean-François
Lyotard calls a *différend* because the protagonists apparently did not share
the same premises. As Suzuki bluntly put it, there are vis-à-vis Zen at least
two types of mentality: "one which can understand Zen and, therefore, has
the right to say something about it, and another which is utterly unable to
grasp what Zen is. The difference between the two types is one of quality
and is beyond the possibility of mutual reconciliation" (Suzuki 1953, 25).
Thus, Hu Shih, as a historian, knows Zen in its historical setting, but not
"Zen in itself" (ibid., 26), and besides, adds Suzuki, "it is not the historian's business to peer into [the latter]" (ibid. , 25). The discussion, however, bears precisely on the validity of the premises of each interlocutor and,
more generally, on the claim to legitimacy of the metaphysical tradition of
Chan on the one hand and of the values of secular humanism as they are
represented by the historical discipline on the other. To what extent is Chan
amenable to a historical approach, if it is indeed? Can this teaching, as
Suzuki thought, traverse the claim of history in the name of its own atemporal character? If not, to what extent is it threatened by the results of the
historical inquiry? Is one entitled to speak of a historical consciousness of
Chan? And if the historical method appears based on Western logic, can
one speak of the rationality of Chan, as Hu Shih argued, or should one stick
to the common perception of Chan as an irrationalism?

Each protagonist in this debate saw the flaw in the adverse argument; but
no encompassing view was reached, and their successors were only able to
repeat, while refining them, the same arguments. Are we then condemned
to use the same dichotomies and to remain forever trapped in the same

discursive hermeneutic dilemma between Suzuki's metaphysics and Hu Shih's historicism? Despite their apparent opposition and the superficial East-West dichotomy that underlies it, symbolized by the name of the journal where it takes place, the two theses in essence presuppose the same discourse of modernity, either to accept or to reject it. In this sense, like the case of Nishida, they are only expressions of this discourse. Suzuki's criticism of historicism calls to mind Leo Strauss's remark that "modern concepts, as that of History with a capital H, are very late, very derived, and . . . due to this, do not allow us to accede to the original thought, which is in no case derived but at the beginning of any tradition" (Strauss 1979, 111). This criticism also resembles the one that Heidegger levels at human sciences, and it may partly explain why the German philosopher saw in the Japanese scholar an intellectual (or rather anti-intellectual) guide (*maître à penser* or perhaps *à ne pas penser*).

Once stripped of its simplistic positivism, the historical approach provides an important insight when it rejects the "foundationalist" position to assert the historicity of truth. According to this model, truth turns out to be, in Nietzsche's famous words, "a mobile army of metaphors, metonyms, and anthropomorphisms—in short, a sum of human relations, which have been enhanced, transposed, and embellished poetically and rhetorically, and which after long use seem firm, canonical, and obligatory to a people" (Nietzsche 1974; see also de Man 1983, 110). Going one step further, one might argue with Maurice Merleau-Ponty that "we do not have to chose between those who think that the history of the individual or society holds the truth of the philosopher's symbolical constructions, and . . . those who think on the contrary that the philosophical consciousness has as a matter of principle the keys to personal and social history": the alternative is imaginary because "those who defend one of these resort surreptitiously to the other" (Merleau-Ponty 1964b, 128–129). This is certainly true, if not of Hu Shih, at least of Suzuki, whose position vis-à-vis history is ambiguous, because he sometimes resorts to a kind of historical discourse to prove his point. Indeed, as Arthur Waley remarks, "Suzuki need not feel he is a sinner (he actually uses the word) if he sometimes dabbled in history, for apart from the mundane there is no transcendental. Still less need he ask Hu to join him in his *peccavi*, for if there were no Hus there would be no Suzukis" (Waley 1955, 78).

Furthermore, not only do the metaphysical or metalinguistic privileges Suzuki grants to himself appear exorbitant, but they also prove insufficient to disqualify history. Far from being always reductionistic, the historical approach can show precisely that the meaning of a given symbolic system, whether that of Western philosophy or Chan Buddhism, cannot be reduced to the circumstances of its emergence and how, despite its historical nature, it "transmutes its situation of departure into a means to understand itself and to understand others" (Merleau-Ponty 1953, 179).

Admittedly, history, as Merleau-Ponty conceived it and as some historians after Foucault attempt to practice it, is not Hu Shih's triumphant historicism, which Suzuki had some good reasons to judge reductionistic. Suzuki himself, however, like his rival, paradoxically finds a niche within a Sino-Japanese historiographical tradition that, through the study of the Dunhuang documents, significantly contributed to a rewriting of Chan history. Since the Meiji Restoration, how have Japanese historians of Chan come to terms with what, for their Western and Christian historians, often constituted the dilemma between faith and reason? Does the historical method constitute a serious threat for the Chan patriarchal tradition, or can this tradition itself conversely be interpreted as the emergence, within Chinese Buddhism, of a historical consciousness? To be sure, Shenhui's adoption of the twenty-eight (or twenty-nine) Indian patriarchs theory resulted from his awareness of the impossibility of his earlier theory of thirteen patriarchs spanning from Buddha to Bodhidharma, according to traditional computation, over a period of fifteen centuries. But, the fact that this earlier theory was ever considered at all suggests that historical consciousness was still relatively weak at that time within Chan circles. I return to that question in chapter 6.

Despite the resistances it has met from the most traditionalist followers of Zen (in which, as noted earlier, Suzuki himself was perceived as a Westernized intellectual), the type of historical criticism made possible in Japan by the textual study of the Dunhuang documents and the subsequent questioning of the Chan patriarchal tradition has rarely led to a fundamental questioning of the truth claims of that tradition. From a Western standpoint, one could have expected that the apocryphal nature of the works attributed to the "founders" Bodhidharma and Huineng, let alone the quasi-mythical nature of such figures, would considerably weaken a tradition that drew its legitimacy from them. Such was not the case, in part because the impact of historical demythification was attenuated by the shift that had already taken place, during the Tokugawa and Meiji periods, from a "hieratical" tradition relying on the ritual transmission of the Dharma and of its *regalia* (patriarchal robe, text, relics, portrait, transmission verses), to a more philosophically minded tradition, one therefore more detached from its human or material carriers.

The "hieratical" and the "philosophical" tendencies seem to have always coexisted in Chan/Zen, as illustrated for instance by the contrast between works such as the *Chuan fabao ji* and the *Lengqie shizi ji* in Tang China or Dōgen's *Shōbōgenzō* and Yōsai's *Kōzen gokokuron* in Kamakura Japan. By a strange irony of fate a "hieratic" work like the *Shōbōgenzō* is today perceived as a purely philosophical treatise.

Making Chan at times an atemporal "essence," at times a kind of "cultural garden" inaccessible to Westerners and to Westernized and rationalist "Easterners" such as Hu Shih, Suzuki's rhetoric appears steeped in the myth of authenticity and radical differences. At the same time, its patent ideological character draws it closer to its "historicist" rival, inasmuch as both are characterized by an attempt to hide, or simply forget, their localized nature. However, if relating ideas to places is precisely what defines the historical enterprise, we must refuse both the nativist ideology of Suzuki and the historicist ideology of Hu Shih.

I first briefly examine a few strongholds of Chan/Zen historiography, without by any means conceiving that "localization" as a pure determination by sociopolitical or economical factors. I also want to question the "objectivist" character of this historiography, which corresponds to a claim of epistemological and ideological neutrality. Whereas the alleged "unlocalized" character of Chan historiographical discourse bears some resemblance to that of Chan theoretical discourse itself, the "localized" thinking of the critical (and self-critical) historian seems more akin to the "logic of practice" of "popular" culture, a logic that, as I discuss in chapter 5, is also "locative." We must keep in mind that the concepts received from historical scholarship, even that of objectivity, are themselves historically determined and that our activity necessarily takes place within what Gadamer calls a "history of effects." This does not mean, however, as Gadamer seems to imply, that one should endorse the claims of the sectarian tradition under study. If the objectivism of Chan historians results from both their denying to belong to a specific place and time and forgetting the history of their discipline that produces ideological effects, it is necessary, before criticizing this objectivism, to examine more closely the places from which it arises. After an excursus on the Chan scholarship of Hu Shih, I limit myself here to the Japanese historiography of Chan.

Before I proceed, it is perhaps worth recalling that the renewal of Chan historiography finds its origin in a fraud that reveals an unequal relationship typical of Orientalism: namely, the initial acquisition of the Dunhuang manuscripts by Sir Aurel Stein. Ironically enough, by posing as a distant heir of the Buddhist pilgrim Xuanzang, a powerful rival of the early Chan tradition, Stein was able to convince the naive Daoist priest Wang to part with the invaluable manuscripts he had discovered in a Dunhuang cave.[1] Thus, the discourse of Chan historiography, like the reverse Orientalism of Suzuki, presupposed a purloined corpus.

PLACES AND PEOPLE

As the controversy between Suzuki and Hu Shih suggests, the history of Chan/Zen is the product of two distincts milieux, the Buddhist institutions

[1] Here is Stein's description of the event: "The priest [i.e., Wang] was obviously impressed by what in my poor Chinese I could tell him of my devotion to the great pilgrim [Xuanzang], and how I had followed his footsteps from India across inhospitable mountains and deserts"

and the academic world. Serving as relay stations between these two circles are Buddhist institutions such as Komazawa University in Tokyo and Hanazono College in Kyoto, respectively affiliated with the Sōtō and Rinzai sects. Also worth mentioning are Ōtani University (where Suzuki taught) and Ryūkoku University: both affiliated with the Jōdo Shinshū sect, they have their own collection of (more or less authentic) Dunhuang manuscripts. Ryūkoku University in particular has significantly contributed to the research on Dunhuang documents with Fujieda Akira and on the Chan influence on Tibetan Buddhism with Ueyama Daishun. In Tokyo, Taishō University, with ties to the Tendai sect, has also produced important studies on Chan owing to the influence of Sekiguchi Shindai.

With a few significant exceptions, the scholarly production of these Buddhist universities is largely determined by their sectarian adherence. Although openly partisan points of view are generally disavowed in the name of scientific objectivity, apologetical considerations are nevertheless rarely absent, not so much in the explicit content of the discourse itself, but rather *en creux*, in the choice of the topics judged as "scientifically" relevant. Moreover, there is an implicit distribution of territories, and Rinzai Zen is still rarely studied at Komazawa University or Sōtō Zen at Hanazono College. Conversely, scholars often spend their entire career studying "neutral" topics such as Indian Buddhist logic or Abhidharmic thought, as if to deny or redeem their own institutional and religious affiliations. In this context, philology sometimes acquires the value of an exorcistic technique: philological rigour is deemed the best way to defuse attempts at criticism of the content. These seemingly opposing tendencies, technical versus discreetly apologetic, actually reinforce each other. They are reflected in university journals such as Hanazono College's *Zen bunka kenkyūsho kiyō* or *Zengaku kenkyū* and the various publications of Komazawa University (*Shūgaku kenkyū*, etc.); and, above all, in the leading academic journal for Buddhist scholarship, the well-known *Indogaku Bukkyōgaku kenkyū* (Researches in Indology and Buddhology). A review of the themes of the main academic journals—particularly those of the *Indogaku Bukkyōgaku kenkyū* and of the *Nihon Bukkyō gakkai nenpō*—shows the relative scarcity of articles concerning ritual and popular religion, compared to the wealth of studies on doctrine and "philosophical" traditions, and the stress on the periods from the Six Dynasties to the Song (for China) and from Nara-Heian to Muromachi (for Japan), while there is nearly nothing, for instance, on Ming or Tokugawa Buddhism. In the case of

(Stein 1964, 177). "I had taken care to assure him in advance of generous donations for his shrine. Yet he seemed constantly to vacillate between fears about his saintly reputation and a shrewd grasp of the advantages to be obtained for his cherished task. In the end we succeeded [in appropriating the manuscripts], thanks to Chang Ssu-yeh's genial persuasion and such reassuring display as I could make of my devotion, genuine enough, to Buddhist lore and Hsüan-tsang's blessed memory" (ibid., 182).

Chan/Zen, points of condensation or even of fascination are figures like
Bodhidharma, Huineng, and Dōgen. In a way, the lacunae of Buddhist
historiography replicate those of Chan discourse: both are characterized
by their stress on orthodoxy and their essentially regularizing function.
Because of this, and despite the unquestionable good faith and critical
minds of individual scholars, the historiographical discourse on Chan/Zen
as a whole, including most recent Western scholarship, can be said to have
serious ideological effects. The compartmentalization within and among
universities is such that specialists of Indian Buddhism usually almost
completely ignore Chinese and Japanese Buddhism (to say nothing of
Korean Buddhism) and a fortiori other autochthonous religions or systems
of thought, to say nothing of neighboring methodologies or more recent
approaches. Such interdisciplinarity as is timidly practiced in a few semi-
nars, particularly at the Jinbun Kagaku Kenkyūsho of Kyōto University, is
insufficient to remedy this state of affairs and to provoke a real questioning
of traditional hierarchies and ideologies.[2]

The Contribution of Hu Shih

Although Japanese academic circles are very different from those around
which Hu Shih (1891–1962) gravitated, the Chinese historian was largely
influenced by Japanese Zen historiography and an important part of his
studies on Chan constitutes a reaction to the work of his Japanese colleagues, not only to Suzuki. The debate which opposed him to Suzuki,
taking place toward the end of his long career, assumes its full meaning
only when placed against his political and ideological backgrounds. First,
Hu Shih was a man of letters and a historian, and his recurrent interest in
Chan must be interpreted in terms of his global work, particularly his
efforts to rehabilitate Chinese vernacular literature (Ch. *baihua*) and
Chinese classical philosophy, as well as in terms of his active role in Chinese
political life and his interest in philosophical pragmatism, a doctrine he
had studied under John Dewey.[3]

Hu Shih became a student at Cornell University in 1910, three years
after Suzuki, completing a stay of ten years, left the United States. In 1915,
he entered the philosophy department of Columbia University, where he

[2] On the situation of Japanese historiography, see Kuroda Toshio, *Rekishigaku no saisei: Chūseishi o kuminaosu* (Tokyo: Kosō shobō, 1983).
[3] See Hu Shih, *The Chinese Renaissance: The Haskell Lectures, 1933* (New York: Paragon Books, 1963); Jerome B. Grieder, *Hu Shih and the Chinese Renaissance: Liberation in the Chinese Revolution, 1917–1937* Cambridge: Harvard University Press, 1970); Chou Min-chih, *Hu Shih and Intellectual Choice in Modern China* (Ann Arbor: University of Michigan Press, 1984). On Hu Shih's attempt to "reorganize the national past," see Irene Eber, "Hu Shih and Chinese History: The Problem of *Cheng-li kuo-ku*," *Monumenta Serica* 27 (1968): 169–207.

followed the courses of Dewey. He obtained his Ph.D. two years later with a dissertation on "The Development of the Logical Method in Ancient China," published in Shanghai in 1922. Here are already found in germinal form some arguments that Hu Shih will apply to Chan in his *Philosophy East and West* essay. In that same year he also published, in a Beijing journal, the article that brought him fame and made him a leader of the literary revolution that paved the way for the rehabilitation of Chinese vernacular literature. Hu Shih was hired as a professor at the Beijing Univerity, where, given his liberal standpoint, he soon distanced himself from extremist students. He was subject to strong criticism from intellectuals, such as Lu Xun, particularly after he sided with the Guomindang.[4] In the thick of these polemics, guided by his desire to revalorize the philosophical and cultural inheritance of China,[5] Hu Shih first became interested in Chan and discovered, in 1924, the historical figure that was going to fascinate him till the end of his life: the Tang dynasty monk Shenhui (684–758), in whom he saw a "Chinese St. Paul," and a "revolutionary" after his own heart (see Hu Shih 1930, 3–4; and McRae 1988).

In 1927 Hu Shih first met Suzuki, not long after Suzuki's *Essays in Zen Buddhism*, published that same year in London, had been severely criticized in an anonymous review article of the *Times*.[6] This article, which Suzuki attributed to Hu Shih, was actually written by Arthur Waley (see Barrett 1989). The main criticism leveled at Suzuki in this review was his failure to take into account the Dunhuang documents on Chan, which had been recently introduced to a Japanese audience by Yabuki Keiki in his *Meisha yoin*. This criticism led Suzuki to study these documents very closely. In a sense, Suzuki's polemical 1953 article, which was to provoke the above-mentioned debate, may be interpreted as a late settling of accounts—unfortunately aimed at the wrong target.

After returning in 1927 from Europe, where he was able to examine the Stein and Pelliot collections, Hu Shih published during the years 1927–1935 a number of essays on early Chan. Two essays in particular, his "Reflexions concerning Bodhidharma" (*Putidamo gao*, 1927) and "Reflexions concerning the *Laṅkāvatāra* School" (*Lengqiezong gao*, 1935), set the study of early Chan on a new track. The 1927 article was written

---

[4] These criticisms accompanied Hu Shih throughout his life. Thus, in a 1962 article entitled "John Dewey in China," Hu Shih felt compelled to respond to communist attacks against "that 'rotten and smelly' Chinese Deweyan, Hu Shih, and his slavish followers," accused of having introduced into China "the poison of the philosophical ideas of Pragmatism" (see Hu Shih 1962, 766–767).

[5] See Hu Shih, "The Indianization of China: A Case Study in Cultural Borrowing," in *Independence, Convergence and Borrowing in Institutions, Thought and Art* (Cambridge: Harvard University Press, 1937), 219–247.

[6] See Daisetz Teitarō Suzuki, "Essays in Zen Buddhism" (First Series), *The Times Literary Supplement* 25 August 1927, 579; reprinted in Hu Shih 1975, 724.

around the time when Mao Zedong published his tracts and when the Japanese military occupied the Shandong peninsula; the 1935 article was written when China, after becoming prey to civil war, was about to be invaded by Japanese armies. Despite the Sino-Japanese war, Hu Shih managed to keep in touch with some Japanese scholars, including Yabuki Keiki, Takakusu Junjirō, Tokiwa Daijō, and of course Suzuki (whom he had met again in Japan in 1927 and 1933 and in China in 1934) (Yamaguchi Sakae 1973). Nominated ambassador of the Guomindang to the United States in 1938, he returned to China for only a short while before the Communist takeover. During all these years, monopolized by political life, he neglected the study of Chan, but he eventually returned to it in 1952, the year before his controversy with Suzuki. That same year, he published several articles about Shenhui and an article concerning Shenhui's successor, Guifeng Zongmi (780–841).

As one can see, the scholarly work of Hu Shih developed against the background of extremely violent political and ideological fights, and it is not surprising that he differs in his interpretation of Chan from traditionalist scholars like Suzuki. The wonder is rather that two men with such different horizons could have become so close in their enthusiasm for the same texts and the same topics. Hu Shih's political involvement casts a singular light on his "scientific" studies. His Communist opponents, who launched a movement of criticism against him in 1954, did not fail to track down that ideological component in all his writings. One critic in particular, Ren Jiyu, in 1955 published "A Discussion of the Errors in Hu Shih's Studies on Chan History" (see Ren 1963, 168–194; trans. in Ren 1984b). As one might expect, Ren rejected across the board the contributions of Hu Shih to the field of Chan history. He reproached him in particular for having used Chan doctrine, which, in Ren's view, is fundamentally subjectivist and idealist, to promote his own interpretation of pragmatism. Ren stressed the affinities between Hu Shih, a scholar and a politician, and Shenhui, a monk and a politician. He concluded his attack by criticizing Hu Shih for characterizing the role played by Shenhui as a "revolutionary" attempt, whereas Shenhui was engaged in a rather sordid game of one-upmanship with rival Buddhist factions. Thus, Hu Shih's idealization of Shenhui is presented by Ren as a typical product of his "bourgeois" thinking (Ren 1963, 174; 1984b). Without following Ren all the way, there is no denying that the terminology used by Hu Shih concerning Shenhui reveals a kind of transferential relationship, a projection of the present into the past. Significantly, the word "revolution" appears constantly in Hu Shih's writings, and one is perhaps entitled to read, behind formulas such as "the success of Shenhui's offensive against the North" (Shenhui bei fa chenggong; that is, the "submission" of the Northern school to Shenhui), the preoccupations (and wishful thinking) of a Republican concerning Chinese Communists.

Inasmuch as they are denied in the name of the scientific objectivity of the historian, these ideological investments singularly burden Hu Shih's study of the origins of Chan. His Western rationalism, paradoxically reinforcing his nativist outlook on Chinese culture, prompted him to see Chan as the privileged expression of a Chinese rationalist humanism and of vernacular literature. Extolling Chan's "Ockham's razor" that is, its sharp nominalist criticism of Indian Buddhist scholasticism—he interpreted Chan as an instrument of intellectual emancipation from all the "superstitions, beliefs in Buddhas, Bodhisattvas, magical powers, charms, spells," of traditional Buddhism and as a genuine manifestation of the pragmatism of "Chinese mentality" (Hu Shih 1932, 481). These biases led Hu Shih to overlook the complexity of the phenomenon under consideration. In this regard, he is not so different from Suzuki: both were only considering different strata of the same reality and taking a part for the whole. Suzuki is in agreement with Hu Shih insofar as he held that the Chan movement was a product of the "practical" Chinese mentality reacting against the abstract speculations of Indian Buddhism.[7] Suzuki only differs about the extent of the Chan reaction: he saw Chan rather as a consummation of the assimilation process of Mahāyāna Buddhism and insisted that Chan/Zen rejected only the deviations brought on by Mahāyāna, not its cardinal truth, the intuitive wisdom of *prajñā* (Suzuki 1953, 24–26).

Significantly, Hu Shih did not show any interest in other Buddhist schools (Tiantai, Huayan, Faxiang, Pure Land, Zhenyan) contemporaneous with early Chan: if he mentions them, it is only to disparage them as being "colonized" by "India's complex philosophy"—referring, for example, to Xuanzang's "falling into the great spider's web" of Yogācāra idealism and unable to escape it (Hu Shih 1970, 42–43; see also McRae 1988, 22). Likewise, popular Buddhism or "religious" Daoism are conspicuously absent from his horizon. Not surprisingly, he privileged the period of "classical Chan," the so-called Golden Age, that is, broadly speaking, the Tang period. He seems to have taken for granted the theory according to which, after the Tang, Buddhism suffered an irreversible decline and a doctrinal corruption that expressed itself as popular "syncretism."[8]

For Hu Shih, therefore, the history of Chan is a purely Chinese phenomenon that must be interpreted in terms of a larger problematic, that of Chinese culture, politics, and philosophy. In this he differs for instance

---

[7] See *Philosophy East and West* (April 1953): 40–41; Foulk 1987, 28.

[8] For a thorough criticism of this model, as prevalent today as it was at the time of Hu's writings, see Welch 1968.

from Yanagida Seizan, for whom Chan is a radical departure, from not only Indian Buddhism but also the mainstream of Chinese thought: despite their undeniably Chinese character, early Chan monks were "outsiders" in Chinese society. At any rate, whether as a Chinese reformation or a revolution within Buddhism, Chan was inscribed by Hu Shih in a teleological schema slightly different from that of Japanese historians, which takes Zen as its implicit or explicit *telos*.

In a letter to Yanagida, Hu Shih wrote: "You are a first rate Buddhist, a first class Zen scholar, while I am a 'student' of the history of Chinese thought, someone who does not believe in any religion. That is why our fundamental standpoints differ and cannot be perfectly reconciled."[9] Hu Shih's positivism made him incapable of doing justice to the religious elements in Chan and led him to interpret it as a kind of "psychological method" destined to effect, through frustration and wanderings, a mental catharsis. On this point, Suzuki was justified in his criticism of Hu, although he himself tended to overemphasize the psychological element in Zen. To Hu Shih, the "sudden enlightenment" of early Chan shares affinities with Western Enlightenment in that both allow one to see through superstitions. Hu Shih and Suzuki shared a vision of Chan as an antiritualist trend in Chinese religions. However, if a certain dose of "rationalism" in the Weberian sense is indeed present in Chan, it cannot be reduced to Hu Shih's rationalism.

Hu Shih's work has greatly stimulated that of later scholars, most notably Yanagida, who is indebted to Hu for his ability to distance himself to a certain extent from sectarian scholarship. Hu Shih's contribution is above all philological, as exemplified by his critical edition of Shenhui's works; his work was continued in Japan by Suzuki and Yanagida (Suzuki 1936; Yanagida 1967) and in the West by Jacques Gernet, Paul Demiéville, and, more recently, John McRae (Gernet 1949; Demiéville 1952; McRae 1986, 1990). One must also stress Hu Shih's rediscovery of the fundamental role played by Shenhui in the constitution of Chan as orthodoxy, as well as his study of early Chan and the so-called Laṅkāvatāra tradition, which was rebaptized "Northern school" and was superseded by Shenhui's "Southern school."

Thus, on the basis of the Dunhuang documents, Hu Shih initiated the rewriting of the history of early Chan, by replacing the traditional narrative of the "Histories of the Lamp" with a critical "historical" narrative. Although the latter obviously represents a scholarly advance, one has to question its claim to supersede the traditional narrative and to provide *the* historical truth about Chan/Zen. What has been gained, ultimately, by

---

[9] Letter dated 15 January 1961, in *Zengaku kenkyū* 53 (1973): 162–170; reprinted in Hu Shih 1975, 614–665. See Yanagida's reply in *Zengaku kenkyū*, 53 (1973): 170–172.

replacing one narrative with another? The historical narrative is inherited by Hu Shih's critic, Ren Jiyu, who, while starting like Hu Shih from the premises of a "secular humanism," merely takes the opposite view when he stresses the religious (and therefore, according to him, purely ideological) character of Chan: "What the Chan sect knew as independent thinking and bold skepticism were activities which could be carried out within the narrow confinements permitted by its own religious viewpoint" (Ren 1984a, 53).

THE RISE OF CHAN HISTORIOGRAPHY IN JAPAN

The methodology of the Japanese historiography of Chan/Zen is to a large extent a product of the Meiji and Taishō periods. The Meiji Restoration permitted the importation of the Western philological methods to which Buddhist historians, among other Japanese scholars, were to resort. The growing interest in philology and historicism permitted a renewal of the study of Buddhism on a basis that claimed to be scientific. It was necessary to regenerate the Buddhist tradition, severely hit by the Meiji "cultural revolution" with its motto "Discard the Buddha, cast out Śākyamuni" (*haibutsu kishaku*) and its policy of separating Buddhism and Shintō (*shin-butsu bunri*) (see Ketelaar 1990; Collcutt 1986). In trying to distance themselves from popular "superstitions" and redefine Buddhism as a philosophical system, Buddhist scholars adopted *volens nolens* the secular humanism that formed one of the main ideological components of the Restoration. Rationalization and demythologization were considered necessary to counterbalance the negative image of Buddhism as a religion of "worldly benefits" (*genze riyaku*), and this ideological clean-up led to a drastic reinterpretation of the Buddhist tradition. While the "irrational" elements of traditional Buddhism were downplayed as "skillful means" (Sk. *upāya*, J. *hōben*) for deluded masses, the Buddhist Middle Way became the solution to the dilemma of idealism and materialism. In both East and West, the historical Buddha was presented as a humanist of sorts, a rational critic of the Hindu tradition. Buddhist notions of emptiness (*śūnyatā*) and codependent origination (*pratītya-samutpāda*) suddenly took a scientific character, and the *Heart sūtra* was even compared to Planck's constant! In search of a new legitimacy, Buddhists looked for allies in Western disciplines such as the (then) newly fledged history of religions: thus, around the same time that the Zen master Shaku Sōen left for the United States, soon to be followed by the young Suzuki, Nanjō Bun'yū and a few other young Buddhist scholars became the disciples of Max Müller.

During the Taishō era, a period compared by Watsuji Tetsurō to a Buddhist Renaissance (LaFleur 1990, 246), Japanese scholars accepted the

challenge of Western scholarship and attempted to capitalize on their native knowledge of East Asian Buddhism. This challenge was first formulated in 1918 by Watanabe Kaigyoku, who had studied from 1900 to 1910
at the University of Strasburg, then under German occupation. In his *Ōbei
no bukkyō* (Buddhist Studies in Europe and America), Watanabe argued
that Japanese scholars should bend their efforts toward overtaking Buddhist studies (Stone 1990, 222–223). Buddhist studies were thus perceived
as a unique vehicle for Japan's contribution to world culture and Japanese
imperialism. Takakusu Junjirō, who had studied at Oxford and other
European universities, was able to publish with Watanabe the Taishō edition of the Buddhist *Tripiṭaka* (1924–1934)—an achievement that pushed
Japanese scholarship well ahead of its Western counterpart. After initially
contemplating, under Western influence, a return to "original Buddhism,"
the Taishō revival attempted to reassert Japanese Buddhism by isolating the
"fundamental Buddhism" (*konpon bukkyō*) common to both Hīnayāna
and Mahāyāna.[10]

However, after the iconoclasm of the "dark age" of Meiji Enlightenment—an iconoclasm compared by Watsuji to that initiated by Paul's
criticism of pagan idolatry—the Taishō period did not see a "restoration of
the idols,"[11] in the sense that Buddhism remained an intellectualist tradition. Taishō was seen as "a new era" in which, like in the Renaissance, the
"restored idols," once rescued from darkness, "did not revert to being gods
to be worshipped but were now appreciated as a work of art" (LaFleur
1990, 239). As Watsuji put it: "[In the Renaissance] the restoration of the
old images [of Greece and Rome] ushered in a very powerful materialist
view of things and was also the stimulus for scientific activities" (Watsuji,
12–13, quoted in LaFleur 1990, 239). Watsuji was also instrumental in
promoting Dōgen to the status of one of Japan's great "philosophical"
minds.[12]

Forerunners

Although the "objective" study of the history of Chan would probably not
have been possible without the "epistemological break" of Meiji, this
break was itself prepared by a series of epistemological landslips during the
Edo period. As Michael Pye noted, "It may be argued that the influence

[10] See, for instance, Anesaki Masaharu, *Konpon bukkyō* (Tokyo: Kokusho kankōkai,
1982); and Murakami Senshō, *Bukkyō tōitsuron* (Tokyo: Kinkōdō, 1901–1905).
[11] See Watsuji Tetsurō, "Restoring the Idols" [*Guzō saikō*], in *Watsuji Tetsurō zenshū* 17:
3–224.
[12] Despite his cosmopolitanism, Watsuji was wary of abstract, philosophical universalism,
which he saw as a disguised Eurocentrism, and he became increasingly nationalist (i.e., anti-
American); LaFleur 1990, 255.

which Max Müller and others exercised in the nineteenth century was effective in Japan only because of the prior development of modern critical ideas" (Pye 1983, 576). Precursors of rationalism can be found in the so-called *karagokoro* or "Chinese mind" denounced by nativists, such as Hirata Atsutane, and in Japanese thinkers apparently free of any Western influence.

The best known case, as concerns Japanese Buddhism, is probably that of Tominaga Nakamoto (1715–1746), who, in his *Shutsujō kōgo* (Emerging from Samādhi), wrote that "the Mahāyāna sūtras are not the direct utterances from the Golden Mouth of the Buddha" and who saw in the various Buddhist doctrines merely the "constant efforts by different groups to supersede each other" (Pye 1983, 569). Tominaga's rationalism is well expressed in the following passage that brings to mind the kind of the Chan iconoclasm so appreciated by Hu Shih: "The tendency peculiar to Buddhism is magic. . . . Indian people like it. In preaching a way, or in teaching people, if a good dose of magic is not mixed, people will not believe and follow. Therefore Śākyamuni itself was good at sorcery. In fact it was for learning this art that he entered the mountains and trained himself for six years" (*Okina no fumi*, quoted in Katō 1967b, 207). Tominaga attributed this taste of the Indians for magic to their "national character," just as he characterized the Chinese by their taste for literature and the Japanese by their taste for simplicity (see Tominaga 1990, 105).

Concerning the Chan transmission, Tominaga first gives side by side several lists of Indian patriarchs, ending with that of the *Baolin zhuan* (dated 801). He then points out their contradictions and the apocryphal nature of the *Baolin zhuan*'s list. All these theories, according to him, do not deserve any credit. He goes on by pointing out the paradox inherent in the notion of a patriarchal tradition: are not Chan followers always repeating that there is no other Buddha, no other patriarch, than one's own mind? Tominaga gives a radically deflated image of Bodhidharma, whom he sees as an unlucky missionary, who had left India—where Buddhism was on the decline—in the hope of proselityzing China, but was unsuccessful and met a tragic end. "In my opinion," says Tominaga, "this Bodhidharma is the most pitiable figure that ever existed in the whole world." Tominaga concludes that the posthumous success of Bodhidharma's teaching, which explains all the interpolations done in his name, only underscores his tragic fate.

At a time when everyone advocated a return to the purity of origins, Tominaga offered a refreshing, if somewhat historicist and polemical, vision of the emergence of religious traditions: "As a rule, since antiquity, those who have preached their way and established a religion have always tended to present their own doctrine as that of a first founder, while trying to supersede those who had preceded them" (*Okina no fumi*). However, as

Jean-Noël Robert rightly points out, "By its systematic character, the method of Tominaga diminishes the distance with those he criticizes rather than increasing it" (Robert 1980–1981, 213).

Although it was eventually coopted by Buddhists as representative of a modern reinterpretation of Buddhism, Tominaga's historical refutation of Buddhism was the work of an outsider. However, a critical approach to Chan history could also be found at times within the Chan/Zen tradition itself. To give a brief overview of antecedents before this period of Western influence, one could go much further back in time and find—in someone like Guifeng Zongmi, the first "historian of Chan"—manifestations of a nascent critical historical mind. At a time when Chan was still divided by the controversy between the Northern and Southern schools, Zongmi gives indeed a relatively precise description of the doctrines of the various Chan trends. However, sectarian stakes are not absent from his discourse, and the "tropical," or metaphorical, character of his writing appears clearly when Zongmi ranks the teachings of the main Chan schools, for instance when he resorts to the metaphor of the bright pearl—that is, ultimate truth—whose brightness, though unchanging, is perceived differently by different individuals when it reflects various colors.[13]

Under the Song, Buddhist historiography progressed by drawing its inspiration from dynastic histories, but it also inherited the prejudices of the latter and rarely went beyond the level of the chronicle (see Jan 1964). Here again, sectarian preoccupations remained in the foreground. Most Chan historical writings of the period were written in response to criticisms from other schools, in particular the Tiantai school and Confucianism. The most well-known "Chan histories" are the works of Qisong (1007–1072) and Huihong (1071–1128). Both were excellent writers, and their style, measured against the standard of Confucianist scholars like Han Yu and Ou Yangxiu, was admired even among detractors of Chan. However, owing to the demands of sectarian polemics, much of their effort was spent proving the authenticity of the Chan patriarchal lineage, a task not conducive to a critical history.[14] These genealogical concerns strongly

[13] Zongmi takes the example of the black color (symbolizing dark ignorance): "Either one recognizes that the bright pearl is a reflective substance and is unchanging [viewpoint of the Hoze school of Shenhui, advocated by Zongmi], or one says that only the black is the pearl [viewpoint of Mazu Daoyi and the Hongzhou school]. One searches for the pearl apart from the black [Northern school], or both the bright and the black are non-existent [Ox-head school]." *Chanmen shizi chengxi tu*, in ZZ 2, 15, 5: 437b; quoted in Jan 1972, 53. On the "tropics" of historiographical discourse, see White 1978.

[14] Individual examples suggesting the existence of a critical historical approach can be misleading. Take the following passage of the *Biyanlu*: "According to the tradition, master Zhi died in the year 514, while Bodhidharma came to the Liang in 520; since there is a seven year discrepancy, why is it said that the two met? This must be a mistake in the tradition. As to

influenced Chinese Confucians, as well as the Japanese *Tennō* ideology. The same sectarian tendency is at work in the *Genkō shakusho* (1322), a "Buddhist history" written by the Japanese Zen master Kokan Shiren (1278–1348). It is reflected, for instance, in the offhand way in which Shiren deals with the Sōtō school or the Darumashū. In all these cases, although critical historical elements seem present, they often apply only to rival schools. Because this tendency also characterizes more recent studies, one should therefore keep in mind the eminently "performative" nature of historical criticism and of "scientific" objectivity. In the Sōtō tradition, the philological and editorial work of scholars such as Manzan Dōhaku (1636–1715) and Menzan Zuihō (1683–1769) is informed by their sectarian devotion to the founder and by the desire to restore orthodoxy and "moral order."

In the Rinzai sect, a figure who paved the way for an "objective" study of Chan by his prodigious philological accomplishments is Mujaku Dōchū (1653–1745). Although less well known than his contemporary Tominaga, Mujaku deserves a place of choice in the portrait gallery of the precursors of the "scientific" historiography of Chan/Zen. Mujaku, however, was ostensibly neglected by a Rinzai orthodoxy, which, because of its motto of "non-dependence on the written letter," thought it good form to slight scholarly research and compare it to as worthless a religious practice as "stringing beads" (*kokuzu*, counting the "black beads" of a rosary). For this reason, Mujaku is often unfavorably contrasted with his contemporary Hakuin Ekaku (1685–1768). A history of Myōshinji, for example, explains that although Mujaku devoted himself to the administration of this monastery, it was Hakuin who achieved a renewal of the Myōshinji branch of Rinzai Zen. Although similar views were expressed by various historians, a more sympathetic approach to Mujaku's scholarship was that of Matsumoto Bunzaburō. More recently, an attempt to rehabilitate Mujaku was undertaken by Yanagida Seizan, who emphasized the "international," eclectic nature of Mujaku's immense erudition and the almost "scientific" character of his philological criticism of Chan and Zen texts.

Mujaku was to a large extent free from the dogmatic or moralizing tendencies of commentators such as Imakita Kōsen (1816–1852), a Zen master imbued with neo-Confucianism. He nevertheless remained a sectarian figure for whom the orthodox tradition could be no other than the so-called *Ōtōkan* branch of Rinzai Zen, a branch deriving its appellation from an abbreviation of the names of the Zen abbots Daiō Kokushi (Nanpo

---

what is recorded in the tradition, I will not discuss this matter now. All that's important is to understand the gist of the matter" (Thomas Cleary and J. C. Cleary 1977, 5). The gist of the matter, incidentally, may be that, by the Song, the Chan and Tiantai school had become enmeshed in a bitter doctrinal conflict, and the earlier legends establishing connexions between them were no longer needed. Hence this sudden and isolated burst of "objectivity."

Jōmyō, 1235–1309), Daitō Kokushi (Shūhō Myōchō, 1282–1338), and Kanzan Egen (1277–1361). Mujaku's sectarian spirit is particularly apparent in his severe criticisms of Dōgen and Ingen Ryūki (1592–1673), the founders of two other Zen sects, Sōtō and Obaku: according to him, these masters are particularly dangerous precisely because they succeed in passing themselves off as representatives of Zen orthodoxy. Mujaku mercilessly examines passages of the *Shōbōgenzō* in which Dōgen seems carried away by the spirit of sectarian polemics. Despite his conclusion that "those are not the words of an awakened master," Mujaku felt obliged to step back and suggest that these passages may be later interpolations. Despite its flaws, his work shows a familiarity with the method of "inner criticism" that was to become the hallmark of Western philologists. Mujaku's erudition, however, differs from Tominaga's through its stress on correct Zen practice. His critical approach, highlighted by Matsumoto and Yanagida, finds here its limits. An example suffices to illustrate these limits. Kokan Shiren had pointed out in his *Genkō Shakusho* the anachronism of a tradition that has the Tiantai master Nanyue Huisi (515–577) reborn in Japan as Prince Shōtoku (574–622), when Shōtoku was born three few years before Huisi's death. Mujaku criticizes Kokan for this because Huisi, like any true Bodhisattva, is evidently capable of appearing simultaneously in different places to save sentient beings. Shōtoku just happened to be one of these avatars. *Quod erat demonstrandum.*

Post-Meiji Chan/Zen Historiography

The "critical" history of Chan in the Western sense should perhaps begin with Sakaino Kōyō's *Shina bukkyōshi kō* (1907) and Matsumoto Bunzaburo's *Daruma* (1911). Although these works, predating the discovery of the Dunhuang manuscripts, are limited by their sources, they are in many respects more detached from traditional prejudices than later studies like Nukariya Kaiten's *Zengaku shisōshi* (A History of Zen Thought, 1923–1925), a work whose periodization alone ("Hīnayāna Zen," "preparatory period," etc.) is patently biased toward "classical Chan." In another work that constitutes the first "history" of Korean Chan (Sŏn), *Chōsen zenkyōshi* (1930), Nukariya summarily condemns Sŏn as a deviation from Chan orthodoxy. He seems unaware that Sŏn remains in many respects much closer than Japanese Zen to the inclusive spirit of early Chan.

A ground breaking "objective" history of Chinese Chan was Ui Hakuju's *Zenshūshi kenkyū* ("Researches on the History of the Chan School"). In contrast to most other historians of Chan, Ui's scholarship covered the entirety of the Buddhist tradition, and he is well-known for his contributions on the history of Indian philosophy and on Indian and Tibetan Buddhism.[15] His approach of Buddhism reflects his assimilation of Western scholarship during his formative stay in Europe. Ui's history of Chinese Chan is particularly valuable for its attempt to reassess early Chan and more particularly Northern Chan. Ui was the first to question the characterizations of Northern Chan as gradual and Southern Chan as sudden. On a number of points, he offered a corrective to Hu Shih: for example, in his reevaluation of the role played by Shenhui, whom he judged severely for having betrayed his former master Shenxiu in his ambition to become the heir of Huineng—and by the same token the seventh patriarch of Chan. Ui argued that the main doctrinal difference between Shenxiu and Shenhui had to do with the modalities of cultivating the experience of "sudden awakening," but that, for both Chan masters, such a gradual cultivation was to take place after this awakening. Ui, however, sided with Hu Shih against Suzuki when he denounced the "metaphysical" or ahistorical interpretation of Chan:

> One cannot say that, because there is no Chan doctrine, or because Chan is something that one obtains by oneself, it cannot become an object of research; nor that one cannot express this state of mind through speech or writing. An object of research is not necessarily something that forms a system, neither does scholarly research, because it must be objective, have to avoid speaking about subjective states of mind. If such were the case, something like Buddhist Nirvāṇa could not become an object of study; but such is not the case.

Like his master Takakusu and his codisciple Kimura Taiken (1881–1930), Ui was interested in discussing "original Buddhism" and uncovering the underlying truth common to both the lesser and greater Vehicles (Stone 1990, 229). That Ui also remained influenced by sectarian concerns and the ideology of the Sōtō sect to which he belonged appears clearly in the fact that he limited his history of Chan to chronicling the Caodong (Sōtō) lineage, beginning with Bodhidharma and ending with a relatively obscure Chinese master, Tiantong Rujing (1163–1228), whose main claim to fame is that he happened to be Dōgen's master.[16] It also shows in Ui's

---

[15] A disciple of Takakusu, Ui published between 1925 and 1930 a six-volume work on Indian philosophy, *Indo tetsugaku kenkyū* (Tokyo: Kōjisha shobō), for which he won the Prize of the Tōkyō Imperial Academy. See also his *Indo tetsugakushi* (A History of Indian Philosophy) (Tokyo: Iwanami shoten, 1938). On the development of Buddhist scholarship during the interwar period, see Stone 1990.

[16] Actually, the final chapter of Ui's three volume *Researches* is dedicated to the textual study of a work by Zongmi, which reflects Ui's interest for the "submerged" tradition of *kyōzen itchi* or "scholastic Chan," from which both Northern Chan and the Caodong school may be said to derive. Another important recent work that shows a similar tendency to read the history of Chan in Sōtō terms is Ishii Shūdō's *Researches on the History of the Chan school under the Song* (1987).

preface, in which he reads back into Bodhidharma's theory of the "two entrances"—through principle and through phenomena—Dōgen's conception of the "unity of practice and realization" (J. *shūshō ittō*) ([Ui 1966, 1: 6–8). Thus, Ui's approach is implicitly teleological, seeing in Dōgen's Zen the ultimate form of Buddhism and in the Chan of the Song and Yuan a decline and a corruption of the "classical" teaching of the Tang. This kind of anachronism is reiterated when he reads back into the early Chan group known as the Dongshan school the constitution of a typically Zen monastic community after the model of the Japanese Zen sects (ibid.).

I have already discussed Suzuki's contribution to the Western reception of Zen. Westerners usually remember his psychological approach to Zen and his nativist interpretation of Zen culture. But Suzuki's work is multifaceted, and another aspect deserves consideration. Despite two long stays in the United States (1897–1909 and 1949–1958) and numerous publications in English, his scholarly work is mainly in Japanese, and his real contribution to Chan studies is more philological than historical. Nevertheless, his studies on the *Laṅkāvatāra-sūtra* and his critical editions of various Dunhuang manuscripts have broadly contributed, despite himself, to demystifying the history of early Chan (see Suzuki 1935). It is noteworthy, however, that the type of Chan Suzuki advocated toward the end of his life differs considerably from the Westernized version he had presented in his *Essays*. While, for most Westerners, Suzuki remains the kōan specialist, it is to a large extent as a reaction against the sclerosis of the kōan system in the Rinzai tradition that he turned toward early Chan and Bankei's "unborn Zen," then toward the so-called *myōkōnin*, saints of the Pure Land tradition. As noted earlier, Suzuki's interest for Dunhuang manuscripts was triggered by the criticism he received in an anonymous review of his *Essays* that he attributed to Hu Shih. His contribution to Chan studies was, however, greatly impaired by his sectarian concerns and his somewhat simplistic or idealized vision of the development of the Chan tradition. Although Suzuki's discourse may be more complex than it seems at first, as a whole, from a historical critical perspective it remains unreliable. Moreover, in its emphasis on the ahistorical nature of Zen, it misses the importance of sacred history for the Chan/Zen tradition.

Only after the Second World War did the study of Chan adopt a new outlook, owing principally to scholars such as Sekiguchi Shindai and Yanagida Seizan. A Tendai scholar, Sekiguchi has exerted a great deal of influence on Chan studies through his books on the history of Chan and in particular on Bodhidharma. Taking a resolutely critical approach, he has devoted himself to proving the apocryphal nature of most works attributed to Bodhidharma and the late emergence of the figure of the "founder" of Chan. He has for instance shown that the real author of the *Guanxin lun*

(Treatise on Mind Contemplation), one of the so-called "Three Treatises of Bodhidharma," was Shenxiu, the leader of the Northern school of Chan. Although Sekiguchi's work is at first glance a model of critical objectivity and a salubrious exercise of "desectarianization," several problems remain. One must note first that his objectivity is too localized to be free of sectarian effects. Yanagida has expressed his regret that Sekiguchi did not take the same critical approach toward the history of the Tendai tradition. If Chan scholars have tended to emphasize the specificity (and, implicitly, the superiority) of Chan, Sekiguchi manifested the opposite tendency to search for the origins of Chan in Tiantai—*ad majorem Tendai gloriam*. Thus, his critique of the Chan patriarchal tradition seems inspired by the Tiantai sectarian criticism of Chan during the Song. Critics like Shenzhi Zongyi (1042–1091) delighted in pointing out anachronisms and other weaknesses in the Chan histories written by Qisong and Huihong (see Jan 1964, 369; Kagamishima 1965, 94).

Above all, Sekiguchi's propensity toward hypercriticism raises questions. To be sure, the traditional image of Bodhidharma needed to be reevaluated. With Sekiguchi it flies into pieces, and we are left with "Bodhidharma splinters." In the wake of Sekiguchi's devastating criticism, only forgeries and pious (or not so pious) lies remain. [17] However, as Carl Bielefedt points out, "there is more to the sectarian apologetical tradition than mere obfuscation of history, and . . . what we now tend to view as obstacle to historical understanding can also serve as an opening into religious themes and issues we have hitherto ignored" (Bielefeldt 1988, 4).

Yanagida Seizan

Our understanding of early Chan history has taken a new turn with the publication in 1967 of Yanagida Seizan's *Shoki zenshū shisho no kenkyū* (Researches on the Historiographical Works of Early Chan). Yanagida is a prolific writer and a consummate scholar, who has opened Chan/Zen to a host of new questions, challenging for instance the hagiographical tradition concerning Dōgen (Yanagida 1982). Unlike Sekiguchi, however, Yanagida insists on the specificity of Chan texts ("Histories of the Lamp" and "Recorded Sayings") and on a critical evaluation of these documents as a first step toward a correct understanding of Chan thought. In the preface to his *Researches*, he writes:

---

[17] One of the best (or worst) examples of hypercriticism in Chan history is that of Nagashima's *Truths and Fabrications*, a book recently analyzed by John Maraldo (1986a). Nagashima's frantic demystification calls to mind the work of some medievalist scholars who attempted to prove that Plato's work was merely the forgery of medieval monks. However, Nagashima's work will not have the influence of Sekiguchi's, and Maraldo, unlike Yanagida, misdirected his criticism. His argumentation remains nevertheless valid.

[So far,] researches have had a propensity to uphold sectarian viewpoints, and there have been cases where, albeit unconsciously, one returned to a conservative study that called itself scientific. Sometimes, dazzled by the novelty of the Dunhuang documents, one forgets even the common knowledge of international Sinological studies. Sometimes, on the contrary, because of the specificity of the "recorded sayings" and of the "histories of the Lamp," through an excessive criticism of their absurdities, some tend, either to reject them as fictions or to affirm them all uncritically, with faith and [in accordance with] the tradition. The results of a truly scholarly and conscientious handling of the materials were unfortunately extremely rare. (Yanagida 1967, 3)

Yanagida's attitude toward the Chan tradition has to be contextualized.[18] Born in 1922 with the auspicious name of Seizan ("sacred mountain") as the first son of a Rinzai Zen priest in a village temple of Shiga prefecture, he was destined to succeed to his father. Instead, he chose to "leave the family" by becoming paradoxically a layman, even changing his family name (Yokoi) to that of his wife (Yanagida). This rejection of priesthood took place just after the military defeat of Japan, at a time when, like so many of his compatriots, he was utterly disillusioned about his country and in particular about the Buddhist establishment that had actively participated in the war effort through its "spiritual" propaganda. After considering suicide, he found a solution to his existential predicament by joining the meditation group organized by the Zen layman Hisamatsu Shin'ichi. At the same time, he embarked on reading early Chan texts, in a similar attempt to cut through traditional exegesis and rediscover a "pure" Zen thought, not yet contaminated by the dominant ideology of Song works such as the *Biyan lu* or the *Wumen guan*.

Yanagida's philosophical expertise benefited from his study under Iriya Yoshitaka, a specialist in colloquial Chinese literature. Together with Iriya, Yanagida joined the research team organized by Ruth Fuller Sasaki, a wealthy American woman who had vowed to publish an English translation of the *Linji lu* (Record of Linji) in the memory of her late husband, the Zen master Sasaki Shigetsu, who died in an American internment camp in 1945. The research team, including American scholars (Burton Watson, Philip Yampolsky) and Japanese scholars (Iriya, Yanagida), was disbanded after the death of Fuller Sasaki in 1967—the same year that Yanagida published his *Researches* and Yampolsky his translation of the *Platform Sūtra*. Yanagida's participation on this team contributed to his international reputation. His annotated translation of the *Linji lu* (1961) served for instance as a basis for Paul Demiéville's French translation (1972)—a

[18] The following discussion relies on the autobiographical information provided by Yanagida during a talk at the San Francisco Zen Center in October 1989.

translation superior to the English translation, finally published by Iriya under Fuller Sasaki's name in 1975.

In 1969, Yanagida inaugurated the "Recorded Sayings of Chan" series of Chikuma Shobō by his annotated translation of the *Treatise of Bodhidharma*, followed in 1971 by translations of the *Lengqie shizi ji* and the *Chuan fabao ji*, and in 1973 of the *Lidai fabao ji*—all major texts of early Chan. These translations were permitted by the fact that, almost fifty years after the isolated efforts of Hu Shih and Suzuki, a global view of the Dunhuang documents became for the first time possible with the availability of the microfilms of the Stein and Pelliot collections. Even now, the dissemination of the Dunhuang manuscripts in London, Paris, Beijing, Leningrad, and a few other places delays their study. After teaching at Hanazono College, Yanagida became in the mid-1970s a member of the prestigious Jinbun Kagaku Kenkyūsho at Kyōto University. Now retired, he is the head of a small International Research Institute for Zen Studies at Hanazono College.

The difficult conditions of postwar research explain two aspects of Yanagida's scholarship: his respect for the written text, a text that had to be copied by hand, read out aloud, manducated, tasted like a kōan, word by word, like those Daoist written talismans that must be swallowed and digested to operate; and his discovery with Fuller Sasaki of the method of card filing, which led to what he calls a case of "card illness"—but also to the publication of thorough indexes and to the creation, currently under way, of data bases that will contribute to a renewal of the study of Chan.

One text was to play a major role in the development of these aspects: the *Zutang ji* (K. *Chodang chip*, Record of Patriarchal Halls), a Chan "history" compiled in 952 in the rich harbor of Quanzhou (in Fujian) and incorporated in 1245 in the Korean Buddhist canon of the Haein-sa. Like Dunhuang, Quanzhou was largely open to Western (in this case Arabic) influences, and this international aspect is reflected in the Chan literature produced there. The deciphering and degustation of the *Zutang ji*, which took several decades, made Yanagida more sensitive than Sekiguchi and most other Chan scholars to the literary nature of Chan texts, while the card-filing method, described by Yanagida as a "kind of satori," led to the computerization of Chan/Zen studies that is now taking place at Yanagida's institute. Although it provides new access to the texts, this technology has obvious limitations and perhaps inherent dangers, inasmuch as, like the Zen cards that produced *Zen Dust*—a convenient but misconceived work published by Miura Isshū and Ruth Fuller Sasaki (Miura and Sasaki 1966)—it lends itself to a piecemeal approach that reinforces Zen orthodoxy while delaying the ideological critique.

Yanagida's "international spirit," acquired through his acquaintance with Fuller Sasaki and other Western scholars and through the contact with early Chan texts that were fundamentally crosscultural, has contributed to free the study of Chan/Zen from its Japanese moorings and trappings. The fact that the *Zutang ji*, in particular, was only available in a Korean edition has led to a long overdue reassessment of Korean Sŏn, while the study of the Dunhuang documents has created a new interest in central Asian Buddhism. Yanagida's work has also found an echo in the West, particularly in the United States, where Chan/Zen studies are thriving.

For all its openness, Yanagida's scholarship remains under specific constraints: the importance of the doctrinal texts, the belief in a "pure" Zen, a tendency to focus on Zen (to the detriment of traditional and popular Buddhism), and on Rinzai Zen in particular. In many respects, Yanagida remains very close to the Kyōto school and the aesthetic vision of Zen promoted by Hisamatsu. Although less partial than Sekiguchi concerning his own tradition, Yanagida's scholarship is still informed by an orthodox view of Chan/Zen. It is perhaps significant that he reserves his most severe criticism for the rival Sōtō tradition, and shares with his colleagues an interest in "classical Chan," to the detriment of other trends like Northern Chan, despite the fact that he was one of the first to reevaluate the teaching of this school (Yanagida 1963, 1974b). Yanagida remains active, and it is too early to judge his future orientation and influence on younger Japanese and Western scholars.

THE COST OF OBJECTIVISM

With a few significant exceptions, the history of Chan is generally approached from the standpoint of intellectual history, rarely from that of institutional history, and almost never from the standpoint of what the French *Annals* school has called "Histoire des mentalités."[19] In the light of the few examples considered above, it appears that scholarly positions and interpretations concerning Chan history differ considerably according to individual idiosyncracies, sociopolitical contexts, and institutional or sectarian affiliations. Nevertheless, a number of common points exist; similar features or tendencies, more or less accentuated, can be found in most authors under consideration. We limit ourselves here to a few cases, schematically.

The most obvious tendency is what I call "objectivism." The ideals of

[19] As exceptions worth mentioning are Japanese scholars like Ishikawa Rikizan and Nagai Masashi, whose work, however, remains largely descriptive: they offer new objects, but not yet new methods. In the West, Martin Collcutt and Griffith Foulk have focused on the institutional history of Chan/Zen.

objectivity and scientificity remain the norm for the vast majority of historians, and Nietzsche may have been right when he denounced them as "eunuchs in the harem of history" for their refusal to judge the materials they were dealing with.[20] This ideal found its classical form with Leopold von Ranke, for whom the strict presentation of facts was the supreme law of history (see von Ranke 1983). It finds expression in the use of a "white rhetoric," that is, of an apparently neutral terminology, resorting to methods, philological or otherwise, with a high degree of technicity and an abundance of critical apparatus that permits the reader to verify the minutest allegation. Multiplying of notes and proper names, erasing all marks of enunciation, has what Roland Barthes called a "realistic effect" (*effet de réel*)[21] and aims at achieving the most faithful possible "representation" of reality.[22] Thus, the implicit model is that of mimesis. The "objective" historian tends to deny the poietical (from *poiesis*, creative activity) aspect of his work and to forget that he actively *invents* his object; he fails to "objectify the objectifying relationship, that is, the epistemological rupture that is also a social rupture" (Bourdieu 1980, 46).

In Bourdieu's words, "objectivism constitutes the social world as a show offered to a spectator who, importing into the object the principles of his relationship to the object, acts as if it were destined to be an object only of knowledge, and as if all interactions were reduced to symbolical exchanges" (Bourdieu 1980, 87) Bourdieu insists on the elitist background of this implicit epistemology, which also contains an "implicit sociology" (ibid.). Taking his cues from Wittgenstein, Michel de Certeau shows that the scholar, being "caught" within language, no longer has his own domain, his privileged place. The metaphysic of objectivity is replaced by the strategies of transference. This Copernican revolution, which identifies

---

[20] See Nietzsche 1957. In this respect as well, Chan historians seem to emulate hagiographers, who often made Chan masters look as impassible as the eunuchs of Tang harems: the best-known story is probably that of the bath given by the servants of the Empress Wu Zetian to the Northern Chan master Shenxiu, who, like the Buddha resisting the temptations of the daughters of Māra, remained unmoved by the charms of his youthful bath attendants. *Zuting shiyuan* 1: 12; *Zutang ji*, ed. Yanagida (1974), 348a.

[21] See Roland Barthes, "The Discourse of History," trans. Stephen Bann, in *Comparative Criticism: A Yearbook*, ed. E. S. Schaffer (Cambridge: Cambridge University Press, 1981), 17.

[22] See Certeau 1975, 112. However, as Paul Veyne points out, "The habit of citing authorities or scholarly annotations was not invented by historians but came from theological controversies and juridical practice" (Veyne 1988, 11). Moreover, the hybris of footnotes undermines the narrative it purports to strengthen. One thus gets texts in which "footnotes," pretexted rather than required by a short textual "body," tend to invade the page. Critical apparatus becomes in many respects the main text, resulting in a subversion, a decentring of the "main" text that calls for and prefigures its own deconstruction. For examples of this type of hybris, see Faure 1988, 1989.

scholarly (or philosophical) practice with "popular" poaching—"efficacious meanderings" (Certeau 1984, xviii)—ends the myth of the "epistemological break" and the epistemological privileges of the specialist. It allows the historian to grasp his/her work as "an ensemble of practices in which one is implicated and through which the prose of the world is at work" (Ibid., 11–12). Likewise, Mikhail Bakhtin argues that "metalanguage is not simply a code" and that "it is always related dialogically to the language it describes and analyzes. The epistemology that gives itself the social world as a representation is far from neutral: it is itself socially determined" (Todorov 1984b, 23). This determination, which we noted earlier with respect to Hu Shih and Suzuki, works just as well for Sekiguchi, Yanagida, and ourselves: Chan historiography, by and large, appears to be the product of a certain intellectual group. This genealogical flaw will probably discredit Chan scholarship in the eyes of "authentic" Zen practitioners, who may have a point here; however, these practitioners should pause to consider that their exclusive emphasis on meditative practice and the interiorization process from which it derives are other typical products of intellectual history.

Pure objectivity is not, and never was, possible in this domain. As James Boon points out, "the notion of a neutral analytical locus, equidistant from (and unscathed by) all cultural values, was the most enduring simplification of Enlightenment comparative studies" (Boon 1982, 34). Historical objectivity turns out to be, in the last analysis, a "mise en scène of a (past) actuality," an occultation of "the social and technical apparatus of the professional institution that produces and organizes it. . . . Representation thus disguises the praxis that organizes it" (Certeau 1986, 203). Chan is a "total social fact" (*fait social total*), not only in the Maussian sense of something that is irreducibly religious, economic, aesthetic, and so on, but also in the sense of Lévi-Strauss's remark concerning Mauss's concept: "That the social fact is total does not mean simply that everything that is observed is part of the observation, but also, and above all, that in a science where the observer has the same nature as the observed, the observer is himself part of his observation" (Lévi-Strauss 1987, 29).

The objectivist approach is a logical outcome of the methods of research used. Like most of their Western counterparts, Japanese historians continue to rely on a "narrowly documentary use of sources," a "documentary model of knowledge that is typically blind to its own rhetoric" (LaCapra 1985, 17). This criticism of methodological naiveté is echoed by Hayden White, who sees the historian "wrapped up in the search for the elusive document that will establish him as an authority in a narrowly defined field" (White 1978, 28). In this sense, by indefinitely postponing the closure of the corpus and the critical evaluation of its ideological content, the search for new Chan texts among the Dunhuang manuscripts has had counterproductive effects.[23]

This criticism of historicism is hardly new. Indeed, it has become rather fashionable and may have in turn perverse ideological effects that do not differ so much from those of the historiographical tradition under criticism. My only excuse for attempting it is that it has yet to be applied consistently to Buddhist historiography and, as such, constitutes a preliminary step that cannot be dispensed with. Therefore, its critical value for Chan/Zen studies remains relatively intact. Although the possibility of such criticism derives from an epistemological shift, the effects of which are probably as constraining as those of historicism on our predecessors, this shift does not automatically find expression in historiographical scholarship, and its effects may well be delayed or blunted by the inertia or the active resistance of the historiographical institution. Accordingly, there is now more than ever, "a need for historians to attend to the interaction between order and challenge to it both in the past and in one's own discourse in addressing the past" (LaCapra 1985, 118).

In so doing, however, one must be aware of the constant temptations of "methodological scapegoating": that is, to speak of "fallacies" amounts to positing oneself as correct, orthodox. Pushing the game one step further, one reaches the point at which one may speak of a "self-critical fallacy," a rather fashionable activity that leads us to wallow in self-reflexivity, to lose oneself in the subject instead of in the object. Even when it is not merely to be dismissed as disarming rhetoric, self-criticism tends to solipsism and disaffection with the object, and it is therefore necessary to return, if not to the elusive "things themselves," at least to some soft "objective" reality—if only that of the text—in a dialectical movement from self to object (however problematic that object may remain). The "atopic" or "neutral" objectivity needs to be replaced by a localized "exotopia." That is, the acceptance and objectivation of one's prejudices should provide an alternative to the problematic "participant observation" or the "hermeneutic fallacy" of those who, like Suzuki, believe in a facile "fusion of horizons." Far from being a mere return to the sectarian biases that we found operating in recent historiography, it prevents us from not only replicating these sectarian biases in our work but also rejecting them altogether, through the realization that, "insofar as the sectarian scholarship is itself a product of Zen, it is not the enemy but the object of our study" (Bielefeldt 1988, 6).

---

[23] This tendency is particularly visible in the work of Dunhuang scholars like Chen Zuolong (Ch'en Tsu-lung) who significantly titles one of his books *Finding Pearls in the Sea of Dunhuang Literature*. See Chen, *Dunhuang xuehai tanzhu*, (Taibei: 1979).

THE TELEOLOGICAL FALLACY

By "teleological fallacy" I mean the propensity to read the past in terms of the present, to read early Chan as having its finality in modern Japanese Zen. This fallacy seems at first glance very different from the kind of historicism represented by Leopold von Ranke. If indeed, as the German historian argued, "in the eyes of God all generations are equal" (*Jede Epoche ist unmittelbar zu Gott*), there is actually no ground to privilege one extremity of the historical "process," whether the beginning (*arche*) or the end (*telos*). The historicist scholar, however, tends to forget that the present from which he/she looks back toward the past constitutes a kind of implicit *telos* from which no one can escape. Thus, the same teleological model can be found at work in the two opposite narratives of progress and decline, narratives that privilege either the origin or the end; or sometimes both simultaneously, when the telos is considered as a return to the origin. More generally, this model is found behind all affirmations of a continuity, of a "thread of history" (*fil de l'histoire*), of a perennial tradition.

In actual practice, the effects of the teleological and objectivist fallacies often mutually reinforce each other. Objectivism, for example, leads the historian to believe that he/she stands outside the tradition, at a safe vantage point from where it can be seen to develop from a simple origin (usually a text), toward increasing complexity, followed by periodical attempts to return to the source. Only an "objectivist" illusion, however, allows one to "imagine" an original text, from which an entire tradition derives. There is no such "original" text because every text comes to us mediated by a hermeneutical tradition that no one can bracket or deny. Consequently, even though the "history of Chan/Zen" seems to progress according to a temporal sequence, only a distortion of that sequence enables us to perceive prior distortions imposed (and more or less successfully erased) by the tradition. In the case of Japanese religion, for instance, one of the most damaging distortions is the conception of Japanese Buddhism as a religious tradition distinct from Shintō. Kuroda Toshio has argued that the Meiji "Separation of Shintō and Buddhism" (*shinbutsu bunri*) successfully masked the fact that there never was a "native" Shintō tradition because Shintō was largely a sectarian departure from the worldview of esoteric Buddhism (*kenmitsu bukkyō*). The same argument can be applied in the case of Japanese Zen, a religious movement that, in many respects, was until the nineteenth century a sectarian variant of esoteric Buddhism.[24] The redefinition of Zen as a "pure" tradition was by and large

---

[24] Most founders of Kamakura Zen, with the possible exception of Dōgen and a few Chinese masters, jointly practiced Zen and *mikkyō* (*zenmitsu sōshū*). The most well-known are Yōsai, Enni Ben'en, and Muhon Kakushin, who all claimed to have received the "direct

an ideological fallout of the Meiji era, a period when Japanese Buddhists, having lost and/or repudiated their grounding in local culture, were trying to adapt to the spirit of the time by redefining Buddhism as a "philosophical tradition."[25] The development of Buddhist scholarship, initiated by scholars such as Shimaji Mokurai and Nanjō Bun'yū after models provided by Western scholars such as Friedrich Max Müller led to a redefinition of Zen as a "pure" tradition uncontaminated by a long but superficial "cohabitation" with Chinese and Japanese "popular religions."

Thus, the "history" of Zen that emerged after Meiji had been prepared by several "rewritings" of the tradition: (1) the Tang elaboration of the Chan patriarchal lineage; (2) the Song narratives of the "Transmission of the Lamp"; (3) the Kamakura-Muromachi accounts of the transmission of Zen to Japan; and (4) the Tokugawa sectarian rewritings of Zen orthodoxy, with scholars like Manzan Dōhaku, Menzan Zuihō, and Mujaku Dōchū. The need for a change of perspective derives from the recognition that the standard history of Zen does not find its origins in a distant and mythical past—this *in illo tempore* being Buddhist India for Zen followers, the Tang dynasty for Zen scholars—but presupposes the existence of Japanese Zen as its ultimate goal.

By way of illustration, I discuss two recent cases of "teleological scholarship" that involve the founder of the Northern Chan school, Shenxiu, and one of his disciples, Zhida. Although the opposition between Northern and Southern schools arose with Shenxiu's and Huineng's disciples, it was read back into the teachings of the founders and even into their personalities. Accordingly, the *Platform Sūtra* stressed that, whereas Shenxiu was an eminent scholar, Huineng was illiterate. Although this "sūtra," a term generally reserved to the Buddha's discourses, is traditionally seen as a record of Huineng's sermons, it is a later compilation. Another work attributed to Huineng seems more authentic, but unfortunately, because it is a rather scholarly commentary on the *Vajracchedikā-prajñāpāramitā-sūtra*, it has until recently been neglected as "unworthy" of Huineng. Owing to Sekiguchi's textual criticism of this work, the situation is now changing, and perhaps Huineng's image will be modified thereby. At any

---

transmission." A similar syncretism seems to have characterized various trends of Chinese Chan, and it becomes the hallmark of later Japanese Zen. However, the teleological view has it that Yōsai, the first transmitter of Chan to Japan, practiced reluctantly esoteric rituals because the time "was not ripe yet," while Dōgen, entering a period of maturity, was able for the first time to teach "pure" Zen. See Funaoka 1987.

[25] Although "Zen philosophy" appears as a typical product of modernity, some trends in Zen, informed by Japanese culture, could be labeled postmodern, if by postmodernism we refer to the disappearance of the subject, the decentering of the discourse, the deconstruction of any systematic, architectonic, or abstract thought, in short an opposition to the dominant epistemological structure of modernity. However, we must keep in mind that this apparent lack of system must in turn be construed or objectified as a form of ideological structure.

rate, it seems true that Shenxiu was a prominent scholar, as were many of his disciples. One of them, Daoxuan (J. Dōsen) is credited with bringing the Huayan (J. Kegon) teaching to Japan in 736, along with Chan and Vinaya. As has often been noticed, Huayan formed the philosophical background of classical Chan, and it was predominant at the beginning of the eighth century, at the time when Shenxiu was invited by Empress Wu to teach at the imperial palace. Japanese scholars therefore came to think of Northern Chan as a kind of doctrinal synthesis of Huayan and Chan, the so-called *Kegon-Zen*. So it was not a surprise to them when they found in a catalogue written by the Korean monk Ŭich'ŏn (twelfth c.) that Shenxiu was the author of two commentaries on the *Avataṃsaka-sūtra*, the *Huayan jing shu* (in thirty *juan*), and the *Miaoli yuancheng guan* (Contemplation of the Perfect Achievement of the Subtle Principle, in three *juan*). A new interest in that question arose a few years ago when several quotations of the *Miaoli yuancheng guan* were discovered in the works of a famous Korean scholar-monk of the tenth century, the Huayan (K. Hwaŏm) master Kyunyŏ. More recently, another long quotation of Shenxiu's commentary on the *Avataṃsaka* was subsequently discovered in Japan in the work of a second generation disciple of the Kegon master Myōe, a monk named Junkō. Kegon scholars have focused their attention on the possible influence of the Northern school on Korean Buddhism. The fact that the content of these quotations showed absolutely no Chan influence or that their authors used the translation of the *Avataṃsaka* in eighty *juan*, which was executed at a time when Shenxiu was already past his nineties, did not raise any doubts. In all books published recently on early Chan in Japan, Korea, and China, the Huayan elements in the thought of Shenxiu have been uncritically emphasized.

However, a closer look at Ŭich'ŏn's catalog shows that all the *Avataṃsaka* commentaries mentioned therein belong to the Huayan school and that their authors are listed in chronological order: Fazang (637–714), his disciple Huiyuan (d.u.), Faxian, and then Shenxiu. This seems to imply that Shenxiu was a disciple of Faxian. Indeed, Faxian's biography in the *Song Gaoseng zhuan* mentions that one of Faxian's disciples was a monk of the Huiqi monastery (in Zhejiang) named Shenxiu. The author of the commentary on the *Avataṃsaka* was therefore not the Northern Chan master, but a codisciple of the fourth Huayan patriarch Chengguan (738–839) who flourished in the second half of the eighth century, that is, some fifty years after the death of the Northern school's founder. There is even evidence that this Shenxiu met the Japanese monk Kūkai (774–835), during the latter's trip to China in 804. The "facts" are stubborn, and the scholastic bias of the Chan master Shenxiu, in other words his "gradualism," proves to be another example of scholarly wishful thinking (see Faure 1983).

In Zhida's case, we can see how the "revolutionary" image of Shenhui promoted by Hu Shih came to interfere with the determination of historical chronology. Zhida's name was until recently known only through two works attributed to him, both of which are Dunhuang manuscripts. One of them, the *Dunwu zhenzong yaojue* (The Essential Teachings according to the True Principle of Sudden Awakening), was even translated into Tibetan. This text has a preface dated 712 by a magistrate of Dizhou, Liu Wude, according to which Zhida (a.k.a. Hou Mochen Yan), was a disciple of the Chan masters Huian and Shenxiu. This preface was rejected as a forgery by Japanese scholars because it resembles the preface of another Northern Chan text, the *Zhenzong lun* (Treatise on the True Principle), written by a monk named Huiguang (a.k.a. Dazhao), who had been a disciple of Huian and Shenhui. Arguing from the fact that the doctrinal content of the *Essential Teachings* appears more radical, more influenced by the notion of Sudden Awakening, Yanagida concluded that it is a much later work and represents an attempt to respond to Shenhui's criticism of the Northern school by borrowing some of Shenhui's ideas. This line of argument contains two presuppositions: first, the origin of subitism is to be found in Shenhui; second, the evolution of the Chan doctrine was a steady process, a linear development toward an always more radical position. According to this interpretation, gradualism, the original sin of Zen, was redeemed by the Southern school. Again, some stubborn "facts": among Dunhuang manuscripts was found an apocryphal sūtra, the *Chanmen jing* (Sūtra of the Chan Gate), which emphasizes the notion of Sudden Awakening and is prefaced by a Northern Chan monk bearing the same name as Huiguang, the author of the *Treatise on the True Principle*. As this work was already listed as an apocryphon in a Buddhist catalog, the *Record of [the] Kaiyuan [era]* (*Kaiyuan lu*, dated 730), it clearly antedates Shenhui's polemic of the 730s.

Regarding Zhida himself, I have found sufficient evidence that his main work, the *Essential Teachings*, was indeed written at the turn of the eighth century. Zhida's funerary inscription, found in a little known epigraphical collection, clearly states that he died in 714. This inscription, the source of the preface of the *Essential Teachings*, gives more biographical details about this disciple of Shenxiu. We learn that, having received from his master the oral, that is, esoteric teachings, "he directly taught the essential of *dhāraṇī* (incantations) and spread the principle of Sudden Awakening."[26] Not only was Zhida proficient in the sudden teaching, he was also, like many of Shenxiu's disciples, attracted to the esoteric school of Buddhism (*zhenyan*) recently transmitted to China. Thus, if we were at all costs

---

[26] See "Liuzu Houmochen dashi shouta mingwen," by Cui Kuan; *Manglo zhongmu yiwen sibian*, in *Shike shiliao xinbian* 19: 14263–14265.

looking for "influences," we might have to revert Yanagida's argument and admit that the author of the *Treatise on the True Principle* took his inspiration from Zhida's *Essential Teachings*, and not the other way around. Moreover, if we consider that the preface of the *Treatise on the True Principle* replaces Shenxiu's name with that of Shenhui, we might even conclude that the author of this preface, a disciple of Shenhui, felt the need to plagiarize the Northern school's Sudden teaching.

Whatever the case, the above evidence might suffice to show that, contrary to what Shenhui and the later tradition claimed, the sudden/gradual opposition did not coincide with the Southern/Northern controversy. Is this opposition then still relevant, or does it simply hide a much more complex interaction between the various trends of Tang Buddhism? In other words, how did this conception, when it became the dominant ideology, really affect the behavior and thinking of Chan adepts? What is the function of the Northern/Southern dichotomy and of the genealogical movement that gradually spread to other Buddhist schools and then to other Chinese religious traditions? The answer to these questions requires a nonsectarian, that is, nonteleological, perspective. We must first deconstruct these lineages and retrace the genealogy of these genealogies. Instead of following the details of the controversy, we must understand what made it possible—what from the outset polarized the discourse in which it emerged—and see it unfolding beyond the subjectivity of its protagonists. The doctrinal opposition of the two schools should not be hypostasized, for in fact they might have been interchangeable.

If a manicheist vision of the origins of the Chan school has asserted itself until now, it is because of its various advantages. Indeed, alloting the role of a scapegoat to the Northern school, which had become an emblem of heterodoxy, allowed one to circumscribe in time and space all risks of deviationism (intellectualism, quietism, corruption, secularization), to which Chan/Zen was constantly exposed. Thus, at relatively little cost the tradition was purified of all its gradual elements, and one could hope that the reign of orthodoxy was definitively established. This kind of exorcism has fostered the idealistic conception of Zen as an ahistorical teaching in which all conflicts are, if not suppressed, at least subordinated to the search for a transcendent truth. This is precisely the conception that we have seen at work in Suzuki's discourse.

The Tradition as Metaphor

Underlying the teleological fallacy are epistemological assumptions—to which I return in chapter 6—about the linearity of time, the existence of a temporal axis permitting the linear development of a tradition. Only then can the tradition become the main historical actor, the subject of the narrative engendered by historiography. Therefore, our first task is to question the use of "white metaphors" such as "tradition."

Although, for the sake of convenience, we constantly speak of an early Chan school, it is not at all proved that there was such a thing. We do find evidence of repeated attempts to create a Chan tradition, usually at the cost of "historical truth"—whatever this may be. The emergence of a tradition is simultaneously the sign of a loss and an attempt to deny this loss, to bridge the gap between a devalorized present and an idealized past. These attempts were in most cases the initiative of marginals who, genuinely or not, idealized earlier beliefs and practices. Thus, the emergence of a Chan school resulted from repeated departures from the doctrinal and institutional frame of traditional Buddhism: although the Chan tradition was reasserted after major cultural breaks (early Tang, Song, Kamakura, Meiji), it has no real continuity, or at least it lacks the type of continuity that it claims to have.

As noted in the introduction, the word *Chan* has several referents, and only toward the end of the eighth century did it come to define primarily a "Chan school," although the latter had not yet acquired its institutional independence. The Chan tradition, if we wish to retain that expression, was always plural, a composite; a cluster of diverse and often conflicting attitudes arose at the contact of changing worldviews, practices, and institutional structures. These circumstances explain why one may find Chan "types" outside the Chan/Zen tradition: to name just a few, the Central Asian thaumaturge Sengqie, the Tiantai monks Hanshan and Shide, the Korean Huayan (Hwaŏm) master Wŏnhyo, or the Japanese Tendai master Zōga. Conversely, many elements considered characteristic of Chan actually originated in other traditions. The historian's perception of a tradition results from a perhaps unconscious epistemological choice that shares some similarities with what the art historian Heinrich Wölfflin called "vision in masses."[27] Because, as noted earlier, the main device in the elaboration of the Chan tradition was the constitution of a patriarchal lineage after the model of the genealogical tree, we need to reverse or replace this traditional scheme. This means among other things that, contrary to a common belief, the Chan tradition is seen to develop, not from one single stem to various branches, but rather, retroactively, from the branches to the stem: thus, from the seventh to the ninth centuries, a number of relatively independent movements such as the Laṅkāvatāra school, the Dongshan school, the Northern and Southern schools, the Niutou ("Oxhead") school, the

---

[27] Heinrich Wölfflin, *Principes fondamentaux de l'histoire de l'art* (Paris: Gallimard, 1966, 25–27.

Jingzhong and Baotang schools in Szechwan, and the Hongzhou school, all looked back to Bodhidharma as their founder and attempted to derive legitimacy from their hypothetical connection with Bodhidharma's early community. To avoid being misled by these forged geneaologies, we should perhaps supplement the tree metaphor by other, more appropriate vegetal metaphors like rhizomes, parasitic vegetal, or intertwining creepers.

Another type of recurrent metaphors in Chan has to do with kinship. Thus, the transmission of the Dharma is seen as a "filiation" and the patriarchal line as a "blood lineage" (*xuemo*). Particularly noteworthy is the case of the legacy transmitted from the "uncle" to the "nephew." According to a verse attributed to the Indian patriarch Prajñātāra in the *Zutang ji*: "Although China is broad, it has no particular paths; the essential is to advance following the tracks of the nephews and grand-sons." (see Yanagida 1978, 33). The patriarchal rank was for instance transmitted from Hongren to Huineng—instead of the "legitimate" heir Shenxiu—and from Huineng to Nanyue Huairang (677–744) and Qingyuan Xingsi (660?–740)—instead of Shenhui. The same holds for canonical texts, and Tzvetan Todorov reminds us that "every period canonizes texts that were judged marginal during the previous period" (Todorov 1984a, 32; see also Genette 1966, 167–168, quoting Chklovski). This is certainly true for Chan classics such as the apocryphal *Yuanjue jing* and *Śūraṃgama-sūtra*, or even for Dōgen's *Shōbōgenzō*. It may therefore be more productive to stress filiations that have been labeled collateral by an ulterior tradition and to follow the critical *chemins de traverse*, even if they may sidetrack us.

Leaving aside the metaphorical aspects of the tradition, there is no convincing evidence of the smooth evolution of an "essential" Chan, let alone of a perfect transmission of some atemporal arcana; instead one finds dogmas and local traditions constantly interplaying and more or less successfully replacing each other. "Classical" Chan and Zen can be said to have superseded "early" Chan as much as to have inherited from it. To take a Chan "tradition" or "essence" for granted is to forget that, as Paul Veyne points out, "in this world we do not play chess with eternal figures like the king and the fool: the figures are what the successive configurations on the playing board make of them" (Veyne 1984, 236).

This is not to deny that, at least from a certain point onward, there was indeed a "Chan school," at least in the minds of its "representatives"; but the emergence of this sectarian awareness was gradual, and perhaps only in Japan did it reach its achieved form. This apparent concession to Suzuki and other teleologically minded Zen scholars implies no superiority whatsoever of Japanese Zen over its Chinese or Korean variants. Although it was prepared by sectarian and outspoken figures such as Shenhui and Dōgen, the "Zen sect" as we know it through Suzuki's writings is a relatively late product, dating mostly from the Edo period.

Once this "historical actor" we call "Chan/Zen tradition" was constituted, a "great narrative" on the popular tune "Glory and Vicissitudes of a Great Tradition" became possible, and the "Histories of the Lamp" paved the way for the history (or rather stories) of historians. These two general types, the traditional and the historical narrative, rely on the same presuppositions. Thus, even if one were to accept Ricoeur's arguments in favor of a "return of/to the narrative" (Ricoeur 1984–1988), Chan narratives should be taken with a grain of salt. Early Chan, for instance, can best be described in Pirandellian fashion as "six patriarchs in search of a tradition."

There is therefore an urgent need to examine closely the narrative structures of Chan histories and in particular to question the teleological model: its two complementary narratives of decline and progress include their uncritical use of metaphors such as "Golden Age" or "Classical Age" of Chan. Whereas the narrative of decline finds its extreme expression in the notion of the "Final Dharma," the narrative of progress holds that the tradition perfects itself in the course of time. An example of the latter can be found in Yōsai's *Kōzen gokokuron*, according to which it is only in Japan, on Mount Hiei, that Buddhist traditions formerly separate eventually came together (*T.* 80, 2543: 10b4). The teleological model of historians who want to see in "early Chan" only the forerunner of "classical Chan" calls to mind Roussel's anecdote, quoted by Fredric Jameson, about the man who claimed to have seen, in a provincial museum, "the head of Voltaire as a child" (Jameson 1981, 139). There is clearly a problem with the traditional periodization because early Chan masters did not know that they were "early" or even that they were, strictly speaking, "Chan" (in the sense given to this term by Suzuki). For instance, Daoxin (580–651) certainly never thought of himself as the "fourth Chan patriarch."

Tradition is not a clearly defined, ahistorical, entity: if it exists at all outside the mind of a few people, it is as a fluid network of relationships, an ongoing process. Like that of the author, the traditional advocacy of tradition may also be seen, as the "principle of rarefaction of discourse," as a scapegoating mechanism or an exorcism against loss. In this sense, the historian's or the commentator's emphasis on tradition is never neutral; it is likely to reinforce ideological effects—even when he tries, as I do, to deconstruct them. With the historical actor named tradition, the historian, due to his "temporal agoraphobia," ends up creating a type of narrative continuity that, according to Lévi-Strauss, is "secured only by dint of fraudulent outlines" (Lévi-Strauss 1966a, 261). In this sense, history plays indeed the same function as a founding myth.

Should we, however, merely dismiss it as such, as Sekiguchi did, in an objectivist gesture of demythologization, or rather search for "the tradition" precisely in this mythopoeic activity? It seems better to apply to the tradition the same criteria that Yanagida, in his criticism of Sekiguchi, applied to the "Recorded Sayings": that is, he considered it a *poietic*, performative discourse, rather than a mere collection of lies. A comprehensive history of ideas and practices should see all these discourses as relevant materials.

Unfortunately, with the predominance of the philological model and the discovery of the Dunhuang documents, there has been an increasing tendency in Chan scholarship to subordinate the "history of ideas" approach to one based on textual filiations—texts becoming the real actors on the scene of history. The "grubbing in the archives" mentality has contributed to an eclipse of the biographical approach complacently inherited from the hagiographical tradition and has transformed the texts themselves into historical actors. This tendency is reflected for example in recent scholarship on the *Platform Sūtra* and the *Shōbōgenzō* and in Yanagida's research on the "History of the Recorded Sayings" (Yanagida 1985).

To be sure, we cannot do entirely without periodization, and a discourse without metaphors tends to become insipid. There is no way, and no need either, to eliminate entirely "white metaphors," such as tradition, as long as they are used between quotation marks. This understanding derives from the basic recognition that we cannot completely eliminate narrative structure (plot, actors, etc.). Hayden White's assertion—"there can be no story without a plot by which to make it a story of a particular kind. This is true even of the most self-consciously impressionistic account" (White 1978, 62)—must be complemented with Braudel's remark that "narrative history is not a method or the method par excellence, but indeed is itself a philosophy of history" (Braudel 1969, 13). Let us, then, advocate a "return to the narrative," but with the qualification that it remain a "narrative under erasure," fragmented and nonlinear.

One will object—and perhaps rightly so—that the above discussion, taking the reader from noncritical through hypercritical to "performative" scholarship, is itself fairly teleological. Another scapegoating mechanism seems at work, leading naturally from description ("here is what has been done") to prescription ("here is what should be done"). Because there can be no logical derivation from descriptive to prescriptive discourse (Lyotard and Thébaud 1985, 21–24), it is obvious that my "description" of Sino-Japanese historiography is already prescriptive, hence performative. Simply to present the views of one's predecessors, in an apparent dialogical movement, amounts to criticizing them, without even having taken the trouble of actually refuting them. Although it implies a perspective that they did not—and could not—have, this vantage point, whatever its karmic or sociological determinations, is not transcendental and has therefore its own cost. As there seems to be no way to escape from this predicament, one must work through the dialectics of "blindness and insight" (de Man 1983).

WRITING CHAN HISTORY

The notion that Chan history is essentially a literary artifact, just like the "documents" it studies, has been pointed out by Yanagida, and John Maraldo has recently called for a "radically different approach" to the history of Chan, "one which would focus on the literary nature of the genres of Chan literature" (Maraldo 1986a; see also D. Wright 1992). What is needed is a "literary history" of Chan in both senses: that is, a history of "Chan as literature" and a study of "Chan history" as a literary genre. The criticism of objectivism and the "referential fallacy" leads to the realization that "all interpretation depends upon the antithetical relations between meanings and not on the supposed relation between a text and its meaning" (Riffaterre 1986, 1–22; see also Bloom 1973, 76). The objectivity so valued by historians can itself be shown to be a literary, "realistic" effect induced by the use of patently nonpoetical language and "dead" metaphors. This criticism and the demonstration of the literary nature of the "writing of history" have been made, among others, by Michel de Certeau and Hayden White.[28] White, for instance, argues that the historian is not merely following passively his sources, but actively interpreting them. His interpretation is governed by the rules of his language—a language that is irremediably figurative or rhetorical, even when it appears the least so. Interpretation creeps into historiographical discourse at several levels—for instance, at the time of selecting and decoding the documentation—where texts and contexts, "not less opaque than the texts studied by the literary critics," require all the historian's fiction-writing capabilities (White 1978, 89). Interpretation predominates at the level of the historical narrative, depending on the type of emplotment used. According to White, "most historical sequences can be emplotted in a number of different ways, so as to provide different interpretations of those events and to endow them with different meanings" (ibid., 85). Events are by no means meaningful in themselves; even a "plain" chronicle already implies a selection. The historian endows them with meaning by inscribing them in a specific plot. The rise of Chan, for instance, can be read in a number of complementary or

28 See Certeau 1988; White 1973, 1978, 1987. On the importance of rhetoric and fiction in historiography, see also LaCapra 1985, 15–44.

conflicting ways: as a triumph of individualism, as a Sinicization of Buddhism, as an episode in the demythologization, deritualization, or spir-
itualization of Chinese religion, as a response to the sociopolitical changes
of the Tang—to name just a few. Thus, owing to the "creative" genius of
Hu Shih, the meeting held by Shenhui at Huatai became a "revolutionary
act" that rang the death knell of "deviationist" Northern Chan and paved
the way for Chan orthodoxy. Consequently, the emplotment of the historical narrative is essentially "a literary, that is to say a fiction-making,
operation—and to call it that in no way detracts from the status of a
historical narrative as providing a kind of knowledge" (White 1978, 85).
These affinities between historiographical discourse and literature, owing
to the fact that both derive from a rhetorical, figurative use of language, are
of course something that disturbs "scientific" historians in their attempt to
reach the "zero degree" of historical writing.

History is intrinsically a historio-*graphy*, that is, a kind of writing, and
this writing here is not—it is never, according to Derrida—a secondary
operation. As Ricoeur points out, the first presupposition of a poetics of
historiographical discourse is that "fiction and history belong to a same
class in terms of narrative structure." The second presupposition is that
this convergence of history and fiction allows a convergence of history and
literature. An emplotment takes place, not only at the obvious but superficial level of the explanation of the facts selected as relevant, of the narrated
story, but also at a deeper level in the choice of the category to which the
narrated story belongs. One can in this sense speak of an "explanation
through emplotment." These various choices constitute the linguistic
modes or protocols of historiographical discourse. In White's opinion,
historiographical disputes arise because of a disagreement over the choice
of these protocols or modes of emplotment, rather than because of a
disagreement over the explanatory systems to be applied to the events
(ibid., 133–134). In this light, the controversy between Suzuki and Hu
Shih appears as essentially a question of protocol; and it replicates the
controversy between the Northern and Southern schools, which seem to
have diverged less on doctrinal matters (sudden vs. gradual) than on questions of "style" and rhetoric.

To define these linguistic modes that predetermine the encoding of historiographical discourse, White borrows Vico's system of tropes. He thus
argues that "the plot structure of a historical narrative" (the *why*) and the
formal argument of explanation (the *how*) are prefigured by the original
description of the "facts" in a given modality of language use: metaphor,
metonymy, synecdoche and irony.[29]

[29] See White 1978, 70–73. White goes so far as to find connections between the tropes that
govern these three levels (the fundamental level of linguistic modes and those of the modes of

White concedes that a sophisticated historian does not limit him-self/herself to only one of these tropological strategies, but rather tries to mediate between them. Nevertheless, his determinism appears too rigid, and his "tropology" is less convincing than his general theory of emplot-ment. When he defines the "tropological code" as a determinative level of discourse, White seems to be doing precisely that for which he takes scien-tifically minded historians to task. In his attempt to reach a determination in the last instance, to find a deep-structural meaning determined by the use of figurative language, he arrives at a kind of structuralism that reduces one level of discourse to another (see LaCapra 1983, 72–83).

From the above discussion we retain all the methodological implications contingent upon the literary nature of historiographical discourse and the importance of emplotment—even in attempts to deconstruct the linearity of the traditional narrative. To evaluate correctly Chan/Zen historiogra-phy, I should therefore have taken into consideration the stylistic variations and the various modes of emplotment in the works of the Chan historians discussed earlier. Such a study is, however, beyond the scope of the present work.

It is at least important to acknowledge the epistemological shift(s) that allowed these reformulations regarding the traditional task of history. Something has changed in the field of Chan historiography, and the effects of this change have just begun to be felt. These effects may be more sensible at the periphery than at the center of the field, where "paraseismic" devices and the resistances of traditional historiography are more important. Let me insist again on the notion of transference: like the early Chan tradition, Chan/Zen historiography is characterized by a kind of visualism that priv-ileges writing and literacy to the detriment of orality (W. Ong 1982). It is therefore necessary to emphasize the repressive function of historio-*graphy* vis-à-vis oral cultures (and toward a certain sector of Chan and popular religion). Even if they can no longer be retrieved, the various discourses repressed by orthodox tradition and canonic doctrine should at least be given the chance to fragment and subvert orthodox historiographical discourse.

After this excursus on historiography, and because I have already men-tioned the structuralist approach, it may be useful to examine this alterna-tive methodology for an "explanation" of Chan—before moving on to other methodologies aimed at "understanding." Perhaps, then, we will be in a better position to evaluate the aporias or dialectics between objective explanation and subjective understanding.

---

emplotment and of explanation) and specific ideological positions (anarchist, radical, liberal, conservative) (ibid., 70).

Chapter Four

ALTERNATIVES

AMONG VARIOUS common alternatives to the historical approach, philosophical hermeneutics and structural criticism have played predominant roles. Turning first to the structural approach, I examine at some length the case of the legendary founder of Chan, the Indian monk Bodhidharma.

THE STRUCTURAL APPROACH

> This kind of intimate relationship that I enjoy with Rousseau is one I also feel with Chateaubriand, who is the contrary of Rousseau, yet the same. So the person I feel closest to is neither Rousseau nor Chateaubriand but a kind of chimera, the Janus figure constituted by the Rousseau-Chateaubriand dyad, which offers me the dual aspect of the same man, though they made diametrically opposite choices.
> (Lévi-Strauss, "Claude Lévi-Strauss Reconsiders")

The "Biographical" Illusion

Although Bodhidharma's biography is obscure, his life is relatively well known. This is less paradoxical than it may sound, because hagiography flourishes precisely when historical materials are scarce. Usually, the main task of historians is to try to uncover the facts behind the legend. Hagiographical texts are considered by them to be documents that need interpretation to bring to light their hidden truths. Often enough, after this mortuary washing only a skeleton remains, and it is this skeleton that will enter the museum of history. Often, some missing bones may have to be taken from other skeletons to complete the exhibit. In the case of Bodhidharma, there is not even a skeleton—only one sandal left, according to legend, in an empty grave. In most cases the biographical process is only an unconscious duplication of the hagiographical process. Both are characterized by an "essentialist" attitude in that they consider a figure as some kind of individual entity whose essence is reflected in specific biographical or doctrinal texts.

Several biographies concerning Bodhidharma are found in Buddhist and Chan histories, and several works attributed to him are extant. However, as Sekiguchi Shindai has shown, most of these *Treatises of Bodhidharma* are apocryphal. Only one of them, the *Erru sixing lun* (Treatise on the Two Entrances and Four Practices), is presently considered Bodhidharma's teaching as recorded by his disciple Tanlin. This work also contains a short biographical account concerning Bodhidharma. According to this account, Bodhidharma was a South Indian monk who came to China to transmit the essential Mahāyāna teachings (see Faure 1986, 67). These biographical elements reappear in Daoxuan's *Xu gaoseng zhuan* (Continued Biographies of Eminent Monks), which was written in 645 and revised down to 664, more than a century after Bodhidharma's mysterious death. According to Daoxuan, after his arrival in Southern China (Nanyue) and a brief sojourn in the capital of the Liu Song (420–479), Bodhidharma went to Luoyang, then the capital of the Northern Wei (*T.* 50, 2060: 551b). Bodhidharma's practice, the so-called wall-contemplation (Ch. *biguan*), differed considerably from, and was much more difficult to practice than, the traditional Indian dhyāna then popular among Buddhists in Northern China. Consequently, Bodhidharma is said to have attracted only a few followers, one of whom, Huike, was to become the second patriarch of Chan. A passage in Daoxuan's biography of Huike tells us that Bodhidharma transmitted to his disciple a Buddhist scripture, the *Laṅkāvatāra-sūtra*, as the essence of his teaching (ibid., 552b). Accordingly, the early Chan movement was first known as the Laṅkāvatāra School. An earlier mention of Bodhidharma can be found in the *Luoyang qielan ji* (Record of the Buddhist Monasteries of Luoyang). In this text, however, Bodhidharma is presented as an elderly Central Asian monk who spent several days singing the praises of the great *stūpa* in the precincts of Yongning Monastery (see Yang Hsüan-chih 1984, 20–21). After endless discussions, historians have harmonized these conflicting images of Bodhidharma—the devout and somewhat senile monk, the austere practitioner of some esoteric type of meditation, and the transmitter of Buddhist scriptures—to give a coherent account of his personality, but it diverges greatly from that of the legendary figure of the later Chan tradition.

Yet, all these discussions and the subsequent conclusions may have missed the point. As noted earlier, the historiographical process that leads to the elaboration of this biography bears important resemblances to the hagiographical process on which it relies. Both share the same obsession with filling the chronological gaps by borrowing from various sources. By considering the texts as documents that yield valuable information, historiography completely ignores their worklike or literary nature. Such a facile division between historical and hagiographical components, relying uncritically on the assumption that the earliest sources are *always* the most authentic, does violence to the texts and deprives the historian of valuable information about the evolution of Chan.

It is therefore a rather arbitrary reconstruction that ignores or hides its ideological motivation and simply "submits a literary genre to the laws of another—historiography" (Certeau 1975, 275). In the case of Chan historiography, we have already noted the predominance of a teleological conception of history, one that takes Japanese Zen as the natural outcome of Chinese Chan, thereby making the "search for the real Bodhidharma" meaningful only as a legitimization of the Zen tradition. If Bodhidharma was just an ordinary Central Asian pilgrim, then he is irrelevant to an understanding of the Chan and later Zen traditions and does not deserve the type of attention he has received. Historians should perhaps stop focusing, like Daoxuan, on "eminent monks" and their "biographies." As far as Bodhidharma is concerned, the biographies that do exist have literary but little or no historical value; Bodhidharma should be seen as a textual and religious paradigm, not reconstructed as either a historical figure or a psychological essence.

One may object that we do possess works attributed to Bodhidharma and that his thought, at least, is relatively well known to us. Here again we may be misled by a type of thinking that is too "essentialist." As a working hypothesis, Michel Foucault's definition of the author might be more helpful. According to Foucault, "The author is the principle of thrift in the proliferation of meaning. . . . [He] is not an indefinite source of significations which fill a work; . . . he is a certain functional principle by which, in our culture, one limits, excludes, and chooses; in short, by which one impedes the free circulation, the free manipulation, the free composition, decomposition, and recomposition of fiction" (Foucault 1979, 159).

Such a redefinition of the author may help us avoid the type of historicism still found in recent Chan studies. One case in point is Jan Yün-hua's attempt to reconstruct the thought of the dhyāna master Sengchou (480–560), a contemporary and, according to Daoxuan, successful rival of Bodhidharma (Jan 1983). Sengchou is credited with a number of works, clearly products of a much later period, that reflect the point of view of the Northern school of Chan. A similar reductionism is at work in the biographies of such eminent early Chan monks as Sengcan (d. 606?), Niutou Farong (594–657), Wolun (d.u.), Shenxiu, and Huineng. This traditional type of discussion of authorship calls to mind Borges's fiction about the world of Tlön, a world in which all books are considered products of a single author: "The critics often invent authors: they select two dissimilar works—the *Tao Te Ching* and the *1001 Nights*, say—attribute them to the same writer and then determine most scrupulously the psychology of this interesting *homme de lettres*" (Borges 1964, 13). As literary critic Gérard

Genette points out, "fundamentally, Tlönian criticism is not the *contrary* of our positivist criticism, it is rather its hyperbole" (Genette 1966, 129).

Structural Analysis

> Supernumeraries, necessarily! for in the ideal painting of the stage, everything moves *according to a symbolic reciprocity of types among themselves, or relatively to a single figure*.
> (Stéphane Mallarmé, "Crayonné au théâtre")[1]

One might extend to Chan masters what Georges Dumézil suggested for Indo-European gods, that is, to "study them in their relationship with each other, find and interpret their habitual groupings; that is, draw the limits of their respective domains before undertaking their individual monographs."[2] Moreover, because we are dealing with written documents, it seems appropriate to treat Bodhidharma's "life" as a literary piece belonging to the hagiographical genre, a genre characterized by a "predominance of explanations concerning places over explanations concerning time" (Certeau 1975, 285). The first step toward understanding its meaning or relevance, then, is to ask what this genre is and by what rules it is governed. In other words, what is its syntagmatic structure, "the actual link between various functions in a given text"? The second step is to examine the paradigmatic structure of the hagiographical text, "the virtual relations between analogous or opposed functions, from one text to the other, in the whole corpus under consideration" (see Ducrot and Todorov 1972, 139–146). This leads us to ask whether the meaning of the hagiographical text itself has ever been fixed once and for all. According to Ferdinand de Saussure: "To imagine that a legend begins with a meaning, has had since its first origin the *meaning* that it now has, is an operation beyond my understanding. It seems to suppose really that there have never been any material elements transmitted on this legend through centuries" (quoted in Starobinski 1979, 8). Saussure contends that in any particular legend each of the characters "is a symbol for which one observes variations of: (a) name, (b) position vis-à-vis others, (c) character, and (d) function and actions. If a *name* is transposed, it could follow that part of the action is reciprocally transposed or that the whole drama is entirely changed by an accident of this kind" (ibid., 5–6).

---

[1] "Comparses, il le faut! car dans l'idéale peinture de la scène, tout se meut *selon une réciprocité symbolique des types entre eux ou relativement à une figure seule*" (Mallarmé 1945, 301; quoted in Barthes 1983, 279).

[2] See Françoise Desbordes, "Le comparatisme de Dumézil: Une introduction," in *Pour un temps: Georges Dumézil*, ed. Jacques Bonnet (Paris: Centre Georges Pompidou/Pandora Editions, 1981): 52.

This, I believe, provides a good starting point from which to examine Bodhidharma's life as a narrative. It is, for example, more flexible than Vladimir Propp's theories concerning the folktale, which do not take into consideration the semantic value of the hero's name and provide somewhat too systematic an approach for our purpose (Propp 1968). The same may be said of Roland Barthes's and Claude Brémond's attempts to analyze the logic of the narrative, not to mention Lévi-Strauss's study of myths (see Brémond 1964, 1973; Barthes 1983; Lévi-Strauss 1963, 1969, 1974). Although recent developments in the field of textual analysis may yield significant results if applied to Buddhist hagiographical materials, hagiography is a hybrid narrative that offers more resistance to structural analysis than either the folktale or the myth.

Let us reconsider by focusing on two of its elements, Bodhidharma's function and his name, Bodhidharma's "life" in the light of Saussure's earlier definition. In the *Xu gaoseng zhuan*, Bodhidharma is contrasted with the dhyāna master Sengchou, whose method of meditation, characterized by Daoxuan as of a rather inferior type, was apparently quite popular. Says Daoxuan: "Thus, when we look at the two tenets [of Sengchou and Bodhidharma, it is clear that] they are like the two wheels of the same cart. [Seng]chou embraced the [practice called] the 'foundations of mindfulness,' a model of purity to be venerated. Bodhidharma relied on the teaching of emptiness, whose purport is obscure and deep. Due to this fact, his principle was intrinsically difficult to comprehend, while Sengchou's model was easily accessible" (see *T.* 50, 2060: 596c).

The contrast drawn by Daoxuan between the two men is a typical literary device that tells us more about him than about them. It is reminiscent of the opposition between Shenxiu and Huineng, the putative founders of the Northern and Southern schools of Chan, who became paradigms of the two main types of Chan practice—gradualism and subitism. Any later Chan monk became, as it were, a Huineng or a Shenxiu. In all these cases, the contrast was clearly exaggerated for hagiographical purposes. More than this contrast itself, what I want to emphasize is that Bodhidharma and Sengchou, or Huineng and Shenxiu, are symmetrical figures that imply each other. They constitute together what Terence Turner calls a single "narrative actor." According to Turner, "an 'actor' may become polarized into two contrasting figures, sharing one attribute but opposed upon one or two others" (T. Turner 1977, 155). The hagiographical text forms a whole, and the literary device used by the author clearly affects the biography of each character. It is therefore artificial to dissect this kind of composite "biography" and to keep only what concerns one or the other of its protagonists, for instance Bodhidharma or Sengchou. Even if one objects that the polarization between the two figures exceeds a simple literary device and reflects a preexistent connection between them at the level of collective representations, this does not invalidate the structural model; on the contrary, the polarization supports the structural approach.

A variant of this model is provided by Roland Barthes's hypothesis that many narratives "set two adversaries in conflict over some stake; the subject is then truly double, not reducible further by substitution; indeed, this is even perhaps a common archaic form, as though narrative, after the fashion of certain languages, had also known a *dual* of persons" (Barthes 1983, 279). Note that the French word *duel* means both *duel*—that is, a contest—and *dual*, the category in Greek grammar intermediate between singular and plural. One protagonist of the *duel* may change, but the *duel* itself remains. Thus, the contrast between Bodhidharma and Sengchou is structurally analogous to the alleged rivalry between Huineng and Shenxiu, which appears as its sectarian hyperbole. It reflects the opposition and complementarity between the two levels of truth, absolute and conventional, or between sectarianism and eclecticism, that is, in Zen terminology, between the standpoints of the "special transmission outside of the Scriptures" (J. *kyōge betsuden*) and of the "harmony between Zen and the Scriptures" (J. *kyōzen itchi*).

The syntagmatic contrast between Bodhidharma and Sengchou is obvious in Daoxuan's notice. The paradigmatic equivalence between them can be found in the fact that the two men were attributed parallel theories concerning the "two entrances" and that both were posthumously considered candidates for the position of "first patriarch" by the early Chan school. Both, in Saussure's terms, have the same function in Chan hagiographical discourse, in which they are each represented as some kind of Daoist immortal: Bodhidharma had achieved immortality through the so-called deliverance from the corpse, while Sengchou was "immortalized" for taming two tigers and causing the spurt of a "divine spring" (see Yanagida 1967, 596; Faure 1989, 28–30).

Sengchou appears therefore as the main double of Bodhidharma: on the syntagmatic axis of the hagiographical narrative, he is a rival; on its paradigmatic axis, he is a substitute. Both Sengchou and Bodhidharma were apparently regarded by Jingjue, the author of the *Lengqie shizi ji*, as the patriarchs of the two main trends of early Chan (see *T.* 85, 2837: 1284c; and Yanagida 1967, 518). When one judges from a poem by Cen Shen (715–770) about a foreign monk who concentrated on the *Laṅkāvatāra-sūtra* and who had subdued two tigers and a dragon (an allusion to the "divine spring" guarded by the dragon), clearly the amalgamation of the two figures was achieved around the same time.[3]

On the paradigmatic axis of Bodhidharma's hagiography, we find leg-

[3] See "Taibo huseng ge" (Song of the Barbarian Monk of Mt. Taibo), in *Quan Tang shi*, *juan* 199, ed. Sheng Zu (Taibei: Hongye shuju, 1977), 1: 2057 ff.

ends related to other thaumaturges such as Baozhi (418–514) and Fu Xi (a.k.a. Fu *dashi*, or "Fu the Mahāsattva," 497–569). These two characters served as models for a certain trend in Buddhism that considered the practice of dhyāna to be a way to acquire supranormal powers (*abhijñā*). Fu Xi, the "Chinese Vimalakīrti," is also (like Sengchou) considered a precursor of the Tiantai school. The famous encounter, another typical example of *duel*, of Bodhidharma with emperor Liang Wudi is a variant of that between Fu Xi and this emperor (see *Biyan lu*, in *T.* 48, 2003: 140a). In both cases, Baozhi plays the role of a clairvoyant witness who reveals to the perplexed emperor the real identity of his interlocutor—Fu Xi being a manifestation of the future Buddha, Maitreya (Ch. Mile), Bodhidharma an avatar of the Bodhisattva Avalokiteśvara (Ch. Guanyin). Another hint at the parallelism between Fu Xi and Bodhidharma is provided by the sectarian comment of the Tiantai patriarch Zhanran, according to whom the "incarnation from Tuṣita Heaven" (Fu Xi as Maitreya) surpasses the "coming of the Indian saint [Bodhidharma]"; in plain words, Tiantai teaching is superior to Chan (*Zhiguan yili*, in *T.* 46, 1913: 452c). The logic at work here is clearly sectarian, but the sectarian interpretation does not do justice to the dynamism and complexity of the legend.

If we now consider the role played by Bodhidharma's name in the evolution of his legend, then we come to an even more complex situation. The substitution of names is, according to Saussure, one of the "two types of historic modification of legend which might well be considered the most difficult to accept."[4] The most obvious confusion of names is the one between Bodhidharma and the Kashmirian monk Dharmatrāta, who flourished in the beginning of the fifth century and who was (incorrectly) attributed the authorship of a *Dhyāna-sūtra* (Ch. *Damotuolo chanjing*, *T.* 15, 618). Not only did Dharmatrāta's lineage become Bodhidharma's lineage and the basis of later Chan patriarchal tradition, but Bodhidharma himself also eventually became known in Tibet as Bodhidharmatrāta.[5] Interestingly, in the Tibetan tradition, he became, along with the Northern Chan master Moheyan [Mahāyāna], one of the two figures added to the list of the sixteen arhats (Lévy and Chavannes 1916). Moheyan himself is usually represented in the company of a tiger, a possible resurgence of Sengchou's figure.

Bodhidharma's name sometimes appears truncated as Bodhi, or more often as Dharma (Damo). In the first case, it may be confused with another of his rivals, Bodhiruci. Incidentally, Bodhiruci (d. 527) was a translator of the *Laṅkāvatāra-sūtra*, although in a recension different from the one

---

[4] The other type of historic modification defined by Saussure is "a change of *motive* or *aim* for an action which remains unchanged." Quoted in Starobinski 1971, 7.

[5] For a traditional discussion of Bodhidharma as Dharmatrāta, see Qisong, *Chuanfa zhengzong ji* (*T.* 51, 2078: 780). The question is treated in detail in Demiéville 1978, 43–49.

supposedly transmitted by Bodhidharma to his disciple Huike. According to legend, Bodhiruci and another monk, Guangtong (alias Huiguang, 468–537), jealous of Bodhidharma's fame, tried several times to poison him and eventually succeeded.[6] Huiguang, himself a disciple of Sengchou, had also studied on Song shan at the famous Shaolin monastery.

This monastery had been built by emperor Xiao Wen of the Northern Wei for another Central Asian monk named Fotuo or Batuo (the Chinese transcription of Buddha or Bhadra) (see Pelliot 1923, 262–264). Only much later, owing to specific historical circumstances such as the development of Northern Chan on Song shan, did Bodhidharma's name come to be associated with the Shaolin monastery; thus, he became the posthumous founder of the martial art known as "Shaolin boxing" (J. *shōrinji kenpō*). From the Song shan gazetteers, we can assume that there was an apparent amalgamation of the lineages of Fotuo/Sengchou and Bodhidharma/Huike. Bodhidharma came to play the same function as Buddha (or Bhadra), that of the patriarch of the Shaolin monastery (see *QTW*, *juan* 514, 11: 6619). Batuo is also the abbreviated transcription of Guṇabhadra (394–468), the first translator of the *Laṅkāvatāra-sūtra*. It was precisely Guṇabhadra's translation that was transmitted by Bodhidharma to Huike. In the *Lengqie shizi ji*, Guṇabhadra is presented as the master of Bodhidharma (*T.* 85, 2837: 1284c), and this biographical interpolation may have resulted from either his role as transmitter of the *Laṅkāvatāra-sūtra* or a confused linkage between Bodhidharma and the founder of the Shaolin monastery, the dhyāna master Batuo. Although the relationship is inverted in a later work of the Laṅkāvatāra tradition, a work in which Bodhidharma becomes Guṇabhadra's master, the dual/duel structure remains (see Faure 1989, 60).

Thus, the different elements of a legend reinforce each other and are in fact rather difficult to distinguish. However inconclusive or impressionistic this argument may seem, all these clues point toward the same conclusion: that is, Bodhidharma's "life," a hybrid textual construction, is only a part of a larger structure that also includes the lives of masters at first glance as different as Sengchou, Baozhi, Fu Xi, Fotuo (Batuo), Guṇabhadra, and Bodhiruci. All these personages should be seen less, if at all, as historical figures than as textual paradigms. Their relevance for the historian is not primarily in their historicity but in the significant modulations achieved by their "lives."

However hagiographic they may be, patriarchal biographies are not simply legends or myths, and they are more resistant to a structural analysis than are those in the latter genre. The approach we have taken here cannot be applied indiscriminately. It will prove most useful with certain

---

[6] The story first appears in the *Lidai fabao ji* (ca. 774). See *T.* 51, 2075: 180c.

types of traditional figures, like the alleged founders of Buddhist schools or
the leaders of certain religious movements. Significantly, most founders
have a very dim historical existence. Many Buddhist schools started in
relative obscurity and were organized by a second- or third-generation
successor, who, I would argue, was in most cases the actual founder. The
first patriarch was retrospectively promoted to his honorific rank to give
more legitimacy to the new school. His name defined a blank space upon
which one may conveniently project all the necessary "biographical" elements. In other words, the patriarchal tradition has no real origin, no real
"founder." The personage who happens to play that role is, to use Lévi-
Strauss's expression, a "virtual focus," a virtual object whose shadow
alone is real (Lévi-Strauss 1969, 5). His "biography" is a "trace" in the
Derridean sense. It will proliferate around this obscure source, and whatever "historical" details may have been preserved will soon turn into
legend.

Two other well-known embellished biographies, which provided the
missing links in the Chan patriarchal lineage, are those of the third and
sixth patriarchs, Sengcan and Huineng. The main purpose of this lineage
itself was to artificially link several independent schools. The first school,
called the School of Bodhidharma (*Damo zong*), probably originated with
Huike or with a later Laṅkāvatāra master named Fachong (587–665?).
The second school, the so-called Dongshan or Eastern Mountain School,
developed around the fourth patriarch Daoxin (580–651) and his successor Hongren and drew its legitimacy from Sengcan, an obscure figure
who was subsequently promoted as Daoxin's master. The first detailed
biographical account on this future "third patriarch" is found in the *Lengqie shizi ji* (*T*. 85, 2837: 1267b). The third school, the famous Southern
school, probably originated with Shenhui and not, as is usually believed,
with Huineng, whose chief merit was probably to be relatively unknown.
The lives of these three Chan masters (Bodhidharma, Sengcan, and
Huineng) are reconstructions dating from the eighth century, at a time
when sectarianism was on the rise.[7] Likewise, the "classical" Chan of the
ninth century traces its source back to two unknown disciples of Huineng,
Nanyue Huairang and Qingyuan Xingsi.

Brought into being as paradigms for orthodox practice, these Chan
masters should be treated as such and not given false psychological identity
through misguided erudition. Indeed, "such is the victorious power of
sheer position, whether among warriors or words" (Jean Paul Richter,
quoted in Freud 1976, 49). Consequently, all variants of a hagiographical
topos should first be considered from a synchronic perspective, without
trying to sort out the historical kernel from the shell of legend. By thus

---

[7] On the formation of these hagiographical accounts, see Yampolsky 1967, 3–88.

widening the scope of our study and downplaying, at least in the case of the founding fathers, the obsolete concept of historical individuality, we might get closer to the underlying structure that regulates the transformations of actual biographies. However, this might not suffice to explain why we get, for example, the type called Bodhidharma as the first patriarch of Chan, instead of other possible types such as Sengchou or Fu Xi. In the last resort, it seems that we must reintroduce the historical or diachronic dimension to make sense of these apparent contingencies. To interpret hybrid texts, our method must itself be hybrid. Although it works to stress a kind of structural analysis, it must at the same time be undermined by an awareness of the failure of all systems that claim in their perfection to transcend history. Only by rejecting all methodological extremes may we come to understand, if not the *meaning*, at least the *significance* of "Bodhidharma's coming from the West."

THE HERMENEUTIC APPROACH

> "When *I* use a word," Humpty Dumpty said, . . . "it means just what I choose it to mean—neither more nor less."
>
> "The question is," said Alice, "whether you *can* make words mean so many different things."
>
> "The question is," said Humpty Dumpty, "which is to be master—that's all."
> (Lewis Carroll, *Through the Looking-glass*)

The above-mentioned debate between Hu Shih and D. T. Suzuki could be interpreted in the classical terms of Western hermeneutics as deriving from the opposition between *explanation* (*erklären*) and *understanding* (*verstehen*), with the qualification that, for Suzuki, understanding does not rely on a hermeneutical method but is purely intuitive and belongs to a meta-empirical wisdom called *prajñā*. Nevertheless, both Suzuki and the champions of hermeneutics tend to criticize the objectivism of explanation in the name of a search for meaning or truth. The hermeneutical approach derives from the will to take seriously the truth claims of tradition and the literary or philosophical nature of Chan texts, inasmuch as these texts, contrary to mere "documentary" texts (although the difference, as we have seen, is not obvious), question the reader, "solicit" him, and require in turn that they be "solicited"; thereby the activity places the reader in an eminently dialogical situation. Gérard Genette suggests that "hermeneutic criticism might speak the language of the resumption of meaning and of internal recreation, and structural criticism that of distant speech and intelligible reconstruction. They would thus bring out complementary significations, and their dialogue would be all the more fruitful, on the condition that one could never speak these two languages at once" (Genette 1982, 15).

Are these two approaches simply complementary, or are they mutually exclusive? A text explained (or understood) in purely historical terms is deprived of its truth claim. By merely placing the text in a network of determinations (author, influences, context), one tends to forget that the written text transcends its conditions of production and becomes contemporary with all its readers, by addressing them dialogically. In the scholar's stance of distantiation and "neutrality," there is a kind of existential resignation and a very real ideological prejudice.

We must assume, therefore, that any Chan text is open to multiple readings, none of which is ultimate. In the case of Dōgen's *Shōbōgenzō*, one can show, for example, that the philosophical reading, currently so fashionable, misses the dialogical nature of the work. The question, however, remains: "How is it possible for a cultural text which fulfills a demonstrably ideological function . . . to embody a properly utopian impulse, or to resonate a universal value inconsistent with the narrower limits . . . which inform its more immediate ideological vocation?" (Jameson 1981, 288).

An important sector of Japanese scholarship regarding Chan continues to practice, consciously or not, hermeneutics as defined by Schleiermacher and Dilthey. This amounts to trying to understand the meaning of the words of an author through identifying oneself with him; thus, Chan practitioners try to understand the intent (or meaning) of Bodhidharma's coming from the West.[8] Considering, however, the doubtful character of many attributions of authorship, this kind of identification remains at best precarious, and Japanese scholars like Sekiguchi have thrived in denouncing the abuses committed in this domain.

Hermeneutics, however, has evolved since Dilthey, in particular with Heidegger, Gadamer, and Ricoeur.[9] An important point is for instance Gadamer's notion of "effective history," which allows him to assert that any encounter with a literary or historical document is part and parcel of our history of interpretations (Gadamer 1982, 267–274). If Gadamer is

[8] The Chinese term *yi* is usually translated as "intent" or "meaning." While the notion of "contextual meaning" is contrary to that of "authorial intention," the Buddhist theory of "skillful means" (*upāya*) and of the four *siddhānta* as strategical hermeneutics may provide a mediating position. The *locus classicus* is the *Da zhidu lun* in which the Buddha declares that he offers four kinds of teaching (*siddhānta*) depending on his listeners's capacities: (1) the mundane (*laukika-siddhānta*); (2) the individual (*prāpavruṣika-siddhānta*); (3) the therapeutic (*prātipākṣika-siddhānta*); and (4) the absolute (*pāramārthika-siddhānta*). See Lamotte 1944–1980, 1: 27–55.

[9] For a description of the evolution from Romantic hermeneutics to post-Heideggerian hermeneutics, see Ricoeur 1981, 43–128.

right to point out that the "hermeneutical act" is dialogical—an implication of a reciprocity between the reader and the text or tradition, a dialog that might lead to a "fusion of horizons"—then he tends however to idealize both the tradition and its interpreter. He is insufficiently sensitive to the radical ambiguity that characterizes most traditions and fails to take into account the possibility of a "systematically distorted communication" taking place in the tradition (see Tracy 1987, 66–81). Therefore, he also fails to recognize the need for the kinds of critique of ideology provided by the great "hermeneutics of suspicion." The difficulty of the "fusion of horizons" is not only owing to the flaws of the tradition, but also to the fact that the validity of Gadamer's hermeneutical model requires man's transparency to himself, a condition admittedly rarely met.[10]

Ricoeur's "hermeneutical wager" seems based on a more inclusive model than Gadamer's. Starting from the fact that the symbol "gives to think" (*donne à penser*), Ricoeur finds the duplicity of symbolic double-entendre to be a semantic feature common to all domains of interpretation. More sensitive than Gadamer to the conflictual dimension of the hermeneutical field, he has attempted to take this "conflict of interpretations" seriously; however, he never gave up the hope of overcoming the old dichotomy between "explanation" and "understanding" and of finally reaching a "secondary naiveté" or "secondary immediacy" beyond criticism and suspicion. Ricoeur ends up stressing the complementarity of distantiation and identification (*erklären/ verstehen*), taken as characteristic of social sciences and hermeneutics, respectively.[11] In this case, too, the "conflict of interpretations" may result not so much from a disagreement over the content than a disagreement over the form itself, that is, from the style adopted and in particular from the place given to rhetoric. Despite his longstanding interest in rhetoric, Ricoeur never developed the notion of "metaphorical truth," and his style remains nonmetaphorical and linear. Not surprisingly, over the role of metaphor he most violently opposes Derrida (see Ricoeur 1977, chap. 8; Derrida 1978; LaCapra 1983, 118–144).

An important point, stressed equally by Ricoeur and Derrida, is the relative autonomy of the text, what Derrida calls the "iterability" of the sign (Derrida 1988, 200). The constant process of contextualization and

---

[10] See Jacques Derrida, "Guter Wille zur Macht (1)," in *Text und Interpretation: Deutsche-Französische Debatte*, ed. Philippe Forget (Münich: Wilhelm Fink, 1984); Fred Dallmayr, "Hermeneutics and Deconstruction: Gadamer and Derrida in Dialogue," in *Critical Encounters* (Notre Dame: University of Notre Dame Press, 1987).

[11] Ricoeur writes for instance: "So if there is a hermeneutics . . . , it must be constituted across the mediation rather than against the current of structural explanation. . . . Then truth and method do not constitute a disjunction but rather a dialectical process" (Ricoeur 1981, 92–93).

decontextualization to which both the sign and the text are subjected ends the fetishisms of the "original text" and the "authorized interpretation" and allows a broader understanding of the tradition. However, it can also engender an interpretive drift, as is apparent, for example, from the way some critics have misread Derrida's notion of "deconstruction," despite the fact that Derrida was the first to recognize that all interpretations are not equal. We must be wary of misinterpreting Derrida as advocating a "free play of meaning." Just as, for instance, Nietzsche's cryptic sentence, "I forgot my umbrella," remains forever open to interpretation (Derrida 1978, 103–113), so do Zen kōan—if only because "meaning is contextual but context is boundless" (Culler 1982, 123). This does not imply that the kōan may mean just anything, but that one can always imagine new contexts, new interpretations of the "generalized text." Although there is no single "true" reading, and even though interpretation can be considered a "generalized misreading," some misreadings remain within the scope of the text and reveal its complexity and heterogeneity, while others simply do violence to the text—reducing it to one of its levels, impoverishing its polysemy, or trying to check its dissemination. Even if it is not always easy to walk the middle way between the "affective fallacy," a relativism that loses the text in the reader's response, and the "intentional fallacy," which loses the text in the author and its idealized intention, there is still plenty of room to argue that some misreadings are authenticated by their fruitfulness. A case in point would be the way in which Dōgen seems to have misread his master Rujing's words as *shinjin datsuraku*, "dropping off body and mind," instead of a more traditional "dropping off the mind's dust." This, again, does not mean that misreading implies true reading. In this case, the misreading has proved more original and fruitful than the supposedly "original" reading. When Alice objects to Humpty Dumpty's arbitrary definitions, "That's a great deal to make one word mean," Humpty Dumpty replies: "When I make a word do a lot of work like that, ... I always pay it extra" (Carroll 1960, 187). The deconstructionist tempted to behave like Humpty Dumpty must realize that his freedom of interpretation has a cost.

According to Ricoeur, the abolition of a first order reference that takes place when a text is decontextualized is what allows the freeing of a second order reference. Thus, the meaning of a work "is not something hidden behind the text, but something disclosed in front of it" (Ricoeur 1981, 218), and this meaning, in turn, produces a "self-understanding in front of the work" (ibid., 142). In Chan terms, Ricoeur may be said to adopt a "gradualist" standpoint when he argues that "we understand ourselves only by the long detour of the signs of humanity deposited in cultural works" (ibid., 143). This type of interpretation frees the text from not only the author but also a too narrowly dialogical situation. As Bakhtin already pointed out, there exists neither first nor last discourse, and the context does not know any limit.

The obvious danger here is the temptation to attribute to the authors' intention the "excess of meaning" and the deconstructive aspects of his work that emerge in later recontextualizations. Here again, Dōgen's work may be a case in point. The interpretation cannot limit itself to the narrow dialogical situation that produced the text; neither can this situation be entirely ignored, for it remains sedimented in the text itself. Even if there is something to be gained by bringing a twelfth-century work like the *Shōbōgenzō* into the field of contemporary Western philosophy, this does not make Dōgen first and foremost an "incomparable philosopher" (Kasulis 1985). Even though meaning is contextual and context boundless, some contexts remain more relevant than others. Although not entirely illegitimate, the current attempt to interpret Dōgen as a modern (or even postmodern) thinker either relies too often on an "intentional fallacy" where the critic claims to understand what "Dōgen" meant by such and such an expression or tends to turn into a half-baked "poietic production" disguised as commentary, that is, a subjective fiction that refuses to tell its name. Better to write, then, as the Japanese writer Inoue Hisashi did, a play in which the fictional nature of the main actor, Dōgen, is evident?[12]

Like Gadamer, Ricoeur introduced a moment of distantiation in the hermeneutical process. According to Ricoeur, distantiation is the condition of understanding at all levels of analysis (Ricoeur 1981, 144). Although it may be useful to free the reader from the fetishism of the author, some texts are nevertheless eminently "authorial," and it seems difficult to dispense entirely with their author. The text is determined by the structures of language *and* by the author. The author is bound by his language, but also has within his bondage a certain freedom. He can be played by language when he thinks that he controls it, but he can also play with language while seeming to surrender to it. Thus, it is possible neither to reduce one of these levels—language and author—to the other nor to dispense with either. Significantly, after attempting to do away with the notion of the author in his theoretical period, Foucault returned to it in his later work.

Even though it pays more attention than Gadamerian "philosophical hermeneutics" to the possibility of "systematic distortion" in traditions under study (Tracy 1981, 137), the "hermeneutics or retrieval" advocated

[12] See Inoue Hisashi, *Dōgen no bōken* (The Adventures of Dōgen) (Tokyo: Shinchō bunko 1971). The play opens in a mental institution with a psychopath, who suffers from a recurring dream in which he is a thirteenth-century monk named Dōgen. The scene then shifts to Dōgen, telling his disciples that he has this recurring dream in which he is a psychopath in a mental institution. The play unfolds through these constant shifts between two levels of reality; the dramatic effect is reinforced by the fact that Dōgen's disciples and the psychotherapists are played by the same actors.

by Ricoeur does not dwell on the aporia defined as the "conflict of interpretations." Arguing that misunderstanding is "homogeneous with understanding and of the same genre" (Ricoeur 1981, 83) does not allow him to consider seriously the possibility of what we could call, taking our cue from Jean-François Lyotard, a "*différend* of interpretations." For Ricoeur, "the assertion that misunderstanding is supported by a prior understanding is a pre-eminent meta-critical theme" (Ricoeur 1981, 77). Like Gadamer, Ricoeur relies on the model described by Schleiermacher, according to which the *grammatical* level of interpretation (i.e., understanding the utterance as a fact of language) and the *technical* level (i.e., understanding the utterance as an individual act) have equal status (ibid., 47). However, he ends up hierarchizing those levels; he gives the hermeneutical approach (the *technical* level) precedence over the structural approach (the *grammatical* level) and thereby gives the hermeneutics of retrieval the precedence over the hermeneutics of suspicion. Ricoeur integrates these approaches through a two-tiered, hierarchical model, a kind of "militant syncretism" that calls to mind the Two Truths theory and the doctrinal classifications (Ch. *panjiao*) of Chinese Buddhism (Ricoeur 1981, 161). Claiming to overcome the dichotomy between understanding and explanation (truth *or* method) by presenting the hermeneutical endeavor as a dialectical process that reconciles "truth *and* method" (*Warheit und Methode*), Ricoeur is oblivious to the fact that his use of the conjunction *and* still retains the old metaphysical hierarchy and implies that method is, if not ancillary, at least second to truth (Ricoeur 1981, 92–93). He does not consider the other obvious possibility, one that links method *and* truth— where truth, in a Nietzschean sense, is always the product of a specific discourse inasmuch as the means necessarily affect the end. Although Ricoeur seems able to integrate at little cost—as two complementary moments of the (meta)hermeneutical process—the structural and hermeneutical critiques, he may find it more difficult to integrate—as he claims he is doing—the hermeneutics of suspicion with the hermeneutics of faith or retrieval, for both are exclusive and unsynthesizable.[13]

The "hermeneutics of suspicion" to which Ricoeur pays lip service finds a more serious advocate in the Marxist critic Fredric Jameson. From the outset, Jameson stresses what Ricoeur, in his attempt at a synthesis, has tended to forget: namely, that this type of hermeneutics is exclusive; it refuses to be reduced to a dialectical moment leading toward a final reconciliation in the "conflict of interpretations." Jameson thinks that the ideological critique must have the final word. If ideology, as defined by Ricoeur, is the "allegedly disinterested knowledge which serves to conceal an inter-

---

[13] David Tracy too makes a claim for the greater adequacy of the hermeneutical model because the latter is able to incorporate the formalist moment without abandoning the priority of reception. See Tracy 1981, 136, 147–149; 1987, 28–46.

est under the guise of a rationalization," hermeneutics remains ideological to the extent that it forgets or occults its own performance or
performativity.[14]

However, the critique of ideology is itself based on a normative vision, which is not, as in the case of traditional hermeneutics, located
"upstream," in an origin such as the tradition, but ahead of us—
"downstream." It is therefore itself performative, to the extent that it does
not acknowledge this. Jameson seems to remain influenced by Ricoeur's
notion of the "two hermeneutics," and he aims at simultaneously practic-
ing what he calls *ideological* and *utopian* analysis (Jameson 1981, 235,
281–299). After quoting Walter Benjamin's famous aphorism, "there has
never been a document of culture which was not at one and the same time a
document of barbarism" (ibid., 281), Jameson suggests that the reverse
may equally be true: there is after all a *utopian* intent in every ideological
discourse. However, despite Jameson's stress on the equivalence of the
ideological and the utopian moments of his analysis, the negative connota-
tion of the term *utopian* suggests that, contrary to Ricoeur, he doubts that
the positive hermeneutics deriving from these utopian impulses has the
same claim to unveil reality as does the negative, "ideological" hermeneutics. On the one hand, Jameson considers that the text's main goal is to
solve, on the symbolical or imaginary level, the conflicts of an essentially
agonistic reality, conflicts understood in terms of class struggle. Thus,
ideals are the inverted image of reality and play a wish-fulfilling function.
In the end, however, Jameson considers that the task of the interpreter is to
bring a hermeneutical *coincidentia oppositorum*: "To think dialectically is
to invent a space from which to think these two identical yet antagonistic
features together all at once" (ibid., 235).

In most cases, however, neither the text nor the reader seem able to come
to terms with what remains an aporia. A case in point is a text entitled
Keisei sanshoku (The Sounds of the Valley Stream, the Forms of the Mountains), putatively a collective instruction delivered by Dōgen in 1240 and
later included in the *Shōbōgenzō*. In the second half of this piece, one finds
a passage that has embarrassed many commentators and that seems at
odds with the highly poetical and philosophical content of the first half.
After describing various cases of awakening at the contact of natural
phenomena—these phenomena being perceived here as manifestations of
the *Dharmakāya* or Cosmic Body of the Buddha—Dōgen proceeds to
discuss the historical circumstances of the transmission of Chan. Suddenly
changing his tone, Dōgen vehemently attacks two Chinese Buddhist priests
named Bodhiruci (d. 527) and Huiguang (468–537), two figures who

---

[14] On ideology, see Ricoeur 1981, 223–246. Louis Althusser defines the term as "the
imaginary representation of the subject's relationship to his or her real conditions of existence.
See Althusser 162.

played important roles under the Northern Wei as translators and scholastics of the epistemological tradition (Yogācāra) (*T.* 82, 2583: 41a). A native of central India, Bodhiruci is considered to have been the foremost translator of that period, and Huiguang is regarded as one patriarch of the Vinaya school. Dōgen's contempt for these two men is not just prompted by their intellectual and mundane character, but rather by the sinister role that they had supposedly played in the assassination of Bodhidharma. While several contemporary Chan masters questioned that story, Dōgen uncritically accepted it. What is surprising, however, is not his acceptance, but the extreme passion with which he denounces these two men, whom he calls "curs" and whose attachment to wealth and honor he compares to the defilement of excrement. Commenting on this passage, the Zen master and scholar Mujaku Dōchū felt compelled to write in his *Eihei Shōbōgenzō Senpyō*: "To insult monks by calling them 'curs' is not the language of someone who has reached awakening" (Kagamishima 1961, 229).

Let us, therefore, reexamine the key role of this passage in the general economy of the *Keisei sanshoku*. The text is composed of two parts: the first, essentially descriptive, takes as its themes nature and awakening, or more precisely awakening *through* the perception of nature and *as* an event of nature. In the second part, the style of which is clearly prescriptive, Dōgen exhorts his disciples to produce the thought of awakening (J. *bodaishin*, Sk. *bodhicitta*) and to repent their past errors, and he warns them against various obstacles on the path. His strong language is sometimes interpreted as an expression of the incisive eloquence of a preacher concerned with detracting his listeners from the wrong path.

The relation between the two parts of the text is not clear, and commentators have tended to read them separately and emphasize the first. Thus, the interpretation renders the text asymmetrical. Interestingly, a similar asymmetry is said to characterize Dōgen's entire work, the first phase of which (until 1242) consists of more "philosophical" material, whereas sectarian preoccupations and disciplinary rigorism seem to prevail in the second phase (1243–1253). One could therefore argue that the radicalism of youth gave way to the conservatism of maturity, and that *Keisei sanshoku*, written in 1240, is a transitional text. Despite its plausibility, this interpretation leaves a number of questions unanswered. This interpretation does not help us account for Dōgen's abrupt change of mind (and of language), and it is able to give coherence to his thought only by neglecting the second part of *Keisei sanshoku*—or worse, of his entire oeuvre. It is clear, however, that Dōgen was trying to base his prescriptive discourse on the ontological description of the world of awakening that is provided in the first part of that text and that the two parts were for him indissociable. In other chapters of the *Shōbōgenzō*, like *Sansuikyō* (The Sūtra of Mountains and Rivers), the descriptive and prescriptive passages are more intimately mixed, and only by doing violence to the text can the interpretation separate them. We seem therefore justified in shifting the text's center of gravity toward the second part and, more precisely, toward the most violently polemical passages. Here lies the heart of the problem, for Dōgen as for his interpreter.

This rhetorical violence reveals the essentially agonistic nature of Chan/Zen. According to Dōgen, the "harmony of Chan and the teachings" (*kyōzen itchi*) advocated by his contemporaries—and rivals—is superficial, and the antagonism between true Chan and other teachings is properly "spiritual." Hermeneutics must take this fact into account, not attempt to elude it. Thus, in spite of the appearances, the first part of *Keisei sanshoku* (descriptive utterance) derives from the second (prescriptive discourse), not the other way around. Consequently, the entire text, including the ontological/poetical "description" of the world of awakening, is ultimately performative, rhetorical, and dialogical.

An obvious danger in the various types of hermeneutics examined above is hermeneutical overkill: for the hermeneutical critic, as for the psychoanalyst, nothing is left to chance; everything is saturated with meaning. In his *Empire of Signs*, Barthes remarked that "the West moistens everything with meaning" (Barthes 1982, 70). The opposite attitude, exemplified by Barthes in the same book, is to reduce everything to the free "play of the signifier" (in this case Sino-Japanese characters) and to fail to understand the constraints imposed by the signified on the readers (except on Barthes himself, for lack of linguistic competency).

From "within" the hermeneutical tradition as it were, Derrida has been a powerful critic of the dialectical, teleological, and totalizing hermeneutics. Derrida's notion of "dissemination" prevents the interpreter from gathering "the totality of a text in the truth of its meaning," and it marks out the irreducible and generative multiplicity of the text (Derrida 1972b, 62). Derrida also pointed out the existence of two "interpretations of interpretation" that are absolutely irreconcilable, even if we live them simultaneously actually and reconcile them "in an obscure economy": the one seeks to decipher a truth or an origin free from freeplay; the other affirms freeplay and is no longer turned toward the origin, the full presence (Derrida 1970, 264–265).

The above discussion has alerted us to both the dangers of a facile eclecticism and the limitations of the two-tiered hermeneutics advocated by Ricoeur. But, instead of leading to some neutralized neutrality, the historical, structural, and hermeneutical approaches may provide a convenient arsenal for a performative scholarship that remains sensitive to the various contexts of the tradition considered. Thus, one may chose to use either history against philosophy when confronted with essentialist theories such as the "philosophical" interpretation of Dōgen or philosophy against history when confronted with historicism (see Culler 1982, 129). These methodological choices call to mind the Buddhist "skillful means" (*upāya*). The paradigm is provided by the Buddha himself, who preached eternalism to the partisans of nihilism and emptiness to the partisans of eternalism. Accordingly, by limiting the meaning of a complex literary text like the *Shōbōgenzō* to ideas appropriate to a specific historical period (Kamakura), we would merely reduce a (complex) text to another, apparently simpler, (con)text, forgetting in the process that this context is still a text. In the last analysis, even Dōgen's life, his bio-*graphy*, has only textual existence for us. In Derrida's words, history belongs to the "generalized text."

Despite its prefix, post-structuralism does not so much imply a posteriority (hence superiority) as the abandonment of any teleological (and metaphysical) perspective. Deconstruction, as a simultaneously and paradoxically hermeneutical and antihermeneutical procedure, has been defined as a "careful teasing out of warring forces of signification within the text" (Johnson 1980, 5). Deconstruction seeks primarily to reveal "the asymmetrical opposition or value-laden hierarchy that structures the text" and to question "whether the second term of an opposition, treated as a negative, marginal or supplementary version of the first, does not prove to be the condition of possibility of the first" (Culler 1982, 213). We have seen, for instance, how a text like the *Shōbōgenzō* "differs from itself" in "points of condensation" where its polemical intent surfaces. The submerged voice seems in this case to be that of the rival Darumashū (often designed in the *Shōbōgenzō* as the "Senika heresy"). Thus, the teachings of the Darumashū form the pre-text, the hidden matrix, the elusive discourse on which Dōgen's own discourse is surreptitiously grafted (see Faure 1987a, 1987b).

Another exponent of deconstruction, Paul de Man, has analyzed the way in which literary language prefigures its own misunderstanding and how texts allegorically demonstrate the inadequacy of their readers' possible interpretive moves (de Man 1983, 102–141). It would be interesting to examine in this light certain chapters of the *Shōbōgenzō*; for example, in *Kattō* ("Vines," a metaphor for the entanglements of words and passions), Dōgen declares: "Generally, saints set out in their practice to cut off the roots of the vines, but they do not realize that cutting off means disentangling the vines, nor do they know how to entangle the vines. Thus, how could they understand that the transmission is achieved through vines, and in the midst of vines? Rare are those who know that the transmission of the Dharma is not distinct from these vines" (Terada and Mizuno 1975, 1:25). According to de Man, texts thematize interpretive operations and thus represent in advance the dramas that give life to the tradition of their interpretation. One can think, for example, of the way in which the so-called *Treatise of Bodhidharma* established a dialectical tension between reliance on and independence from the written word, a dialectic that soon collapsed with the emergence of conflicting interpretations such as the theories of the "special transmission outside the Scriptures" (J. *kyōge betsuden*) and of the "harmony of Chan and the Scriptures" (*kyōzen itchi*).

TOWARD A PERFORMATIVE SCHOLARSHIP

Before proceeding to a discussion of yet another alternative, it may be useful to briefly review the considerations that prompt a departure from existing modes of Chan/Zen scholarship. We have seen that to establish itself historiographical discourse replicated or reinscribed many discursive strategies elaborated in the course of the Chan tradition. If we want now to rethink that tradition, it is clear that our conception of scholarship also has to change to a certain extent. Past scholarship affects our understanding of Chan, and in turn, our understanding of Chan affects the type of scholarship we may perform—hence the transferential relationships between the scholar and its object. This circular causality is a fact that one may choose to regret or to affirm, but to acknowledge it already implies a radical departure from traditional Chan studies.

The shift from the hermeneutical model to the performative model is suggested by the evolution of Chan itself: as we will see, the use of kōan can be "interpreted" (or "performed") as a departure from the traditional Buddhist standpoint based on commentary and referential truth, toward a rhetorical use of the scriptures aimed at the production of an apparently "free-floating" truth. The hermeneutics of suspicion itself, by teaching us to look for a deep, hidden meaning behind the surface of the text, had already loosened the bond between meaning and "content" (thereby permitting a shift from "latent" or deep meaning to more "formal" and "superficial" meanings). Jameson, in particular, taught us to read a text as revealing social conflicts (Jameson 1981). The dialogical tensions in the *Shōbōgenzō*, for example, revealed a doctrinal—as well as social—conflict between Dōgen and the adepts of the Darumashū.

We could now, as Michael Riffaterre has done for poetry, say that the point of a Chan text or a kōan lies not so much in its superficial or deep meaning as in its *significance* (Riffaterre 1984, 2–3). Like poetry and literature (and possibly all discourse), kōan often say one thing and mean another, let alone mean one thing and achieve another. Thus, a pragmatic or performative analysis of discourse is needed to reintroduce the dialogical dimension often neglected by hermeneutics. However, there can be no simple determination by context, because the context itself, at least in the case of Chan discourse, remains largely textual and dialectically related to the "literary" text. With regard to the textual paradigm "Bodhidharma," we have already noted the necessity to take the historical contingencies into account even while taking the structural approach. Assuming the "iterability of the sign" (Derrida 1988, 200)—that is, the endless "recontextualization" of any utterance, text, or recorded event—we have to conclude that all religious, ideological, or scholarly standpoints are eventually reinscribed in new, complex, and at times conflicting, strategies. The Chan advocacy of spiritual freedom, for instance, has paradoxically sometimes led to assert the most conservative aspects of the tradition; and the assertion of the "pleasure of the text," the interest in marginality or the denunciation of ideologies such as Orientalism in contemporary scholarship have rendered specific payoffs and reinforced existing structures. Not unlike some recent trends in Western philosophy, literary criticism, or anthropology, Chan soon lost its subversive power to become another powerful, hence repressive, institution. To avoid this kind of routinization, it is insufficient simply to condemn it loudly, for such condemnations merely replicate or reinforce the scapegoating mechanisms that characterize the dominant orthodoxy; nor is it sufficient, a fortiori, to simply endorse that orthodoxy, with or without awareness of its ideological effects.

The performative aspect of discourse, whether that of Chan or of scholarship, derives from its rhetorical nature. As Nietzsche pointed out, no language is purely constative. Often in spite of itself, scholars waxe metaphorical, even though they tend to resort to "white metaphors" to keep a pretense of scientificity. Chan and scholarly texts constitute therefore two types of symbolic and metaphorical discourse. Not only is it important, therefore, to unravel the symbolic configurations that structure these discourses, but one must also bring to light their performative dimension. Like ritual, according to Stanley Tambiah, any text or speech-act "symbolically and/or iconically represents the cosmos and at the same time indexically legitimates and realizes social hierarchies" (Tambiah 1981, 153). But precisely, as Marc Augé puts it, the difficulty is to think simultaneously these two dimensions—symbol and function (Augé 1982a, 32).

It appears that interpretation itself is an act, a performance. Therefore, hermeneutics is not the impartial method it claims to be; it becomes a "performative ritual," which not only has (or deciphers) a meaning but also performs a specific social and ideological role (see Sullivan 1986, 28–30). To return to Dōgen's example, the mere fact of reading him as an "incomparable philosopher" or a "medieval religious/sectarian figure" significantly affects the emerging subfield labeled Dōgen Studies and its various academic stakes. There is no denying that scholars are people who have vested interests in promoting their personal interpretations of such apparently remote phenomena as Kamakura Zen or Japanese religion/philosophy. While Bourdieu, with his notion of "socio-analysis" (Bourdieu 1979, 595), and Lyotard, with his performative use of Wittgenstein's notion of "language games" (Lyotard and Thébaud 1985), also point out various aspects of the problem, perhaps the most thorough analysis of this phenomenon was that attempted by Foucault, who rejected the hermeneutics of suspicion and its attempt to reach a deeper meaning. Foucault was no longer interested in revealing, like Jameson, the implicit ideology of discourses, for even behind his own "will to truth," he discerned the workings of power. It is not sufficient to characterize a type of discourse as ideological because that characterization is itself performative (Dreyfus and Rabinow 1983, 123–125, 180–182). Foucault therefore constantly rejected the temptation of "deep hermeneutics"—whether of belief or of suspicion—by showing that these may be strategies of power that maintain the subject "subjected."

According to this analysis, hermeneutics remains a case of what in Chan parlance one might call "seeking in the depths what one has left behind in the shallows." One is reminded of Linji and many other Chan masters stressing that there is no Dharma to be found, nothing to understand or to obtain. According to this (non)interpretive model, Chan, as it developed around the ninth century, can be characterized as a rhetorical tradition, that is, a tradition turned forward—in contrast with the exegetical tradition always looking back toward the original text and the originary truth it allegedly hides and reveals (Charles 1985). To be sure, many Chan texts still refer to a primordial truth, a perennial Dharma to which the adept must conform, a mythic origin that must be reenacted in individual practice through a meeting "face to face" with the ancient patriarchs. As is well-known, much of Chan doctrine derives from the Tathāgatagarbha tradition and its speculations on the Buddha-nature, and early Chan had strong "essentialist" overtones. The dynamic reinterpretation of this model paradoxically led Chan adepts to affirm pure spontaneity and to see the Dharma as being "performed," "actualized"; an actualization that does not imply, however, any previous "latence." Despite the reference to the past patriarchs, the tradition was seen (at least by some) as constantly emerging, as a kind of ongoing revelation taking place through the "live words" of Chan masters. Although the distinction between "live word" (Ch. huoju) and "dead word" (siju) seems to have developed primarily in Chan as a hermeneutical tool, it implied a distinction between the "performative" and the "communicative" functions of language and, in this sense, paved the way to a departure from hermeneutics (see Buswell 1988).

We seem to move, at least with this strand of Chan sometimes labeled "classical," toward a performative conception of truth, the best expression of which may possibly be found in the ritualized "encounter" between master and disciple.[15] This breakthrough, however, was not and probably could not be definitive, and, perhaps due to routinization, the hermeneuti-

cal model soon resurfaced. Toward the Song, the iconoclastic utterances of
the patriarchs themselves became enshrined as icons in the "Recorded
Sayings" (*yulu*), and the mood returned to a veneration of the words of
"past Buddhas," a Chan "hermeneutics of retrieval." The dialectic between the hermeneutical and the performative tendencies remained, and all
later masters felt compelled to adopt a performative "style," even when
adding their own orthodox comments to the sedimented glosses (*jakugo*)
of their predecessors. At any rate, because Chan texts, perhaps more than
any other texts, embody this dual tendency, there is clearly a need for
another "reading" that would not be strictly hermeneutical.

The performative nature of Chan texts derives from their strategic or
tactical use, which appears to take precedence over their actual content.
Thus, Chan performers came to use the "dead words" of the Buddhist
scriptures as "live words." This technique is already at work in early Chan
texts such as the *Guanxin lun*, a treatise in which Shenxiu, while offering a
"reinterpretation" of various rubrics of traditional Buddhism, seems at
first glance to remain formally bound by the hermeneutical model but has
already moved beyond it.[16] In the Chan controversy over subitism, scriptures such as the *Laṅkāvatāra-sūtra* and the *Vajracchedikā* became used as
emblems or rallying symbols of the two protagonists, namely, the Northern and Southern schools. This dichotomy between schools and texts was
uncritically accepted by many modern scholars, among whom was D. T.
Suzuki, who contrasted the "gradualist" content of the *Laṅkāvatāra-sūtra*
with the "sudden" content of the *Vajracchedikā* (Suzuki 1977, 60–62).
The *Laṅkāvatāra-sūtra*, however, was apparently transmitted in the early
Chan school more as a talismanic text than as a doctrinal scripture, and its
doctrinal content was not really a matter of great interest to Chan practitioners (Faure 1988). Even Chan "classics" such as the *Platform Sūtra of
the Sixth Patriarch*, the *Shōbōgenzō*, and the "Recorded Sayings" (*yulu*) of
most Chan/Zen masters, served primarily as emblems of legitimacy. Applying to these texts Tambiah's insights on ritual, we might say that they had a

---

[15] As Tambiah as shown in another context, ritual, being simultaneously symbolic and
performative, has a duplex structure. It can be said to be performative in three senses: in the
Austinian sense, in its staged performance aspect, and in its value as an index. This definition
seems to apply to the "encounter" ritual, to the very extent that it became a ritual, that is, lost
some of its alleged spontaneity (Tambiah 1981).

[16] It may be argued that Shenxiu's "spiritual interpretation" of Buddhist scriptures resembles the allegorical interpretation of Christian Scriptures and, as such, remains entirely within
the framework of traditional hermeneutics. Whereas the allegorical interpretation of Christian texts attempted to reduce textual discrepancies to the unique authorized interpretation of
the Church, Shenxiu's "allegorical" interpretations actively reinterpret traditional Buddhist
notions in an idiosyncratic and unwarranted fashion—to serve the purposes (didactic or
otherwise) of the "interpreter."

duplex existence as a symbol and an index; they simultaneously represented truth and contributed to social differentiation.[17]

It may therefore be legitimate to adopt what Roman Jakobson calls the "performative model of discourse," that is, to consider Chan discourse as an apparatus for the production (and simultaneous rarefaction) of "meaning" rather than for communication.[18] As I discuss in chapter 7, language in Chan was not considered a transparent medium. The performative (or, more precisely, *perlocutionary*) function of language derives from its metaphorical nature.[19] Therefore, Chan discourse is not simply reflecting realities or expressing truths; it is actively producing them, "impressing" them on an audience. Likewise, the Chan practitioner does not so much try to discover his true hidden self (in Socratic fashion) as to invent or "produce" himself.[20] Truth is produced, not revealed, in a dialogical encounter that brings to mind the "authentic" dialogues analyzed by Gadamer, in which, like in a game, something that transcends each participant's will takes over and words "reveal" to them what they are thinking.

This process is somewhat similar to what sometimes takes place in poetical writing and even in such prosaic endeavors as scholarly writing. Therefore, a consciously performative scholarship becomes more concerned with the "content of its form" (White 1987), and the recognition of its literariness prevents its author from claiming the objectivity of "representation," the neutrality of the commentary. Not unlike recent trends in literary criticism, Chan writers (or locutors) achieved (or tried to achieve) a "freedom from the signifier." There ensued a kind of weightlessness, a feeling of elation conspicuous in some of the *Recorded Sayings* literature, although it eventually turned into its opposite with the ritualization of the

[17] An interesting, although somewhat different, example of performative use of a scripture is that of the *Heart Sūtra*, a predominantly philosophical text that came to be used as a *dhāraṇī* (see Lopez 1990). This sūtra, an epitome of Mahāyāna doctrine, is nowadays recited in the temples of all Japanese Buddhist sects, including Zen. The risk here is to reproduce the metaphysical distinction that opposes "philosophy" (as truth) to "dhāraṇī" (as superstition) and considers the final dhāraṇī of the *Heart Sūtra*, or the use of the whole text as a dhāraṇī, as a later interpolation or deviation. A number of other scriptures, like the *Laṅkāvatāra-sūtra* and the apocryphal *Śūraṃgama-sūtra* were also used in Chan primarily for their dhāraṇī.

[18] The term *meaning* is used here in a broad sense, as the result of what Austin called the "perlocutionary" force of language, because dhāraṇī have such a performative meaning (or better, significance), while often being deprived of linguistic meaning.

[19] Austin defines perlocutionary acts as "what we bring about or achieve by saying something, such as convincing, persuading, deterring, and even, say, surprising or misleading" (Austin 1962, 109).

[20] Conversely, Socrates' emphasis on retrieving the hidden self constituted a departure from the archaic Greek way of expressing the self by "acting out, publicly, in an altogether unreflexive manner" (Stroumsa 1990, 28).

genre. Unfortunately, this feeling has not yet had a chance to pervade Chan/Zen scholarship.

However, as Paul de Man pointed out, the realizations that there is no purely constative language as scientifically-minded scholars like to believe, that all language is an act, and that all constative language is performative, puts us in a strange predicament. For, once we become aware that "deconstruction states the fallacy of reference in a necessarily referential mode" (de Man 1983, 125), we cannot simply replace knowledge by performance or hermeneutics by deconstruction. Regarding the aporia between performative and constative language, de Man argues that "the differentiation between performative and constative language is undecidable: the deconstruction leading from the one model to the other is irreversible but it always remains suspended, regardless of how often it is repeated" (ibid., 130).

Might this be the very aporia of the kōan? We return to this question. For the time being suffice it to note that Chan dialogues, like Chan scholarship, are language games that "one can enter into but not play," for they are "games that make us into their players" (Lyotard and Thébaud 1985, 51). One is thus, according to Lyotard, always caught up in one (or several) pragmatics of language.[21] Unable as we are to make up a new game and to leave behind the discourse of Western metaphysics or Buddhism, we must content ourselves with making up new moves in an old game, using these two sets (Western and Buddhist) of language games to check each other.

According to Derrida, the deconstructive reading recognizes the "essential" nature of a seemingly accidental occurrence when the latter is bound to occur; that is, it blurs the metaphysical distinction between essence and accident by revealing the "essential" contamination of any pure essence (Derrida 1988, 218; see also Staten 1984, 124). When applied to the tradition read as a text, this insight shows that phenomena such as routinization or syncretism cannot be simply characterized as secondary, derivative occurrences. Nevertheless, while this reading also discloses the literary, metaphorical, and "fundamentally" performative nature of all scholarship, it does maintain the polarity between the constative and the performative, the literal and the metaphorical. It never attempts to reduce discourse to its metaphorical or performative aspects. The cognitive and communicative aspects retain their logical (or illogical) priority. If, to paraphrase Laozi, all truths seem paradoxical, it does not follow that all paradoxes are true; even true paradoxes still need a *doxa* to depart from. Likewise, in the Two Truths theory, the identity of the relative with the

[21] In contrast to the syntactical and semantical standpoints, which correspond broadly to the formal/structuralist and hermeneutical approaches described above, pragmatics describe the ways in which interlocutors who aim at affecting each other can use formulas (see Ducrot and Todorov 1979). It therefore subordinates structure and symbol to function.

absolute does not collapse the distinction; instead, it retains the "logical" priority of the absolute. To affirm the opposite, as some radical interpreters of Chan have done, is to reduce everything to the relative and end up advocating a "naturalist" position that loses the Middle Path. The characteristic of the Two Truths theory is perhaps, paradoxically, that they are not hierarchizable, and in this sense the "naturalist" position might be partly justified. Despite the subitist claim, the two truths cannot be seen simultaneously (see Faure 1991, 53–78). In similar fashion, as noted earlier, the rival hermeneutics of suspicion and of retrieval resist to synthesis. But, of course, to say this is already to make way for an evasion of the aporia, a resolution of the *différend*.

Through the transferential relationship between the scholar and his object, the shift from the hermeneutic model to the performative model, which characterized the evolution of Chan during the Tang, may reappear in Chan/Zen scholarship.[22] Although it is true that scholars tend to project surreptitiously their own thought categories on their object of study, one can also hope that, *par la force des choses*, the resilient object—here the Chan tradition—in turn projects its structures onto the theoretical approach. The unmasking of the performative nature of scholarly discourse eventually reaches its own limits, if it does not want to dissolve into fictional discourse, thereby erasing the generative tension between the two poles. As Derrida once remarked, "A text is not a text unless it hides from the first comer, from the first glance, the laws of its composition and the rules of its games" (Derrida 1981, 63). Ultimately, revealing is always hiding; any insight generates its own blindness; any deconstruction is always already a reconstruction.

---

[22] As LaCapra points out, "in a transferential relation one tends to repeat in a displaced way the very processes that are active (at times uncritically) in one's object of inquiring. . . . The point is not simply to indulge in transferential relations or to deny them. It is to 'work through' them in a 'dialogic' fashion that strives for empirically and critically controlled reciprocity in an exchange" (LaCapra 1988, 682–683).

PART TWO

Chapter Five

SPACE AND PLACE

> Compassion is the total opening in which the Buddha had
> neither ground nor territory. . . . Whereas passion seizes
> upon a territory and holds on to it, he taught a dharma
> devoid of passion, devoid of aggression.
> (Chogyam Trungpa, *Myth of Freedom*)

> Identify yourself with space and there is no place
> that you will not embrace.
> (Shenhui)

IN THIS CHAPTER, I examine how two very different types of religious discourse—those of Chan and of "local religion—interacted; more precisely, I study how these discourses invested a particular geographical and/or mental space and what they have to say specifically about space. By so doing, I hope to understand how "the field and the gaze are tied to each other by codes of knowledge," in what Foucault called the "deep structures of visibility" (Foucault 1963: 89). In China, these epistemological and ideological structures were drastically modified during the Tang, and this modification coincided with sociopolitical changes, in particular with imperial centralization. The rise of the "Chan patriarchs" as foci of veneration, at the turn of the eighth century, contributed to the creation of a new "sacred geography." A network of cultic centers loosely structuring the wanderings (*anxing*) of the "clouds and waters" (*yunshui*)—as Chan monks were called—were superimposed on and tended to supersede traditional pilgrimage sites. Chan may therefore be seen as part of a larger movement of "spatialization of thought," and this spatialization was also a "delocalization." Another aspect of this phenomenon was the Tantric "mandalization" of space, which integrated all the various places and deities of local traditions into the abstract space of the maṇḍala. A similar logic presided to the reorganization of the imperial capital, according to a model derived from traditional Buddhist cosmology, but also the Yin/Yang theories of Han cosmology. Another Buddhist model of spatial/political organization was the Huayan conception of the universe as a hierarchized, centralized, interpenetrating reality, with the Tathāgata/emperor at its center. Thus, the symbolic mapping achieved by Buddhism during the Tang dynasty clearly had a strong sociopolitical impact.

Unlike "great traditions," such as Buddhism, local religion fails to provide an elaborate theoretical discourse: its voice is often repressed and can be heard only indirectly in the echoes of legend and hagiography. In particular, stories staging a Buddhist monk and a local god—the latter often in animal form (snake, tiger, dragon)—seem to express the confrontation of two incommensurable, yet coexisting visions of the world: the unlocalized (or "utopian") conceptions of Buddhism as universal doctrine and the localized (and "locative") beliefs of local religion as ritual practice.[1] I shall argue that this—always localized—tension between localizing and unlocalizing tendencies, between a specific *place* and abstract *space*, predates any polarization into "great" and "little" traditions or whatever other paradigm we may use; moreover, it is essential to the vitality of a tradition like Buddhism.[2]

CHAN AND LOCAL SPIRITS

Since the time of the Buddha, monks have been known to convert snakes or dragons (*Nāga*) to the Buddhist Dharma and/or to receive protection from them. In most cases, these snakes are the form assumed by a local deity who, once converted, decides to protect Buddhism.[3] The best-known example is that of the Nāga Mucilinda, who protected the newly awakened Śākyamuni from a storm by providing him shelter under his eightfold hood. The legitimizing role of the converted Nāga as guardian of a particular territory is well documented for Indian Buddhism (see Bloss 1973; Rawlinson 1986). In China, dragons and tigers came to perform the same function of *genii loci*.[4]

[1] I use Jonathan Z. Smith's terminology in a slightly modified fashion. In his book *Map is Not Territory*, Smith defines the *locative* vision as emphasizing place and the *utopian* vision as stressing the value of being in no place (1978, 101). He further defines the former as a normative, imperial worldview, while the latter reflects a peripheral, disruptive tendency (1978, 293, 309). I believe that, in the cases of Chan Buddhism and of Chinese popular religion considered below, the roles were soon inverted: "utopian" Chan represented the normative tendency; "locative" popular religion (or whatever we may call it), the disruptive tendency.

[2] Also worth mentioning in this respect is Augustin Berque's distinction between the "topic" dimension of a given milieu (that is, its belonging to a *specific place*) and its "choretic" dimension (that is, its inscription in an abstract space). Characteristic of "great traditions" such as the Confucian state ideology or Buddhism, the choretic dimension presupposes among other things "a territorial competence able to transpose certain elements of reality that are foreign to the places receiving them, and also to integrate these places into a whole" (Berque 1986, 159).

[3] See also *Da zhidu lun*, a Buddhist compendium in which the Buddha is described as a dragon-tamer, where the dragon is in this case, a symbol of the brahmans. Lamotte 1944–1980, 1: 188. See also de Visser 1913 and Vogel 1926.

[4] On snakes and dragons in Japan, see Higo Kazuo, *Kodai denshō kenkyū* (Studies in Ancient Traditions), 2d ed. (Tokyo, 1943); de Visser 1913; Cornelius Ouwehand, "Some

Chan's first significant contacts with local religion and Daoism occurred during the heyday of the Northern school of Chan, which had developed on Song shan, the "Central Peak," a mountain that had been until then a stronghold of Daoism. The sacred mountains of Daoism were believed interconnected by an array of caves (*tiandong*, litt. "grotto-heavens") that formed the gateways to the Daoist underworld (or Heavens).[5] Mapping both the outer space and the inner space of the body (where countless colorful gods dwelt), Daoist mythology was utterly spatialized. The mountain was a text to be deciphered, a succession of "practiced places" that encapsulated mythological time (see Certeau 1984, 117; Grapard 1982, 1988). A quick glance at the toponymy of Song shan reveals a wealth of mythical associations: Cave of the Precious Jade Girl, Red Cooking Basin, Jade Mirror Peak, White Crane Peak, Three Storks Peak, Jade Man Peak, and so on. Although it was saturated with mythical references and over-populated with spirits, the mountain appeared deserted to profane visitors and profanators. According to the description of a Westerner in the early twentieth century, "Verily the place is all but empty, though by no means swept and garnished. As the old faiths give way, what is to come? Devils worse than before, or the good news of a Heavenly Father?"[6]

Long before the arrival of the Western missionaries, the "devils" of local religion had been enrolled, dismissed, or subdued repeatedly by Daoist and Buddhist priests. Song shan became in the early Tang a retreat for eminent Daoist masters of the so-called Mao shan school. Although Daoists shared with literati and Chan monks a similar elitist contempt for the people, their attitude toward folk beliefs differed in that they accepted the symbolic system of local traditions and regarded it only as an inferior level of their spiritual hierarchy.[7] Chan monks, however, felt compelled to convert or subdue the local deities, to erase the memory of the places, to desacralize or reconvert spaces, to decode and re-encode legends.

Influenced as it was by Huayan theories such as the "interpenetration of phenomena" (*shishi wu'ai*), Northern Chan has often been accused of intellectualism. However, Shenxiu and his disciples were complex religious figures, and another side of their personalities—a side largely ignored by

---

Notes on the God Susa-no-o," *Monumenta Nipponica* 14, 3–4 (1958): 138–161; and Kelsey 1981. On dragons and snakes vanquished by Western saints, see Le Goff 1988, 159–188.

[5] According to a Daoist *Chart of the True Form of the Five Peaks*, "The Central Peak presides in the world over mountains and rivers, gorges and valleys, and simultaneously over oxen, sheep and all rice-eating beings. Such are the things in his jurisdiction." Quoted in Chavannes 1910, 418. See also Soymié 1956 and Chavannes 1919.

[6] Geil 1926, 181. See also Joseph Hers, "The Sacred Mountains of China: Sung-shan the Deserted," *China Journal* 24, 2 (February 1936): 76–82; Alexander C. Soper, "Two Stelae and a Pagoda on the Central Peak, Mt. Sung," *Archives of the Chinese Art Society of America* 16 (1962): 41–48.

[7] Such is still the case today in Taiwan, where mediums and Daoist priests perform hierarchized rituals side by side.

the later Chan tradition—accounts for their popular appeal: they were renowned for their supranormal powers (*shentong*), in particular for their clairvoyance and their control over demonic apparitions. Before moving to the capital and near-by Song shan, Shenxiu had spent several years of ascetic practice on another mountain, Yuquan shan (Mount of the Jade Spring). As the story goes, "When Shenxiu arrived near Yuquan shan, a huge snake came from the ground. Shenxiu remained seated without fear, and the next day, he found a treasure hidden at the foot of a tree; with this treasure, he was able to build a temple."[8]

The snake appears in this story as a potentially harmful, yet ultimately beneficent messenger of the invisible world. The spiritual power acquired through meditation allows Shenxiu to vanquish fear and obtain the tribute of the local god. In many other stories, a snake or some other wild animal reveals to a Buddhist monk the presence of a spring that will make possible the foundation of a monastery. In some cases, the snake is a malevolent spirit that must be pacified in order for an existing community to survive. One story takes place on Song shan, in the community of the Northern Chan master Puji. Puji once scolded a monk for failing to take proper care of his begging bowl; Puji told him that this bowl was his life. Some time later, the bowl was accidentally broken by another monk. Overcome by anger or frightened for having taken his master's words literally, the owner of the bowl died. The following night, Puji warned the monks to remain in their room. In the middle of the night, a large snake appeared: this wrathful apparition was actually a reincarnation of the dead monk who had come for revenge. Unmoved, Puji eventually appeased the snake with a sermon on karmic retribution and foretold the former monk's rebirth as a human girl in a family of the neighboring village (*Shenseng zhuan* 7, *T.* 50, 2064: 991a; also Doré 1914–1938, 8: 526–529).

In several other stories bearing a strong structural resemblance, a Northern Chan monk converts the god of Song shan by conferring the Bodhisattva precepts on him. Although the god is not represented as (by) a snake, these stories clearly belong to a cycle of legends dealing with the transmission of local jurisdiction from a local god to a Buddhist priest.[9] In most cases, the disruptive power of a *local* spirit is pacified by the Buddhist teaching, that is, by the revelation of a higher understanding of reality, one

[8] *Shenxian tongjian* 14, quoted by Doré 1914–1929, 7: 205. For other legends dealing with the relations between Guan Di and Buddhist monks on Yuquan shan, see Duara 1988, Hansen 1990.

[9] See for example the case of Huian in *Song gaoseng zhuan*, *T.* 50, 2061: 823b. A similar meeting takes place between Yuangui, a disciple of Huian, and the tutelary god of Song shan. The story is somewhat more elaborated, and reports the dialogue between the monk and the god. See *Song Gaoseng zhuan* 19, *ibid.*, 828c–829a. The story is translated in Doré 1914–1929, 7: 294–296; 1914–1938, 8: 490–492. Many other cases are found in the later tradition, namely in Sōtō Zen.

that implies an overall, *unlocalized* vision. Sometimes, the initial disruption is provoked by the Buddhist monk, rather than by the autochtonous god or spirit. A case in point is that of the Chan master Duo, better known as Pozao Duo, "Duo the stove-breaker." His nickname alludes to the following episode. There was on Song shan a shamaness who sacrificed to the stove-god and performed exorcisms. One day Duo visited her, and while striking the stove, he said: "Whence comes the deity? Where are the miraculous spirits?" When he eventually demolished the stove, everyone feared an instant divine retribution. Instead of this, a young layman in a plain blue robe appeared and bowed respectfully to Duo, saying: "I have suffered many afflictions here. Now by virtue of your discourse on the teaching of *non-birth*, I have been reborn into the heavens. I cannot repay your kindness." Having said this, he departed.[10]

FROM PLACE TO SPACE

These stories reveal the opposition between two visions of space, two different anthropologies: that of Chan Buddhism and that of territorial cults symbolized by the snake, the mountain god, or other autochtonous spirits. The ambiguous nature of these sacred beings has often been pointed out. I would like to emphasize their subversive power vis-à-vis the elaborate discourse of established religions, and the territorial claim of snake symbolism. My purpose, however, is not to attempt a structural analysis of these legends, but rather, to use in a somewhat different sense a term coined by Gaston Bachelard in *The Poetics of Space*, what we may call a *topoanalysis* (Bachelard 1964).

In the process of its official recognition, Chan came at times to hold an eminently conservative discourse. Despite its later popularization, it always remained an elitist teaching, and it is therefore significant that it tended to subdue and displace various symbols of local power. I suggested earlier that the contrast or conflict between the various symbolic systems subsumed under the terms Chan and local religion seems to find its expression in the opposition between different conceptions of space. However, the term *expression* implies that such spatial conceptions are merely derived, ancillary to the two systems in presence, while, on the contrary, I want to underscore what Merleau-Ponty, in another context, called the "primacy of perception" (Merleau-Ponty 1964a). Religious or sectarian polarization

[10] I have summarized several variants of the story. The *Song Gaoseng zhuan* version downplays Pozao Duo's iconoclasm; it argues that the stove fell apart of itself, "not by human power." See *T.* 50, 2061: 828b; and Doré 1914–1929, 8: 338; 1914–1938, 8: 548. The story was also known in medieval Japan, but was then interpreted as a rehabilitation of popular religion. See Morrell 1985, 93–94.

derives in this case from a basic epistemological divergence concerning space—more precisely sacred space. If "a vision of the world is a di-vision of the world" (Bourdieu 1980, 348), perhaps precisely this perceptive difference, grounded in a specific bodily habitus, determines religious practice—rather than the contrary. At any rate, this admittedly relative primacy of conflicting perceptions renders the notion of "epistemological dualism" more appropriate than that of "doctrinal" or "ritual" dualism sometimes used to describe Chinese religion (see Overmyer 1976, 46; 1980).

One could argue that the dichotomy, expressed in spatial terms—such as, precisely, *space* and *place*—is only the projection onto the plane of the dominant Chan discourse of a more fundamental dichotomy between spatial/visual and temporal/auditory metaphors. For instance, David Chidester has suggested that, whereas visual imagery is associated with continuity and spatial simultaneity, auditory imagery refers to discontinuity and temporal sequence (Chidester 1985).

These epistemological dichotomies underlie the antagonism between Chan and local religion.[11] In this light, it is significant that visual metaphors (such as, precisely, "light") still inform our discourse on these religious traditions. This metaphorical bias may be partly compensated by our attempt to stress the *discontinuity* (and therefore the popular or local elements) of the Chan tradition, rather than its synchronic or diachronic continuity.

As noted earlier, the Central Peak was an essential part of the cosmological system inherited from the Han. This system was an ideological construct, the cohesion of which has been somewhat exaggerated by traditional sinologists.[12] In actual practice, Chinese cosmology was never more than a loosely articulated symbolic apparatus, a spatially and temporally discontinuous matrix. Even though it was reinterpreted, adapted, and subverted by local traditions and religious Daoism, its fundamental intuition was never questioned—at least not until the rise of Mahāyāna Buddhism and the emergence of Chan. This intuition was that space is complex and unstable, that it is neither always nor everywhere the same; now diluted, now concentrated, it constitutes a "hierarchized federation of heterogeneous expanses" (Granet 1968, 84). In sharp contrast with the Chan conception of space, two features stand out. First, the qualitative nature of

[11] In another context, Michel de Certeau underscores the opposition between the spatial strategies of the dominant classes and the temporal tactics of "popular" practices. See Certeau 1990, 63.

[12] See, for example, the masterful description in Granet 1968, 75–318. For a criticism of Durkheimian influence on Granet and French Sinology from the point of view of the "logic of practice," see Bourdieu 1977, 230; 1980, 425.

a cosmologically conceived space determines that of its occupants: what you are depends on where you are.[13] Second, such a conception is not dichotomic, and there exist gradations within this space as well as between it and its outside. This means that "the limit . . . must be thought of in terms of a transformational model of relationships between spaces" (Paul-Lévy and Segaud 1983, 41). This hierarchized, gradual model was replaced in "sudden" Chan by a dichotomic model, according to which the limit is "abrupt," without any mediation: only a leap can take you from the fragmented space of ignorance to the unified space of awakening.

Despite the collapse of the Han cosmological structure, the intuition of a "qualitative," heterogeneous space did not disappear. As Lévi-Strauss points out, this intuition is neither specifically Chinese nor premodern: "However rebellious our Euclidian mind may have become to the qualitative conception of space, it does not depend on us that great astronomical and meteorological phenomena affect regions with an imperceptible but indelible coefficient" (Lévi-Strauss 1965, 136; see also Panofsky 1975, 42–43). At any rate, the fragments of the old Chinese cosmology were loosely incorporated and actualized in new symbolic systems, which obeyed different rules, more akin to the "logic of practice" defined by Bourdieu, a logic that "constantly sacrifices the care for coherence to the search for efficacy" (Bourdieu 1980, 426). This is why a structural analysis of local religion proved "systematically" reductionistic. However, the rise of Chan is part of a kind of Copernican revolution,[14] the appearance of a new form of space (and of time), "whose homogeneity abolishes the old heterogeneities of various forms of sacred space" (see Jameson 1985, 374). Like Hamlet, the Chan master claims to be "king of infinite space."

The Other Scene

Whereas traditional Buddhist hagiography was a "composition of places," Chan "histories of the Lamp" ultimately pointed toward an empty or

[13] Consequently, "to be on the Chinese side of the limit is to be in a territory with spatial qualities and it is also to be a human; to be on the other side is to be in a territory without spatial qualities and also not to be a human; to pass to this other side suffices to ensure the loss of human characteristics: as if these characteristics depended less on the beings than on their space" (Paul-Lévy and Segaud 1983, 38).

[14] In *Newtonian Studies*, Alexandre Koyré characterizes the Copernican revolution by: (a) a destruction of the cosmos; (b) a geometrization of space, that is, "the substitution of the homogeneous and abstract . . . space of Euclidean geometry for the concrete and differentiated place-continuum of pre-Galilean physics and astronomy" (Koyré 1965, 6–7). In other words, it is the emergence of a universe whose components all appear to be located at the same ontological level. *Mutatis mutandis*, this characterization seems to fit the "mental revolution" brought about by Mahāyāna philosophy and Chan.

different spiritual space.[15] Likewise, Chan monasteries defined a new domain, a "*utopian*" space that, contrary to the hidden paradises of popular "heterotopies," was a *non-lieu* and the scene of religious *non-lieux*;[16] a cultic center, yet decentering or displacing the old spatial frame; a concrete institution, depending on society for its subsistence, yet presuming "to represent the entire cosmos, society included" (Boon 1982, 202); a place ruled (in theory) by the law of emptiness and functioning as a kind of negative field in which all worldly values were canceled, dismissed, or inverted.[17] Ideally belonging to another order of reality, the ideal space of the Chan monastery was a negation of the dense and pluralistic space of local religion.

As Jameson suggests in the case of temporality, "this abstract structure . . . clearly cannot emerge until the older traditional activities, projects, rituals through which time was experienced . . . have broken down" (Jameson 1981, 261). Apparently, the epistemological break that, according to Karatani Kōjin, transformed the perception of nature in nineteenth-century Japan (Karatani 1988, 619; Brett de Bary 1988, 598–602) was already prefigured in the rationalizing tendencies of Chan. In this sense, one could perhaps see in Chan/Zen masters like Dōgen the distant precursors of modern Japanese "mountain climbers," if, as Karatani points out, "the existence of mountain climbing as a sport in Japan is predicated on a qualitative transformation and homogeneization of space which had traditionally been held as 'separate' on the basis of religious values and taboos."[18]

In Chan hagiography, this epistemological shift is usually expressed indirectly, but sometimes it is also stated more explicitly in doctrinal terms. The story of Yuangui's conversion of the Song shan god is in this respect significant. According to this story, when the god threatened to kill Yuangui for his lack of respect, the monk replied: "Since I am unborn, how

[15] See Michel de Certeau, "Hagiographie," in *Encyclopedia Universalis* (Paris, 1968) 8: 207–209; and Certeau 1988, 280.

[16] The term *non-lieu* should be taken both literally as a denial of place and in the juridical sense of "dismissal of a case for lack of evidence."

[17] This tendency to spatial abstraction, however, seems to find a counter-example in the cartography of Chan and other Buddhist monasteries: to read the indications on the map, the reader must project himself mentally onto its center and turn successively toward the four cardinal directions. This orientation already implies a hierarchization of space. After the Tang, there developed a cosmic/human symbolism of the monastery, the main buildings of which were seen to correspond to the parts of the human body.

[18] Karatani 1988, ibid. It is perhaps no mere coincidence that the first English translation of Dōgen's *Shōbōgenzō Sansuikyō* (Sūtra of Mountains and Rivers) was published in a collection of essays concerning mountains and alpinism. See Bielefeldt 1979. Nevertheless, Dōgen's conception of the mountains remained largely "mystical," albeit in a way different from later Sōtō masters such as Keizan Jōkin.

could you kill me? My body is empty and I see myself as no different from you: how could you destroy emptiness, or destroy yourself?" Eventually, after conferring the Bodhisattva precepts on the god, Yuangui explained to him that the true supranormal power (*shentong*) is no other than emptiness: "That there is neither Dharma nor master [to follow] is what is called no-mind. For those who understand thus, even the Buddha has no powers: he can only, through no-mind, penetrate all dharmas" (*Song gaoseng zhuan, T.* 50, 2061: 828c). Likewise, Pozao Duo converted the stove-god of Song shan by preaching to him the truth of the "unborn," the "sudden teaching" superior to all gradual "skillful means" (upāya), the ultimate truth that subsumes and cancels all conventional truths. The coercive nature of this "sudden teaching" is revealed by the physical violence of Duo's smashing of the stove—a violence euphemized in later variants. "Non-birth" (*wusheng*, Sk. *anutpanna*) is the equivalent for the Mahāyāna cardinal tenet of emptiness (*śūnyatā*): things are called "unborn" because they are intrinsically empty, like space. Having only an illusory existence, all phenomena are therefore deprived of any ontological status. As Horkheimer and Adorno pointed out in another context, "The destruction of gods and qualities alike is insisted upon. . . . It is the identity of the spirit and its correlate, the unity of nature, to which the multiplicity of qualities falls victim" (Horkeimer and Adorno 1972, 8–10). Likewise, the essentially pluralistic nature of local religion was negated by Chan and replaced by an abstract vision. The contrast between the two views is well expressed by Michel Serres:

> To be pluralistic means that truths are always local, distributed in a somewhat complicated way in space. In other words, there are *always* singularities. The opposite of pluralism is to say that a single truth obtains for the entire space. . . . There is a difference between a homogeneous space, entirely occupied by a single truth, and a complex space where the whole task consists in passing from one singularity to another. . . . On the other hand, to have everything all at once, to occupy the whole space abruptly, . . . this is what these ideologies do. After all, what does it mean, a universal space: a specialist tries to occupy the whole field. It is an imperialism.[19]

The strategy of the *all-at-once* or sudden doctrine advocated by early Chan masters no longer allowed "the joy of alternances and reincarnations, the joyful relativity, the joyful negation of identity and of single meaning, the negation of the stupid coincidence with oneself"—all qualities that, according to Bakhtin, characterize popular culture (Bakhtin

[19] Michel Serres, in an interview for *Le Monde* (10 May 1981), reprinted in *Entretiens avec Le Monde*, Vol. 1, *Philosophies* (Paris: La Découverte, 1984), 198–199.

1970, 49). This bird's-eye vision, emanated from an intellectual elite, met the ideological needs of the higher strata of Chinese society.[20] However, Chan was never as monolithic as its most radical tracts imply, and we should be wary of confusing the model derived from these theoretical statements with the reality—thus adopting ourselves a bird's-eye view of Chan. Perhaps, as Hegel remarked, "Only when one stands on high ground can one survey the situation and note every detail, not when one has to peer up from below through a small bottle (*durch das Loch einer moralischen Bouteille*)."[21] Or perhaps this vision is too imperialistic and blind to its own conditions of possibility. As with all idealisms, the weightlessness of the Chan or Hegelian plunging vision causes one to overlook its groundlessness, or rather its existential grounding in a specific site, in a sociological and biological reality—the body, "the sentinel that stands silently under [our] words and [our] acts" (Merleau-Ponty 1964c, 12). This dream of a social and epistemological flight was also oblivious to the fact that, as James Clifford points out, "there is no longer any place of overview from which to map human ways of life, nor Archimedian points from which to represent the world. Mountains are in constant motion" (Clifford and Marcus 1986, 22). Or, as one of the kōan that constitute the matrix of Dōgen's *Sansuikyō* put it: "The blue mountains always walk on the water" (see Bielefeldt 1979).

At any rate, the mountain is a recurrent metaphor in early Chan texts. It is, for instance, used by the fifth patriarch Hongren to describe his contemplative practice: "When sitting in meditation, you feel like being at the top of a solitary tall mountain, and gazing off into the distance on all four sides—it is limitless. Loosen your body and mind to fill up the whole world and abide in the Buddha realm. The pure Dharmakāya is limitless" (*Lengqie shizi ji, T. 85, 2837*: 1289c). The empty inner space discovered (or produced) by Hongren's contemplation is strikingly different from the densely populated realm of the Daoist body, a microcosmic sacred space where myriads of gods dwell and must be localized, fixed by inner contemplation to insure corporeal longevity.[22] These two types of inner contemplation generate two different bodies; the transparent and often disparaged body of Chan doctrinal treatises and the opaque, mysterious,

[20] In his book *Space and Place*, Yi-fu Tuan points out that "we more readily assume a Godlike position, looking at the earth from above, than from the perspective of another mortal living on the same level as ourselves" (Tuan 1977, 28).

[21] Hegel 1953, 5. See also Merleau-Ponty: "High places attract those who wish to look over the world with an eagle-view. Vision ceases to be solipsist [*simpliste*] only up close, when the other turns back upon me the luminous rays in which I had caught him" (Merleau-Ponty 1968, 78).

[22] Concerning the Daoist body and inner contemplation, see Schipper 1982, 137–153; Robinet 1979; Maspero 1981, 279–286 and 346–373.

sacralized body of local religion and Daoism.[23] The same can be said of
Chan and Daoist conceptions of outer space. In Chan, the Dharmakāya or
Cosmic Body of the Buddha symbolizes the infinite empty space coextensive to the Buddha Dharma. It often appears in Chan dialogues like the
following, in which a monk, scolded by a fellow monk for sitting with his
back to the altar, replies: "Since the Dharmakāya fills the entire space, why
should one sit facing one direction rather than another?"[24]

Prefiguring the structuralist "vision from afar" (Lévi-Strauss 1985),
Chan masters were in fact saying: "Remove everything, so you can see."
The famous (apocryphal) verse attributed to Huineng in the *Platform
Sūtra* stresses that "fundamentally, there is not a single thing [to see]." A
disciple of Shenxiu, the Northern Chan master Zhida, described the
method of "gazing at the mind" or "at the unlocalized":

> All obstacles and errors are created by mind. To gaze at the mind is to gaze at
> the unlocalized. The unlocalized is your mind. Space empty of all entities is called
> "receptacle," in it are the vital principle and consciousness.
>
> Unlocalized means the absence of any mind (or dharma). This unlocalized is
> the awakening of the Buddha, the basis of practice of all Bodhisattvas. By gazing
> at it you will come to *see*.[25]

Zhida defined the vision achieved through his "method" as a nonseeing,
nonthinking, nonattachment to any phenomenon, and he denounced as
mere illusions all other visions or powers induced by meditation. The
importance of noncognitive perception is emphasized repeatedly in early
Chan texts. What seems to underlie the Chan attitude toward worldly
knowledge is a visual and spatial metaphor. Space is empty: all phenomena
are mere "flowers in the sky"—that is, hallucinations. The following anecdote, staging the Northern Chan master Puji, illustrates how early Chan

---

[23] In actual practice, however, corporeality played a central role in Chan, as evidenced in
the cult of relics and "flesh-bodies." See Faure 1991.

[24] See *Jingde chuandeng lu* 27, T. 51, 2076: 435b. A parodic variant runs as follows: "A
monk said to another: 'Since the Dharmakāya fills all space, where in the entire universe can I
find a place to shit?' " See *Chanlin sengbao zhuan*, in ZZ 137, 71. This story calls to mind the
famous passage in *The Journey to the West*, in which the hero, the unruly monkey Sun
Wukong, challenged by the Buddha to show his extraordinary powers, leaps to the end of the
universe, urinates on the five huge pillars he finds there and returns only to realize that these
were the fingers of the cosmic Buddha, whose palm he never left. Here, of course, the abstract
space of Mahāyāna, although significantly diversified on the ground level by the uneven
process of the pilgrims on this Chinese snakes and ladders, is never actually threatened by the
rebellious attempts of popular tradition symbolized by the monkey. See Antony Yu 1977,
1: 174.

[25] *Chanmen fa*, in Suzuki 1936, 1: 90. See also *Dunwu zhenzong jingang banruo xiuxing
da pian famen yaojue*, mss. Stein 5533, Pelliot 2799 and 3922.

attempted to move beyond the imaginary and symbolical systems of traditional Chinese culture:

> Liu Zhongyong, an expert on the *Yijing* (Book of Changes), once visited
> master Puji, who asked him: "Won't you try to guess where my mind is?" Liu
> said: "Your mind is on the seventh inscription of the roof's eaves." When asked
> again, he answered that [Puji's mind] was here or there. Puji told him: "Although
> the ten thousand things cannot avoid the numbers [governing fate], let me try to
> avoid them. Try to fathom me!" After a while, Liu was taken aback. "It is the
> end. Your mind is completely immobile, I can no longer know it." (*Youyang
> zazu*, ed. Imamura Yoshio 1980, 4: 32, 972)

Thus, through nonthinking Chan practitioners are able to enter into the
realm of emptiness, a mental space where no image or symbol remain,
where no cosmology or causality can avail.[26] The tabula rasa created by
Puji's nonthinking is the spiritual equivalent of Pozao Duo's iconoclasm.
The high tide of Chan "ideology" covered all the accidents of the popular
landscape, creating a clean, abstract space that could ideally be embraced
at one glance. The world was seen as a limpid, homogeneous, harmonious
whole. The old boundaries were erased, and boundless space meant
boundless sovereignty. In the words of the Chan master Xuansha Shibei
(835–908), "The entire universe is one bright pearl. What is there to
interpret or to understand?" (Waddell and Abe 1971b, 112) Commenting
on this passage, Dōgen wrote that "even coming and going in the Black
Mountain's Cave of Demons is nothing but the one bright pearl."[27] This
epistemological break implies a departure from hermeneutics: the world,
emptied of symbols, no longer needs to be interpreted. Truth reveals itself
immediately to an unmediated vision. The opaque, ambivalent, and at
times dangerous "enchanted garden" of local religion has been dispelled

[26] It is interesting to note that one of Puji's disciples, Yixing (673–727), one of the foremost Chinese experts in numbers and symbols, elaborated a new calendar. His name has been
recorded in the History of Science and appears among those of Copernicus, Newton, and
many others on the frontispiece of the Sainte Geneviève Library in Paris. Approaching an early
death, Yixing returned to Song shan to take leave of his old master Puji who, as could be
expected, had already foretold his impromptu visit. See *Song gaoseng zhuan* 9, T. 50, 2061:
760c.

[27] See *Shōbōgenzō*, T. 82, 2582: 25c; Waddell and Abe 1971b, 117. However, the "place"
acquires a new importance in Sōtō Zen after Dōgen. Keizan Jōkin, for example, had in a
dream the revelation that the land he just received from donators was, for "geomantic"
reasons, perfect for the foundation of his monastery, the Yōkōji, in Noto peninsula. According
to the hagiographical tradition, he was also guided to the site itself by an emissary of the local
god, a white fox. Sōtō Zen did not spread in an abstract space, but along the lines of force, the
network of the local cults of Shugendō: more particularly that of Hakusan (from Hokuriku to
Ise, along the Biwa lake), a network whose nodal points are sacred mountains. See Faure
1991, 224–226.

by the clear, haughty vision of the enlightened mind (see Weber 1964, 270). Chan "enlightenment" must be understood both in the sense of supreme awakening and in that of an almost Voltairian perception of reality, a Buddhist *Aufklärung* of sorts that blissfully erases an entire domain of religious experience. As noted earlier, Chan leaders shared their contempt for "heterodox cults" with Daoists and Confucian officials.[28] However, "just as the myths already realize enlightenment, so enlightenment with every step becomes more deeply engulfed in mythology" (Horkheimer and Adorno 1972, 11–12). Despite its homogeneity, the epistemological space of Chan is not the amorphous profane space described by Mircea Eliade (Eliade 1959, 23). It is, at least theoretically, yet another type of sacred space. Buddhist emptiness remains a structure, and the Chan vision is still "structured like a language." Chan masters were perhaps justified in their attempt to free space from its empirical limitations; they were mistaken, however, when they idealized space as something "beyond any viewpoint, any latency, any depth, without any true thickness" (Merleau-Ponty 1964c, 48).

CHAN IN-SIGHTS AND DI-VISIONS

The imposition of the Chan worldview on local beliefs was neither a complete nor an enduring success. The ideological tide of Chan eventually had to recede, letting some islands of the popular mental landscape reemerge in the midst of its discourse. The ambiguity of some hagiographical accounts is significant. The above-mentioned story concerning Shenxiu's recognition by the local god (as a snake) was actually introducing another episode which Henri Doré translated as follows:

> The peasants of the place venerated Kuan-kung [a very popular god invoked against devils]. Shen-hsiu destroyed its pagoda. No sooner had the pagoda been destroyed than a black cloud covered the sky, and Kuan-kung appeared in it, riding his horse and holding his sword, to ask Shen-hsiu the reason of his behavior. Shen-hsiu had to rebuild the pagoda, and Kuan-kung ordered him to take up the duty of gate-keeper. . . . Since this event, the tradition has been to place Shen-hsiu as gate-keeper of pagodas. (Doré 1914–1929, 7: 205)

It seems that we are offered here the other side of the picture, one that usually remains unseen. It is likely that the local traditions, far from being purely passive, could at times subvert the authorized discourse of the literati or the clergy. One could easily imagine cases in which the snake, and

[28] Concerning the relationships between the literati and local gods, see Jean Lévi 1986, 1987.

with it the local traditions, was the winner.[29] Unfortunately, only the authorized voice is usually heard through historiographers, who, consciously or not, have imported into their own discourse the biases inherited from the "great texts."

This "popular" interpretation of Shenxiu's tale presents only one inconvenience: it is based on what appears to be a mistranslation. Doré, and in his wake E.T.C. Werner, have misinterpreted the text. According to the source, quoted also by the Zen scholar Mujaku Dōchū, Guangong, not Shenxiu, becomes the protector of the monastery. If I have cared to quote this (mis)translation, it is because it has the merit of drawing our attention to the ambiguity of its source. There is indeed a discrepancy in the narrative: Guangong arrives at the spot of his smashed altar and fulminates against Shenxiu, who hastens to apologize and promises to compensate for his desecration, to worship the god as a protector of the monastery. The narrative's careful staging of Guangong's apparition, reminiscent of that of the statue of the commandatore in *Don Giovanni*, suggests another ending, one less glorious for Shenxiu that might therefore have been erased by the later Chan tradition.[30] At any rate, the enshrinement of Guangong as monastery god (*qielan shen*) can be interpreted as a compromise, if not a defeat of Shenxiu.[31] There is of course no way to conclude, but it is rather ironic that, in my attempt to retrieve popular discourse erased by "great tradition" (see Faure 1987c), I committed the same error as the Jesuit Fathers, intent on belittling the tradition of their Chan rivals.

This legend prompts us to examine some ambiguities of Northern Chan, ambiguities that reflect its hybrid origin. After all, even if this is mere

[29] As in the well-known Dōjōji legend where a monk is pursued by a large snake, actually the angry spirit of a deceived woman, and is eventually calcined by the intense heat of the snake's passion under the bell of the Dōjōji temple where he had taken refuge. Unlike the Japanese character Tamino at the opening of the *Magic Flute*, he is saved neither by the Queen of the Night nor by his fellow monks. Another interesting case shows the Buddhist recuperation of a tale in which ignorant Daoist aspirants to immortality are found to have fallen victims to a huge python. See Miyakawa 1979, 96–98.

[30] According to Zhang Shangyin (1043–1121), Guan Yu (Guangong) appeared to the Tiantai patriarch Zhiyi (d. 587) at the time of the foundation of the Yuquan Monastery. To frighten the monk, he took various threatening forms (tiger, snake, python, spirit soldiers), but Zhiyi remained unmoved. Guan Yu then admitted his defeat and donated the land to him. See Duara 1990.

[31] It is interesting in this respect to note that the Hall of the monastery god (*Garandō*) of Manpukuji, the head temple of the Ōbaku sect of Zen in Uji (on the southern outskirts of Kyoto) is dedicated to Guangong. Although the god is represented in traditional ("popular") fashion, behind him is found a large statue of a figure wearing the cap of a Chinese official and sitting in the posture of a Chan master. According to the monastery records, it is the Bodhisattva Huaguang (J. Kakō Bosatsu). Could it be that the monastery god was an avatar of Shenxiu and that the iconographic tradition has unwittingly retained the other side of the story?

wishful thinking, it would be significant if Shenxiu, the "founder" of a Chan school, were assigned the role of a gatekeeper, that is, of a local god, by a more powerful deity. The threshold is seen in many cultures as a dangerous place, a focal point where space inverts, and Victor Turner, among others, has noted that liminal states and individuals are both ambiguous and dangerous (Turner 1969, 93–111; 1974, 274; see also Bourdieu 1977, 130–132) Shenxiu is the focal point from which a different, inverted conception of space—and a new school—arose. Like the threshold on which he stands (in Doré's version), he allows a transition from one (epistemological) space to another. Not surprisingly, he was, as a transitional figure, rejected by the later Chan tradition, which derived its orthodoxy from this scapegoating process. As the mediating figure of the gatekeeper, however, he may have contributed to the influence of Chan on local religion. Perhaps this piqued my interest in this paradigmatic "lonely captive of the threshold" (*captif solitaire du seuil*, Mallarmé 1945, 69).

These stories can usually be read as attempts by an emerging great tradition to establish its superiority over other great traditions as well as folk traditions. Nevertheless, one cannot exclude the possibility that some of them—or some of their elements—attempt to give voice to the nonelite point of view and constitute a subversion of authorized, clerical discourse. We find ourselves here in what Maurice Freedman has called the "rather tired field of great and little traditions" (Freedman 1974, 36; see also Sangren 1984, 1–24). As Victor Turner pointed out, antitheses such as great/little traditions are of little importance for the founders of protest religious movements; and Chan started as one such movement, at least at the doctrinal level. Admittedly, "great and little traditions were rejected alike as the 'establishment,' as structure, and what was stressed instead was religious experience" (V. Turner 1974, 286). However, as Turner elsewhere admits, these movements tend in turn to become "great traditions" or "structures"—and Chan was no exception in this regard.

Within the Chan tradition itself, one can discern various trends or strata—some more elitist and utopian, others more popular and locative. However, the polarization remains useful: the fact that it does not overlap with a clear-cut sociopolitical division does not mean that the distinction between both types of vision collapses; nor that, as Freedman argues, "elite and peasant religion rest upon a common base, representing two versions of one religion that we may see as idiomatic translations of each other" (Freedman 1974, 37). The analysis must also take into account the ideological representations, for which the distinction between elite and local religion was indeed crucial. Although these two modes of thought or "orderings of reality" are not separated by watertight bulkheads and do not represent two radically different types of minds, they still reflect ten-

sions and conflicts resulting, not only from the very different socioeco-
nomic conditions of two distinct groups, but also, within a single individual, from a subtle epistemological shift, a perceptive change that could
occur, without one being necessarily aware of it.[32]

Therefore, I still use polarities or ideal types such as "great" and "little"
traditions for heuristic purposes. Not only the agonistic relation between
these two poles or ideal-types is logically prior to the terms it relates and
defines, but it is also asymmetrical: whereas the great tradition tends to be
reified into an orthodoxy by its own exponents, the little tradition remains
elusive; its logic, like that of poaching, is nomadic, and its hidden tracks
criss-cross on the preserves of the great tradition (see Certeau 1984, 1986).
Thus, our topo-analysis turns into a "geography of the repressed" (Certeau 1986, 131). The "great/little traditions" paradigm used here to
describe the antagonism between Chan and local religion(s) does not then
refer to an opposition between two juridically or socially distinct parties,
but rather to what Lyotard would call a *différend* between incommensurable perceptions and unequal uses of the same space (Lyotard 1988). Although the common criticism that this paradigm is based on static categories or reified polarities seems usually pertinent, its cost is also very high. By
merely rejecting the antithese, one misses the process of polarization that
"takes place," the crucial split of generative epistemological schemes. This
confusion between the (*noetic*) process and the (*noematic*) product leads
one to overlook the agonistic nature of a religious tradition in situ, the
evasive dynamics of its spatial relationships, and the complex dialectics of
its local and imported components.[33]

Within Chan itself, we also find two trends that should not simply be
construed as two conflicting doctrines (as, for example, the so-called sudden and gradual teachings), but rather as two incommensurable visions,
and more precisely two radically different and differential perceptions of
space and time. They tend to constitute "two worlds whose inhabitants,
while using the same terms, do not speak the same language"

---

[32] Thus, like Lévy-Bruhl and Malinowski according to Clifford Geertz (1973, 120), Freedman becomes, in spite of himself, a reductionist for failing to see that "man moves, more or
less easily, but very frequently, between two visions between which there is no continuity and
which are separated by cultural abysses that one has to jump over in both directions with a
Kierkegaardian leap." See also, concerning this question, Veyne 1983. Note, however, that
Lévy-Bruhl abandoned in his posthumous *Notebooks* (1949) the naive dichotomy between
primitive and civilized thinking he had described in earlier books such as *How Natives Think*
(1975).

[33] When considering the resulting objectified traditions one might distinguish, as does
Dominick LaCapra, between "the hegemonic culture(s) of dominant classes, popular cul-
ture(s), and high culture(s)." See LaCapra 1985, 58. However, there may be no such a thing as
"popular culture(s)," but only a "popular" use of hegemonic and/or high cultures. See also
Certeau, "A (popular) use of religion modifies its functioning" (Certeau 1984, 18).

(Groethuysen 1927, 20). Although Freedman is probably justified in believing that a society so differentiated by social status and power as Chinese society would allow "religious similarity to be expressed as though it were religious difference" (Freedman 1974, 38), the reverse is equally true: Chinese society did at times allow religious difference to be expressed as though it were religious similarity. Hence perhaps the fundamental ambiguity of Northern Chan and of similar transitional, hybrid, "syncretistic" movements. Despite its abstract, intellectualist tendency, early Chan needed to ground itself in local myths in order to establish the legitimacy of its "philosophy," and this is why its hagiographical literature often seems to contradict its theoretical discourse.[34] Only after it was well established did Chan orthodoxy become able—although never for very long—to censure more effectively popular beliefs. This should not surprise us, as we are familiar with similar contradictions or compromises in the Western philosophical tradition.[35]

Paradoxically, while Chan monks were busy desacralizing mountains and imposing the abstract space of their monasteries, they also became engrossed in enshrining relics and erecting funerary stūpa—thereby creating new centers, new sacred spaces or places that were entrusted to the protection of local gods and eventually became identified with them. This phenomenon, however, had its source in highly literate monastic circles and should not be read merely as the subversion of a "great tradition" by local cults. The erection of stūpa paradoxically reflected both the "humanization" of the ancient sacred places and the "sacralization" of Chan. Within the Chan school itself, however, mythology (in the usual sense of stories about gods) was displaced by hagiography, and Chan faith was anchored in the "lives" of eminent anchorites. A superficial resemblance—namely the fact that new places of worship were often the same as those of the autochthonous cults—must not obscure their opposite meaning and the fundamental change that has taken place, at least in the minds of Chan

[34] Another example of abstraction is the genealogical chart, which proved so important in the elaboration of the patriarchal tradition. Bourdieu points out that "genealogies and other learned models are to the sense of social orientation . . . what a map, abstract model of all possible itineraries, is to the practical sense of space" (Bourdieu 1980, 58). The analogy between the genealogy and the map or plan derives from the substitution, in both cases, of a regular, homogeneous space, whether social, historical, or geographical, to the discontinuous space of practical strategies, actualized according to time and context. However, the patriarchal tradition itself was a means through which various popular practices such as ancestor worship were reintroduced in Chan.

[35] Despite Aristotle's comment that "those who, [in philosophy] use myth are not worth being seriously considered" (*Metaphysics*, B.4), Plato and other Greek philosophers, while looking down upon myth, spoke in a space still defined by the discourse of mythology. Studying another crucial phase in the history of Western philosophy, Frances Yates (1966) has argued that the rise of Western rationalism was triggered by the rediscovery of hermetic occultism. Conversely, Descartes's tabula rasa led to theological conclusions.

monks: despite superficial similarities, the worship offered to a stūpa and its relics is not the same thing as that offered to a chtonian power.

Song shan's *mirabilia* came to include the cave where Bodhidharma practiced "wall-contemplation,"[36] the stone with his shadow, the place where his disciple Huike had cut off his arm, and the "forest of stūpa" (*talin*) of the Shaolin Monastery—among which in particular were the stūpa of Shenxiu and Puji. After the decline of Northern Chan, there was also a "cedar of the Sixth Patriarch," supposedly planted by Huineng himself (Li Chi 1974, 140).

At Caoxi (near Canton), in the Baolin (later Nanhua) Monastery where Huineng taught and died at the turn of the eighth century, the marking feature in the landscape was the presence of his "flesh-body"—joined in the early seventeenth century by that of his distant heir Hanshan Deqing (see Faure 1991, 151–153, 162–167). Over the centuries, various other mirabilia were invented. Two numinous places in the monastery were the iron stūpa called "stūpa of the taming of the dragon" (*xianglong ta*) and the "fountain of the planted staff" (*zhuoxi quan*). The first name refers to an episode in which Huineng tamed a dragon by imprisoning it under his begging bowl after having challenged it to reduce its size—a Buddhist variant of a widespread folklorical theme. The iron stūpa allegedly contained the bones of the dragon, but those bones disappeared during the turmoil of the Yuan. The second name refers to a related motif, that of the saint as dowser. The legend has it that Huineng, wanting to wash the robe and the bowl received from the fifth patriarch Hongren, caused a spring to well up by driving his staff into the ground. Since that time, whenever the spring appeared to dry up, it was reactivated by the mere presentation of the patriarchal robe—so great was the supposed efficacy (*ling*) of Huineng's talismanic cloth. Huineng is credited with the creation of several other springs in Northern Guangdong, Southern Jiangxi, and Hunan (see Soymié 1961, 33–35). These legends reveal that the conquest of the place by Chan, as in the case of Song shan, involved some kind of symbolical violence; however, their relative scarcity in the case of Caoxi suggests that the place offered much less resistance, probably because it was not as deeply rooted as Song shan in the local, official, and Daoist symbolical systems.

In the process of relocating or resacralizing its space, Chan universalism was gradually subverted by local traditions and their "finite provinces of meaning."[37] Elaborated in the rarefied atmosphere of social and spiritual

[36] It is ironical that Bodhidharma's "wall-contemplation" (*biguan*), first defined as "theoretical entrance" (*liru*) or contemplation of the absolute (*liguan*), was eventually misinterpreted as a practical meditative technique consisting in "looking at a wall" (*guanbi*) (see Faure 1986a, 23–32]—whereas the wall and the cave themselves turned into a sacred place.

[37] See Alfred Schutz, *Collected Papers*, Vol. 1, *The Problem of Social Reality* (The Hague: Nijhoff, 1962), 231.

summits, the new cultural models imposed by Chan lost some of their purity in the densely haunted valleys of the sacred mountains.[38] In actual practice, all kinds of mediations or "skillful means" were maintained for the sake of less advanced practitioners. Thus, Chan's inner sectarian dynamic, which had paved the way for the emergence of a new space, was the main factor that contributed to the loss of "that special purity" that still characterizes the space of Shintō shrines: "No relics. No images. No iconography. A purity with no hint of death" (Okamoto Tarō, quoted in Tada 1981, 24).

The unmediated vision of Chan, however, did not simply give way to local cults, and the relationships between the two is dialectical. On the one hand, the worship of stūpa, relics, and mummies, while instrumental in the popularization of Chan, implied a "humanization" of the sacred, a kind of "demythologization" that often went against local beliefs in cosmic or divine mediators. Chan mediators were idealized men, masters whose power was manifest in and through their relics. As noted earlier, this evolution, characterized by the replacement of mythical adhesions by hierarchical relationships, set up a new "sacred topography," a new network of pilgrimage centered on sacred sites such as meditation caves and stūpa. On the other hand, the manipulation of sacred relics triggered what we may call a process of sacralization, which transformed the mummified patriarch into a saintly intercessor and ultimately into a god with a wider lay following. Thus, Huineng was no longer seen as a man, but as a Buddha—that is, a god who was superior to non-Buddhistic deities, yet shared with them a number of features. Centuries after his death, he remained a powerful presence at Caoxi, as a protector who could, from his permanent *samādhi*, influence the course of events. Thus, the rise of Chan can be described as the appearance of a new system of "places," a new cutting out of space, the creation of a new sacred geography centered on relics and stūpa, and on living masters. The fact that Chan masters are designated by their *toponym* attests to the *topical* component of their status.

Let us return to our initial theme, the snake—in a circular fashion that is itself symbolized by the *ourouboros*, a snake biting its tail: it is significant that Dōgen, the monk supposed to have brought "pure" Zen to Japan and to have developed a type of religious philosophy highly valued today for its supposedly ecumenical nature, was protected on his way back to Japan by a dragon-king who took the shape of a small white snake that Dōgen put in

---

[38] Tada Michitarō, analyzing this process in the case of Japanese Buddhism, quotes the following passage by Nakamatsu Yashū on the evolution from *ji* to *tera*: "*Tera* . . . was apparently originally used to refer to the crypts used for human remains. . . . In time, the name *tera* for these hollows containing bones spread to include any structure used for this purpose. . . . Perhaps the main reason that Buddhism became so widely accepted all over Japan is that *ji* became like *tera*" (Tada 1981, 22).

his begging bowl (see Durt 1983, 608). In this and similar stories, the snake or dragon is subdued or converted by the monk, who in turn owes it his life or prosperity. With this in mind, we may reconsider the words of Puji to his careless disciple and understand why the begging bowl (and the snake now hidden in it) represents indeed the very life of a monk. Despite the antagonism between the snake and the monk, each one is eventually saved by the other, and it seems that Buddhists were well aware of this interdependence. Thus, despite the inherent risks, it may be vital for any "great tradition," whether Buddhist or Western, to "nurture a snake in its bosom." The subversive and vitalizing power of the snake transformed the logic of Chan/Zen discourse into a plurality of sectarian discourses influenced by local cults' might. This multivocal discourse of the Chan tradition is easier to retrieve now that the uniformity of the structuralist era tends to give way to a "mosaic of fragmentary and regional approaches."[39]

[39] In her book *Deadly Words*, Jeanne Favret-Saada seems to contrast her "localized" approach (and that of the folk practices characterized as witchcraft) to the "unlocalized" (utopian) discourse of both structuralists and post-structuralists (like Derrida, Foucault, Lyotard) who, she claims, have in common the ideal of "speaking from nowhere" and who (not unlike Linji) advocate an *atopical* conception of the subject (Favret-Saada 1977, 26). Although her critique calls to mind the ocularcentrism denounced by Martin Jay as characteristic of modern French thought (Jay 1986, 1989), it should be pointed out that Foucault was the first to analyze and denounce the panoptical model.

Chapter Six

TIMES AND TIDES

Time & Space are Real Beings
Time is a Man   Space is a Woman.
(William Blake, *A Vision of the Last Judgment*)

I HAVE ARGUED above that the "sudden" teaching of Chan imposed a conception of space that differed from that of local religion and that early Chan contributed to a kind of "spatialization of thought." Because it suggested the absence of false notions—the Chan version of Descartes's tabula rasa (with the difference that Chan aims at erasing even the tabula, that is, the cogito)—empty space became a root metaphor in Chan discourse. The emphasis on space in early Chan texts and the anti-historical implications of the primacy of vision lead us to examine the Chan/Zen conceptions of time and history.[1] To the extent that the search for awakening is an attempt to end karma—that is, time—the Chan discourse on time has to be read *en creux*. To the extent that the temporal thinking (or even the atemporal experience) of the individual is a product of history, this discourse also needs to be contextualized (see Pomian 1984, 329). In the West, time and space have been since Kant accepted as a priori categories of perception. Kant actually subordinated space to time by arguing that the relationship between these two a priori forms of sensibility is not symmetrical: whereas space is merely the a priori condition of outer phenomena, time is an a priori condition of all phenomena, both inner and outer (Kant, *Philosophical Works*, quoted in Pomian 1984, 209). The Kantian bias toward time paved the way to reorient knowledge, a shift in emphasis from the past to the future. This prejudice against space, given by Pomian as a characteristic of Western modernity, can be detected in Ernst Bloch's remark that "the primacy of space over time is an infallible sign of reactionary language" (quoted in Fabian 1983, 37).

To what extent is the Kantian conception itself a historical product? Without following Mauss and Durkheim in the detail of their demonstration of the sociogenesis of categories, we can easily maintain the cultural determination of collective representations of space and time. In traditional Chinese culture, the heterogeneous and discontinuous nature of time and

---

[1] The question has been treated in the Western context by Pomian 1984; Le Goff 1977; Gourevitch 1985; Hubert and Mauss 1909.

space prevented these notions from evolving into a priori categories of understanding. The situation, however, changed with the introduction of Mahāyāna Buddhism and the rise of Chan, both of which contributed to the emergence of a homogeneous space. The same tendency can be observed with regard to the representation of time. From the Mahāyāna standpoint of emptiness, all times are equal—and ultimately delusory. In its well-known lines, the *Heart Sūtra* denies the twelve-linked chain of causation of early Buddhism in the name of ultimate truth, stating that, for the enlightened mind, there is no such thing as birth and death, aging and suffering. Like Plato's reconciliation, in *Timaeus*, of Heraclites' notion of universal flux and Parmenides' notion of unchanging being, the Mahāyāna theory of the Two Truths allowed to hierarchize two levels, the ultimate level in which there was no time, and the conventional in which a homogenized time reigned. Thus, according to the Chan master Dahui Zonggao, "Past, present, future, are all delusions," for the three periods "are ultimately empty and still" (Cleary and Cleary 1977, 24–25).

By immersing themselves in the "pure experience" of samādhi, Mahāyāna practitioners claimed to transcend time and change. As Huiyuan (334–417) made it clear in a letter to the emperor, "He who seeks the first principle is not obedient to change" (*Hongming ji, T. 52, 2102: 29–32*). This claim was often judged extravagant, even in Buddhist circles, and it was believed by some to bring immediate karmic retribution. An interesting case in point, often quoted in Chan literature, is that of the encounter between the Chan master Baizhang Huaihai and a fox. Appearing as an old monk, the fox tells Baizhang that he was formerly a Chan master himself, but for once saying that the enlightened master is not subject to the law of change, he was condemned to be reborn in this animal form during five hundred lifetimes. His unhappy fate, however, is eventually canceled by the realization obtained when Baizhang tells him that the enlightened man does not oppose change (see, for instance, *Shōbōgenzō Shinjin inga, T. 82, 2582: 294b*). The lesson of the story is ambiguous because, by claiming to submit to change, Baizhang actually transcends it. At any rate, by stressing the point of view of ultimate emptiness, Chan monks attempted to mentally transform the world into a utopia like Samuel Butler's *Erehwon*, where time and change do not exist. Yet, paradoxically, to express this "sudden" transcendence over time, they had to use spatial metaphors. This Chan "never-never land" was the realm of "pure experience," a state prior to the differentiation between being and becoming, time and space, or being and time. Isolated attempts to solve these aporias can be found in Buddhist theoreticians such as Nāgarjūna and Dōgen (or, more recently, Nishida Kitarō and Nishitani Keiji), who, instead of evading the seeming contradiction between the two levels of truth, take this very tension or chiasmatic intertwining as constitutive of the paradoxical nature of reality.[2]

CONFLICTING MODELS

However, the Chan attempt to transcend and/or homogenize time ultimately failed, owing perhaps to the variety of the models used, a variety resulting in a plurality of "homogeneities" that did not look too different from the earlier heterogeneity. As men of their time(s), Chan monks lived simultaneously in different temporalities; consequently they had to resort, more or less explicitly, to different models of time. These seemingly incommensurable models usually coexisted in the mind of the monks, and their intertwining bears witness to the sedimentation of different temporal strata in collective representations. Let us therefore attempt to retrieve the conceptions of time found in our corpus and examine their consequences for the development of the tradition(s) under study. Taking my cues from Krzysztof Pomian, I distinguish between three topologies of time: the linear, the circular, and the stationary (Pomian 1984, 50).

Chinese interest in history is often contrasted with the supposedly total lack of historical sense in Indian culture—a culture centered on the cyclical time of the *kalpa*. Like all such dichotomies, this one needs to be nuanced: in India as in China various temporalities always coexisted. Joseph Needham has argued that the Chinese conception of history is linear.[3] The Chinese sense of time remained essentially cyclical, however, and "historical" time only reflected a cosmic time marked by the rhythms of Yin and Yang and of the "five phases" (*wuxing*). Whereas space, belonging to the earth, was conceived as square, time, belonging to heaven, was conceived as circular. Chinese "correlative thinking"—just a local form of analogical thinking—has been well studied, by among others Granet (1968), Durkheim and Mauss (1963), and Needham (1974–1983). In a general way—although this summary judgment warrants many qualifications—it seems that, at least in its Confucian or Daoist versions, Chinese traditional thought attempted to make psychological and "historical" times coincide

[2] Rhetorical concepts such as "time-being" or "bodymind," used by Dōgen, call to "mind" what Arnold van Gennep imprudently labeled "Hitler's principle"—that is, "juxtaposing contradictions and imposing on its 'subjects' composite terms that, since they have no meaning, permit to think anything." Van Gennep gives the example of Wilhelm Wundt, who, finding it impossible "to distinguish clearly between *Mythus* (myth) and *Märchen* (folktales), invented the terms *Mythusmärchen* and its opposite *Märchenmythus* which denote neither the one nor the other yet somehow denote both simultaneously while also distinguishing between them without actually doing so." Quoted in Belmont 1979, 143.

[3] See Joseph Needham: "Le temps et l'homme oriental," in Needham 1977, 201.

with the paradigm of religious (cosmic, liturgical) time. It differed therefore from the Western notion of a historicity conceived as radically contingent and irreversible. Chinese "historical" works, for instance, were meant primarily as a collection of exempla illustrating dynastic cycles, not as an objective account of what actually happened (see Balasz 1961). Despite Chinese influence, Japanese official histories such as the *Jinnō shōtōki* (Chronicle of the Direct Lineage of Gods and Ancestors) by Kitabatake Chikafusa (1293–1354), relied on the model of a linear sacred time marked by the regular succession of imperials reigns. The emperors were no longer metaphorically "Sons of Heaven" (*Tianzi*) like their Chinese counterparts, who reigned only as long as they had the Mandate of Heaven (*tianming*), but true descendants of the Sun Goddess Amaterasu. While emphasizing Japan's essential difference, the *Jinnō shōtōki* also introduced Japan into universal (that is, largely Buddhist) history (see Durt 1988, 22).

Linear Time

Together with a circular notion of cosmic time (kalpa) derived from Hindu cosmology, Buddhism developed that of a linear time (chronology of Buddha's life, "Dotted record" of the Vinaya transmission) into Chinese cyclical time.[4] As Durt points out, "one can detect in almost all Buddhist countries a relation between monastic discipline and historiography" (Durt 1988, 5). The historical consciousness in the Vinaya school derived from the necessity to trace back the emergence of monastic rules to particular events in the life of the Buddha. B. G. Gokhale also points out that the emergence of a cult of relics created a need for a history of these relics and led to the compilation of chronicles such as the *Thūpavaṃsa* (Gokhale 1965, 356). Thus, in early Buddhism as in Chan, historical consciousness developed hand in hand with hagiography, and it is not synonymous with secular consciousness. The fact that the founder of the Vinaya school, Daoxuan (596–667), contributed more than anyone else to "mythologize" Chinese Buddhism—by initiating, for example, cults of the tooth relic of the Buddha or of the Arhat Piṇḍola—must be understood as an attempt to link Chinese Buddhism with the sacred time in which the Buddha lived. For Daoxuan, the sacred character of mythical time was reported on the historical origin.

Linear temporality, which forms the basis of the narrative, implies that

---

[4] The "Dotted Record" (*Shengdian ji*) was a copy of the Vinaya transmitted to China; it was allegedly written down at the First Council and subsequently dotted at every annual assembly (*pravāraṇā*). It is quoted twice in the *Lidai sanbao ji* [T. 49, 2034: 23a, 95b]. The number of dots allowed scholars to reconstitute the date of the Nirvāṇa of the Buddha as 485 B.C.E. On this question, see Durt 1988; Pachow 1965.

tradition (or whatever else is the subject of the narrative) is perceived as an individual entity. In this linear model, temporal change might be interpreted as either progress or regression, instead of the transcendence or trans-*gression* of the stationary model valued by "sudden" Chan. Although it seems initially derived from the cyclical kalpa theory, the ideology of the "decline of the Law" (Ch. *mofa*, J. *mappō*) was used in China and Japan to establish a linear periodization (Durt 1988, 5). This ideology, prevalent in Chinese Buddhism from the sixth century onward, reached its climax in Japanese Buddhism after the tenth century.

Nevertheless, the notion of progress was also present in Buddhism. It justified the founding of the new schools of Chinese and Japanese Buddhism, whose "doctrinal classifications" (*panjiao*) were based on a teleological model that gave primacy to one school over all others. It was prevalent, for example, in Japanese Tendai, as is clear from the works of Annen (841–?) and of Yōsai (d. 1215). Despite his role in the introduction of Rinzai Zen to Japan, Yōsai apparently never pretended to innovate but simply to return to Saichō's syncretism of Tendai, esoteric Buddhism (*Mikkyō*), Vinaya, and Zen—a unique conjunction of teachings perceived as the outcome of a unique historical conjuncture. As noted earlier, while departing from Annen's exclusive emphasis on Mikkyō, Yōsai echoed his claim that only on Mount Hiei had it been possible for all these trends to come together (*T.* 80, 2543: 10b). This teleological conception affected geographical notions as well: the earlier model, in which India, not China, was the "central kingdom,"[5] while China and Japan were perceived as peripheral, barbarian countries, was gradually abandoned.[6] Actually, the main effect of the ideology of the three countries (*sangoku shisō*) was to relativize the importance of China in Japanese perceptions and, consequently, to increase that of Japan (Durt 1988, 11). With Dōgen, we can even discern the transition from this earlier model to a second model where Japan becomes the center.[7] This strategic move is reinforced by a phenomenological emphasis on meditative practice, in which the present moment becomes the supreme instance, while the origin is displaced in Dōgen's

[5] See, for example, Guṇabhadra's statement in the *Lengqie shizi ji*: "This land [China] is located at the Eastern outskirts, and [its inhabitants] do not have a method to cultivate the Way. . . . In my middle Kingdom there exists an orthodox Law, but it is secret and is not transmitted [at random]" *T.* 85, 2837: 1284a. See also Dōgen's *Shōbōgenzō Shizen biku* (*T.* 82, 2582: 299c; Yokoi 1976, 163).

[6] See, for example, Saichō's *Naishō buppōsō jō kechimyakufu* in *Nihon daizōkyō* 75, 349; Gyōnen's *Sangoku buppō denzū engi*, in *DNBZ* 62, 467; and Yōsai's *Kōzen gokokuron*, *T.* 80, 2543: 16a.

[7] This model, reinforced at the time of the Mongol invasion by the nativist notion of Japan as "divine country," paved the way for the nativist Shintō theory that reverted the *honji-suijaku* model, the so-called *han-honji suijaku*. This theory argued that Japan (Shintō) was the root, whereas China (Confucianism) was the branches and India (Buddhism) the fruit.

notion of *gyōji*, a perpetual, circular "sustained practice" (*Shōbōgenzō Gyōji, T.* 82, 2582: 127a–144b).

As noted earlier, Indian Buddhism inherited from Hinduism the idea of a *circular* time, cosmic and individual. The notion of *saṃsāra*, the cycle of births and deaths, implied that the span of human life was only the visible face of time. With the popular interest in the "hidden face of time," that is, with the desire to know more about the other destinies (Sk. *gati*) offering or imposing themselves on man, linear time lost some of its significance. Because the ultimate goal, the eternity of Nirvāṇa, was too distant to be of much relevance, people were satisfied to hope for a better rebirth and tended to revert to the old temporalities.[8]

Another response, more appealing in the Chinese context, was to introduce "leaps" on the path to shorten the distance from here to infinity. Finally, with the development of Mahāyāna, there emerged the notion of a suprahistorical, irreversible time, in which man, once he has produced the thought of awakening (*bodhicitta*), transcends the circular, reversible time of saṃsāra and eventually surmounts all the obstacles in this cosmic game of snakes and ladders. This conception of a suprahistorical time calls to mind the case of Christianity, in which an intermediary time, the *aevum*, emerged between the Parmenidian realm of immutability (*aeternitas*) and the Heraclitean realm of change (*tempus*). The aevum differed from cosmic time in its linearity and irreversibility. There seems to be in Buddhism a conception of intermediary time, whether individual, as in the case of the "Stream-enterer" and other advanced practitioners who gradually escape the whorl of saṃsāra, or collective, for example what we may call the "sacred history" of esoteric Buddhism or Chan. Mediating between the apparent immobility of Nirvāṇa, labeled the "dark pit" by Chan,[9] and the endless cycle of saṃsāra, this intermediary time may be conceived as suprahistorical—although it seems in some cases to mark a return to cosmic time.[10] The notion of a "sacred history" is clearly present in early Chan texts such as the *Chuan fabao ji* (ca. 712), a chronicle of the "Transmission of the Dharma-Jewel." Another, rather extreme, example is provided by a Dunhuang text (Beijing collection, *xian* 29) in which the patriarchal transmission is said to take place in the Adamantine Realm (*Vajradhātu*), that is, on the plane of spiritual or suprahistorical history:

[8] Melford Spiro has attempted to distinguish between what he calls "Nirvanic" and "Karmatic" Buddhism (Spiro 1982, 12). These notions have a certain heuristic value as ideal-types, but they should not be taken, as he does, as referring to specific social groups (monks vs. laymen, for example).

[9] See, for instance, C. Cleary 1977, 29. Early Chan texts, influenced by the Tathāgata-garbha tradition, attempted to redefine Nirvāṇa positively as an exact opposite of the Four ⟨...⟩ oncerning saṃsāra, that is, as a state that is "permanent, blissful, personal and ⟨...⟩e wo jing)" (Faure 1989, 110–111); however, this conception did not prevail.

"The saint Bodhidharma, being at the Bodhisattva rank of the eighth *bhūmi*, received the ultimate teaching from the Bodhisattva Vasubandhu. Ascending to the Adamantine Realm [of Vairocana], he received the transmission and obtained perfect awakening" (Xu Guolin 1937, 2: 139–140). The same scenario is repeated for the six patriarchs, down to Huineng.

A compromise between linear and circular time may be found in the ritual conception of the patriarchal lineage, a conception illustrated by the diagrams of the *kirigami* of the Sōtō tradition. According to these esoteric documents of transmission, while the transmission seems to develop historically in linear fashion from the past Buddha Śākyamuni to the present master, it returns to Śākyamuni in suprahistorical fashion at the moment of individual awakening. The schematic representation is therefore ultimately circular. The linear succession of patriarchs corresponds to the tangential points between time and eternity because each "historical" awakening is described as a face-to-face encounter with the primordial, ahistorical Buddha and takes place *in illo tempore*. In this sense, every awakening is a ritual reenactment of the Buddha's awakening.

If the Dharma transmission takes place on the plane of suprahistorical history, then does the Chan denial of the linearity of time imply a denial of history? The Chan emphasis on immediacy seems to derive from the traditional notion that knowledge has to be immediate and is therefore limited to the present.[11] The past can only be an object of faith; it cannot be the object of a mediate (for instance historical) knowledge because such knowledge is epistemologically depreciated.[12] According to Pomian, the development of historical consciousness can take place only when knowledge is not conceived as necessarily immediate but can be mediated through the written or oral tradition (Pomian 1984, 20). We return in chapter 8 to the role of writing in Chan. Nevertheless, the rise of a Chan historiography under the Song seems to reflect the growth of a Chan historical consciousness. This phenomenon is not isolated; it is part of a larger societal change between the Tang and the Song. Among many other factors, the growing use of currency, like that in Europe, probably con-

[10] See, for example, the return to the cosmological schemas of the *Yijing* and neo-Confucianism in the Sōtō tradition.

[11] There are, however, some cases in which a direct perceptual knowledge of past or distant events is deemed possible, namely, through the supranormal powers (*abhijñā*) acquired by advanced practitioners (see Gokhale 1965, 359). Needless to say, Chan masters felt obliged to devalorize these powers. On this question, see Faure 1991.

[12] The problem reappears in the Suzuki/Hu Shih controversy, owing to the fact that the two men relied on different epistemologies, different conceptions of knowledge and of time. In the case of Suzuki, one can clearly discern conflicting temporalities: his nostalgia for origins, itself derived from his modernity, contradicted his notion of ahistorical Chan. The same can be said with regard to the notion of supra-historical history advocated by representatives of the Kyōto school like Nishitani Keiji or Abe Masao.

tributed to undermine the world of immediacy and face-to-face relationship and to modify the attitude toward time. However, this evolution did not affect equally all sectors of society and all collective representations. It did not reduce, and perhaps only reinforced, the diversity of temporalities found in Chan. If Chan followers seem to become more interested in a mythical past, they remain almost untouched by eschatological themes or ideologies such as the entrance into the period of the Final Dharma and the coming of the future Buddha Maitreya. The Chan emphasis on the phenomenal world, through its assertion of the phenomenal qua absolute, amounts to an escape from finitude: man being in truth infinite and living in an eternal present, it follows that transiency, death, and ultimately time itself, belong to the realm of delusion; they result from epistemological mistakes and are devoid of ontological reality. "Sudden" awakening marks a rupture with time, a denial of temporality: it is not simply "faster" to obtain, but it is properly atemporal. Significantly, the definition of sudden awakening as a simultaneous perception of the Two Truths is commanded by a spatial rather than a temporal metaphor. The "gradualist" metaphor of the path (*mārga*) itself is often spatialized, for instance in the parable of Sudhana's pilgrimage in search of truth.

History, at least individual history, is further denied by the ritual demarcation, in profane time, of specific periods invested with a special soteriological meaning. As Henri Hubert points out, critical junctures are equivalent to the intervals they limit because "what must take place over the entire period is realized at its beginning, at least in representation" (Hubert and Mauss 1909, 203). Thus, the entire process leading to awakening, the fifty-two stages of the so-called Bodhisattva career, is subsumed in the inaugural moment of the "thought of awakening" (*bodhicitta*), the initial resolution to save all sentient beings. In Sudhana's story, this point is illustrated by the fact that young Sudhana, at the end of his initiatic journey, realizes that the last stage was already contained in the first, that his last interlocutor, Mañjuśri, is no other than the first. All contingencies have been cleared from the pilgrim's process, which, unlike other spatial metaphors such as the game of snakes and ladders, can be retrospectively seen as perfectly homogeneous. The gradualism of the path and the uncertainties of the future have been, as it were, canceled by the inaugural act, the thought of awakening, or in some cases, by the prediction (Sk. *vyākaraṇa*) made by the Buddha of his disciple's future awakening.

Historical Consciousness

Despite the self-proclaimed atemporal nature of Chan, reiterated by Suzuki, there is no denying that, even before the rise of Song historiography, the early Chan patriarchal tradition reflected a conventional type of

"historical consciousness." As in Chinese ancestor worship, the enumera-
tion of patriarchal generations is a fundamental aspect of Chan monks'
relation to time. This relation is also reflected in the importance of early
Chan epigraphy and in the Chan fascination with relics and funerary
rituals. Funerary inscriptions recording the dates of death and the age
reached by the monks seem to indicate that Chan followers, for all their
official contempt for life and death, perceived life as a precious opportunity
and death as a momentous event. Many funerary stelae of Northern Chan
masters record the seven patriarchal generations, spanning from the Indian
monk Bodhidharma to Shenxiu's disciples. The historical anchoring of
Northern Chan is particularly significant in Li Yong's inscription for
the Chan master Puji (d. 739), according to which these seven generations
were the equivalent of the seven imperial generations of the Tang dynasty
(see "Dazhao chanshi taming," in QTW 262, 6: 3360; McRae 1986, 65;
Faure 1988, 132). However, it was not sufficient to trace the Chan lineage
back to its inception in China; soon, it became necessary to establish the
genealogical link with Śākyamuni, the founder of Buddhism himself. After a few hesitations and anachronisms—such as Shenhui's early theory
of thirteen generations of Indian patriarchs—a consensus was eventually reached with the theory of twenty-eight Indian patriarchs, from the
Buddha to Bodhidharma. Another aspect of the growth of historical
consciousness in Chan is the development of prophecies in the sectarian arena: unlike the earlier predictions of Buddhahood, which canceled
the hazards of the search and leveled the path, these Chan prophecies
refer to times when the true Dharma and/or the life of its representatives will be endangered. The fact that prophecies of this type were
usually made ex post facto is not important here. Upon transmitting
the Laṅkāvatāra-sūtra to his disciple Huike, Bodhidharma warned him
that, four generations later, this scripture would no longer be understood
(see Faure 1989); the Fifth Patriarch Hongren, upon transmitting the kā-
ṣāya to Huineng, predicted that the destiny of Chan would be "hanging by
a thread" forty years after his death (presumably an allusion to Shenhui's
exile); likewise, the Japanese master Yōsai predicted that, fifty years after
his death, his teaching would be endangered—an ex post facto apocryphal
prediction implying a criticism of the Darumashū on the part of Yōsai's
disciples.[13]

Psychological Time and Memory

By opening a breach in the cosmic time of Indian thought, Buddhism
contributed to the growth of both psychological time and individualism.

[13] See the *Miraiki* [Record of the Future], a prophecy annexed to Yōsai's *Kōzen gokokuron*,
in Ichikawa, Iriya, and Yanagida 1972, 96–97.

Although the notion of impermanence (Sk. *anitya*, J. *mujō*) was in early Buddhism closely related to that of no-self (*anātman*), it tended to increase the existential awareness of the individual. This tendency reached its climax in Japanese Buddhism, where this notion of impermanence merged with the (apparently) native notion of *mono no aware* to achieve an almost Heraclitean sense of time. The practice of meditation probably increased, in some respects, the feeling of being caught "*in lubrico tempore*" (Augustine) for monks who, by reciting day and night that "time flies like an arrow," were constantly aware that every passing moment diminishes the chances of reaching awakening in this life.

Psychological time is closely associated with memory, that is, with the persistence of mental images.[14] In early Buddhism, while memory played a crucial role in preserving the teachings of the Buddha, the identification with individual memories was seen as the cause of the false notion of a self. Early Chan shows a strong tendency to do away with all mental images, in an attempt to reach the blissful state of nonthinking (Ch. *wuxin, wunian*).[15] Along with an emphasis on the present moment as locus of the "pure experience," this ideal of anoetism may explain the Chan rejection of memory: awakening is not a Platonic *anamnesia* or a Proustian remembrance of things past, nor a Jātaka-like knowledge of past lives. There was apparently in Tang China a growing mistrust toward the Buddhist claim that meditation gave the power to remember past lives (see Demiéville 1927). However, we have seen that "classical" Chan implied a departure from the earlier ontological model defined as "seeing one's nature" (Ch. *jianxing*, J. *kenshō*), toward a more performative model privileging awakening *in actu* and giving precedence to the mind's "integral function" over its essence. Perhaps against such a backdrop we should read the enigmatic three-sentence motto of the Chan master Wuxiang (K. Musang): "No remembrance, no-thought, no forgetting" (*wuyi wunian mowang*).[16] Along with a growing distrust of the hermeneutical model came the insight that memory cannot be trusted: although apparently "hermeneutical" in its retrieval of the past, it is actually performative or constitutive—actively producing the past, projecting it from the present (just as the memory of a dream recreates or perhaps creates it). When asked about his age by Empress Wu, the Chan master Huian claimed that he had completely forgotten it. Nothing surprising, from a man who was allegedly

---

[14] Mental images constitute for instance the basis of the mnemotechnical methods described by the Jesuit Matteo Ricci in his *Memory Palace*, in Spence 1986.

[15] Although *wunian* is nonattachment to thoughts rather than the production of a "blank mind," the latter being criticized in Chan as a Hinayanist state of mind, the constant comparison of mind with empty space leads to similar conclusions.

[16] See *Lidai fabao ji*, in Yanagida 1976, 143. Wuxiang equates no remembrance with *śīla*, no thought with *samādhi*, and no forgetting with *prajñā*. See also ibid., 200.

almost 120 years old at the time! However, the metaphor used by Huian is significant: "Isn't this body subject to the endless cycles of saṃsāra? What is the use to remember, as long as these cycles have not ended? . . . All these are only false notions, like looking at bubbles that appear and disappear. What months, what years should we remember?" (*Song gaoseng zhuan*, T. 50, 2061: 823c).

Temporal Conditions

In contrast with the "spatial" metaphors of the path (*mārga*) and of the "other shore," there is a Buddhist root metaphor that is essentially temporal—namely, the organic metaphor of germination and maturation. In Mahāyāna, the Buddha nature was conceived as a germ that would grow and in due time bear the fruit of Nirvāṇa. Associated with that of the "mind-ground" (Ch. *xindi*),[17] this metaphor came to play an important role in the Chan "verses of transmission" (Ch. *chuanfa jie*, J. *denbōge*). From Bodhidharma to Huineng, the *Jingde Chuandeng lu* describes a versified sequence that seems to prefigure Japanese linked verses (*renga*), a sequence unfolding from the famous line attributed to Bodhidharma: "One flower opens five petals, and the fruit ripens of itself" (see Yampolsky 1967, 177). Time in this context is essentially the cosmic and liturgical time of the agricultural calendar. The importance of the calenderic conceptions in Chinese culture may explain the success of the Buddhist notion of "temporal conditions" (Ch. *shijie yinyuan*, J. *jisetsu innen*), an expression referring to the proper time when a breakthrough toward awakening may be attempted. The *locus classicus* is a scriptural passage according to which: "If you want to understand the meaning of the Buddha nature, you must observe the temporal conditions" (quoted in *Shōbōgenzō Busshō*, T. 82, 2582: 92c). Because "times and tides wait for no man," the "crossing to the other shore" had to take meteorological conditions into consideration. The expression seems therefore to refer to not only the maturity of the practitioner himself but also the "quality of time."[18] In contrast with agricultural metaphors, the use of maritime metaphors such as the "crossing to the other shore" remained relatively rare in a largely land-locked tradition. Consequently, it was essential for a Chan master to distinguish the different stages of maturation of his disciples—as did the Buddha himself, who devised four modes of teaching (*siddhānta*) to take into account the capacity of his interlocutors (see Lamotte 1944–1980, 1: 27–

[17] The early Chan teaching was apparently known as the "teaching of the mind-ground" (*xindi famen*). Depending on the context, "mind-ground" refers to the Buddha nature or to the content of the awakening transmitted by Bodhidharma. See, for example, Fuller Sasaki 1975, 11, 26.

[18] On the notion of "quality of time," see Hubert and Mauss 1909, 209.

55). Many Chan texts attempt to define various levels of understanding and appropriate methods of teaching. In the *Lengqie shizi ji*, for example, the "first patriarch" Guṇabhadra discusses four types of mind (*T.* 85, 2837: 1284b), while the "fifth patriarch" Daoxin distinguishes between four categories of disciples (ibid., 1287c).

However, this "discernment of minds" was later denied by the rhetoric of the "sudden" teaching, which asserted the innate perfection of the Buddha Nature and privileged the ultimate standpoint. According to this teaching, there is no need to wait for a future event called awakening because the temporal conditions are always already fulfilled and everyone is fundamentally awakened. This stance was taken up by Dōgen in his advocacy of "sitting-only" (*shikan taza*). In a hermeneutical sleight of hand that allowed him to read the passage "*If* [or *when*] the temporal conditions are ripe" as "*Since* the temporal conditions are ripe," Dōgen denied the organic growth metaphor associated with the notion of "temporal conditions" (*T.* 82, 3582: 92c–93a).

Although Dōgen's idiosyncratic gloss is usually read as a criticism of Dahui Zonggao and his Japanese followers, Dahui shared with Dōgen a desire to go beyond the gradualist understanding of "temporal conditions." According to Dahui: "If you want to get so you aren't following times and seasons, simply abandon it at once" (J. C. Cleary 1977, 78). In another passage, Dahui quotes side by side two apparently contradictory poems by Lingyun Zhiqin (d.u.) and Xuefeng Yicun (822–908).[19] Lingyun's poem, concerning his awakening upon seeing peach blossoms, is followed by this comment from his master, Guishan Lingyou (771–853): "When you enter [the path] in accordance with circumstances, there will be no regression."[20] Xuefeng's poem reads: "If you attain from causal circumstances, / It begins and ends, forms and disintegrates. / If you don't attain from causal circumstances, / It endures through the ages, everlasting and solid." Dahui pointed out the seeming contradiction between the two poems: "Tell me, are the viewpoints of these two venerable adepts the same or different? If you say they're the same, one man considers attainment from causal conditions right and one man considers it wrong. If you say they're different, it's impossible that the two great elders were setting up divergent sects to confuse later people with doubts." Dahui tried to show the difference between the two verses with another verse alluding to the Two Truths: "Although the two exist because of one / Don't even keep the

---

[19] Lingyun's poem about his awakening, an awakening reached after seeing peach blossoms, is also commented on by Dōgen. The strategical role of this poem in Dōgen's *Shōbōgenzō* is clearly related to its importance in the texts of the Darumashū. See, for example, *Hōmon taikō*, in Shinagawa Kenritsu Kanazawa Bunko 1974, 219.

[20] To this well-known story, Dōgen later added his own comment: "Who could enter without following circumstances, and who could ever regress?" See Faure 1987a, 125.

one! / When the one mind isn't born, / The myriad phenomena are without fault." Dahui eventually side-stepped the contradiction with a light-hearted comment ("Bah!")—thus rhetorically placing himself above the "temporal conditions" (see J. C. Cleary 1977, 117).

The notion of "temporal conditions" paved the way for the "encounter dialogues" (*jiyuan*) that were essentially attempts to create or seize "opportunities" (Ch. *ji*, J. *ki*)—a notion that calls to mind the Greek *kairos*.[21] With the institutionalization of these agonistic dialogues, a gradual shift took place, from the submission of psychological time to cosmic patterns toward an assertion of the individual and a forceful creation of (sometimes inopportune) opportunities. In the ritual context of the dialogues, the time of Chan became a permanent spring or autumn, the monastery an enchanted garden where temporal conditions were always ripe, flowers always ready to open, fruits always ready to fall. However, the notion of organic growth did also lend itself to a "naturalist" reading that undermined the necessity of spiritual practice. Against the backdrop of such a "naturalist heresy" we must place Dōgen's famous discussion of time.

DŌGEN AND HIS TIMES

Dōgen's "ontologization" of time is also a "spatialization": everything is time, but time is, as it were, spatialized. In various passages of the *Shōbōgenzō*, time is described as perfectly coextensive with the phenomenal world: "The fact that horses and sheep are arrayed as they are throughout the whole world is also due to the dwelling [of everything] like this in its own dharma-position, ascending and descending up and down. Rats are time. So are tigers. Sentient beings are time, and buddhas are too."[22] Paradoxically, time can only be perceived in its spatial extension.

For heuristic purposes, we might distinguish several conceptions of time coexisting in Dōgen's work. Dōgen inherited from the Buddhist tradition a basic polarity that calls to mind the Western opposition between *aeternitas* and *tempus*. In his case, however, this binary schema eventually turns into a ternary one because three conflicting or complementary models seem at work in the *Shōbōgenzō*: the linear, the stationary, and the cyclical conceptions of time.

The linear model derives from the conception of the transmission of the

[21] On the notion of *kairos*, see Detienne and Vernant 1974, 212–214. As regards the notion of *ki*, it seems to point to not only an unpredictable event but also the return of a very rare and brief occurrence—like the blooming of the Udumbara flower (on which see *Shōbōgenzō Udonge*, T. 82, 2582: 236–237).

[22] See *Shōbōgenzō Uji*, T. 82, 2582: 122. Note here the shift from time to space permitted by the use of the zodiacal symbols, tiger or rat, to express real animals.

Shōbōgenzō (a term referring here to ultimate truth itself) as taking place in a kind of sacred history. One could argue that Dōgen allows some progress to take place, if not in the content of truth itself, at least in its conditions of transmission. Dōgen saw himself as the first to have introduced authentic Buddhism to Japan: the name of the monastery he founded in Echizen, Eiheiji, refers to the *Yongping* (J. *Eihei*, 57–75 C.E.) era of Emperor Ming, who was allegedly the first Chinese ruler to convert to Buddhism. Dōgen also draws an analogy between Bodhidharma and himself, as transmitters of the true Dharma in China and Japan, respectively.[23] He even goes so far as to claim that, contrary to the tradition depicting Bodhidharma as a solitary ascetic, the Indian monk, like himself, came to China as a member of an official mission. This claim may explain why Dōgen and the Sōtō sect seem to have consciously ignored the legend, accredited by Kokan Shiren's *Genkō shakusho* and the Rinzai tradition, that Bodhidharma had come to Japan (see Faure 1988, 159–160). At any rate, the notion of a progress is clearly at work here, with the assumption that the esoteric transmission of the Buddha Dharma, the "Treasure of the Eye of the True Law" (*Shōbōgenzō*) has reached its perfection in Japan with Dōgen.

However, Dōgen emphasizes a stationary model of time when he claims that there is an essential identity of the Dharma (*Shōbōgenzō*). As noted earlier, the immediacy of awakening also implies a stationary topology of time, a denial that spirituality could be determined by spatio-temporal conditions that had supposedly brought the decline of Buddhism in the period of the "Final Dharma" (*mappō*). The stationary, as it were, dotted, topology of time seems to exclude any prediction because there is no link between what precedes and what follows; each individual awakening (and, more generally, each event) takes place *in illo tempore*, in the atemporal realm of Suchness (*tathatā*).[24] The main difficulty raised by this variation on the "nature origination" (*xingqi*) theory (a theory deriving from speculations on the *Tathāgatagarbha* and other variants of the Buddha nature) is that it undermines the traditional karmic causality. Thus, although Dōgen attached a great importance to causality and karmic retribution, he relied on a conception of time that implicitly denied it.

[23] However, Dōgen seems to have hesitated between these two images of himself, as a transmitter of traditional Buddhism (inaugurating a new *yongping/eihei* era) and as a second Bodhidharma, transmitter of "true" Buddhism (Chan).

[24] Although Chan is characterized by a denial of traditional divination, early Chan masters such as Shenxiu, Puji, and Yixing were famous for their predictions. In theory, there is no way to foretell the future, unless the notion of *dun* ("sudden"), inasmuch as it means simultaneity, simultaneous perception of the principle and the phenomena, implies a knowledge of the future as a juxtaposed present. All evolution would thus be denied as illusory, in the name of a simultaneity of cause and effect. See *Shōbōgenzō Shinjin inga*, T. 82, 2582: 294–296. See also Pomian 1984, viii.

Although transmission implies a linear time, there seems to be a cyclical pattern in Dōgen's replay in Japan of the introduction of Buddhism into China. This cyclical pattern also appears in Dōgen's conception of religious practice, as illustrated by his discussion of the "sustained practice" (gyōji):

> The great way of the Buddhas and Patriarchs involves the highest form of exertion, which goes on unceasingly in cycles from the first dawning of religious truth, through the test of discipline and practice, to enlightenment and Nirvāṇa. It is sustained exertion, proceeding without lapse from cycle to cycle. . . . Thus, it is through our exertions that these benefits circulate in cycles to others, and it is due only to this that the Buddhas and Patriarchs come and go, affirming Buddha and negating Buddha, attaining the Buddha-mind and achieving Buddhahood, ceaselessly and without end. (Tsunoda, de Bary, and Keene 1964, 250)

Dōgen attempted to reconcile the sacred and time by "timing" the sacred, deploying it in time "as an uninterrupted chain of eternities" (Hubert and Mauss 1909, 226), thereby allowing a shift from the stationary to the linear model. Although time had to be stationary if the "Treasure of the True Dharma Eye" (Shōbōgenzō) was to remain intact, Dōgen could not help acknowledging that the tradition had a—sacred and profane— history. While refusing the ideology of the "Final Dharma," he used the periodization provided by another prevalent ideology, that of Buddhism's "eastward penetration" (tōzen) in the "Three Countries" (India, China, and Japan), in what looks like an attempt to reconcile the linear and cyclical models into a kind of spiral pattern. This reconciliation, however, was never realized in his writings, and there is no proof that the discrepancy we see between these heuristic models was ever experienced as such by Dōgen himself. On the basis of a superficial similarity between the title of one of Dōgen's sermons, Uji (a binom usually translated as "Being"/time), and Heidegger's epoch-making Being and Time, comparativist scholars have tended to see in Dōgen an existentialist philosopher avant la lettre, who emphasized, against his predecessors, the essential impermanence or finitude of the phenomenal world. For Dōgen, even the Buddha Nature is impermanent, or rather impermanence itself is the Buddha nature. He gives time a philosophical importance unprecedented in Chinese and Japanese Buddhism (with the exception of Sengzhao). Time becomes ultimate reality. However, as noted earlier, Dōgen's collapse of time and reality, of the present and eternity, led him to deny the traditional understanding of "temporal conditions." In Shōbōgenzō Busshō, elaborating on the Platform Sūtra's notion that "impermanence is the Buddha nature" (T. 48, 2008: 359), Dōgen writes: "Therefore, the very impermanence of grass and trees, thicket and forest, is the Buddha nature. . . . Nations and lands, mountains and rivers, are impermanent because they are Buddha nature"

(*T*. 82, 2582: 95a). And he concludes by quoting the famous line: "If you wish to know the Buddha nature's meaning, you should watch for temporal conditions" (ibid.; see also Terada and Mizuno 1970, 1: 102). In *Uji*, Dōgen stresses the immutability of things: "As the time right now is all there ever is, each being-time is without exception entire time. . . . Entire being, the entire world, exists in the time of each and every now" (Waddell 1979, 118). In another passage, he writes: "We set the self out in array and make that the whole world. You must see all the various things of the whole world as so many times" (ibid., 117). He returns to this point in *Shōji*: "It is a mistake to think you pass from birth to death. Being one stage of total time, birth is already possessed of before and after. Being one stage of total time as well, cessation of life also is possessed of before and after. Thus it is said, extinction itself is non-extinction" (ibid., 79). This almost Parmenidian notion, also found in *Genjō kōan* (*T*. 82, 2582: 24a), was actually strongly influenced by the Huayan philosophy of "mutual interpenetration of phenomena" (Ch. *shishi wu'ai*) and by Sengzhao's notion of the "immutability of things."[25] By resorting to the hermeneutical theory of the Two Truths, Dōgen (and Sengzhao) substituted permanence for impermanence, immutability to change; they spatialized time by visualizing it as concrete, unchanging stages: wood, ashes, and so on. This visual arraying is associated with a claim for returning to the original (or perennial) teaching of the Buddha—a claim that seems to confirm Ernst Bloch's remark, quoted earlier, that the primacy of space over time characterizes reactionary language.[26] For all its lofty philosophical style, Dōgen's conception of time and of the Buddha nature appears to have specific ideological and sectarian stakes. As I have tried to show elsewhere (Faure 1988, 55–61), Dōgen's notion of Buddha nature as impermanent might be seen partly as a criticism of the Darumashū's notion of a permanent self/Buddha Nature and of its "naturalist" advocacy of the natural ripening of temporal conditions.

Sectarian Time

The sectarian background of Dōgen's conceptions of time becomes apparent in *Keisei sanshoku*, a chapter in which Dōgen takes up the notion of "circumstantial Buddhas" (*pratyeka-buddha*), a term referring to those who have awakened by themselves, owing to precisely the natural "fru-

[25] According to opening line of the *Zhao lun*, "That birth and death alternate, that winter and summer succeed each other, that all things glide along and move is a generally accepted proposition. But to me this is not so" (Liebenthal 1968, 45).

[26] Although the "original" teaching of the "historical" Buddha may never be retrievable, it seems that, contrary to Dōgen's claim, the doctrine of early Buddhism gave the primacy to time over space.

ition" of their karma, the ripeness of "temporal conditions." As it turns out, Dainichi Nōnin, the founder of the Darumashū, claimed to have awakened by himself, "without the guidance of a master" (*mushi dokugo*). Unlike Yōsai and Dōgen, Nōnin had not crossed over to the "other shore" of China and had only received indirectly the Dharma transmission from Fozhao Deguang (1121–1203), a disciple of Dahui. Nōnin's autodidacticism was the main object of the criticism leveled at him by his rivals,[27] and Dōgen was the most adamant in emphasizing the necessity of a face-to-face transmission from master to disciple. Unlike his successor Keizan, who recognized various modalities of awakening, Dōgen denied the authenticity of a solitary awakening, although, ironically enough, such was precisely the type of awakening realized by Śākyamuni under the *bodhi* tree (See Durt 1987, 1224). In *Keisei sanshoku*, Dōgen examines famous cases of awakening brought about by "temporal conditions"—such as the sound of a mountain stream for the Chinese poet Su Shi, the sound of a stone on a bamboo for Xiangyan Zhixian (d. 898), the blossoming of peach flowers for Lingyun—to show, precisely, that all these apparent cases of "natural" awakening were actually initiated by an encounter with an authentic Chan master. He points out, for example, that, in Su Shi's case, awakening took place when the resonance of the words of the Chan master Fayin on the "preaching of the non-sentient" (J. *mujō seppō*) merged at night with the sound of the valley stream.

Dōgen was probably justified in seeing, behind the "naturalist" interpretation of "temporal conditions," the threat of "quietistic" conceptions, "heretic" teachings that criticized Chan practice for doing violence to natural rhythms and "temporal conditions." At first glance, the "sitting only" (*shikan taza*) practice advocated by Dōgen seems itself rather passive, at least more so than the perpetual rumination of the kōan. However, in spite of their differences, both techniques were seen by their detractors as variants of "voluntarist" meditation, a form of practice characterized for instance by commentators of the *Yijing* as "immobilizing the hips and stiffening the sacrum."[28] As it was enforced in most monasteries, Chan meditation was perceived as an attempt to stop the flow of thought (and therefore of time), to force the course of things instead of merely following it, as the *Yijing* and the theoreticians of "nonaction" (Ch. *wuwei*) recommended.

[27] See, for example, *Genkō shakusho*: "Bragging of [Fozhao's] courtesy gifts, Nōnin began to spread Chan teachings. But since he lacked a direct transmission from a master as well as a disciplinary code, the people of the capital scorned him" (*DNBZ* 62, 76).

[28] This criticism of Buddhist meditation is found in a gloss of the hexagram *gen*, "the mountain," or "Immobilization of the back" (*Yijing* no. 52). Significantly, this hexagram was chosen by the Confucianist Lin Zhaoen to summarize his conception of spiritual practice. See Berling 1980, 116–121.

THE RITUALIZATION OF TIME

After this review of the conceptions of time at work in the theoretical discourse of Chan/Zen, it may be time to examine briefly how these conceptions organized the practice of Zen monasteries. "Sudden" Chan eventually became the doctrine of an institution centered on liturgical time. The time of the monastery is fundamentally utopian, and as such constitutes a denial of history. Its main purpose seems to transform the transient human existence, with its trail of sufferings, into the cyclical and ultimately stationary time of ritual. Buddhist spiritual practice entails a departure from the agonistic and finite reality of ordinary life, although to a lesser extent than the theoretical discourse of Chan. Both the theory and the practice are essentially utopian inasmuch as they imply a claim to achieve an ideal of harmony that hides the real relations of power. Presupposing a cyclical topology of time, Chan meditation and liturgy achieve a significant "humanization" of time: their ritualized time mediates between the apparent linearity of psychological time and the stationary time of an awakening conceived as a full awareness of the eternal present, yet it also implies a denial of mythical time and historical time (see Pomian 1984, 243).

The imbrication of different temporalities is reflected in the rhythms that regulate monastic life—as they can still be observed in Japanese Zen monasteries today. Particularly striking in this respect is the ritualized alternation of activity and quietude in the daily routine: for instance, the contrast between the immobility of *zazen* and the frantic cadence of meals and alms rounds. Many ritual details—such as the burning of incense sticks during meditation, the beating of wooden blocks, the sound of bells and drums—point to the importance of the measure, or rather the rhythm, of time in monasteries. Here again, the cyclical time of ritual intertwines with the linear time of the tradition, with the ritual recitation of the entire sequence of patriarchs, from the Buddha to the present abbot. Whereas the stress on the cult of the patriarchs and, more generally, on the cult of the dead seems to anchor Chan/Zen in the past, this past, becoming mythical, has lost its historical dimension. The practice of Rinzai Zen, entirely bent toward the distant or imminent breakthrough, seems also to divert the practitioner from his/her present (and often painful) experience. This may be one reason for the Sōtō refusal to consider awakening as a future event and for its attempt to place it upstream, at the very source of the practitioner's consciousness.[29] The two different soteriologies and types of practice found in

[29] Nevertheless, there is an undeniable sense of transiency in Zen and the urgency of intensive practice is constantly stressed in daily ritual. Also significant is the daily recitation of the *Enmyō jikku Kannongyō*, a sūtra (or rather dhāraṇī) concerned with longevity, a concern

Rinzai and Sōtō are traditionally opposed as *kanna zen* (Zen focused on kōan, disparaged by its critics as *taigo zen*, "waiting for awakening" Zen) and *mokushō zen* ("silent illumination Zen"). Despite the polemical connotations of these labels, it is clear that the two approaches to awakening that they define imply two different temporal orientations. According to Yanagida Seizan, whereas the Rinzai sect emphasized techniques based on time (the kōan), the Sōtō sect (after Dōgen, and to some extent against him) emphasized visual and spatial techniques—among which was the use of complex diagrams relying on the "Five Ranks" theory and influenced by neo-Confucian cosmology.[30] Perhaps the divergences between the two sects in regard to time might derive from the fact that the "spatialization of thought" was more advanced in Sōtō than in Rinzai. To prove this point, however, would require more research, and such proof is beyond the scope of this programmatic chapter.

To sum up, it appears that early Chan tried to impose, as it did with space, a homogenous conception of time against the qualitative, heterogeneous time of popular consciousness; however, the tension between alternative models of time contributed from the outset to generate a disparity and to reintroduce a qualitative and heterogeneous time. The popularization of Chan/Zen and the growing importance of funerary rituals probably played an important role in the "reenchantment" or "remythologization" of time and space that took place in Chan/Zen monasteries.

I have tried to tease out the multiple—and often contradictory—implications of the early Chan privilege given to visual/spatial metaphors over temporal metaphors. To the extent that writing also implies a "spatialization of thought," this leads us to examine the relations that developed in Chan between scriptural and oral/aural metaphors. We have to keep in mind, however, that the Chan/Zen tradition is multivocal, sometimes even discordant, and that different trends, at various times, have emphasized some virtualities over others. The term "multivocality" points to our own use of "logocentric" metaphors and to the fact that our present understanding of Chan/Zen might itself depend on similar shifts from the visual/spatial metaphors of hermeneutics (such as the Gadamerian "fusion of horizons") to antivisual or nonspatial metaphors (see Jay 1989, 61). It is too early, at this point, to provide anything but a cursory "glance," lacking the historical fine tuning necessary to contextualize my arguments. As we turn in the next chapters to the question of language and writing, we might

---

that seems at first glance to undermine the emphasis on the present moment and on the denial or undoing of karmic causality.

[30] Yanagida argues for instance that the founder of Nō, Zeami (1363–1443), who elaborated the notion of *ma* (space, interval), was strongly influenced by medieval Sōtō. See Yanagida 1984a, 128.

predict (fore-*tell* or fore-*see*) that the emphasis on performative language that seems to characterize "classical" Chan is a (temporary) departure from the visual primacy of early Chan. Perhaps, as Jorge Luis Borges once suggested for Western philosophy, the history of Chan/Zen is only the history of a few metaphors.

Chapter Seven

CHAN AND LANGUAGE: FAIR AND UNFAIR GAMES

> Whether one trusts speech absolutely or, on the contrary, one
> distrusts it absolutely—the ignorance of the problem of
> speech is here that of any mediation.
> (Maurice Merleau-Ponty, *The Visible and the Invisible*)

> All *kōan* are the utterance of *satori* without
> any intellectual mediation.
> (D. T. Suzuki, *Essays in Zen Buddhism*)

IT IS OFTEN SAID that in China between the seventh and eighth
centuries Chan/Zen emerged as a new form of Buddhist practice aimed
at (or deriving from) "sudden awakening." It was first and foremost,
however, a *discourse* on practice and a discursive practice. In the words of
Dahui Zonggao, "Chan discourse is coextensive with Chan practice" (see
Buswell 1987, 336). Although Chan masters (and scholars like Suzuki),
often claim that this discourse is unlocalized, it is more likely to be subject
to specific epistemological, cultural, and sociopolitical constraints. Its fundamental "duplicity," despite (or because of) its attempt to merge into a
unified vision the two planes—absolute and relative—of reality with notions such as the identity of saṃsāra and Nirvāṇa, or of passions and
awakening, derives perhaps from the necessity of ordinary language,
which reintroduces the overwhelming presence of everyday life—a life in
which saṃsāra *is not* Nirvāṇa; passions *are not* awakening. The moral
imperative to convey through language the insights gained in samādhi
implies the impossibility of remaining on the plane of "pure experience."
As Berger and Luckmann point out, "the reality of everyday life retains its
paramount status even as such 'leaps' take place. If nothing else, language
makes sure of this" (Berger and Luckmann 1967, 26).

Chan Buddhists tried to solve this linguistic predicament in various—
and sometimes conflicting—ways. They had first to decide whether to try
to reach transparency to oneself and communication with others through a
symbolic system or on the contrary through the absence of such a system.
The prevalent understanding was that awakening begins where language
and mental functions end. A recurrent description of awakening is that
"the path of language is cut off, all mental functions are extinguished."

However, language was also perceived as having an infinite depth.[1] Therefore, the possibility of an awakening taking place *within* language could not be excluded. Perhaps this alternative is at the background of the famous opposition drawn by Dōgen between Linji's notion of the "true man without a rank" (Ch. *wuwei zhenren*, J. *mui no shinnin*)—who has awakened outside (and without) language—and his own advocacy of the "true man with a rank" (Ch. *youwei zhenren*, J. *ui no shinnin*)—who has awakened with and within language.[2] One compromise was to purify language from its ontological and dualistic elements, to "give a clearer meaning to the words of the tribe" (Stéphane Mallarmé)—for instance, by adding apophatic markers. An alternative solution was to use language in an essentially performative and oblique way, thus acknowledging the failure of linear, sequential, discursive thinking. This may explain the breaking of syntax and logic in the kōan. To grasp the discursive strategies of Chan/Zen, we need to examine how conceptions relative to ordinary or poetical language (and writing), when grafted onto Chan discourse, came themselves to play a specific semiotic or ideological role. The question is never that of language *in abstracto*, but always that of *legitimate* language and of the power from which it derives and to which it gives access. I limit myself here to trying to reassess the role(s) played by the prevalent Chan conceptions of language in fields such as Chan poetry, kōan, and "encounter dialogues."

Chan is often defined by the motto "No dependence on the written letter, a special transmission outside the Scriptures" (Ch. *buli wenzi, jiaowai biechuan*, J. *furyū monji, kyōge betsuden*). This motto appeared in the eighth century and was not found in earlier texts such as the *Damo lun* (Treatise of Bodhidharma), although similar points are already made in this anthology of early Chan (see Yanagida 1969, 32; Faure 1986a). The debasement of writing(s), to which I return, derived from a fundamental skepticism regarding language and its capacity to express reality. Words have been condemned on various grounds in China, and this attitude is already reflected in the famous opening verse of the *Laozi*—with its pun on Dao—and in Zhuangzi's well-known comparison of words with a fishnet.[3] In the Chan case, this approach was also indebted to the *via negativa* of

[1] According to the *Taittirīya Brāhmana* (II.8, 4–5), for example, language is "endless, beyond all creation, immense" (Calcutta 1859).

[2] See *Shōbōgenzō Sesshin sesshō*, in *T.* 82, 2582, 181c. On the expression "true man with a rank," see *Linji lu*, in *T.* 47, 1985, 496c; Fuller Sasaki 1975, 3.

[3] See *Laozi*, section 1: "The Dao that can be spoken of (*dao*) is not the constant *dao*." Trans. Lau 1963, 57. The *Zhuangzi* passage runs as follows: "The fish-trap exists because of the fish; once you have gotten the fish, you can forget the trap. The rabbit snare exists because of the rabbit; once you've gotten the rabbit, you can forget the snare. Words exist because of the meaning; once you've gotten the meaning, you can forget the words" (Ed. Sibu beiyao 1973, 9: 6a; Watson 1968, 302).

Buddhism's Madhyamika school. Daoists and Buddhists agreed that words, incapable of expressing ultimate truth, can only express conventional truth. One cannot, however, rule out the possibility that the common assertion according to which neither the Dao nor awakening can be spoken of reflects the reluctance of a spiritual or artistic elite to disclose its esoteric knowledge and constitutes an attempt to preserve its social distinction and symbolic capital (see Bourdieu 1979). The obvious difficulty, and perhaps impossibility, of conveying truth through language should not prevent us from suspecting some unwillingness on the part of those who have a specific interest in remaining the privileged holders of ultimate truth.

At first glance, the only way out of what Nietzsche called the "prison-house of language" appears to be silence. In Wittgenstein's words, "Whereof we cannot speak, thereof we must remain silent."[4] In his idealized description of Japan as an *Empire of Signs*, Roland Barthes wrote that "all of Zen . . . appears as an enormous praxis destined to *halt language*, . . . to empty out, to stupefy, to dry up the soul's incoercible babble" (Barthes 1982, 74). For Barthes, satori was "a panic suspension of language, the blank which erases in us the reign of the Codes, the breach of that internal recitation which constitutes our person" (ibid., 74–75). Perhaps then the success of Zen in the Empire of the Signs was owing to the fact that Zen silence itself became a paradigmatic signifier?

There are, however, many kinds of silence.[5] The particular kind that Chan practitioners tried to emulate was the "thundering silence" of the mythical Indian layman Vimalakīrti in response to Mañjuśrī's question about nonduality (see Lamotte 1962, 317–318). Of course, some must have been aware that the praise of silence still takes place within language and could not fail to realize the inherent paradox of the via negativa, that is, the "unacceptable character (the nonsense) of any proposition that attempts to escape toward 'that which cannot be said.'"[6] As Emile Benveniste points out, "the characteristic of linguistic negation is that it can cancel only that which is uttered, that it must grant explicitly in order to suppress, that a judgment of non-existence has also necessarily the status of a judgment of

---

[4] Yet, as Fredric Jameson points out, "the famous sentence, in that it can be spoken at all, carries its own paradox within itself." See Jameson 1972, 12. The same point has often been made concerning Laozi's five-thousand-word apology of silence.

[5] See, for example, Father Dinouart's analysis of *The Art of Keeping Silent* (1771), reedited as Dinouart 1987. Interestingly, it appears that Dinouart plagiarized another work attributed to Father Jean-Baptiste Morvan de Bellegarde, *Conduite pour se taire et pour parler, principalement en matière de religion* (Paris: Simon Bénard, 1696). However, one might argue that plagiarism is perhaps one way to remain silent, to "speak without speaking," a technique not totally unknown to Chan masters.

[6] Certeau 1984, 10; quoting Wittgenstein. See also Staten's comment on Wittgenstein: "There is no sign whose signification is 'that which is beyond signification'" (Staten 1984, 71).

existence. Thus negation is first of all admission" (Benveniste 1974, 1: 84). To avoid this paradox, then, the negation of language had to be attempted in nonlinguistic ways, through "skillful means" (*upāya*) and "body language" (blows, shouts, gestures, facial expressions) or some kind of "qualified" or paradoxical silence. According to Barthes's perceptive remark, "It is not a question of halting language on a heavy, full, profound, mystical silence, or even on an emptiness which would be open to divine communication . . .; what is posited must develop neither in discourse nor in the end of discourse" (Barthes 1982, 74).

According to the founding legend of Chan, Śākyamuni, desiring to transmit the "essence of the True Dharma," held up a flower in front of the assembly of his disciples. No one understood his gesture, except Mahākāśyapa, who smiled and was consequently declared by the Buddha to be his true heir. The problematic aspects of this transmission are vividly expressed by Wumen Huikai, the author of a famous kōan collection entitled *Wumen guan* (The Gateless Pass, 1229):

> Yellow-faced Gautama, acting as if there were no one near him, forced good people into slavery, and hanging up a sheep's head, sold dog meat instead. . . . But if at that time everybody had smiled, then how could he have transmitted the treasure of the true *dharma* eye, or if Mahākāśyapa had not smiled, how could he have transmitted the treasure of the true *dharma* eye? If he says there is a transmission of the true *dharma* eye, then that yellow-faced old geezer would be cheating country bumpkins. But if he says there is no transmission, then why did he approve of Mahākāśyapa alone?[7]

In the same vein, the tradition records that when Bodhidharma asked his four main disciples to demonstrate their understanding, three of them came forward with various doctrinal explanations; only Huike stood at his place and made a deep bow—thereby becoming the second Chan patriarch.

This kind of silent response did not always work. When the Japanese monk Kakua (1143–?), upon returning from China, was asked by the emperor about Zen, he simply played his flute. Not surprisingly, his attitude was judged inappropriate. Ignoring the rules of the Chan game, the emperor wanted an explanation, not a flute solo. This story points to a basic problem with the nonverbal approach: that is, words were still needed if Chan was to make new converts. An emperor takes neither a nonverbal answer nor a verbal nonanswer for an answer. Not only did Kakua lose one important convert, but he also missed the opportunity to become the first Japanese patriarch of Zen.

[7] *Wumen guan*, T. 48, 2005, 293b; see translation of this passage in Schmidt 1974, 240. Incidentally, Dōgen considered Buddha's silent gesture much superior to Vimalakīrti's silence.

Likewise, Bodhidharma's famous reply—"I don't know"—to the emperor Liang Wudi's question—"Who is standing in front of me?"—may be a model of Chan apophasis, but, had that exchange actually taken place, it would have greatly endangered the future of Chan. The legend acknowledges the point when it tells us that Bodhidharma had to leave in haste for another kingdom, the Northern Wei. Despite its potentially self-defeating effects, however, the nondiscursive strategy had on the whole obvious advantages for those masters who, having nothing to say, could always pretend that they were emulating Vimalakīrti's silence. During the Tang, the situation even reached a point where an imperial edict had to make it clear that monks, when questioned on the Buddhist doctrine, could no longer sit silently in dhyāna without jeopardizing their clerical status.[8]

ON THE WAY TO LANGUAGE

> Whether you can speak or whether you can't,
> you cannot escape.
> (Layman Pang, *Recorded Sayings*)

To convey their teachings to the powers that be, Chan masters were eventually led to forsake the via negativa. By the mid-Tang, language was recognized by them as a necessary evil and granted a provisional value—as a signpost or a "skillful means' (*upāya*). Thus, when Linji Yixuan was asked to instruct the prefectural governor and other officials, he accepted the invitation in the following terms:

> Today, I, this mountain monk, having no choice in the matter, have perforce yielded to customary etiquette and taken this seat. If I were to demonstrate the Great Matter in strict keeping with the teaching of the Patriarchal School, I simply couldn't open my mouth and there wouldn't be any place for you to find footing. But since I've been so earnestly entreated today by the Counselor Wang, why should I conceal the essential doctrine of our school? (Fuller Sasaki 1975, 1)

To be sure, Linji's "answers," consisting mainly of shouts, blows and enigmatic utterances, seemed highly unconventional. Even Linji, however, had to comply eventually with the rules of the discursive game, and he ended up giving relatively straightforward answers, which, as he was acutely aware, would be put on "record."

Linji's strategic denial of language is therefore all the more revealing, as well as his complex relationship with his eccentric (and ex-centric) acolyte Puhua. By simulating madness, Puhua was able to remain until the end

---

[8] See decree of 20 July 724, in *Tang huiyao* 49: 6b; quoted in Demiéville 1952, n. 1, p. 113.

outside the discourse of Chan—or at least on its margins. The following "dialogue" is in this respect significant:

> One day Puhua was eating raw vegetables in front of the Monk's Hall. The Master saw him and said: "Just like an ass!"
> "Heehaw, heehaw!" brayed Puhua.
> "You thief!" said the Master.
> "Thief, thief!" cried Puhua, and went off. (Fuller Sasaki 1975, 42)

The contrast between Linji and Puhua is, among many other things, one between two different approaches to language. Although initially aimed at ending all quirks, Linji's words themselves were in turn reduced to quirks that merely increased the grip of his discourse on the listeners (or readers). But by merely echoing the words of the interlocutor, Puhua's *glossolalia* apparently allows him to escape this predicament. Breaking the communicative function of language, his feigned madness prevents him from becoming a master and taking a position in the authorized discourse. Because of his reluctance to accept a patriarchal seat, he strikes us as the "true man without a rank" idealized by Linji.[9]

Among the three ways defined by Vladimir Jankélévitch to elude the obstacle of inexpressibility—namely, the euphemism, the apophatic inversion, and the "conversion to the ineffable" (Jankélévitch 1977, 60)—Puhua clearly chooses the third, while Linji seems to oscillate between the first and the second. This oscillation is not specific to Linji; it reflects an ambiguity already at play in early Chan. One scriptural authority of the Chan tradition, the *Laṅkāvatāra-sūtra*, distinguishes between *siddhānta-naya*, the personal and nondiscursive experience of reality, and *deśanā-naya*, the realization obtained through an external teaching (see D. T. Suzuki 1977). While emphasizing the complementarity of these two approaches, which overlap with the Two Truths of the Madhyamika tradition, the *Laṅkāvatāra-sūtra* also constantly underscores the inexpressibility of truth. It claims that, during his fifty years of teaching, the Buddha "never spoke a single word": his sermons were mere "skilfull means," "golden leaves to stop the crying of an infant," empty talk from a "golden mouth." In his biography of one main representative of the *Laṅkāvatāra* tradition, Fachong (587–*ca.* 665), Daoxuan makes an interesting distinction between Bodhidharma's two disciples Huike and Daoyu (see *Xu Gaoseng zhuan*, in T. 50, 2060: 666). Whereas Daoyu, "having received the Dao, practiced it in his mind and abstained from talking about

---

[9] However, Puhua himself was not without spiritual posterity: he was later "tamed" by the Zen tradition, which promoted him as the "founder" of the Fuke (ch. Puhua) school, a relatively obscure school introduced to Japan by the flute player Kakua and Muhon Kakushin (1207–1298). On Puhua, see Faure 1991, 119–121; on the Fuke school, see Sanford 1977.

it," Huike apparently did try to express his realization.[10] Again, the denial of language and its "homeopathic" use appear to play rather ambiguous roles in sectarian strategies.[11]

Speaking the Truth

Let us now turn toward a radically different conception, in which language is seen, not just as an imperfect tool, let alone a trap or a prison-house, but as a full expression of reality—as ultimate reality itself. During the Tang, one witnesses in Buddhism a gradual shift from apophatic to "kataphatic" or positive discourse (See Gimello 1976). Many linguistic and extra-linguistic factors, both inside and outside Buddhism, have probably con-tributed to this change. To limit ourselves to linguistic factors, among them was perhaps the reassertion of the old idea that, as Emile Benveniste has pointed out in his critique of Saussure, "for the speaking subject, there is between language and reality a complete adequacy: the sign covers and commands reality; better, it *is* this reality" (Benveniste 1966–1974, 1: 52). The power of invocations and incantations was well known to the Chinese, and the notion that the name is the thing, or at least is, in an almost Cratylian fashion, mimetically related to it, was commonly accepted since the time of Confucius.[12] According to Granet, Chinese words are emblems rather than signs (Granet 1968, 42); consequently, the Saussurian theory concerning the "arbitrary nature of signs" would have seemed inappropri-ate to the ancient Chinese. For Cratylus as for these Chinese, names are *eponyms*; that is, they are simultaneously deictic (like a personal name) and meaningful. As Lu Xie, the author of the *Wenxin diaolong*, put it: "The reason why words can arouse the world is that they are the *wen* ("pat-terns") of the Dao" (quoted in Jullien 1982b, 86). During the Tang, esoteric Buddhism, recently introduced, provided a further rationale for this ten-

[10] The *Xu gaoseng zhuan* further divides Huike's disciples into two groups: those (Seng-can, Sengna, etc.) who "expounded the principle orally and did not produce any writing," and those who wrote commentaries on the *Laṅkāvatāra*. Fachong himself, when asked by his disciples to explain the deep meaning of the sūtra, declared: "The meaning is no other than the principle. Oral explanations are already too summary, how then could it be written down!" But, the chronicle continues, "despite his reticence, he eventually wrote a five scroll commentary, titled *Personal notes*, which is nowadays very popular." See *T*. 50, 2060: 666b.

[11] For more details on these strategies, see Faure 1988.

[12] In *Cratylus*, Socrates attempts to find a middle way between the two positions repre-sented by Hermogenes, who holds the "conventionalist" thesis that names result from agree-ment and convention, and Cratylus, who holds the "naturalist" thesis that every object has received the "just denomination" that was due to it naturally. See Plato, *Cratylus* 387c–d; Genette 1976, 11.

dency to extol words with its stress on mantra (a Sanskrit term translated in Chinese as "true words") and dhāraṇī.

Another theoretical justification for language was provided by the Mahāyāna teaching of nonduality. If everything is a manifestation of Suchness (*tathatā*), if every being, sentient and nonsentient, possesses a Buddha-nature, then any speech or writing is liable to express ultimate reality. According to the *Lengqie shizi ji*, the "third" Chan patriarch Huike held that "everything affirmed about the true Dharma is reality as such" (*T.* 85, 2837: 1286a), while the "fifth" Chan patriarch Daoxin (580–651) taught that "if only one sentence impregnates the vital principle, [this principle] remains forever incorruptible" (ibid., 1289a).

Mazu Daoyi's famous dictum, "The ordinary mind is the Dao," might be taken to imply that even words uttered in a deluded frame of mind have ontological nobility. According to the early Chan "historian" Zongmi (780–841), Mazu taught that:

> All dharmas, whether existent or empty, are nothing but the absolute nature. . . . Things such as language and action, desire and hatred, compassion and patience, good and evil deeds, suffering and enjoyment, all these are the Buddha-nature within yourselves; they are the original Buddha apart from which there is no other Buddha. . . . [All actions such as] the arising of mind, the movements of thought, a snapping of the fingers, a sigh or a cough, or taking up a fan, all are the functionings of the whole substance of Buddha-nature. (*T.* 48, 2015: 402a; Jan 1972, 39)

In the Japanese context, the traditionally exalted status of poetical language also contributed significantly to the rehabilitation of "true words" (Ch. *zhenyan*, J. *shingon*). Esoteric Buddhism and its theory of language significantly influenced early Chan and later Japanese Zen. The antinomian position deriving from the theory of the immanence of truth in all things found critics even within the Chan school. However, the basic premise of that theory, namely the ontological value of language, was shared even by some of these critics. Dōgen, for instance, addressed the question of representation in *Shōbōgenzō Gabyō* through a gloss on the old proverb, "The painting of a rice-cake (*gabyō*) does not satisfy hunger" (see *T.* 82, 2582: 165a–167a). This proverb had been used in early Chan texts to depreciate the oral teachings vis-à-vis sitting meditation.[13] In one of his hermeneutical sleight-of-hands, however, the probably well-fed Dōgen inverted the hierarchy between reality and representation and concluded that

---

[13] For example, in an apocryphal sūtra influenced by Chan theories, the *Faju jing*, we find the following comment: "If names were reality, one should be able to satisfy the hunger of people by talking to them about food. And if one could satisfy them in this way, all food and drink would be useless. Why? Because he whose hunger can be satisfied by talk about food is not really hungry" (*T.* 85, 2901: 1432b).

"only the painting of a rice-cake can satisfy hunger." To use another of his expressions, "only a painted dragon can bring rain." The paradoxical statement attributed to the Northern Chan master Shenxiu—"Although the body disappears, its shadow does not"—suggests that a similar reversal was already effected by early Chan masters (*Lengqie shizi ji*, T. 85, 2837: 1290c). By so inverting the traditional hierarchy between reality and representation, truth and language, these statements actually depart from the Buddhist "metaphysics of presence" and its correlative downplaying of words as ancillary to "pure experience."

The term Shōbōgenzō (Ch. *zhengfa yanzang*), which Dōgen took for the title of his main work, implies a radical reevaluation of language. This "essential repository of the true Dharma" is linguistic. According to the legend that Dōgen took as historical event and often quoted, although Śākyamuni *silently* transmitted that repository to his disciple Mahākāśyapa, he nevertheless felt obliged to state that he was doing so. The entire episode appears as a performance, in both the Austinian sense of "doing what one says" (see Austin 1962) and the theatrical sense of impressing a somewhat gullible audience. This is, at least, how the author of the *Wumen guan*, in the passage quoted above, seems to have interpreted the story.

Another famous case of transmission is that of Linji, who, as he was about to die, asked his disciple Sansheng to show his understanding of the truth. When Sansheng shouted, Linji praised him in Chan fashion by declaring: "Who would have thought that my True Dharma Eye would be extinguished upon reaching this blind ass!" (Fuller Sasaki 1975, 62). We do have a few words here, but they need to be taken with a grain of salt: language is still used, but in a self-depreciating fashion, with apophatic markers. Such is no longer the case with Dōgen, who asserts the ultimate value of words: not those of ordinary language, however, but words vivified, transmuted by a spiritual realization. To characterize this ability to use language in a new key, Dōgen uses the neologism *dōtoku* (lit. "to be able to speak," used here in the special sense of "voicing the way"]. Thus, "every Buddha and every patriarch is able to voice the Way" (see *Shōbōgenzō Dōtoku*, T. 82, 2582: 163a; Sakamoto 1983, 91).

Another related strand of thought in the *Shōbōgenzō* is the notion of the "preaching of the non-sentient" (J. *mujō seppō*). According to the Chan tradition, this preaching cannot be heard in an ordinary way but requires a synaesthesia of all senses: thus, its sounds must be perceived through the eyes, not through the ears. The point, is that the whole world has become a sacred text or discourse, the "sūtra of mountains and rivers" (*sansuikyō*). Consequently, everything in the universe does reveal the Buddhist truth, and words and scriptures are no exceptions in this regard. According to Dōgen, "There is nothing but scriptures everywhere in time and space.

Thus, everything we perceive . . . is the letters of the scriptures, the outer coverings of the scriptures" (*T. 82*, 2582: 194b). Whereas early Mahāyāna masters taught that only sentient beings have a Buddha-nature, for Sōtō Zen masters everything *is* the Buddha-nature and consequently every word—as such—*is* the Dharma. But admittedly, it takes an enlightened master like Dōgen to realize and express this.

In *Keisei sanshoku*, Dōgen quotes the following poem written by the Chinese poet Su Shi (*a.k.a.* Su Dongpo) on the occasion of a visit to Lushan:

> The sounds from the valley stream are from [the Buddha's] great tongue,
> The forms of the mountains are his pure body.
> The eighty-four thousand verses heard during the night,
> How should I tell them to the people the next day?
>
> (*T. 82*, 2582: 38c)

Although Su Shi may not have been able to convey the truths he has heard, he still intended to convey a message through the use of "apophatic inversion." Dōgen is aware of this when he comments: "By telling this to men, Su Shi leaves them far behind and proceeds alone" (ibid., 41b). Although the truth is inexpressible, it has to be—and has just been—expressed by Su Shi. The very obstacle to its expression becomes the channel or instrument of its expression. The fact that the medium is a poem is not insignificant: whereas the instrumental words of prose, as Zhuangzi already pointed out, can be forgotten when their meaning is understood, the words of poetry are remembered and they can be reactualized every time the poem is recited. Poetic words have a resonance that cannot be exhausted with one hearing because, as Paul Valéry said, "the poem is a prolonged hesitation between sound and meaning" (quoted in Jakobson 1963, 233).

A similar resonance may be found in the words uttered by a master. Thus, the day before he became enlightened, Su Shi had a conversation with the Chan master Changzong Zhaojue about the preaching of the nonsentient. The words of the master had to sink deeply into his mind before he could understand them, or rather, before he could be moved, transformed by them. Dōgen offers the following comment on that conversation: "Although at the time these words could not cause in him any reversal, the sound of the valley stream, when he heard it, seemed like the tide assaulting heaven. But was it the sound of the valley stream that seized him in this way, or the words of Zhaojue flowing into him? One may wonder whether the latter's words on the predication of the non-sentient, which were still resonating, did not secretly merge with the sound from the valley" (ibid., 39a).

POETICAL LANGUAGE IN CHAN

The question of resonance—that is, of the repercussion of words within the mind—leads us to examine briefly the role(s) imparted (or denied) to poetry by Chan followers. Not surprisingly, we find in their evaluation of poetry the same ambiguities that characterized the Chan attitude toward language in general. At first glance, Chan is characterized by a deep-rooted prejudice against literary pleasure and a disbelief in the power of a poem to express ultimate reality. According to this view, poetry is an ancillary practice, an upāya, at best a starting point; however, it is also considered a double-edged tool, and it can become a stumbling block for the practitioner who forsakes the goal for the means. Consequently, two different kinds of poetry are distinguished: one leads toward a higher goal; another detracts from it. Although the latter, purely profane, use of poetry as a form of aesthetic pastime is of course discouraged, the status of poetry as a religious means remains uncertain. The *locus classicus* on this matter is Bai Juyi's famous statement about "wild words and specious phrases" (Ch. *kuangyan qiyu*, J. *kyōgen kigo*): "May the wordly writings of my present life, with all their wild words and specious phrases, serve in future ages as the inspiration for hymns of praise extolling the Buddha's teachings, and turn the Wheel of the Dharma forever."[14] In another poem, however, the Chinese poet complains that, although he has "gradually conquered the wine devil," his indulging in poetry remains a source of "mouth karma" (see Watson 1988, 114; Waley 1949, 207; LaFleur 1983). Even though this passage is largely rhetorical and Bai Juyi is not really willing to atone for his poetical sin, it illustrates the ambiguous status of poetry for him and his followers.

Su Shi provides a complex set of justifications for poetry. Like Bai Juyi, he seems at first to have considered poetry as a means to an end, a mere stepping stone toward spiritual realization:

> [The] monk Sicong at the age of seven played the lute well. At twelve he gave up the lute and studied calligraphy. After he became skilled in calligraphy, in ten years he gave it up and studied poetry; in his poems there are extraordinary passages. Then he read the *Avataṃsaka-sūtra*, and entered into the Realm of Reality and the Sea of Wisdom. . . . I have heard that when one's thoughts are trained so they are reaching close to the Dao, the *Avataṃsaka*, the Realm of Reality and the Sea of Wisdom are only way-stations; and this is even more true of calligraphy, poetry, and the lute. No matter how hard he tries, no student of

---

[14] See Waley 1949, 194. A similar attitude is found in Mujū Ichien, the compiler of the *Shasekishū* (Collection of Sand and Pebbles). See Plutschow 1978, 208. On *kyōgen kigo*, see also LaFleur 1983, 8; and Childs 1980.

the Dao achieves it if he starts from nothing. . . . If Cong does achieve it, his lute-playing and calligraphy, and above all his poetry, will have had something to do with it. Like water, Cong will be able to reflect all things in one, and his calligraphy will become still more extraordinary. I will keep watch on them, and take them as indications of how profoundly Cong achieves the Dao. (see March 1966, 387–388)

Poetry is presented by Su Shi as not only a valuable practice and a condition of enlightenment but also a legitimate expression of the enlightened mind. These two aspects are characteristic of the Buddhist "skillfulness in means" because the upāya is a means for both the believer to get closer to reality and the Bodhisattva to convey the truth to others. Such is precisely the skillfulness with which Su Shi, in the poem quoted by Dōgen, obliquely intimated the reality of the *Dharmakāya*—that is, the omnipresence of the cosmic body of the Buddha—to his fellow men. A similar rhetorical device is often used by Buddhist poets, for instance by the Tang poet Hanshan when he writes: "My mind is like an autumn moon, / An emerald pool, clear and pure. Nothing will afford comparison . . . / Tell me, how should I explain?" (Iriya 1973b, 57).

Another justification Su Shi provided for poetry is that it is an expression of that which in man transcends the limitations of the human condition; in other words, the irrepressible spontaneity that bears witness to the wonderful workings of nature (the Dao, or, in Buddhist terminology, the Buddha nature) within man. This naturalness—the ultimate goal (and underlying principle) of both Chan and poetry—becomes the hallmark of the true and poetically gifted practitioner, a distinction that exempts him from following the rules established for common men. Using a vivid metaphor Su Shi describes his poetic writing: "My writing is like a ten-thousand-gallon spring. It can issue from the ground anywhere at all. On smooth ground it rushes swiftly and covers a thousand *li* in a single day without difficulty. When it twists and turns among mountains and rocks, it fits its form to the things it meets: unknowable. What can be known is, it always goes where it must go, always stops where it cannot help stopping—nothing else. More than that even I cannot know" (March 1966, 385).

Su Shi shifts from the notion that words are an attempt, flawed from the start, at *expressing* some inner reality, to the idea that poetry is a transcendent speech-act, the joyful outpouring of samādhi, reality itself at work (at play). Poetical speech/writing is the intransitive act of *realizing*, although there is actually *nothing* to be realized or expressed. In the words of Valéry, "Poetry means to reach a state of perpetual invention. / He who dances does not intend to walk" (Valéry 1973–1974, 2: 1077).

Su Shi makes a last, possibly more important, claim for poetry when he writes: "In salty and sour are mixed a host of preferences, / But in their middle there is a great taste, everlasting" (Schmidt 1974, 232). He is alluding here to the theory of the "taste beyond taste" (*weiwai wei*) advocated in the ninth century by the poet Sikong Tu (837–908), who was apparently the first to argue, as later Su Shi, that poetry reflected the poet's grasp of the Dao (Liu 1975, 35). Sikong Tu compared the resonance of the poem in the sensitive mind to the subtle taste that a gourmet can find even in insipid foods. This notion can be traced back to Laozi's *logia*: "The five tastes injure man's palate"; "Music and food will induce the wayfarer to stop, while the Dao in its passage through the mouth is without flavour" (see *Laozi* 12 and 35; in Lau 1963, 68, 94). At any rate, Su Shi elaborated on Sikong Tu's notion by distinguishing between the "center" and the edges of a taste: "According to Buddhists, 'it is like when people eat honey; they find that everything is sweet, at the center as well as on the edges.' When people taste the five flavours they all distinguish between the bitter and the sweet; but rare are those who, for the same flavour, can distinguish between the center and the edge" (see Jullien 1982b, 88).

Like foods, poetic texts have an aftertaste, or rather a center that may be reached only after a long process of savoring, after leaving the edges of words and meanings. The same is true of the *huatou*, the essential part of the "dialogues" (*wenda*) used in Chan maieutics, often a single word, which can be approached in two ways (depending on the level of the practitioner): by focusing on its meaning, an approach usually described as "investigating the dead word"; or by focusing on (and eventually breaking through) the word itself, an approach to the "live word" described as "tasteless." With the poem as with the huatou, the savouring amounts to a rejection of all superficial, "peripheral" interpretations elaborated by the intellect. At the center of the tasteless resides an infinite savor; at the core of the word can be found an infinite "meaning" that is no longer a meaning— Bodhidharma's "marrow" or Rabelais's "*substantifique moëlle*." The "infinitude" of the phenomenal world, well expressed by Dōgen in *Genjō kōan*, is also that of the word or the poem (see *T.* 52, 2582: 24b). Dōgen was well aware of the semantic depth of words, of what we may with Merleau-Ponty call the "ontogenic nature of language"; like Su Shi, he recognized the "two sources"—natural and cultural—of poetry. He himself wrote poems, which have been collected in *Sanshō dōei*, and seems to have participated in *waka* meetings. Despite, or because of, his poetic activity, he rejected poetry as an idle pastime, an attachment to the world of form. In its semantic richness, Dōgen's prose seems at times closer to poetry than his formal verses. Although Dōgen would probably have endorsed Su Shi's claim for "naturalness" and seems sometimes to yield to what some critics have called his "linguistic genius," his ornate style derives from the Chinese literary form known in Japan as *shiroku benrei*,[15] which seems too literary to be spontaneous.

The Identity of Chan and Poetry

The theory of the harmony of Chan and poetry developed during the Tang and the Song, when many monks and poets certified that "poetry and the Dharma don't obstruct each other." The similarities were drawn on various grounds, in terms of the underlying principle of both endeavours, or of their process. Thus, according to Han Ru (d. 1135):

> Studying poetry, you should be like one starting to study Ch'an:
> Before you are enlightened, you must meditate on various methods.
> But one day when you are enlightened to the true *dharma* eye,
> Then trusting your hand, you draw it out and all the stanzas are ready-made.
>
> (Schmidt 1974, 232)

There was also some resistance to this trend. According to Liu Kezhuang,

> Poets take as their patriarch Shao Ling, who stated that "words don't surprise men, death does not stop"; Chan followers take as their patriarch Bodhidharma, who advocated the "non-dependence on the written letter." What poetry considers to be wrong is precisely what constitutes Chan, what Chan considers to be wrong is precisely what constitutes poetry. . . . Essential words have a subtle meaning, which does not reside in words and letters. By abandoning truth in order to search for delusions, grudging the near and yearning for the distant, for a long time forgetting to return, I fear that, although your Chan may progress, your poetry will recede. (*Liu Kezhuang houcun daquan, juan* 99, quoted in Du Songbo 1976, 365)

However, these dissenting voices were obscured by those who compared poetical incitation and Chan intuition, searched for Chan in poetry, for poetry in Chan, and eventually collapsed the distinction between the two.[16] According to Meng Jiao, "Poetical thought is found among the bamboos, religious mind arises above the pine-trees" (quoted in Demiéville 1962, 330). Poetry became the expression of samādhi and prajñā, an "extasis of the brush." For Li Zhiyi, "the awakening of the brush is similar to the awakening of Chan," while Ge Tianmin considers that "in

---

[15] This style was a combination of four and six character parallel sentences widespread under the Tang, despite the attempts of Han Yu and a few others to return to the "ancient style" (*guwen*).

[16] As François Jullien has shown, the term "incitation" seems more appropriate than "inspiration" in the case of Chinese poetry. See Jullien 1982a, 31–71.

poetry like in Chan there are not two methods: you must return to the dead snake the venom of life" (ibid., 331). In his famous treatise on aesthetics, the *Canlang shihua*, Yan You (1180–1235) declares: "As the entire principle of Chan is in subtle awakening (*miaowu*), so is the principle of poetry exclusively in subtle awakening. . . . There is in poetry a certain quality that has nothing to do with the written letter, a certain taste that has nothing to do with reason" (Demiéville 1962, 330). Likewise, Shen Deqian writes: "Whereas refined poetry has a Chan principle and a Chan tendency, vulgar poetry uses a Chan terminology" (quoted in Du Songbo 1976, 326).

Mujū and Poetry

The equation between Chan and poetry became a commonplace in Japan, particularly in the so-called literature of the Five Mountains (*gozan bungaku*). The Zen master Mujū Ichien resorts, however, in his *Shasekishū* (Collection of Sand and Pebbles) to a different kind of argumentation. Retaining from traditional Buddhism and from Bai Juyi an ancillary conception of language as upāya or *kyōgen kigo*, Mujū declares in his prologue: "Coarse words and refined expressions both proceed from the First Principle, nor are the everyday affairs of life at variance with the True Reality. Through the wanton sport of wild words and specious phrases, I wish to bring people into the marvelous Way of the Buddha's teachings" (Morrell 1985, 71). Here, as in other parts of his work, one argument invoked is the fundamental Mahāyāna tenet of the nonduality between sacred and profane, principle and phenomena. But the insistence with which Mujū tries to legitimize the Way of poetry shows that he was well aware of the precariousness of his position in the light of traditional Buddhist doctrine: "Now we refer to the poetry of 'wild words and specious phrases' as 'defiled poetry, because it lures us to attachment, imbues us with vain sensuality, and decks us out with empty words. But poetry may express the principles of the Holy Teaching, accompany a sense of impermanence, weaken our wordly ties and profane thoughts, and cause us to forget fame and profit" (ibid., 163). Accordingly, language itself is neutral; its value depends on the moral intent of the speaker/writer (and not, as Dōgen would argue, on his degree of spiritual realization): "If one levels the charge that poetry is 'specious talk,' he should be aware that the fault lies in the defiled mind of the subject. Even the sacred teachings, when exploited for prestige and profit, generate evil karma. This is *man's* defect" (ibid., 165).

Mujū deems necessary to reinforce this conception with notions derived from Japanese literary theories and esoteric Buddhism. The equation between Japanese poetry (in particular the *waka* genre) and esoteric dhāraṇī

(J. *waka soku darani*) is a recurrent theme in medieval Japanese Buddhism, and the syncretistic theories (*honji suijaku*) of esoteric Buddhism played a significant role in the Buddhist legitimization of poetry. Mujū's defense of *waka* poetry deserves to be quoted at some length:

> When we consider *waka* as a means to religious realization, we see that it has the virtue of serenity and peace, and putting a stop to the distractions and undisciplined movements of the mind. With a few words, it encompasses its sentiment. This is the very nature of mystic verses, or *dhāraṇī*.
>
> The gods of Japan are Manifest Traces, the unexcelled Transformation Bodies of buddhas and bodhisattvas. The god Susa-no-o initiated composition in thirty-one syllables with the "many-layered fence at Izumo." Japanese poems do not differ from the words of the Buddha. The *dhāraṇī* of India are simply the words used by the people of that country which the Buddha took and interpreted as mystic formulas. For this reason the Meditation Master Yixing in his *Commentary on the Great Sun Sūtra* says: "The languages of every region are all *dhāraṇī*." Had the Buddha appeared in Japan, he would simply have used Japanese for mystic verses." (ibid., 163–164)

No wonder then that Japanese deities, reinterpreted in esoteric Buddhism as "manifestations" (*suijaku*, lit. "manifested traces") of the Buddhas and Bodhisattvas (*honji*), all delight in poetry (ibid., 179). Not only does Mujū advocate the Way of Poetry as an upāya, a preliminary method, but he also considers it as the most excellent religious practice, the one that subsumes all others and allows the practitioner to enter into formless reality: "It is the state of mind attained in the Zen sect through the *kōan*, and in the esoteric sects through contemplation on the letter *A*" (ibid.). This is why, says Mujū, this Way has been practiced from antiquity by the Buddhas who have "manifested their traces" in Japan as *kami*. Mujū also alludes to the practice of oneirical poetry, poems revealed in a dream: "Such instances of poems being revealed in dreams are known from antiquity."[17] However, Mujū could not fail to acknowledge that "that which is spoken by the mouth we should not call *zen*, but rather, the serenity after having set aside all thoughts from the mind." Clearly, he is at contradiction with himself, and this contradiction seems to stem from his joint allegiance to Zen orthodoxy and to the syncretistic theories of esoteric Buddhism. In the end, Mujū seems unable to solve his doubts concerning the possible sinful nature of poetry and admits reluctantly that poetry must be ultimately forsaken.

A recurrent theme in "literary Chan" (*wenzi chan*) is that, despite appearances, the words of poetry, being the expression of Chan awakening, have a

---

[17] Ibid., 171. An interesting example is that of the oracular poems (in *manyōgana* script) received in a dream by the Sōtō master Keizan from Japanese *kami* (see Faure 1991, 209).

higher status than ordinary language. They are not the language of a deluded subjectivity that would create a hiatus in the natural flow of things, but rather the language that nature speaks through man. Like the words of the Chan master Xuefeng Yicun (823–909), the words of poetry are said to leave no traces or tracks.[18] According to a Chinese poetical cliché, the poet is "like to the antelope hanging itself by its horns to the branches of trees."[19] For the poet Wu Ke (d. *ca.* 1174), "dead poetry is a poetry the language of which is still language; live poetry is a poetry the language of which is no longer language."[20] "Live words" become in this way a kind of hierophany, the "preaching of the non-sentient," the speech-acts of the cosmic Buddha. According to Wang Shizhen, such words (or songs) "perfectly correspond to the ineffable situation in which Śākyamuni held up a flower and Kāśyapa smiled at him" (Jullien 1989, 271). Whether in Chan or in poetry, spontaneous speech in response to things is seen as proof of awakening. As soon as spontaneity itself becomes an ideal, however, its nature changes drastically; like the kōan, it is eventually appropriated by performative discourse and tends to become a form of mystical mystification.

How to Do Things with the Kōan

The analogy between the poem and the kōan is far-reaching. Although the kōan, at least in "classical" Chan, was originally part of an unfolding dialogue (Ch. *wenda*, J. *mondō*), its (unspoken) rules, like those of poetry, are usually considered to be "obstacles to discourse."[21] Considering the proliferation of discourse around kōan and their ritual, mantric, or incantatory use, we may wonder whether they are really "words destined to put an end to words." This, in turn, raises the question of their actual function in the general economy of Chan spirituality.

[18] See *Laozi*, section 27: "One who excels in travelling leaves no wheel tracks; one who excels in speech makes no slips" (Lau 1963, 84).

[19] According to Han Yu: "What is called 'not touching the path of reason (*li*) nor falling into the trammel of words' is the best. . . . The poets of the High T'ang relied only on inspired feelings (*hsing-chü*), like the antelope that hangs by its horns, leaving no traces to be found. Therefore, the miraculousness of their poetry lies in its transparent luminosity, which cannot be pieced together; it is like sound in the air, color in appearances, or an image in the mirror; it has limited words but unlimited meaning" (quoted in Liu 1975, 39) See also Wang Shizhen's *Daijingtang shihua*, quoted in Jullien 1989, 268, 271–272.

[20] See Demiéville 1962, 330. According to Wang Shizhen, this passage is based on an aphorism of the Chan master Dongshan Liangjie (807–869): "A word that contains speech is a dead word; a word that no longer contains speech is a live word" (*Daijingtang shihua* 3, par. weiyu, quoted in Jullien 1989, 266).

[21] Strictly speaking, *mondō* and *kōan* should be distinguished as two different genres, but for the moment we can consider them together. Notice the difference between the "progressive" or linear dialogues of early Chan and the "disruptive" dialogues of "classical" Chan.

I have already mentioned what we may call the "gustatory" interpretation of the *huatou*. The common interpretation of the kōan as an irrational riddle designed to create in the practitioner a kind of psychological double bind—Hakuin's "great doubt"—that will eventually force him to bypass or break through his intellectual hindrances, is not entirely convincing. This interpretation would not allow the taste of the kōan to linger in a sensitive palate, and it was indeed rejected on various grounds within the Chan/Zen tradition itself. The psychological elaboration provided by Suzuki for well-meaning psychoanalysts is clearly a further rationalization that significantly contributed to the development of a "false consciousness" and some enduring misunderstandings concerning Chan practice.

The "gustatory" conceptions of the huatou and the kōan presuppose the hermeneutical belief that behind the surface meaning (or lack thereof), there lurks some *deep* meaning to be retrieved, some profound insight to be gained. This may indeed be the case in some dialogues borrowed from Buddhist scriptures or from the "recorded sayings" (*yulu*) of famous Chan masters; however, the possibility of retrieving the contextual meaning of the kōan (let alone its "essential" meaning) through some hermeneutical "fusion of horizons" seems rather dim, insofar as their "discourse situation" or dialogical context is most of the time irremediably lost. The chances of misunderstanding increase when the cultural setting has became radically different, as it was in Japanese Zen where kōan became utterly systematized, ritualized, and routinized. Like ritual or poetry, kōan turned into a practice that was an end in itself, and this is why, barring a too unlikely "mind to mind transmission," the "hermeneutics of retrieval" proves inappropriate here.

Why would the Chan tradition have perpetuated an interpretation that does not—or at least neither always nor entirely—account for the actual practice? There is probably no single answer to such a naive question. I merely submit a few working hypotheses that suggest the necessity of taking into account the social and historical contexts of the various conceptions of language underlying Chan practice. This approach does not invalidate the truth claim of these conceptions because one cannot disprove that they originally reflected some genuine insight. The fact remains, however, that when these conceptions became rigidly systematized, Chan masters tended to become just another interest group, and at this ideological level our analysis might legitimately focus.

More important for our purpose than the meaning of the kōan is its performative nature. If Chan dialogues often end with blows (*coups*), it is because they are themselves "*coups*," that is, hits or moves in a game (Certeau 1986, 79). One might argue that they were not so much intended to express a meaning, as to impress an interlocutor, to gain the upper hand in a contest where all moves were allowed (*tous les coups sont permis*). Like

rituals or language games, they work simultaneously on several levels—
what we could call the semantic, the syntactic, and, more important, the
semiotic or pragmatic levels. Kōan are, to use Austin's terminology, essentially performative: they are *illocutionary* insofar as they create an "event"
and necessitate some kind of social ceremonial and *perlocutionary* insofar
as they indirectly produce effects that are not always perceived by the
protagonists.[22] They also imply a shift from the ontological standpoint
that conceives of truth as already there, *ab aeterno*, toward a conception of
truth in the process of emerging, in constant actualization. Such might be
the "actualized kōan" (*genjō kōan*) advocated by Dōgen, an "enacted"
truth that is never separate from a specific historical situation or sectarian
position (see Faure 1987b, 30–54). This conception of truth can be traced
back to the story in which the Buddha, holding a small bird in his hand,
asks his disciples whether the bird is alive or dead. Of course, this turns out
to be a losing game for the disciples (and possibly for the bird as well) (see
Biyan lu 9; Cleary and Cleary 1977, 1: 64). One cannot simply overlook
that truth may be the outcome of a will to power, instead of its denial.
According to Jean-François Lyotard, "to speak is to fight, in the sense of
playing, . . . and language acts belong to a general agonistic" (Lyotard and
Thébaud 1985, 23).

The agonistic or conflictual nature of Chan "dialogues," sometimes
called "Dharma battles," has often been pointed out,[23] but it is usually
downplayed as a "skillful means" used by the master to test and awaken his
disciple. Clearly, this interpretation cannot simply be taken for granted in
the case of those masters whom Linji called "blind shavepates and wild
foxes." Quite possibly, many of them were symbolically, socially, or psy-
chologically empowered by their confrontations with novices. In these
encounters, as in the discursive challenges described by Jeanne Favret-
Saada in her book on witchcraft, what matters is "less to decipher utterances or what is being said—than to understand who speaks, and to
whom" (Favret-Saada 1977, 26). The encounter produces a winner and a
loser; and the gain and the loss are very real: like the "deadly words" of
witchcraft, the dialogue seems to activate quasi-magical forces. According
to Favret-Saada, "a force is 'magical' in that it cannot be contained in the

22 See Austin 1962. On this question, see also "Performative Utterances," in ed. Paul
Edwards, *The Encyclopedia of Philosophy*, (New York: Macmillan, 1967), 6: 90–91; Jacques
Derrida, "Signature, événement, contexte," in Derrida 1972a, 382 ff.; and de Man 1979,
119–132. Notice however that, contrary to Austin's definition, Chan "speech-acts" are
polysemic, irreducible to a single meaning, and do not imply a self-controlled intentionality.
See Derrida 1972a, 384.

23 In a round table on Chan, Nishitani Keiji stated for example that these encounters,
"different from the dialogues that take place in schools or elsewhere, . . . were direct body
attacks," while his interlocutor, Shibayama Zenkei, compared their protagonists to "two
swordsmen fighting with real swords." See *The Eastern Buddhist* 8, 2 (October 1975): 70 sq.

system of names; by this very fact, it produces its effects without passing through the ordinary symbolical mediations" (ibid., 261).

Vire-volte

After arguing heuristically that Chan dialogues could at times become deadly serious language games, turning now to the opposite interpretation, I want to suggest that they could also be seen as a ludic activity, the parodic purpose of which was too often lost on later practitioners. I take my cues from Bakhtin, for whom "there never was a . . . single type of direct discourse . . . that did not have its own parodying and travestying double, its own comic-ironic contre-partie" (Bakhtin 1981, 53). The following "Dharma battle," set in an entirely different context, may serve as a counterpoint. It is found in Book Two of Rabelais's *Pantagruel* entitled "How Panurge Confounded the Englishman who argued by Signs." In this chapter, Panurge engages in a debate against the English scholar Thaumaste on behalf of his master Pantagruel. I cannot unfortunately quote the passage in full and in its original language, the flavor of which is considerably diminished by translation, but a "taste beyond taste" might still be found in this excerpt:

> Then, with everyone attending and listening in perfect silence, the Englishman raised his two hands separately high in the air, clenching all the tips of his fingers in the form that is known in the language of Chinon as the hen's arse, and struck the nails of one against the other four times. Then he opened them and struck the one with the flat of the other, making a sharp noise. Next, clenching them again, as before, he struck twice more and, after opening them, yet another four times. Then he joined them afresh and laid them one beside the other, as if offering up devout prayers to God" (Rabelais 1970, 234)

Panurge answers in a similar way, and the silent dialogue intensifies gradually, leading toward its climax:

> Next [Panurge] put the thumb of his left hand to the corner of his left eye, extending his whole hand like the wing of a bird or the fins of a fish, and flapping it very daintily this way and that, afterwards repeating the action with his right at the corner of his right eye.
>
> Thaumaste began to tremble and grow pale, and made him this sign. . . . (ibid., 235–236)
>
> Then Panurge struck one hand against the other and blew in his palm. After which he once more thrust the forefinger of his right hand into the ring made by his left, pushing it in and drawing it out several times. Then he stuck out his chin and looked intently at Thaumaste. . . .
>
> Thaumaste now began to sweat great drops, and had all the appearance of a man rapt in high contemplation. (ibid., 237)

Finally, Thaumaste admits his defeat and tells the bystanders how Panurge has opened to him "the true and encyclopaedic well and abyss of learning" (ibid., 238). This typically Rabelaisian contest calls to mind certain Chan "encounters," although the parodic intent here is more obvious.[24] The point of these stories is that the esoteric signs used by the protagonists have no referent; they are empty. The "meaning" of the kōan is not to be found at the semantic or syntactic levels, but at the semiotic or pragmatic levels. According to Barthes, what is recommended to the apprentice working on a kōan is "not to solve it, as if it had a meaning, nor even to perceive its absurdity (which is still a meaning), but to ruminate it 'until the tooth falls out'" (Barthes 1982, 74). Likewise, Thomas Merton argued that "the acts and gestures of a Zen master are no more 'statements' than is the ringing of an alarm clock. . . . Usually the Master is simply 'producing facts' which the disciple either sees or does not see. . . . In so far as the disciple takes the fact to be a sign of something else, he is misled by it" (Merton 1968, 50). Merton then criticized the Western tendency to "interpret" everything: "Nothing is allowed just to be and to mean itself: everything has to mysteriously signify something else" (ibid.). Merton himself, however, following Suzuki, still "interprets" the master's actions as stemming from his "will to truth," without questioning the various possible strategies in which this "will to truth" might be inscribed—thereby becoming a "will to power."

By suggesting heuristically the multiplicity of possible emplotments of these "dialogues" or "cases," I want to seriously (yet playfully) question the traditional hermeneutical approach. This criticism is not meant, however, to reject entirely this approach, but merely to relativize it. It is significant that what may (or may not) have been at first spontaneous encounters or "raids on the unspeakable," to use Merton's metaphor, eventually became a literary genre—that is, a highly ritualized form of discourse with a given sociocultural setting and specific role expectations. To hear the manifold echoes of the "sound of one hand," we have to remain aware of the "difference within repetition"; that is, the process of differentiation is always at work between various "cases" or various uses of the same "case."

[24] One well-known Zen story has been translated in English under the title "Trading dialogue for lodging" (Reps 1957, 38–39). However, the parodic intent appears is even more obvious in the Rakugo story entitled "Konnyaku mondō," in which the traveling monk Takuzen engages in a dialogue with Rokubee, a *konnyaku*-root seller whom he mistakes for a Zen priest. Like Panurge confounding Thaumaste, Rokubee is able to mystify the scholarly monk with a few cryptic gestures. This exhilarating critique of scholarly hermeneutical overkill seems to draw upon a widespread folkloric motif because the Zen story finds another Western counterpart in the (allegedly ancient) dialogue between a fool and a Greek doctor, recorded in *Schimpf und Ernst*, an exempla collection that might have been known to Rabelais. For a full translation of the Rakugo story and a discussion of its parallels and antecedents, see Morioka and Sasaki 1990, 52, 192.

Despite (or because of) its denial of language, Chan was first and foremost a new "art of speaking." Not only are there many kinds of silence, but there are also many ways to speak and to avoid speaking. While admittedly some of them may be genuine, others turn out to be rhetorical strategies. Insofar as they serve more distant ends or achieve more complex effects than straightforward communication, most, if not all, are essentially performative, or more precisely *perlocutionary* (see Austin 1962, 121). Remember Linji's words: "Officially, a needle is not permitted to enter, privately, carriages can go through" (Fuller Sasaki 1975, 61). It is therefore essential to qualify the Chan denial of language by examining, whenever possible, the ways in which it has been appropriated by various "speakers." I suggest just one possibility: the rejection by early Chan masters of "language as absolute" may be seen against the background of their ambivalence toward Tantric speculations on sound and toward Daoist and Confucian belief systems; however, the verification of this hypothesis is beyond the scope of the present chapter. If, as Pascal believed, "nature abhors the void," we should keep in mind that the emptiness (*śūnyatā*) that theoretically underlies the Buddhist experience and legitimizes Chan discourse is an elusive reality, all too easily reified; and Chan discourse itself—let alone scholarly discourse on Chan—is always running the risk of becoming empty talk.

Chapter Eight

IN-SCRIBING/DE-SCRIBING CHAN

> We must put an end to this superstition of texts and of
> *written* poetry. Written poetry is valuable once, and after it
> should be destroyed. . . . Beneath the poetry of texts there is
> poetry pure and simple, without form and without text.
> (Antonin Artaud, *Selected Writings*)

THE IDEOLOGY of the "live word" examined in the previous chapter raises the question of the place of writing in the Chan/Zen tradition. At first glance, the Chan motto "Non-reliance on the written letter, a special transmission outside the scriptures" (Ch. *buli wenzi jiaowai biechuan*) seems to make the debasement of writing and scripture a central feature of Chan. Even though both speech and writing were considered utterly inadequate to describe or express the "direct vision" of awakening, writing, a further remove from "pure experience," was regarded as inferior to speech. Like philosophical writing according to Richard Rorty, Chan writing was in principle aimed at putting an end to writing. This situation also calls to mind Derrida's analysis of writing and "logocentrism" in *Of Grammatology*. This analogy must be examined closely, if only because of the high status of writing in Chinese culture.

A QUALIFIED ANTI-INTELLECTUALISM

Despite attempts—inscribed/described earlier—to redeem poetical writing as an aspect of Chan practice and realization, the fundamental suspicion toward writing (and reading) was never questioned within the mainstream of Chan/Zen. The notion of a "harmony between Chan and poetry" (Ch. *chanshi yizhi*, J. *zenshi itchi*) derived from that of a "harmony between [canonical] teachings and Chan" (Ch. *jiaochan yizhi*, J. *kyōzen itchi*), first advocated by Zongmi (780–841) to counterbalance that of a "special transmission outside the scriptures." These two trends, which can be traced back to the *Damo lun* (Treatise of Bodhidharma), developed in parallel after the Tang (see Furuta 1965; Kagamishima 1965). Although the radical, exclusive motto always remained the hallmark of orthodoxy, the inclusive tendency became very influential in various times and places—for example, Song China, Koryŏ period in Korea, Kamakura period in Japan. Japanese scholars like Kagamishima Genryū have pointed out that the Chan claim of independence from the written word was merely a reaction against the scholastic tendencies prevailing in Chinese Buddhism during the Six Dynasties and the Tang and did not imply a rejection of the Scriptures as such (Kagamishima 1965, 88–100). The process, however, was not always as dialectical as Kagamishima describes it, and it lent itself to an anti-intellectualist drift that still characterizes large sectors of the Zen tradition.

The tension between the two tendencies explains the ambiguity of many Chan texts in regard to writing, that is, to their own status as *written* texts. An early work like the *Chuan fabao ji*, compiled at the turn of the eighth century, is typical in its paradoxical rejection of writing:

> [In] our [school,] the true *Dharmakāya* is what a Buddha obtains as Dharma: it is apart from that which is transmitted in written characters as the spoken word of the metamorphic Buddhas. . . . How can those who grasp causality and investigate phrases and meanings be able to enter therein? Thus, the [self-] realization [Ch. *zongtong*, Sk. *siddhānta-naya*] spoken of in the [*Laṅkāvatāra*] *sūtra* means to advance by relying on what one has obtained by oneself. It discards all false notions [deriving from] the spoken word and written characters. (Yanagida 1971, 331)

Even an advocate of the "harmony between canonical teaching and Chan" like Zongmi felt compelled to emphasize the "non-reliance on the written letter" in the preface to his *summa* on Chan—a hundred *juan* work that unfortunately was lost or perhaps never written. The paradoxical status of such works, which claim to transmit the ultimate teaching of Chan, has been pointed out by many critics (see, for example, *Fozu tongji*, in *T.* 49, 2035: 188c). Within Chan itself, the process that transformed the apophatic teaching of Bodhidharma into the "literati Chan" (*wenzi chan*) of the Song was seen by many as a deviation. Dōgen, for instance, rejected both the "special transmission" and the "harmony" theories as departures from the true Chan teaching, false dichotomies resulting from a loss of insight (Kagamishima 1965).

One thing to bear in mind is that Chan conceptions of writing, however theoretical they may appear, were always dialogical and performative—in the sense that they imply an interlocutor or a third party who is at times carefully erased from the text. Variations along the doctrinal spectrum owe perhaps less to textual and doctrinal influences than to subtextual, epistemological shifts and to extratextual, sectarian concerns. To ignore these hidden agendas—or rather *legenda*—is perhaps to miss the point, let alone the comma or the inverted commas. However, in the actual state of the documentation, retrieving these changing contexts would prove a daunting task, beyond the scope of this book, and here I want only to suggest a few directions for further research.

In the Japanese context, the dialogical nature of the "nonreliance on the written letter" motto appears clearly in the *Kōzen gokokuron*, a work written by Yōsai to establish his orthodoxy against the claims of the rival Darumashū. The following (and fictitious) dialogue is significant in this respect:

> Question: Some say, "This school, since it claims 'not to depend on the written letter,' is almost like those who erroneously seize upon emptiness and those who have a 'dark realization.' If such is the case, it has already been refuted by the Tendai school, since it is said in the "Shikan shakkan fushigikyō" that: This is not something that the 'dhyāna masters with dark realization' and the 'Dharma masters [attached to] the letter' can understand."
>
> Answer: "Like the ocean rejecting corpses, our Zen school loathes the 'dhyāna masters with dark realization,' and abhors those who hold on to emptiness. Merely to rely on the perfected stage and to cultivate the sudden-and-perfect, outwardly through discipline to abstain from any transgression, inwardly through compassion to benefit others, this is what is called the Zen school, this is what is called the Buddha Dharma. Those whose Zen is blind and who erroneously grasp emptiness do not understand this, they are bandits within Buddhism." (*T.* 80, 2543: 7b–c; Ichikawa, Iriya, and Yanagida 1972, 39–40)

Despite his claim to Zen orthodoxy, Yōsai's position is more akin to the Tiantai/Tendai teachings than to the mainstream of Song dynasty Chan, represented in Japan by his rival Dainichi Nōnin and his followers. The expression "masters with dark realization" (*anshō shi*) goes back to Zhiyi's criticism of a certain category of Chan practitioners—perhaps Bodhidharma's disciples—who advocated a strict antinomianism. Actually, as the quotation makes clear, Zhiyi rejected both the Chan claim of independence from the letter of the Scriptures and the exegetes' attachment to the letter, in the name of a hermeneutics based on mind contemplation (Ch. *guanxin shi*).[1] This type of hermeneutics was also characteristic of Northern Chan, a school that had a strong influence on Saichō and Japa-

---

[1] Zhiyi compares the type of meditation that rejects any doctrinal understanding to seizing a torch (mind) without knowing how to hold it and the type of doctrinal study that neglects meditative practice to holding a sharp knife (the intellect) without knowing how to hold it: in both cases one will harm oneself. See *Fahua xuanyi, T.* 33, 1716: 686a; also *Mohe zhiguan, T.* 46, 1911: 132a. A story, found in the Tendai encyclopaedia *Keiran shūyōshū*, stages Zhiyi and Bodhidharma and attributes to Zhiyi a strong criticism of Bodhidharma's rejection of the Scriptures: "Whereas the spirit of Bodhidharma has only contempt for the scriptures, in the spirit of Tendai, the teaching and the contemplation are equally real" (*T.* 76, 2410: 532b, 533b). Interestingly, a tradition recorded in Dunhuang manuscripts ridicules Zhiyi for his alleged (and typically Chan) rejection of the Scriptures. Encountering on a mountain a young girl who lived as a recluse in a cave and noticing that she kept some sūtras, Zhiyi admonished

nese Tendai and, through the latter, on Yōsai himself and the subsequent Zen tradition (see Faure 1988).

CHAN LOGOCENTRISM

To perceive the implications of the Chan debasement of writing, it is necessary to understand the fluctuating status of writing in Chinese culture and more precisely in Tang China when this position was first advocated. If, as Derrida has argued, the Western tradition is "logocentric" because of the preeminence it gives to the spoken word, it would seem at first that such is not the case in China, where writing always had a superior ontological status. Derrida himself remarks that not all languages are logocentric, and he finds in "largely nonphonetic scripts" such as Chinese or Japanese the testimony of a "powerful movement of civilization developing outside of all logocentrism" (Derrida 1974, 90). Perhaps his argument should be more nuanced because the quasi-totality of Chinese characters contains a phonetical element.

Chinese Writing

The invention (or rather, "discovery") of writing in China is traditionally attributed to Cang Jie, a scribe of the mythical Yellow Emperor. By observing the traces of birds and animals on the ground, Cang Jie realized their differences and created graphic signs that permitted differentiation of ranks and professions and therefore the ordering of society after the model allegedly provided by nature. Writing seems to derive from mimesis, but it is also the metaphysical principle of all things that connects the different planes of reality. This purely spiritual "arch-writing," to borrow Derrida's expression, was perceived as the source of a quasi-Plotinian procession from the metaphysical realm to the physical. Depending on whether such a procession is seen as a degeneration or as a process toward completion, the "invention" of human writing becomes a negative (for Daoist philosophers influenced by Laozi and Zhuangzi) or a positive event (for Confucianists). Chinese writing seems to derive largely from divinatory practices, and, like the power of deciphering oracles, the knowledge obtained through writing had a hermeneutical character (see Vandermeersch 1974; Lagerwey 1985). It was not simply hermeneutical but also performative. Every character of

---

her: "In the *prajñā*, the letter is of no use: what is the use of paper and brush? Trying to free yourself, you are binding yourself; by destroying delusion, you merely delude yourself." To which the girl replied: "That from which the letter itself is deliverance, is this not the *prajñā*? When you see deluded people outside your own mind, you are youself deluded!" (see Demiéville 1961, 15).

writing was an emblem relating realities of various orders. Because "the graphic emblem records (or pretends to record) a stylized gesture, words never became mere signs. The written word had a power of *correct* evocation, for the gesture it figured (or pretended to figure) was a gesture that had a *ritual* value (or, at least, was perceived as such)" (Granet 1968, 50).

At the risk of oversimplifying, one may distinguish two basic kinds of writing, radically different in their effects (and perhaps in their social origins): the philosophical writing of the rationalist trends in Confucianism and in Daoism and the oracular writing of "religious" Daoism, Han cosmology, and so-called popular religion. Not only did these two types of writing bring about fundamental epistemological changes, but they were also from the outset stakes of power.

If writing is the source of social differentiation, then its rejection in the name of a Daoist or Buddhist "metaphysics of presence" implies a criticism of the social order. This criticism, in the case of Chan, would apply to not only Confucianism but also certain trends of Daoism and "popular religion." Likewise, if oracular writing is a means of communicating with gods and spirits, then its rejection implies that of the cosmological (and thereby social) worldview of "official" religion. We need therefore to attend to these two aspects—epistemological and ideological—of writing in the Chan context.

Let us examine briefly the semantic field of *wen*, a word closely associated with writing in the Chan motto *buli wenzi* (no dependence on the "written letter," *wenzi*). The etymological associations of wen (marks, "figuration") and its symbolical value (the wen as participating in cosmic order and serving as mediator between the spiritual and the human world) lead to the notion of culture (wen) as an offshoot of (instead of opposition to) nature. According to François Jullien, when the term *wen* came to designate the graphic sign, then the written text, it already had a long cultural past. Early Confucian speculation reinforced the connotations of this word by emphasizing its cosmologico-moral relationships with the world (1984, 44).

The mediating role of wen, permitted by its polysemic play, leads Jullien to stress the absence of mimesis in Chinese culture and to contrast the Western conception of literature as imitation of reality to the Chinese notion of the literary wen as an unfolding or display (*déploiement*) of the natural wen. According to Jullien, the fault line between speech and writing, which reflects that created by Western mimesis between reality and its representation, is also absent in the Chinese case. The inner intuition of truth and its oral or written expression are perfectly continuous.[2] Because

---

[2] See, for example, Lu Xie's *Wenxin diaolun*, ch. 1: "Man is the jewel of the Five Phases; / He is the spirit of Heaven and Earth; / The spirit manifests itself and language is founded, / Language is founded and the *wen* appears. / This whole process is perfectly natural" (quoted in Jullien 1984).

the Dao is at work from one end of the chain to the other, culture is the consummation of nature. A "metaphysics of presence"—analogous to that which Derrida holds characteristic of Western logocentrism—pervades the entire system; yet the lack of any break or hierarchy between intuition, speech, and writing seems to undercut logocentrism. In contrast to the Western tradition, for which writing is ontologically deficient, the "Chinese" tradition considers writing to be ontologically (*Dao*-logically) efficient (Jullien 1984).

Jullien's interpretation, however, reflects (or furthers) that of its Confucianist sources, in particular that of the *Wenxin diaolong*. To what extent can this interpretation be applied to other currents of Chinese culture? Even in the Confucian case, does this discourse reflect the reality of practice, or merely distort it? We cannot simply assume that there is no discontinuity, no ideological inversion, between the literary theory and the common representation or practice. Unfortunately, the question of ideology is conspicuously absent in most scholarly interpretations of Chinese thought.

It is easy to find counterexamples in other Chinese traditions. In Daoism, for instance, there was indeed a rupture, or at least a degradation, between the "arch-writing" of the Dao and human writing. Because the Chan denial of writing implies a rejection of the canonic tradition, let us consider now the semantic field of the word *jing*, a term usually translated as "classics," sacred or canonic scriptures, and used by Chinese Buddhists to translate the Sanskrit *sūtra*.[3] Concerning the notion of jing in the Lingbao tradition of Daoism, Isabelle Robinet mentions the existence of three kinds of scriptures: the celestial jing or "Dragon-scriptures," made of original breath; the divine or "spontaneous" scriptures, written by the gods and kept in heavens; and the "human" scriptures written down by Cang Jie. These correspond to the three levels of reality: the level of principles, the immaterial level, and the material level, respectively (Robinet 1979, 34). Revealed scriptures were only the projection or "trace" of divine and celestial scriptures: the result of a threefold process of materialization, they were only a pale reflection of truth. Nevertheless, like the wen, they still revealed the ultimate structure of the world—and simultaneously sustained it. The etymology of jing, "warp," "texture" (hence text) alludes to this ordering function. Because these scriptures were an emanation or embodiment of the Dao, they also provided principles for governing oneself and ruling the world (*Yunji qiqian* 3: 13b, in *TT* 677–702; Robinet 1979a, 36). In the case of the revealed scriptures used in the Southern Mao shan tradition, however, the "procession" or emanation from the Dao more clearly entails a degradation. In this school of Daoism, writing was closely related to

---

[3] As is well known, the term sūtra referred originally to the words *spoken* by the Buddha, words eventually written down to constitute the essential part of the "Triple Basket," that is, the Buddhist canon.

cosmogonical speculation. Long before the "invention" of writing, at the time of the separation of Yin and Yang, there was an "arch-writing" or primordial writing called the "Writing of the Eight Assemblies of the Three Primordials" (*sanyuan bahui*). From this derived the writing of the *deva* in the eight directions of space and the writing of the "Spiritual light of the Seal-Cloud of the Eight Dragons" (*balong yunzhuan mingguang*). The latter two, used in the revelations granted to the medium Yang Xi, were at the origin of the school. But with time, the Writing of the Eight Assemblies was transformed into the "Writing of the Dragon and the Phoenix," thus losing its original perfection and unity. This "fragmented" writing, scattered in the various regions of the universe and composed of sixty-four hexagrams, in turn gave birth to impure human writing (see Strickmann 1981, 118–119). From the above examples, it appears that the debasement of writing in Daoism implies a degeneration that takes place within writing itself. In contrast to the West, it did not originate in the fundamental dichotomy between speech and writing—at least in the mainstream tradition.

Although influenced by Daoism, Chan Buddhism was part of another epistemological trend in which speech is undeniably considered prior and superior to writing. The Chan master Linji is clearly logocentric when, (mis)quoting the Indian patriarch Vasubandhu, he declares that: "The act of speech, displayed without, merely informs about the mental activities manifested within. Depending upon mental activities there are thoughts. All these are mere robes [i.e., outer coverings]" (see Fuller Sasaki 1975, 31).

Is this to say that there is no logocentrism, in the Derridean sense, in Chinese culture? We should not hasten to conclude that Linji's logocentrism was due only to Indian (and Buddhist) influences. As noted earlier, we cannot simply assume, as Derrida does, that Chinese language, for lack of a *logos*, entirely escapes logocentrism and refuses to lend itself to a "metaphysics of presence." The "philosophical" Daoism of Laozi and Zhuangzi clearly recognized the logocentric insufficiency of writing to express the fullness of the truth. Thus, in an apologue from Zhuangzi, a wheelwright tells Duke Huan that what the latter is reading is "nothing but the chaff and dregs of the men of old" (*Zhuangzi* 12.7; Watson 1968, 153). Likewise, the early Confucian tradition relied on a "logic of the supplement" similar to that analyzed by Derrida in the case of Rousseau and Western logocentrism: Confucius is quoted in the *Zuozhuan* for saying that: "According to ancient treatises, speech serves as complement of the content of consciousness and *wen* as complement of speech. Without speech, how could one know the content of [someone's] consciousness; and if speech does not have *wen*, it cannot go far and wide" (quoted in Jullien 1984, 47).

Despite his brilliant insights, Derrida seems therefore mistaken when he limits logocentrism to an "ethnocentric metaphysics" related to the history of the West (Derrida 1974, 79). His idealization of the Chinese tradition amounts to a case of reverse ethnocentrism not unlike that for which he reproached Lévi-Strauss (ibid.). Commenting on Derrida's *Of Grammatology*, the Chinese literary critic Zhang Longxi argues that the Aristotelian hierarchy between speech and writing applies to not only phonetic writing but also nonphonetic. According to him, the Chinese debasement of writing "is based on the same considerations as in the West: written words are secondary signifiers" (Zhang 1985, 394). Against Derrida (and indirectly Jullien), Zhang argues that "the dichotomy of meaning and word, content and form, intention and expression, and so forth, is deeply rooted in the thinking of both the East and the West"; and consequently, China is to be included in the tradition of the metaphysics of presence because logocentrism, "far from being specific to the West, is constitutive of human thinking" (ibid, 395). Nevertheless, Zhang also argues that the Chinese language has always provided the possibility of a deconstructive turn: "In the Chinese tradition, however, the power of writing as such avenged itself the very moment it was debased; the metaphysical hierarchy was thus already undermined when it was established. Perhaps this is precisely where the *tao* differs from the *logos*: it hardly needed to wait till the twentieth century for the dismantling of phonetic writing, for the Derridean sleight of hand, the strategy of deconstruction."[4] Admittedly, in Chan this deconstructive turn was most notably found, before being, not unlike Derridean deconstruction itself, coopted by the hierarchies it meant to subvert.

Even if Linji's logocentrism is more Chinese than Indian, many doctrinal characteristics of Chan can be traced back to Indian Mahāyāna—a teaching that is largely the product of a phonetic language, Sanskrit.[5] In his book *Derrida on the Mend*, Robert Magliola argues that Chan derived from one trend of Indian Buddhism, the Madhyamika school founded by Nāgārjuna, whose "deconstruction" of Buddhist logocentrism proves even more thorough than Derrida's deconstruction of Western metaphysics (Magliola 1984, 93). Here I question neither Magliola's understanding of Derrida

---

[4] Zhang 1985, 397. Interestingly, a similar argument has been made in Japan for for Japanese thought, namely for a Tokugawa thinker like Motoori Norinaga. See Karatani 1988, de Bary 1988. One may wonder if these are not also cases of reverse ethnocentrism that reinforce nativist discourse.

[5] What of the relationship between Zen and Japanese writing, a mixture of phonetic and nonphonetic signs? The *kana* syllabary derived from the Sanskrit phonetic system known as *siddham*, through the intermediary of esoteric Buddhism (hence its attribution to Kūkai, the founder of the Shingon school). The siddham had some influence on early Chan, as can be seen from a Dunhuang text known as *Xitan zhang* or *Chapter on Siddham*. [T. 85, 2779] It would be useful to examine if—and to what extent—this characteristic of the language affected Zen teachings. The mystical power attributed to Sanskrit letters played an important role in nativist esoteric speculations concerning *kotodama*, and its influence can also be found in the *kirigami* of the Sōtō tradition. On siddham, see van Gulik 1956.

nor his interpretation of Nāgārjuna's "Middle Path." His distinction between two trends in Chan/Zen, "[logo]centric" and "differential," and his criticism of the former as dominant orthodoxy, may still serve our purpose, even if Magliola himself relies too much on D. T. Suzuki's presentation of Zen when he equates "(logo)centric" Zen with the Yogācara trend in Chan. Although heuristically useful, the very distinction between (logo)centric and differential Chan becomes counterproductive when it hardens into a rigid opposition between two historically well-defined trends such as Northern and Southern Chan.[6] By so doing, it merely replicates the scapegoating process of logocentrism denounced in another context by Derrida. Differential Zen eludes or subverts logocentric Zen, rather than opposing it; and these two forms of Chan/Zen must remain virtual poles or ideal-types.

Methodological Caveats

To aim at a correct evaluation of Chan presupposes that we know what kind of teaching we are dealing with. But how do we know it? Are we not "reading" into this teaching, with our literary, intellectual expectations, things that are not there? Conversely, how can we be sure of not missing crucial aspects? Is the paradox of writing down a teaching that rejects writing as paradoxical as it looks (or "sounds," to use an auditory rather than visual metaphor)? To begin with, are we so certain that Chan masters were really denying or downplaying writing? It was suggested earlier that their denial was highly selective and nuanced. But to what extent is the Chan teaching *written*? How can we distinguish the formulaic components of oral discourse from the intertextuality of written texts? In a *book* like this one, where visual metaphors tend to impose themselves, it is not so easy to sort out our own presuppositions from those of the tradition under study. We have for instance noted earlier the Western/Christian prejudice in favor of doctrine and against ritual; that is, we emphasize the semantic/hermeneutical level of language to the detriment of its pragmatic/performative level. Not surprisingly, the Chan tradition has until now been studied mainly from the viewpoint of its doctrinal/philosophical content, while its ritual content has been largely neglected.

Two basic models are available when attempting to evaluate the relative importance of literacy and orality in a tradition like Chan: one model,

[6] To give just one example, Magliola quotes Keizan's teaching as a case of differential Zen (Magliola 1984, 99). However, Keizan was a representative of the "inclusive" Zen so despised by intellectuals who delight in the subtleties of Madhyamika thought. Magliola would perhaps see in Dōgen an example of "absolutist" or logocentric Zen, and he might be right. In reality, we find in the Chan/Zen tradition in general, or in Dōgen and Keizan in particular (and probably in Nāgārjuna as well), only combinations of these ideal-types.

privileging orality (and the discourse of popular culture[s]), can be found in the works of such scholars as Walter Ong, Jack Goody, or Michel de Certeau; the other, privileging an extended concept of writing and literacy (and the teaching of the "great tradition"), has been advocated by Derrida.

Taking our cues mainly from Walter Ong, let us apply the first model to Chan. Paradoxically, Ong's approach may help us realize that there is both more orality and more literacy in Chan than is generally assumed. What are then the implications of the oral/aural and/or written aspects of Chan? Does the tension between two types of Chan, translated doctrinally (that is, at the level of literacy) as the sudden/gradual controversy, reflect a deeper fault between orality and literacy? And if so, is the sudden teaching automatically on the side of orality, or does it, on the contrary, represent in its "secondary" form a revenge of intellectualism?

Significantly, one founding myth of Chan is the poetical contest that allegedly opposed Shenxiu and Huineng for the position of Sixth Patriarch. Whereas Shenxiu's verse was written by himself, the illiterate Huineng had to dictate his verse to a monk. Like today's *dazibao*, the two poems were written on a wall, and their reading gave perhaps a new meaning to Bodhidharma's "wall-contemplation." Shenxiu is thus made into a paradigm of literacy, Huineng of illiteracy and/or orality. Shenxiu was also an elder monk of noble Chinese extraction, while Huineng was a layman and a commoner, who may have descended on his mother's side from a Southern "barbarian" ethnic group, the Liao. Whereas Shenxiu's verse is characterized by the use of concrete metaphors—the tree for the body, the mirror for the mind, dust for the passions that cloud the mind, polishing the mirror for meditative practice—Huineng's verse rejects all images in the name of emptiness. Thus, if we follow Ong's argument that orality is characterized by concreteness, Shenxiu's verse seems closer to the oral world, whereas Huineng's reveals a higher degree of intellectualism and therefore of interiorized literacy. The relation of the two verses to orality and literacy turns out to be the reverse of that provided by the common hagiographical characterization of their authors.

If we consider that, as a "commitment of the word to space," writing "restructures thought" (Ong 1982, 7), what might have been the epistemological effects of writing in the case of Chan? At first glance, most Chan texts present a number of features characteristic of orally based thought or expression: namely, a certain redundancy, a closeness to the human world, and a tendency to be agonistically toned and situational rather than abstract (ibid., 34). As Ong remarks, "Many, if not all, oral or residually oral cultures strike literates as extraordinarily agonistic in their verbal performance and indeed in their lifestyle" (ibid., 43). Moreover, "by keeping knowledge embedded in the human lifeworld, orality situates knowledge within a context of struggle (ibid., 44). These remarks could apply to Chan "dialogues" (*wenda*) and kōan. For the Chan practitioner engaged in a "dialogue," and for the orally minded individual, the meaning of words depends entirely on their context, a context that "includes also gestures, vocal inflections, facial expression, and the entire human, existential setting in which the real, spoken word always occurs" (ibid., 47). Neither is interested in definitions: their thinking is situational, not categorical (ibid., 52). Like the riddle, the kōan seems to belong in the oral world: it cannot be solved by rational thinking, a faculty derived from (or enhanced by) literacy. The performative aspect of the kōan may indicate that it is a product of what Ong, quoting Marcel Jousse, calls a "verbo-motor culture," that is, a culture that retains "enough oral residue to remain significantly word-attentive in a person-interactive context (the oral type of context) rather than object-attentive" (ibid., 68). Typically, a Chan master often answers a question by asking another, and, like the orally minded individual, he "never lets down his oral guard."

If we follow this line of thinking further, then we may come to see the irruption of the "sudden teaching" into traditional, philosophical, literate Buddhism as a resurfacing of aural/oral elements within literacy.[7] Ong argues that the predominance of the auditory sense permits a sudden, unifying, intuitive experience, whereas vision tends to be sequential, analytic, and objectifying (ibid., 72). This analysis (intuition, in-*sight*?) seems justified in the case of early Chan texts like the *Dasheng wusheng fangbian men* (Treatise of the Five Unborn *Upāya* of the Great Vehicle), in which sudden awakening is described through auditory metaphors.[8] One might also argue just the opposite; namely, vision is simultaneous while sound is sequential, and therefore "sudden" awakening is fundamentally visual, as implied by the visual metaphor of "illumination." In this sense, then, the "sudden" teaching might derive from a kind of total vision of space that, according to Ong, constitutes a by-product of writing. Again, a number of texts describe sudden awakening in visual terms, and I have connected earlier the rise of subitism with the primacy of space and vision in early Chan. Visual and auditory metaphors can be found side by side in the context of Chan awakening, and it is not clear whether they refer to different aspects of the same experience or to different experiences. Nevertheless, so-called awakening implies the vision of an inner self, and the existence of such a subjectivity, or its interiority, seems to presuppose writing. In the Western context, for instance, "introspection and greater and greater internalization of conscience mark the entire history of Christian asceticism, where their intensification is clearly connected with writing" (ibid.,

---

[7] Paradoxically, like *différance/différence*, the aural/oral distinction between *oral* and *aural* cannot be heard (spoken), it has to be *read* (written).

[8] *T. 85, 2834, 1274b–1275a*; see also Demiéville 1952, 49–50; and *Lengqie shizi ji*, in *T. 85, 2837: 1290c*.

153). Chan is the product of a tradition of asceticism that, in this respect, offers striking analogies with the Christian tradition.[9] In both cases, renouncing the world leads to the discovery of an inner self. Whether Christian or Buddhist, self-analysis "requires a certain demolition of situational thinking. It calls for isolation of the self" (ibid., 54). The fact that traditional Buddhists practiced this kind of introspection just to prove the emptiness of the self, while Chan monks apparently rejected it, does not mean that the latter could simply return to a state prior to the emergence of the self and thereby erase the effects of writing on their thinking (or nonthinking). The Buddhist/Chan mind is not a palimpsest.

ORALITY IN CHAN

> Visus, tactus, gustus in te fallitur;
> Sed auditus solo tuto creditur.
> (Thomas Aquinas)

Whereas early Chan texts were "theoretical," later texts are characterized by their concreteness. If the interest in theory, a typical by-product of literacy, also reflects, as Bourdieu argues, a social ascension, then perhaps the ambiguous role of writing in early Chan derives from the transitional situation of this school toward the mid-Tang, a time when its social position was half-way between the largely illiterate masses and highly literate circles and therefore characterized by semi-orality or semi-literacy (depending on the viewpoint).

In some respects, the growing importance of writing in Chan did not reduce orality but rather enhanced it, as it did in the West for rhetoric: hence the well-know importance of "dialogues" in Chan (Ong 1982, 9). At the same time, whatever orality there was in early and middle Chan became soon subjected to an increasing literarization. I illustrate this in dialectical fashion with reference to a few Chan genres such as genealogies, hagiography, philosophical "dialogues," "recorded" sayings, and kōan. In what follows, I heuristically attempt to de-scribe and re-inscribe Chan texts, that is, to read/hear them alternatively as predominantly oral or literary, hermeneutical or rhetorical.

De-scribing Chan

My first gesture consists both in emphasizing the oral components of what have usually been considered "philosophical" writings—as found for ex-

---

[9] On the philosophical side as well, one may argue that, although Chan masters, like Plato, debased writing, "the philosophical thinking [they] fought for depended entirely on writing" (Ong 1982, 24).

ample in the Dunhuang literature—and in analyzing the evolution of Chan as a shift from a purely oral situation to a residually oral and eventually literate situation. Their textual presupposition has led philosophically minded interpreters like myself (my earlier self), trying to account for similarities, to talk of intertextuality; perhaps one should even talk of *homotextuality*, so great is the family resemblance of most of these texts. Conversely, an oral presupposition would have led these scholars to notice the possibly formulaic nature of such passages and to realize that such texts were inscribed in a network of practices and therefore meant to be used performatively. Thus, in an allegedly "philosophical" work like the *Dasheng wusheng fangbian men*, the ritual introduction that frames the text has been neglected in favor of the doctrinal content, although the doctrine cannot be understood apart from its ritual context—or perhaps is conveyed primarily by the ritual itself. Texts such as the *Laṅkāvatāra-sūtra*, the *Platform Sūtra*, or the *Shōbōgenzō* were not revered primarily, as we tend to believe today, for their doctrinal or "philosophical" content. They also played a crucial role in a ritual of transmission by legitimizing the patriarchal lineage. Likewise, when the teachings of early Chan were transmitted in didactic songs such as *Yao dao ge* (Enjoying the Way), *Xinglu nan* (Hard is the Road), or *Wugeng zhuan* (The Five Watches), their effect changed drastically (see Xu Guolin 1937, 1: 92-93). Although these songs are usually attributed to famous Chan masters, as with the work of legendary "authors" like Homer or Laozi, the formulaic nature of such texts radically thwarts the process of hermeneutic retrieval.[10] Whatever the genre of the text—whether Chan treatises, hagiographical works, *Recorded Sayings*, or didactic songs—these formulas can usually be shifted around without interfering with the teaching or the narrative (see ibid., 58–59).

The oral/aural components of early Chan treatises can be inferred from their dialogical structure. These texts usually stage two or more interlocutors, whose fictitious nature is sometimes explicitly stated. Here again, the comparison with the Western tradition is suggestive. In the West, "early writing provides the reader with conspicuous helps for situating himself imaginatively. It presents philosophical material in dialogues." Later, however, "writing will present philosophical and theological texts in objection-and-response form, so that the reader can imagine an oral disputation" (ibid., 103). This approach, however, entails some logocentric nostalgia. It leads to the acknowledgment of a gradual loss, a decline of orality. At best,

---

[10] As Milman Parry has shown, Homeric poems "were made up not simply of word-units but of formulas, groups of words for dealing with traditional materials, each formula shaped to fit into a hexameter line." See Milman Parry, *The Making of the Homeric Verse: The Collected Papers of Milman Parry*, ed. Adam Parry (Oxford: Clarendon Press, 1971); quoted in Ong 1982, 58. Many scholars have also pointed out the formulaic nature of the *Laozi*, but little has been done to understand the implications of this formulaic approach.

the early Chan tradition constitutes a residual orality that increasingly gives way to literacy. This literarization goes together with a ritualization, which seems to preserve a residually oral situation permitted by writing: thus, in medieval Japan, kōan ended up being routinely read at funerals by the Zen priest officiating in front of the coffin (and on behalf of the dead) (see Bodiford 1989).

Re-inscribing Chan

With the emergence of the Chan patriarchal tradition, what was in the beginning a simple list of six or seven names of patriarchs (or would-be patriarchs) soon gave rise to complex diagrams including collateral lineages. One of the first attempts at schematic spatialization may be found in Zongmi's *Chanmen shizi chengxitu* (Diagram of the Chan Lineage, in ZZ 1, 2, 15). These genealogical diagrams tended to replace the first narrative genealogies, which, although they already show the ascendency of writing, still reflected an orally framed tradition—a tradition in which, "instead of a recitation of names, we find a sequence of 'begats,' of statements of what someone did. . . . This sort of aggregation derives partly from the oral drive to use formulas, partly from the oral mnemonic drive to exploit balance . . . , partly from the oral drive to redundancy (each person is mentioned twice, as begetter and begotten), and partly from the oral drive to narrate rather than simply to juxtapose" (Ong 1982, 99). Thus, according to an early Chan chronicle, the *Chuan fabao ji*, "The Great Master [Bodhidharma] transmitted [the Dharma] to [Huike] and left. Huike transmitted it to Sengcan, Sengcan transmitted it to Daoxin, Daoxin transmitted it to Hongren, Hongren transmitted it to Faru, and Faru transmitted it to Datong [Shenxiu]" (see Yanagida 1971, 337; McRae 1986, 257). In the subsequent Buddhist histories, this pseudo-narrative has been replaced by a mere list of names and charts. The use of diagrams increased in the Caodong tradition with the speculations—partly inspired by the *Yijing*—on the "Five Ranks" (*wuwei*) (see W. Lai 1983b). In Japan, this evolution led to the *kirigami* of the Sōtō tradition and turned Sōtō Zen into a form of "diagrammatic Buddhism" based on a semi-written "oral tradition" (*kuden*).

With regard to hagiography, the epistemological changes brought by literacy may have significantly contributed to the growing realism that characterizes Chan "histories" after the Tang. Writing allowed to mobilize knowledge and memory without resorting to the heroic feats and wonders that were characteristic of the oral tradition (Ong 1982, 71). The shift of focus toward ordinary life that characterizes Chan literature after Mazu Daoyi may therefore reflect as much a literarization as a popularization of Chan.

Despite the apparent oral/aural nature of the master-disciple relation-ship, the development of Chan "dialogues" derives perhaps from a grow-ing interiorization of writing, a process that led from the earlier, largely fictitious dialogues to the "recorded sayings" of the masters and the col-lected "Histories of the Lamp."[11] Chan masters often warned, but appar-ently to no avail, their disciples that their words should not be recorded because the soteriological purport of their *dialogue* (wenda) was limited to a single occurrence. However, the shift from dialogues to kōan (Ch. *gongan*, a term that evokes the "public cases," which served as precedents in Chinese legislation) shows an increasing tendency to publicize and pub-lish these words. This process culminates in later Zen anthologies such as the *Zenrin kushū* (A Collection of Sentences from the Forests of Chan), an anthology of answers to famous "cases" from which the Zen practitioner may select his own answer to the age-old kōan—probably selected from a similar collection by the master.[12] Even if these verses or sentences, ar-ranged by number of characters, derive from a formulaic tradition, their use has been enhanced by literacy.[13] At the same time, the emergence of a graphic space reveals the multiplicity of what was assumed to be a unified teaching. It engenders conflicting interpretations and attempts at reconciliation—thus paving the way for new doctrinal developments. By modifying mental structures, the new technology of writing affected, not only Chan doctrine, but also the very content of Chan practice, and per-haps ultimately Chan awakening itself.

In most cases, admittedly, "recorded sayings" were compiled long after the death of a master and copiously edited by his disciples. Even if it was a faithful rendition of the master's words, the very act of writing these words down drastically transformed them and modified their impact, producing "reencoded" sayings. Like the recording of European oral traditions by the Grimm brothers, Andersen or Perrault, the recording of Chan *logia*, although purporting to preserve them as "live words," resulted in a rather deadly fixation of flexible thought processes and versatile speech-acts. Of-ten enough, the master's tongue "had no bones," and his teaching could

[11] Even to deny writing, early Chan resorted to metaphors of interiorized textuality. Commenting on Wuzhu's antinomianism, Shenqing, the author of the *Beishan lu* (Record of Northern Mountain), writes: "Therefore, only when images are abandoned and the sūtra discarded can it properly be called the sudden teaching. If one has anything to expound, he should determine the text from within himself. What need is there for exegesis and commen-tary?" And Shenqing notes: "This corresponds to the present-day practice of improvised dialogues" (*T.* 52, 2113: 612c).

[12] See, for instance, Yoel Hoffman, trans. *The Sound of the One Hand: 281 Zen Koans with Answers* (New York: Basic Books, 1975); and Shigematsu Soiku, comp. and trans., *A Zen Forest: Sayings of the Masters* (New York: Weatherhill, 1981).

[13] They constitute, for example, the entries of several reference works produced during the Tokugawa period by Mujaku Dōchū (1653–1744). On this man and his work, see App 1987.

vary according to circumstances. Once a statement is removed from its oral context, however, it tends to be interpreted in terms of logical truth. Although its utterance was characterized by the essential ambiguity of what Bourdieu calls the "logic of practice," it is now judged in terms of conventional logic (or its inverted image, Chan "irrationalism"). This is why Mazu Daoyi puzzled some of his students (and modern interpreters) by saying at times that our mind "is the Buddha" and at other times that "it is not the Buddha." Hermeneutical theories such as the Two Truths are necessary to reconcile such contradictory statements by introducing a difference of level between them. Both the contradiction and the need to solve it were to a large extent by-products of the technology of writing, which transformed a fecund ambiguity into a sterile dichotomy or a neutralized synthesis.

Thus, the recording of oral discourse alters it considerably, by restructuring it in a subtle way along lines of literacy, not orality. However, the impact of writing is not necessarily as negative as nostalgics of orality would have us believe. If, on the one hand, writing tends to prevent the renewal of the oral tradition and to generate dogmatism, on the other, it frees the text from its context and allows an inexhaustible "surplus of meaning" to emerge. As Ong points out, "the paradox lies in the fact that the deadness of the text, its removal from the living human lifeworld, its rigid visual fixity, assures its endurance and its potential for being resurrected into limitless living contexts by a potentially infinite number of living readers" (ibid., 81). The importance of decontextualization is also underscored by Paul Ricoeur, who discerns a threefold autonomy of the text: with respect to the intention of the author; with respect to the cultural situation and all the sociological conditions of the production of the text; and finally, with respect to the original addressee. In this way, the text is capable of decontextualizing and recontextualizing itself (Ricoeur 1981, 91). Furthermore, "the distantiation revealed by writing is already present in discourse itself, which contains the seeds of the distantiation of the said [meaning] from the saying [event]."[14] Contrary to Ong, Ricoeur sees the movement from orality to textuality as a gain.[15] The structural semantic gained by textualization, and the "hermeneutical function of distantiation" (Ricoeur 1981, 131–144) are achieved at the cost of the performative dimension of discourse and more precisely of its rhetorical richness. Of the three levels of performative discourse described by Austin—locutionary, illocutionary, and perlocutionary—only the first two may be reinscribed in the text. The

[14] See Ricoeur 1981, 92. The last point had been made, in a slightly different fashion, by Derrida, for whom "the *spacing* of speech already makes it a writing" (Derrida 1974, 139). On "iterability," see also Derrida 1988, 200.

[15] Both, however, accept the existence of a hierarchy between orality and literacy/textuality, whereas that hierarchy is precisely what Derrida denounces as ideological.

perlocutionary level, essential in Chan discourse ("dialogues," kōan), disappears in the written text. This loss was perhaps one reason for the Chan distrust toward writing and the "gradual" hermeneutics it implies. If, however, there is no way to retrieve the original perlocutionary effects once the initial dialogical context is erased, new perlocutionary effects might emerge from new contexts.

CHAN AS A KIND OF WRITING

My first gesture, focusing on the oral components of Chan, suggested that these components were gradually "literarized." My second gesture contradicts ("counter-writes") or counterbalances the first by emphasizing the intrinsically literary character of all Chan "literature"—even when the latter seems to record residually oral situations. We now insist on taking Chan texts for what they are, that is, *written* texts, and not for what they claim to be, that is, recordings of verbal performances. After all, the opening and legitimizing line ("Thus I have heard") of Mahāyāna scriptures never tricked scholars (and not always Buddhist adherents) into believing that these were truly "recorded sayings"—and not apocrypha.

Let us, then, heuristically consider Chan discourse as a text resulting from a "writing-act" rather than from a speech-act and focus on the implications of such a "textuality." If the reader, when she/he reads a Chan/Zen text, usually presupposes that it has a primarily mimetic function, he/she is not entirely responsible for that assumption. Whatever one may say about the absence of mimesis in Chinese literature, it is clear that many early Chan texts claim to describe spiritual or physical, sacred or profane reality. Most Buddhist literature is of that kind, and it does not matter too much that this "descriptive" account is implicitly prescriptive, giving the reality it describes as a goal for the practitioner.

What matters, however, is that, despite its dialogical markers, the "description"—for example that of an "encounter dialogue"—is from the outset written. It is produced as a text, and as such it has to obey rules of text production; these rules differ in significant ways from those of oral speech. What we witness in the case of the "Recorded Sayings" of Chan is a merely *literary* turn to orality. This means that, however straightforward and "realistic" it may appear, the text should be read as a *self-referential* literary work. Literary writing "replaces referential meaning with references of words to texts and of texts to texts, it replaces literalness with literariness. The *praxis* it demands of the reader is therefore the awareness that the text always refers to something said otherwise and elsewhere, the continuous experience of a verbal detour" (Riffaterre 1986, 138).

The rules of text production have been carefully studied by Michael

Riffaterre. Although Riffaterre is mainly concerned with literary genres such as poetry, which openly claim their literariness, the conclusions he draws from these "experimental" models can apparently be extended to a large part of Buddhist literature. This is true even when such literature shuns literariness, as in the Chan case. Early Chan texts and later yulu are primarily different literary genres, concerned less with "reality" than with their own structural rules. At this point, we need to introduce Riffaterre's distinction between *meaning* and *significance*—a distinction that overlaps with that between the mimetic and semiotic levels of a text. Whereas the *meaning* is the information provided by the text at the mimetic level—that is, what the text seems to say about a referent—*significance* is the meaning emerging at the semiotic level—that is, what the text is really about, its subtle, hidden implications. Produced by a device called *indirection*, that is, the fact of "displacing, distorting or creating meaning," significance always threatens *mimesis*, that is, the literary representation of reality (Riffaterre 1986, 2). Like the perlocutionary effects of the speech-acts studied by Austin, Riffaterre's analysis of significance points to the necessity of looking beyond the apparent, referential meaning of Chan texts, which often say one thing and mean (or do) another. Thus, the relations between one text and others—intertextuality—and the relations within the text itself—its structural constraints—come to predominate over the relations between the text and the (inner or outer) reality. Far from being a mimetic representation or even a spontaneous expression of such a reality, the text and its significance result from a transformation of a *matrix*—that is, a word or a minimal sentence, usually hidden or reduced to a marker— around which the text will develop its arabesques. To use Riffaterre's metaphor, "the significance is shaped like a doughnut, the hole being the matrix" (ibid., 13). It is "produced by the *detour* the text makes as it runs the gauntlet of mimesis, . . . with the aim of exhausting the paradigm of all possible variations of the matrix" (ibid., 19). This unfolding and revolving of the text is permitted by the two basic rules of conversion and expansion (ibid., 22).

ANOTHER DIFFEREND

In our analysis of the epistemological and stylistic constraints brought about by the technology of writing, we have followed Ong a long way and accompanied Riffaterre on a significant *détour*. It is time to return to Derrida, whose grammatological model has been criticized by Ong as a typical product of interiorized literacy. Ong himself, however, seems to fall victim to the criticism that Derrida addresses to the way in which Lévi-Strauss, in *Tristes Tropiques*, romantically elaborates on the binary opposition between speech and writing. In so doing, Derrida argues, Lévi-Strauss makes a scapegoat of writing and fails to see in orality the very same chacteristics that he condemns in writing (Derrida 1974, 101–140; see also LaCapra 1985, 51). One could also argue that the logic of writing is already at work in Ong's attempt to objectify orality and that the embalming gesture that gives orality "the beauty of the dead" is heir to a long tradition of violence (see Certeau 1986, 119–136).

In this confrontation between two conceptions of writing, as with the sudden/gradual "controversy," we may be in presence of a *différend*, that is, of two discourses that do not share the same premises and therefore never meet on the same ground. Given the impossibility to decide, two models might be better than one, and perhaps, as Lévi-Strauss himself argued in another context, it is precisely in the play (or lag, *jeu*) between these two models that some insight might be gained. Ong is justified to point out that writing involves power and that classical Chinese was one of those "chirographically controlled, sex-linked languages" that were spoken by males only (Ong 1982, 114). To be sure, although Chan literature is a mixture of classical and colloquial Chinese, there is probably no single Chan text written by a woman. Due to the Chinese educational system, access to written Chinese—and therefore to the Buddhist canon—was reserved to men. But I have also pointed out in the case of the kōan that the spoken word itself is not always innocent in relation to power. Moreover, writing had not always had a rationalizing effect, nor did it necessarily lead to abstraction. Oracular writing in particular, as practiced in Daoism or local cults, had the opposite effect. Lagerwey argues that "Buddhism, coming from a civilization with an alphabet, a civilization entirely addicted to the discourse, had an overwhelmingly oralizing and rationalizing impact on Chinese culture. . . . [For] all its orality, [it] shared the visual prejudice of pagan idealism in general. . . . In this regard, Buddhism confirmed and deepened the visual bias of the civilization of the written sign" (Lagerwey 1985, 319). Oracular writing seems to have played an important role in Chan/Zen—particularly with the Ōbaku school in Tokugawa Japan (see Strickmann 1990). As regards Japanese Buddhism, one has noted earlier the crucial role played by the so-called oral transmission (*kuden*)—a secret transmission that in fact was produced through written documents, the kirigami (see Sugimoto 1982). Originating in esoteric Buddhism (*mikkyō*), this (semi-literary) genre was also important in Zen (particularly Sōtō) and Pure Land sects. Dealing with the inner rules of the monastery, these kirigami were defined as the "letter of oral resolution" or "letter transcending the letter." Characterized by complex diagrams, they constitute, half-way between the oral and written traditions, what we could call a form of "diagrammatic Buddhism," and they attest to the importance of charts and lineage in Chan/Zen.

All this leads us to the conclusion that we should not put too much weight on the opposition between orality and literacy. Taking these terms as ideal- types rather than realities, we should above all avoid debasing writing and idealizing oral culture and those aspects of Chan that seem to derive from or point toward it, for it would mean repeating Chan and Western prejudices. As Derrida convincingly argues:

> The ethic of the living word would be perfectly respectable, completely utopian and a-topic [*utopique et atopique*] as it is (unconnected to *spacing* and to differance as writing), . . . if it did not live on a delusion and a nonrespect for its own condition of origin, if it did not dream in speech of a presence denied to writing, denied by writing. The ethic of speech is the *delusion* [*leurre*, lure] of presence mastered. . . . To recognize writing in speech, that is to say *différance* and the absence of speech, is to begin to think the lure. (Derrida 1974, 139)

Derrida helps us out of the lure or delusion of an authentic culture or of a pristinely pure experience that would have been irreversibly corrupted by writing. In this sense, there is indeed no *hors-texte* because all thinking, and even the unconscious are always already differed and differential, that is, textualized. The generalization of writing may have indeed brought radical changes, but to interpret these changes as an absolute loss is to misunderstand the nature of what was lost (let alone of what was gained), as well as to misunderstand the nature of writing. Insofar as they spatialize human experience, even the most "primitive" classifications are a form of writing. In this sense, there is no pure oral/aural culture, and there never was. Therefore, if the anthropological "writing of (oral) culture" by anthropologists does not neccessarily produce a radical distortion of pristine orality (Clifford 1986, 118), neither perhaps does the "textualization" of Chan experience.

In the last analysis, if there is such a thing, the emphasis on the two models presented above (Chan as residually oral vs. Chan as written; or, put differently, hermeneutical Chan vs. rhetorical Chan) and the decision to read the texts as predominantly oral or written constitute in themselves rhetorical and ideological moves—and not, as I claimed earlier, purely heuristic ones. These two ways of arbitrarily interpreting or "mobilizing" the same corpus, however, are never entirely the free choice of the reader: they reinscribe in the individual the conflictual interpretive strategies of past rival groups or traditions. Thus, genres are not purely theoretical: they are historical artifacts that allow the institutionalization of certain practices. The ideology of orality cannot simply be dismissed as such, for it did in a number of cases produce real effects; for instance, it engendered a logocentric Chan that rejected the dead letter in the name of the "live word." Conversely, there is some evidence for the existence of a "differential" Chan that severed its umbilical cord with the mythical founder(s) and let go of the myth of pure origins (see Faure 1991, 11–31). This trend appears more clearly when we emphasize Chan as a rhetorical tradition.

CHAN RHETORIC

In my earlier discussion of Chan/Zen scholarship, I have privileged the performative model over the hermeneutical model. This move was dictated by my interpretive choice to read the "high" Chan tradition as a departure from the Buddhist canon. This choice is not entirely arbitrary: the new Chan style of the Tang seems indeed to reflect a growing awareness of the fact that the hermeneutical tradition, despite (or because of) its claims to adhere to the letter of the scriptures, had actually engendered a burdensome doctrinal proliferation. Any Chinese Buddhist who read through the commentaries and subcommentaries of a treatise such as the *Awakening of Faith (Dasheng qixinlun)* would eventually realize that commentary is endless and that, like the horizon line, the "original" meaning of a text constantly recedes. In that particular case, he would have had some reason to suspect that the original meaning was problematic because that work, like many other Chan scriptures of the Tang, is apocryphal. The very notion of apocryphal scriptures, however, became problematic in that context. At any rate, the Chan criticism of all interpretations as "secondary" in the name of a "first order meaning" (*diyiyi*, J. *daiichi gi*) implied a denial of referential truth. Interpretation is perceived as a blind alley because ultimately nothing in the foundational text is not already an interpretation (see Dreyfus and Rabinow 1983, 107).

The rhetorical discourse of Chan was partly a response to this exegetical excess, which was itself an attempt to overcome the closure of the Buddhist canon.[16] Exegesis can be analyzed in terms of the dialectic of canonization, a dialectic described by Jonathan Z. Smith as a process of limitation or rarefaction followed by an overcoming of the limits through ingenuity. To overcome the rarefaction of materials caused by the closure of a canon, exegetes multiply ingenious readings of this canon, thereby causing a proliferation of meaning. Although Smith is concerned mainly with exegetical manipulations, these manipulations can also be rhetorical. In his study of Western medieval literature, Michel Charles contrasts the commentary to rhetoric, which keeps its distance from the text and develops as a discourse of "mastery over language and over oneself" (Charles 1985, 47). In the

[16] I follow Dominick LaCapra's definition of rhetoric: "(1) [It] involves a dialogical understanding of discourse and of 'truth.' (2) [It] includes 'performative' uses of language that make a difference in one's relation to the object of study. (3) [It] highlights the problem of how one reads texts. (4) It exceeds not only documentary or referential but all utilitarian, workaday, and instrumental functions of language, etc." See LaCapra 1985, 36.

rhetorical tradition, the canonical text has lost its authority and has become a *pre*-text. No longer seen as a distant origin and a receding horizon, as with the commentary, it merely reinforces discourse with markers of authenticity.

Opening the Canon

At the risk of producing yet another fraudulent linear narrative, let me endeavor to describe how the transition from the hermeneutical to the rhetorical model in Chan might have taken place.[17] One discerns in early Chan an attempt, still in the hermeneutical manner, to reinterpret "spiritually" the traditional rubrics of Buddhism. This attitude is exemplified by a Chan commentary on the *[Foshuo] Faju jing* (Pelliot 2192). The word *jing* ("scripture," "sūtra", but also, etymologically, "warp") in the title is glossed as follows: "The body of the six *skandha* is the loom, the six senses are the warp, the six consciousnesses are the woof, the six types of sense data are the shuttle, the mental states of grasping and rejecting are the thread, and the conditionalities of craving are the weave. With these, each sentient being weaves his own karma of rebirth in hell or heaven" (see McRae 1986, 203). The hermeneutic *habitus*, lingering in a number of Linji's sermons, undercuts his most radical statements. For instance, his famous incitation to spiritual murder—"If you meet the Buddha, kill the Buddha; . . . if you meet your parents, kill your parents!"—is qualified by the following comment: "Ignorance is the father . . . , covetousness is the mother. . . . [If] in the midst of the pure *dharmadhātu* you haven't a single thought in your mind . . . , this is called 'shedding the blood of the Buddha'" (Fuller Sasaki 1975, 35–36).

Early Chan also witnessed a flourishing of apocryphal scriptures such as the *Jingang sanmeijing*, the *Faju jing*, the *Yuanjue jing*, the *Shoulengyan jing*, and so on (see Buswell 1989). This attempt to give to the new Chan teaching the authority and legitimacy of Buddha's words shows that the latter were still highly respected. One last apocryphal Chan scripture is "Sūtra of the Gate of Chan" (*Chanmen jing*). Written by a follower of the Northern school some time before 730—that is, several years before Shenhui launched his offensive against the "gradualism" of that school—it already takes a radically "sudden" standpoint. As a genre, however, this type of apocryphal scripture had almost lost its purpose.[18] Chan, which

---

[17] David Chappell distinguishes three hermeneutical phases in Chinese Buddhism: (1) the discovery of a new interpretation and practice that solves a personal crisis; (2) their integration with the established tradition; (3) their systematic propagation; See Chappell 1988, 176. Although early Chan was still inscribed in this hermeneutical process, it was already pointing beyond it.

[18] Two exceptions are the *Śūraṃgama-sūtra* (*Shoulengyan jing*) and the *Sūtra of Perfect Enlightenment* (*Yuanjue jing*). Forged during the Tang in circles close to Northern Chan and

had at first smacked of heterodoxy, had become by the eighth century the dominant orthodoxy, and its followers were growing confident. This confidence is reflected in the title of a work attributed to Huineng, the *Platform Sūtra*, the first Chinese Buddhist text to vindicate openly for itself the status of a sūtra. Chan patriarchs were now seen as equal to the Buddha himself. Consequently, interest shifted from the Indian paradigms (Śākyamuni, Bodhidharma) to purely Chinese patriarchs like Huineng. In this light, the motto "a special transmission outside the scriptures" might perhaps be read as a departure, not only from the Buddhist canon, but also from the apocryphal literature of early Chan.

A further step toward independence from the canon was taken with what is improperly called "classical" Chan. In the "dialogues" between master and disciples, canonical Scriptures are often decontextualized and treated as "cases," just like the sayings of earlier Chan masters. In this way, Chan contributed to "re-oralize" the scriptural tradition. The antiscriptural frame became an integral part of the yulu genre. It is true, as Judith Berling points out, that the yulu genre has contributed to "bring the Buddha down to earth" (see Berling 1987), but the "earth" was itself sanctified by this process, and so were the patriarchs it carried. Chan sayings became oracles, hierophanies.[19] In the most radical instances, the hermeneutical model is completely discarded. Reading is interrupted by textual fragmentation, and textual debris of the Buddhist canon is used (or abused), mobilized, reactivated in entirely new language games. Like the enigmas of the Sphinx, kōan could interpellate someone abruptly, like no traditional scripture did, and give him/her the impression to be faced with a living transcendence. They could also legitimize him/her through their ritual performance. Gradually, they functioned more like gems or relics, signs of legitimacy, talismans, or proof of one's participation to a superior power. As noted earlier, the cryptic language of the kōan, ritually used during funerals in Japan, was taken as evidence that the Zen master who performed it during a funerary ritual had conquered death (see Bodiford 1989).

Although Chan discourse, by the end of the Tang, claimed to have become autonomous, this autonomy was soon questioned. The hermeneutical model survived in the theory of the "harmony between the [canonical] teachings and Chan" (*jiaochan yizhi*), as it was developed by Zongmi and his emules, and became at times dominant in Korea and Japan. In the "syncretistic" literature of this "canonical" Chan, the proliferation of au-

---

Zongmi, these two scriptures played an important role in Song Chan and Japanese Zen. On the *Shoulengyan jing*, see Demiéville 1952, 43–52.

[19] In this sense, although Léon Wieger's description of the kōan as "exclamations which escaped from the stultified [monks], momentarily drawn from their coma" is blatantly polemical, he was not entirely unjustified to interpret them as "oracles of the Brahman, which the other monks scrutinize to occupy themselves" (Wieger 1927, 530).

thoritative quotations creates a situation in which several voices are heard in a single discourse, and the author's discursive strategies are achieved by a discrete manipulation of these quotations. In this sense, we have not only a synthesis of the teachings (*jiao*) and of meditation (*chan*), of the letter and the spirit, but of the hermeneutical and rhetorical models as well.

The hermeneutical model also resurfaced in "extra-canonical" Chan (*jiaowai biechuan*) itself, with the canonization of Chan masters and texts. Paradoxically, the rejection of the Buddhist canon allowed the canonization of Chan patriarchs. As mentioned earlier, the exegetical tradition was an attempt to open the Chinese Buddhist canon, which had been closed after the completion of authoritative translations during the fifth through seventh centuries. Chan rhetoric constituted an alternative and a further response. Its flourishing discourse, however, was soon submitted to a similar process of limitation, which resulted in the creation of a Chan canon. This tendency can be observed already in Zongmi, who wrote the preface to the Chan canon that he envisioned, but was apparently unable to compile the latter. Once a Chan canon reached its own closure, toward the Song, a return to exegesis as a means to overcome that limitation was needed again (see J. Z. Smith 1982, 36–52). The infinite variations of exegesis allowed the multiplication of layers of glosses ("capping phrases," *jakugo*) in texts such as the *Biyan lu*. After their earlier criticisms, Chan commentators could not simply return to traditional exegesis. Thus, despite its intrinsic conservatism, Chan exegesis retained at least an appearance of freedom and displayed a strong rhetorical tendency; it was a rhetorical exegesis. The exegetical trend triumphed in the Sōtō tradition with the attempts of Dōgen's successors to "return to the text" of the *Shōbōgenzō*. Many commentaries on this difficult work were written in the course of centuries, but they are yet another proof that commentaries increase the difficulties rather than resolving them and achieve a canonization of the original text rather than its understanding.

A Rhetorical Treasure

Ironically enough, the *Shōbōgenzō* itself can be included in the rhetorical tradition. This work (or rather, the various texts subsumed under that title) illustrates a type of rhetorical use of scriptural authorities, a type in which, instead of resulting from a montage of quotations, the text grows from or proliferates around a "textual matrix"—like a pearl around a grain of sand. We recall that, according to Riffaterre, "any text can be shown to be generated from a minimal sentence or *matrix* . . . in accordance with the two rules of expansion and conversion" (Riffaterre 1984, 22). In the *Shōbōgenzō*, one such matrix may be the early Chan logion (later used as a kōan) "This very mind is the Buddha" (J. *sokushin zebutsu*), held by

Dōgen as the characteristic teaching of the rival Darumashū. Dōgen's major disciples came from that school, and they are the addressees of many sermons collected in the *Shōbōgenzō*. It is easy to see how each element of the sokushin zebutsu theme is developed by Dōgen into a more complex form and how the semantic value is systematically modified to present a standpoint opposite that of the Darumashū.

Other traditional kōan constituted textual matrices of the *Shōbōgenzō*. Despite the usual interpretation that sees Dōgen as an enemy of the so-called *kanna zen* (Ch. *kanhua chan*)—a form of Chan based on the study of kōan and developed by Dahui Zonggao—the *Shōbōgenzō* looks like an extended and rather free-floating "commentary" on kōan. The title of the work replicates that of a kōan collection compiled by Dahui, the *Zhengfa yanzang*, and it seems that Dōgen also compiled a *Shōbōgenzō* in Chinese (*Mana* or *Shinji Shōbōgenzō*)—actually a collection of three hundred kōan (hence its other title, *Sanbyaku soku*) (see Suzuki et al. 1989, 5: 124–275).

More than a commentary in the traditional sense, the *Shōbōgenzō* in Japanese (*Kana Shōbōgenzō*) is rather a rhetorical "mobilization" of these kōan. The "sayings of the ancients" (*kosoku*) usually serve more as a pretext for the spinning of infinite variations. The best example is the way in which Dōgen "interprets" the above-mentioned logion by permuting its four Chinese characters (*soku/shin/ze/butsu*) against all grammatical rules and deriving elaborate "philosophical" meanings from these permutations. This hermeneutical/rhetorical device, often used by Dōgen, has led many commentators to praise his "linguistic genius." Dōgen is rightly famous for his neologisms and personal style. Indeed, if these permutations are brilliant exercises of style, one would be mistaken to take them too literally. Despite Dōgen's frequent admonitions against literary "sin," he is easily caught in the "act of literature." For the most part, the seduction exerted by the *Shōbōgenzō* is owing less to the originality of Dōgen's ideas than to his felicitous choice of metaphors and his mastery of ornated Chinese prose—the so-called *shiroku benrei* style.

One may object that emphasizing the rhetorical, literary and dialogical nature of the *Shōbōgenzō* drastically and unduly reduces its value as a spiritual document. Such would indeed be the case if the text were, as it is usually presented, an authentic description of a certain spiritual state transcending culture and history. Dōgen himself argues that words are valuable, not because of their capacity to represent reality (mimesis), but because of their power to produce it. Truth has no essence; it exists only through its effects and in particular through speech: such is the "enacted" or "realized" kōan (*genjō kōan*). The rhetorical nature of the *Shōbōgenzō* does not diminish its truth claim in the eyes of its author and its early commentators. On the contrary, even if Dōgen's conception of truth may appear singularly sectarian and self-serving to us, we must leave him the benefit of the doubt. We must realize how superficial (or even unthinkable) our Platonician conception of an objective truth transcending history would have appeared to Dōgen. Despite his conservatism and his nostalgia for Buddhist origins, Dōgen was in his rejection of ontological foundationalism very close to the most "differential" tendencies in "classical" Chan. For him, the world of nature and awakening was through and through historical and therefore sectarian. We would be misled by Dōgen's "language games" if we considered it an essentially "philosophical" text and his author a humanist of sorts. The *Shōbōgenzō* is indeed a "text that belongs more to the verbal arts than to philosophical dialectics" (Lyotard and Thébaud 1985, 4).

For Dōgen as for other representatives of "differential" Chan/Zen, the primary function of language was not communication, but persuasion; truth does not precede words, but it comes into being together with speech. Chan texts are necessarily rhetorical in the sense that they imply a departure from an ontological conception of truth toward a more performative and dialogical conception. Perhaps the coexistence in Chan of two antithetical (and complementary) discourses—hermeneutical and rhetorical—paradoxically contributed to the balance of the system. Eventually, through the dialectical process of canonization and decanonization, these two discourses regularly overflowed into each other; thus, it has become more difficult to distinguish between what, *pace* van Gennep, we could call exegetical rhetoric and rhetorical exegesis (see above, note 2, 177).

Chapter Nine

THE PARADOXES OF CHAN INDIVIDUALISM

> A being within being? *Homo duplex*! Come now! Different
> tendencies reveal different motives, that's all
> (Flaubert, *Bouvard and Pécuchet*)

MARCEL MAUSS once pointed out the need for recensing the categories that have informed human experience. Among them he singled out one epistemological configuration that has played a great role in Western culture: that of the self or person; or, in slightly different terms, of a form of individualism usually expressed as a humanism. Significantly, Chan/Zen has often been praised (and sometimes decried) by Western observers for its rugged individualism. Paul Demiéville, the eminent sinologist and masterful translator of the *Linji lu*, was for instance attracted to the ninth-century Chan master Linji by the latter's "typically Chinese humanism." According to Demiéville, Linji proves in this respect "almost Confucian" because "he reduces everything to man" (Demiéville 1972, 17–18).

THE WESTERN CONFIGURATION OF THE SELF

Is individualism then a useful category in understanding Chan? Put differently, to what extent can the emergence of Chan be seen as that of a new (conception of the) self? I use here the expression "configuration of the self" to design the broad semantic field structured by terms such as subjectivity, individuality, person, man, soul, substance, or agent. Because a number of related, yet distinct, problematics derive from the complex semantic evolution of these terms, each term needs to be defined by its contrary (self-not-other, individual-not-society, individualism-not-holism) and by its correlates (cogito, reason, madness, free will, responsibility).[1] Although the social or philosophical history of the *person* (as described by Mauss) is not exactly the same as the conceptual evolution of *man* (as described by Bernard Groethuysen) or of *individualism* (as

---

[1] Merleau-Ponty, for example, contrasting the conceptions of the self found in various Western philosophers such as Descartes, Pascal, and Kierkegaard, argues: "Why make of these discordant "subjectivities" the moments of a single discovery?" (Merleau-Ponty 1964b, 152–156).

described by Dumont), these notions are intimately related. Because none of them can really subsume all the others, they must be studied as part of a larger semantic field. The apparent disagreements among scholars who have written on these topics result in part from the localized character of studies dealing with different strata of a complex "subjective architecture," as in the Indian parable of the blind men groping for the elephant.

By assuming that there are analogies between Buddhist or Asian and Western approaches to the question of self, our understanding of the evolution of the Western side of the issue may help us understand what is at stake in the Asian, and more precisely Chan/Zen, contexts. Therefore, I first consider the epistemological shift that may have caused the emergence of a "configuration" of subjectivity and then proceed to examine the possible linkage between changing concepts of self and power. Before exploring how the Western configuration of the self informs our perception of Chan "individualism," it is necessary to take a glimpse at the semantic evolution of the main terms defining that configuration.

The Genealogy of Man

In his ground-breaking study on the genealogy of the so-called human sciences, *The Order of Things* (in French *Les mots et les choses*; literally, Words and Things), Michel Foucault stated provocatively that man, the elusive object of these sciences, is a "quite recent creature" that did not exist before the eighteenth century (Foucault 1966, 308). This is obviously true in the sense that the full-fledged configuration of man, person or self, such as we know it and take it for granted today, is a product of both the Classical Age and the Enlightenment. Various strands of the conception could be traced back to the Greco-Roman beginnings of Western culture, and to this task Foucault consecrated his last writings. To understand the necessity of this shift in Foucault's work, a detour through the work of Bernard Groethuysen may be useful.

In his *Philosophical Anthropology*, Groethuysen offers a master-narrative of what he calls the "dialectics between life and knowledge," that is, the hiatus between our objective knowledge of the self and our subjective relationship with ourselves. Whereas the objective approach is exemplified by Aristotle, for whom man—being merely an object, a "case," or a type—belongs entirely to the "order of things," the subjective relationship to oneself is characteristic of the Greco-Roman "philosophy of life" (Cicero, Seneca, Epictete, Marcus Aurelius). Plato seems to have oscillated between these two approaches. Although he first considers the story of a human life as the story of a soul—this eternal element in man that is more himself than he is—in its nostalgia for the World of Ideas, in his later political theory, Plato comes to reconsider man from a legislator's point of view, as a creature of nature and a citizen. From this Platonician dilemma derived two distinct anthropological types: (1) a utopian or mythical conception of man as a soul searching for itself; (2) a "locative" conception of man conceived as a physical being ranked in the physical, social, or cosmic wholes to which he belongs. Whereas the first conception was developed by neo-Platonicians and Augustine, the second was systematized by the Aristotelian tradition. Both motifs—man as a soul and man as a creature— were reinscribed in the anthropology of medieval Christianity.

With the Greco-Roman "philosophy of life," Groethuysen argues, man came to be perceived as a specific personality, and what became important to the Stoician was his relationship with himself. Like early Buddhism, this philosophy aimed at making the self independent from the world, by controlling its passions and its representations of things. Man now found his values in himself. Aristotle's optimism, which saw nature working and reaching perfection in all beings, was replaced by a fundamental pessimism—one that found its full expression in Augustine and his epigones. For Augustine, man is fundamentally sinful and full of contradictions, lost in an inner world of tensions and struggles that he does not understand: "Quis in me seminavit hoc bellum?" Through his very sin, however, man ceased to be a creature of nature and became a real individual and by the same token the subject of sacred history. Paradoxically, by thus entering into a personal relationship with God, he acquires primacy over the cosmos.[2] Augustine completely rejects Plato's "mythical" conception of man as well as the "humanist" conception of the Stoicians. He integrates the earlier motifs (soul, nature, personality) into a religious whole and shapes a new human type that Groethuysen defines as "religious man." However, after Augustine, the three motifs enter into further combinations that determined variant anthropological figures: the "mythical type" reappears with Renaissance thinkers such as Pico della Mirandola and Marsilius Ficino, the "religious type" with Nicholas Cusano, Paracelsus, and Luther, the "humanist type" with Erasmus and Montaigne. Significantly, Groethuysen stops on the threshold of the Classical Age, which for Foucault marks the "great divide" that produced modernity. Although the above outline does not do justice to the complexity of Groethuysen's account and argumentation, it suggests the various kinds of "grand narratives" attempted by Western thinkers and emphasizes the onesidedness of any approach that considers man only as an object. In this sense, while it is never mentioned as a direct influence by Foucault, Groethuysen's work can be seen as a precursor of Foucault's analysis of "individualization."

    [2] As Gedaliahu Stroumsa (1990, 34) remarks, "The new interest in the self had a price, which should not be ignored. Diving into oneself meant the end of the soul's immersion within the universe, which had always been the core of astral mysticism in the ancient world."

The Category of the Person

As noted earlier, the person became a much-discussed epistemological object since the publication in 1938 of Mauss's ground-breaking essay "A Category of the Human Mind: The Notion of Person; The Notion of Self."[3] Although he did not limit himself to the great philosophical texts, Mauss's sociohistorical study is in many ways reminiscent of Groethuysen's "philosophical anthropology." I will not dwell on the evolutionism that leads him from the "primitives" to Kant, with only a side glance at India and China. Mauss cannot escape Orientalist prejudice in his summary treatment of Indian and Chinese cultures, cultures that, "so to speak, invented [the notion of person], only to allow it to fade away almost irrevocably" (Carrithers, Collins, and Lukes 1985, 13). More problematic, however, is the discursive strategy that permits him to assert the identity between self and person. While in the first part of his essay Mauss speaks mainly of the *self*, in the second part, a linguistic drift leads him to focus on the *person*. His use of the image of the Roman ritual mask (*persona*), determined by the etymology, allows him to negotiate a transition between the two parts of the essay—a transition that is at once geographical (from primitive to civilized societies), historical (from antiquity to modern times), and methodological (from anthropology to intellectual history). Mauss seems to make his the motto of the Roman actor, "*Larvatus prodeo*," as he himself "proceeds masked." The mask metaphor enables him to make the crucial connection between self and person, history and anthropology. This rhetorical advantage has a cost, however, because it causes Mauss to locate in Roman society the emergence of the persona. Rome thus becomes not only the focal point of the essay but also the pivot of Mauss's evolutionary model. If, instead of focusing on the person, Mauss had chosen to explore notions such as man or self, he would have had to trace their origins as far back as Plato and Aristotle.

Despite the intrinsic methodological difficulty of justifying the criteria that represent the subjective configuration and the periodization deriving from them, one may retain from Mauss's essay his distinction between a universal "sense" of the self and a specifically Western concept of the self. His disciple Louis Dumont similarly distinguishes between the empirical self and the self as value, the latter also a Western invention. By bracketing the empirical self to focus on the social history of the concept or value, Mauss and Dumont overlook the dialectical process, the intertwining of the two aspects (subjective and objective) of the self analyzed by Groethuysen. By objectifying the self as a concept, they forsake the "rela-

[3] One recent contribution to this debate is a collection of essays, *The Category of the Person: Anthropology, Philosophy, History*, in which Mauss's essay is translated. See Carrithers, Collins, and Lukes 1985, 1–25.

tionship to oneself" as a subjective/objective sense. If the dichotomy between the two aspects (subjective/objective) of the self is precisely what marks the emergence of modern man, taking one of its poles as a starting point for a retrospective reflection seems questionable. For example, his objectifying approach leads Mauss to define the Christian person by what is perhaps the least specific about it: the permanence of an individual "substance," the soul, which was already a characteristic of Platonism or neo-Platonism—or even, mutatis mutandis, of Hinduism. Mauss thus neglects the original nature of the Christian relationship between man, as a unique individual, and his personal God—a relationship that bears some analogy with the *bhakti* of Hinduism and the devotion to Amida in Japanese Buddhism. These remarks, however, should not mask the importance of Mauss's approach; it paved the way to Dumont's reflection on individualism and holism.

The Cost of Individualism

Louis Dumont pays more attention than Mauss to the problem of crosscultural comparisons. His basic assumption is that, in contrast to Western societies that valorized the individual, most other societies remain fundamentally holistic and hierarchical. Therefore, the focus of Dumont's reflection is the passage between the two antithetic universes of thought—the two mutually irreconcilable ideologies that he calls holism and individualism (Dumont 1985, 94). Taking his cues from Indian culture, Dumont connects the emergence of the individual as *value* to the advent of a new figure, the renouncer or *outworldly individual* (as opposed to the "man-in-the-world"). Renunciation supposedly leads to social and cosmic deliverance—an emancipation from the bonds of society and, more broadly, from saṃsāra or transmigration: "It seems that the individual becomes real only at the end of the transmigration that made him pass through all the unreal positions of the system" (Dumont 1966, 338; 1971, 47). The complementarity of the notions of transmigration and deliverance is for Dumont proof that both have their origin in the speculations of the renouncer. Rather than ethnocentrically projecting Western conceptions of individualism onto non-Western holistic societies, Dumont attempts to use the Indian model to understand the meaning of the Western individual. He argues that, "if individualism is to appear in a society of the traditional, holistic type, it will be in opposition to society and as a kind of supplement to it, that is, in the form of the outworldly individual" (Dumont 1985, 96). What characterizes Western society, however, is the shift from the "outworldly" to the "inworldly" individual. To explain this shift in the light of the Indian paradigm, Dumont resorts to a grand narrative describing the "Christian beginnings of modern individualism." Beginning with an analysis of the early Christian conceptions of the otherworldly individual, he then focuses on the political dimension and describes the relations between Church and State. In this way, he explains the transition from a typically hierarchical, almost "Indian," model (as elaborated by Pope Gelasius, ca. 500) to one that perverts hierarchy by stressing the spiritual *and* temporal superiority of the Church. The Church became more worldly, while the political realm was made to participate in absolute, universalist value (ibid., 111). Initiated by the Church, this unification of the two spheres— spiritual and temporal—resulted in a full legitimation of the mundane world and to a "transfer of the individual *into* this world." Thus, Dumont attributes a fundamental and unique epistemological event, the appearance of the "inworldly individual" of Western modernity, to a somewhat contingent political development, the fact that the Church, toward the turn of the eighth century, aspired to rule the world and consequently redefined the role of the Christian individual to meet this purpose. According to Dumont, this evolution was eventually achieved with Calvin's inworldly individualism. *Petites causes, grands effets* . . . Elaborating on Nietzsche's insight that even "transcendental" categories (such as person, truth, etc.) are culturally and historically bound, this kind of objectifying narrative makes us realize that objectivity itself is a changing concept (see Veyne 1988, 118). Yet, these narratives fail to question their conditions of possibility and confront us instead with the paradox of an individual writing a history of individualism as if standing outside it.

Language and Subjectivity

The linguistic approach searches in language for the conditions of the emergence of a category of *subject* or *agent*. According to Emile Benveniste, subjectivity "is only the emergence within being of a fundamental property of language. To be *ego* is to say *ego*" (Benveniste 1966–1974, 1: 260). The existence and the use of the personal pronoun *I* allows the locutor to constitute himself as subject and to turn language into discourse. By occupying this empty slot, he appropriates language to himself. By the same token, however, he is led to mistake a linguistic reality for an ontological one and to hypostasize a mere figure of speech as a real subject. This "metaphysic of the subject"—the linguistic or Cartesian illusion denounced by Nietzsche—consists in erroneously inferring, "according to the grammatical habit," an agent—"the famous old 'ego'"—behind an activity, a thinker behind the act of thinking (*es denkt*) (Nietzsche 1966, 24). This compulsive belief in a subject, which sociologists like Dumont consider prescribed by society, is now seen as a product of language.[4] At

---

[4] Linguists have often pointed out the absence (or secondary role) of personal pronouns in Japanese. The rise of subjectivity in Japanese literature has been connected to that of the

any rate, in both the sociological and the linguistic approaches—as in Buddhism—the individual or subject is structurally determined; it has no "substance."

To conclude this *tour d'horizon* of the "subjective" approach, let us mention the idealistic viewpoint that attempts to isolate a transcendental self by denying the notions of both structure and substance. Paul Valéry, for instance, defines the self as a pure potentiality, a mere condition of thinking, an origin in a geometrical sense, a virtual or optical focus, or a space of possibilities (Valéry 1973–1974, 2: 289). This space is devoid of any attribute and especially of determinations, which define only a "secondary" and contingent self: "I would not be me if I could not be an other" (ibid., 285). Valéry's perception of the true, "formless," "primary" self as an unlocalized vantage point reminds us of early Chan texts and is, like them, organized by a visual metaphor: "Any individual, by making himself an *integral spectator,—integral opponent*—. . . can consider personality and reactions as accidents, particular cases, *étrangetés*—and declare them to be *phenomena*" (ibid., 318). In various passages of his *Cahiers*, Valéry compares the relation between Self and self to that between whole and part, player and pawn, light and color, potentiality and actuality (ibid., passim).

Homo Duplex

The above discussion has permitted to discern a fault line running in the Western discourse on the self, between the objectifying and subjectifying approaches, which produce two different "objects"—the *self* as "object" and *myself* as "subject." Whereas one view objectifies a "region of being" (soul, self, personality), the other emphasizes a subjective relation to oneself and the apparently unique perspective one has on the world.

The objectifying/subjectifying paradigm is found at work in the recurring opposition (or better, *différend*) between sociohistorical and philosophical approaches (see Allen 1985, 30). The partisans of the sociohistorical argue that even cogito and a priori categories are historical, while the partisans of a philosophical/idealist approach always find that sociological analysis remains naively objectifying or, worse, ideological. Mauss and Dumont take the objectifying (sociohistorical) approach and deal simply with the *person* as object. Groethuysen and Valéry deal with *man* both as subject and object, but Groethuysen's approach remains on the objective side, while Valéry vindicates the subjective approach. Dumont discovers in the *inworldly* individual of Calvinism the outcome of the dialectics between the holistic man-in-the-world and the outworldly individual. The "objective" distinction between philosophical epistemology and a so-

---

"I-novel" (*watakushi-shōsetsu*), which finds a distant precursor in the *Shōbōgenzō* with Dōgen's idiosyncratic use of the pronoun *watakushi*.

ciologically informed history of ideas is problematic because this very gesture of distinction is part of the process in question. This is perhaps why Foucault, after taking an objective approach in his early work, later attempted to show that the duality between subject and object is itself an effect of *modernity*. According to him, the modern episteme is characterized by "the constitution of an empirico-transcendental doublet which was called *man*" (Foucault 1973b, 32). By this, Foucault meant man, "not merely as both subject and object of knowledge, but even more paradoxically, as organizer of the spectacle in which he appears" (Dreyfus and Rabinow 1983, 29). Any inquiry into the question of the self seems therefore condemned to face this "transcendental/empirical doublet" and its variants.[5] Foucault located the cause of this "epistemological break" in a linguistic change—the fact that language has become opaque and no longer permits pure representation—resulting in a unification of the two fields of nature and human nature. After the classical age, man no longer conceives of himself as a microcosm; he has become conscious of his finitude. However, and this is the crucial change characterizing modernity, this finitude is now becoming the very basis of his knowledge (Foucault 1973b, 337).

Toward the end of his life, Foucault began to stress the second component defined by Groethuysen, the "philosophy of life," and came to consider the individualization process, no longer from the viewpoint of social history (as in *Discipline and Punish*), but from that of the individual himself—as a change in the relationship with oneself. However, the empirical/transcendental doublet also calls to mind the gradual/sudden paradigm, and thus it may not be as peculiar to modernity as Foucault believed. Moreover, Foucault's emphasis on the "production of oneself," inspired from Kant and Nietzsche, calls to mind the Chan/Zen emphasis on "performative" or "expressive"—rather than "hermeneutical"—selfhood.[6] Thus, when we consider the hermeneneutic value of these categories (whether they are a priori or culturally bound) for the study of Asian cultures and religions, it makes more sense to compare the *approaches* (subjectifying/objectifying) than the "products" (specific notions of self in West and non-West); or, to use a more Kantian distinction, the *structura structurans* rather than the *structura structurata*.[7] After this long but nec-

---

[5] What Dreyfus and Rabinow (1983, 37–41) call the "retreat and return of the origin" is precisely the constant oscillation between conceptions that see man as a product of a long history whose origin he cannot reach and those that see man as the very source of that history.

[6] See Foucault 1984, 41. As Gedaliahu Stroumsa (1990, 28) points out, Nietzsche "loathed Socrates' attempt at retrieving the hidden self, his recoiling from the archaic Greek attitude of acting out, publicly, in an altogether unreflexive manner, as the healthy way of expressing the self."

[7] Kant, as interpreted by Foucault, provides a good example of the reinscription of the objectifying/subjectifying tendencies, with the tension between, on the one hand, a universal morality and an abstract philosophical system (Kantism) and, on the other, an acute feeling of

essary *détour* through Western conceptions of the self and its *alter egos*, we can now turn toward Asian conceptions.

EARLY BUDDHIST CONCEPTIONS

In India, "philosophical anthropology" has been mainly concerned with the question of the self as a permanent entity (*ātman*).[8] We have seen that, for Dumont, the emergence of the individual/self was the result of a societal change that had permitted the appearance of the "renouncer." Among these renouncers were the Buddhist monks who, paradoxically, denied the existence of the self. Dumont suggests that, by leaving the world, the renouncer "finds himself invested with an individuality which he apparently finds uncomfortable since all his efforts tend to its extinction or to its transcendence" (Dumont 1960, 46).

On the basis of Dumont's work and of Mauss's above-mentioned essay, Steven Collins has taken up the paradox in his book *Selfless Persons*, to which the following discussion is largely indebted. The Buddhist and Western traditions seem to have raised a number of similar questions, although their answers to these questions differ radically. First, the Buddhist conception of no-self (*anātman*) was a radical departure from the Hindu conceptions of self. The acquisition of an individuality by the renouncers was prepared by the ethicization of karma, the shift from cosmological to moral conceptions marking the passage from Brahmanism to Hinduism. The philosophical equation between ātman and Brahman, or between microscosm and macrocosm, gave the renouncer a kind of leverage on the unknown: finding in himself the ātman, a parcel of ultimate reality, allowed him to bypass the social hierarchy (symbolized by saṃsāra, the cycle of birth and death) and to directly achieve union with Brahman, the ultimate principle. Although early Buddhists similarly aimed at escaping saṃsāra, they chose an opposite strategy and denied any reality to the ātman/Brahman.

The notions of self (ātman) and person (*puruṣa*) nevertheless remained in use at the conventional level of Buddhist practice. We seem confronted here with the kind of "affirmation qua negation" described by Jon Elster[9]—if

---

historicity and a Kantian "philosophy of life" (that constitutes one of the first definitions of *modernity*). The debate between Habermas and Foucault on Kant and modernity, unfortunately interrupted by Foucault's premature death, is itself representative of (and replicates) these two tendencies. See Foucault 1984; Habermas 1986; Dreyfus and Rabinow 1986.

[8] On this question, see Collins 1982; Dumont 1971a, 1972, 1973; Bareau 1973.

[9] Elster's comment seem to apply to the idea of "non-self": "If I desire the absence of some specific thought, or of thought in general, the desire by itself suffices to insure the presence of the object" (Elster 1983, 46). Concerning the affirmation qua negation: "A doctrine or an idea can survive only if it has some kind of existence in somebody's mind, be it an existence qua denied only" (Ibid., 49).

only because, as the Buddha explains in the *Da zhidu lun*: "There is
nothing ridiculous in exchanging copper coins against gold coins. Why?
Because this is required by the rules of trade" (Lamotte 1944–1980, 1: 67).
Unfortunately, this mercantile consideration lent itself to theoretical misin-
terpretations, as is the case with the famous last words of the Buddha,
recorded in the *Mahaparinibbana-sutta*: "Dwell making yourself an *island*
(or support), take refuge in yourself." Later commentators have tended to
hypostasize this personal pronoun as an ontological self.[10] What Buddhists criticized was not the ordinary use of these notions as such, but the
"metaphysics of the self" to which they too easily led. Collins argues that
the teaching of anātman plays in technical discourse the role of a linguistic
taboo, "applied *differently* by different Buddhists, according to their position on the continuum from ordinary man to specialist" (Collins 1982, 12,
also 182–183). Although this teaching may play a soteriological role in the
religious life of virtuoso meditators and scholastic individuals, its function
for common people is semiotic, a rallying sign and a symbol of opposition
to Brahmanism (or its later avatars). Collins further argues that "there is a
difference between the way [the denial of self] is appropriated by the monk
earnestly engaged in meditation and the way it was appropriated by the
Buddhist scholastic" (ibid., 13). In other words, we find two types of
emphasis on doctrine—descriptive and prescriptive: as a description of
reality and as an instrument of salvation. Hence the importance of a careful
analysis of the sociocultural setting in which this teaching is advocated, if
we are to understand what role(s) it comes to play in the Buddhist tradi-
tion(s). As a soteriological strategy, it is based on linguistic arguments that
remind us of Nietzsche: early Buddhists denied the ontological reality of a
grammatical subject wrongly inferred from the active verb. They argued
that, although the action described by the verbal form actually takes place,
there is no doer, no agent, behind it. Consequently, the questions asked by
the tenants of eternalism (*śāsvata-vāda*) and of annihilationism (*uccheda-
vāda*)—"Are self and world eternal? Not eternal?"—were considered irrelevant to practice and linguistically ill formed. The queries were left
unanswered by the Buddha, who preached instead the emptiness or dependent origination (*pratītya-samutpāda*) of persons and things (see Lamotte
1944–1980, 1: 32).

Traditionally, Buddhism has resorted to the Two Truths theory to explain the empirical/transcendental doublet: this has led scholars such as
Melford Spiro to distinguish between a "Karmatic" Buddhism that, at the
conventional level, believes in a self, while "Nirvanic" Buddhism, express-

[10] Walpola Rahula (1959, 60–61), for instance, criticizes "those who, wish[ing] to see a
self in Buddhism, interpret the words *attadipa* and *attasarana* as "taking self as a lamp" and
"taking self as refuge." For him, *dipa* definitely means "island," and "the question of a
metaphysical *Ātman*, or Self, is quite beside the point."

ing the standpoint of the ultimate level, denies it (Spiro 1982, 11–14). The tendency to reify these two ideal-types and to identify them respectively with popular and literate Buddhism has obscured rather than clarified the issue. As Collins shows, the imagery of the self (for instance, the use of the house metaphor for the mind/body) is variously contextualized and cuts across scholastic and popular Buddhism. The soteriological strategies analyzed by Collins reveal that ideological stakes are at play in the definition of anātman. Ideology is still present, and controversy over the self is not over; these positions are obvious from the distortions found in recent scholarship, for example in Walpola Rahula's "objective" presentation of early Buddhist thought—a presentation that confuses empirical self and transcendental self under the notion of ātman (Rahula 1959, 51–56). Rahula first asserts the orthodoxy of the anātman theory: "The negation of an imperishable *ātman* is the common characteristic of all dogmatic systems of the Lesser as well as the Great Vehicle, and there is, therefore, no reason to assume that Buddhist tradition, which is in complete agreement on this point, has deviated from the Buddha's original teachings" (ibid., 55). He continues with a polemic against "heterodox" views: "It is therefore curious that recently there should have been a vain attempt by a few scholars [who are designated only in a footnote: 'The late Mrs. Rhys Davids and others'] to smuggle the idea of self into the teaching of the Buddha, quite contrary to the spirit of Buddhism" (ibid.). Rahula's demonstration relies on innuendo, as when he argues, in a rather nervous and condescending tone, that "people become nervous at the idea that through the Buddha's teaching of *Anatta*, the self they imagine they have is going to be destroyed" (ibid., 58). Perhaps his polemical style only points to the paradox of a (necessarily) subjective discourse on selflessness. Significantly, the erasing of the historical determinations of orthodoxy seems to go hand in hand with the assertion of a no-self or an unconditioned self.

Similar discursive strategies, typical of an intellectualist approach, are found in David Kalupahana's vulgarization of Buddhist thought. Kalupahana resorts to a double-edged psychological explanation to dismiss the ātman theory: "The Upaniṣadic theory of an eternal and immortal 'self' seems . . . to have been intended to satisfy this deep-seated craving of man for permanent happiness" (Kalupahana 1973, 38). If such is the case, is it not equally true of the Mahāyāna theory of Nirvāṇa, in which Nirvāṇa is said to be "permanent, blissful, personal, and pure"? Furthermore, can one, bona fide, simply dismiss the Brahmanical tradition as " mundane" and "self-assertive" and assert without justification that the Upaniṣadic theory of self "merely caters to the instincts of the individual"? (ibid., 38–39). Only someone who has never read Plato—or the *Upaniṣad* for that matter—could claim that the theory of an immortal soul (ātman) is "harmful to the religious life in that it tends to generate selfishness and egoism" (ibid., 41). Equally disturbing is the elitist tendency manifest in passages such as the following: "Thus, nonsubstantiality becomes a synonym for causality, and for those who, either in the East or in the West, are conditioned to think in terms of an immortal soul or are engrossed (*papancita*) with the belief in a 'self,' it is a difficult theory to understand" (ibid., 41– 42). Perhaps the concept of ātman is not so simple either. Madeleine Biardeau has pointed out the distinction between the Brahmanistic ātman that is impersonal and the ātman denounced by Buddhists as personal (in Bareau 1973, 95). Kalupahana, however, conveniently subsumes both theories in his criticism.

The social implications of the anātman controversy are brought to light in a recent debate between Frits Staal and J. W. de Jong concerning Etienne Lamotte's characterization of Buddhism as a doctrine of nonself (Staal 1985; de Jong 1987). Although proudly orthodox, the scholastic point of view represented by de Jong clearly reflects a vision of Buddhism from the top. At the lower end, it is obvious, as Staal argues, that most adherents of "popular" Buddhism believe in a self. Their belief cannot simply be dismissed as "non-Buddhist" in the name of some ideal pristine teaching. In defining what constitutes orthodoxy—by chosing the segment of society whose beliefs he sees as representative of Buddhism as a whole—the scholar merely reflects his elitist biases. At the conventional level, where the self is duly acknowledged, one discerns, as in the Western case, two general conceptions of man: either a self warranted by the cosmos, in which it finds a legitimate place; or a free subject facing the cosmos, which it transcends. These two conceptions are perhaps reflected in the two faces of that supreme individual, the Janus/Buddha of popular beliefs, who is both a universal monarch (*cakravartin*) and a radical anarchist, a "world conqueror" and a "world renouncer"—simultaneously accepting (if only temporarily) and denying cosmic order. Thus, the orthodox view of anātman does not do justice to the complexity of the early Buddhist tradition. Pitting in its dichotomic dogmatism orthodoxy against heresy, it supresses the whole range of nuanced answers to the question of the self.[11]

CHINESE CONCEPTIONS

Despite Mauss's expeditive treatment of the Indian and Chinese cultures in his famous essay, the category of the self seems fundamental in these cul-

[11] André Bareau, for example, has stressed the importance of the Vijñānavādin, who adopted a middle way between the Pudgalavādin and the Madhyamika. While opposed to the *pudgalavādin* or personalists, according to whom the *pudgala* transmigrated from one life to another, and remained even in Nirvāṇa, the Vijñānavādin attributed to the *vijñāna* or cognitive function of the individual a permanent nature beyond death and saw in it the link between the various existences and the necessary basis for karmic retribution. See Bareau 1973, 91.

tures. Dominated as it was by Confucian models of human relationships, traditional Chinese society appears holistic at first glance.[12] Chinese religion, similarly, was predominantly ritualistic. Sinologists, however, have been eager to describe what they see as the first blossoming of individualism in China. The most well-known case—one that clearly had an influence on Chan—was of course that of Zhuangzi. Another often mentioned "free-thinker" *avant la lettre* is Wang Chong (ca. 27–100), whose example was followed by Xi Kang and the "Seven Sages of the Bamboo Grove."[13] We are confronted with a teleological model describing the "emergence of self" as a first step in the development of rationality, a first chapter in the narrative, often delayed like any suspenseful narrative, of the emancipation of the individual. This teleological model is questionable on several counts. One may argue that individualism, rationalism or secularism can actually be found at all times and to varying degrees in all cultures. Assuming that a certain development in rationality could be shown to have taken place, one may question the interpretation that sees this as progress. Moreover, the implication of the individual self in various social networks, although it is usually seen as a loss of autonomy and a regression toward holism, does not necessarily diminish or dissolve selfhood, but rather qualifies it, enriches it in relation to its different contexts (see Augé 1982b, 192]. In this sense, the dichotomy between holism and individualism appears too simplistic. The heuristic value of these ideal-types should not lead us to confuse them with an accurate description of reality.

Judith Berling has attempted to show that Dumont's categories do not work in the case of Zhuangzi's individualism. According to Berling, Zhuangzi "rejects the holistic approach *à la* Dumont of the Confucianists, but his attitude is also holistic (mystical fusion with the Dao)" (Berling 1985, 101–119). Referring here to Zhuangzi's famous dream in which his consciousness becomes that of a butterfly, Berling further argues that "the autonomous, perfected self [of Zhuangzi] is free even of the limitations of humanness and physical existence because it has the courage of imagination" (Berling 1985, 109). Apart from that dream, however, the fantastic world in Zhuangzi and the transgression of human limits are merely imaginary and have little cosmological or ontological reality.[14] At any rate, Berling considers that Zhuangzi's response to his wife's death, both loving her and accepting her death, demonstrates that his position is different

[12] See in particular Munro 1985; de Bary 1970; Mark Levin, "Between the Earth and Heaven: Conceptions of the Self in China," in Carrithers, Collins, and Lukes 1985, 156–189.

[13] According to Henri Maspero, the development of Daoism as a religion of salvation marked the rise of individualism in China. See Maspero 1981, 25–37.

[14] His idealism has made Zhuangzi the target of criticism by orthodox Chinese communists, who see in it a typical case of escapism. Despite the abundance of mythological themes and his acerbic critique of rationalist blindness and "trivial" distinctions, Zhuangzi's work may be seen as an attempt at "demythologization," and it shares this feature with its Confucianist rivals or its Communist detractors.

from either holism or renunciation as defined by Dumont: "The Taoist can live in the world and have serious and meaningful relationships with others, but he or she functions in these relationships with a freedom which comes from cultivation of the art of living" (ibid., 115). In this sense, Zhuangzi appears as a precursor of Chan masters. However, as we have seen earlier, Dumont himself defined another, mediating category between holism and renunciation, that of inworldly individualism, which seems to apply here. Berling is justified when she warns against the unilateral interpretations of those who see Zhuangzi as "advocating accommodation with history and the social order" or, on the contrary, upholding eccentricity and withdrawal from society because "neither of these positions does justice to the balance of Zhuangzi's position. One is slanted toward holism (accommodation with society), the other toward radical individualism. Zhuangzi's Taoist, however, leans toward neither side of the dichotomy" (ibid., 117–118). Perhaps does he lean toward both sides, successively or even simultaneously? This would explain the tensions or the somersaults of his thought.[15]

At any rate, one cannot simply associate social values with Confucianism and individualistic values with Daoism (and Zhuangzi). Although Confucianists tend to take a holistic stand and Daoist "renouncers" an individualistic one, many counterexamples could be found, within both ritualistic Daoist religion and Confucianism. For an example of the latter, suffice it to mention the case of Li Zhi (1527–1623), the "accursed philosopher."[16] Clearly, individualism and holism cannot differentiate social groups; instead, they must be seen as trends at work (or at play) within both groups and individuals.

As has often been noted, Buddhism was criticized by Confucianists as an asocial teaching. Allegedly, Buddhist monks did not respect social relations and thrived as parasites. However, the Mahāyāna emphasis on emptiness had two contradictory effects: on the one hand, as can be seen most clearly in Tantric Buddhism and Chan antinomianism, it resulted in a relativization or a reversal of social values; on the other hand, it had an integrative

[15] A striking example of radical individualism, and "the most incisive mockery of Confucianism" after Zhuangzi, can be found in the *Daren xiansheng zhuan* (Biography of master Great-Man) by Ruan Ji, who compares men-in-the-world, trapped in the network of social relationships, with the lice living inside a pair of pants (see Balazs 1968, 119). Also worth quoting, if only for his use of the pants metaphor, is Liu Ling (225?–280?), another member of the group of the Seven Sages of the Bamboo Grove. "Some guests went to visit Liu Ling, at a time when he happened to be stark naked. Ling, laughing, said: 'I have taken heaven and earth for my house and home, and my room and roof for my pants and coat. You gentlemen shouldn't be in my pants in the first place, so now what are you complaining about?' Such was his self-abandon." *Shishuo xinyu* 3A, 37b; Mather 1976, 374; see also Balazs 1968, 120.

[16] Concerning Li Zhi, see Billeter 1979; de Bary 1970, 188–225; and Wu Pei-yi 1990, 19–24.

aspect wherein the Madhyamika interpretation of emptiness as synonymous with dependent origination (Sk. *pratītya-samutpāda*) led to a realization of the relativity of the individual. Accordingly, the individuality of the Buddhist monk was counterbalanced by his strong consciousness of his "position" within the social or religious hierarchy. The Buddhist acculturation in China was significantly determined by the evolution of the relationships of the Buddhist clergy with the State. Between the fourth and seventh centuries, the clergy definitively lost its independence and reluctantly became an agent of the imperial ideology. Thereafter, Buddhist individualism tended to become sectarian (and by the same token tied to political power) or devotional (as in the Pure Land tradition). Only when the political center was weakened, for instance after the An Lushan rebellion in 755, could a kind of libertarian individualism resurface, principally in Chan, but never for very long. Despite its apparent success, Chan antinomianism survived merely as an institutionalized marginality, like Daoist eremitism from which it borrowed a number of features.

THE INDIVIDUAL AND POWER

Just as our perception of ourselves as individuals is socially informed, so too is the renouncer's desire to be free from the bonds of society (Dumont 1980, 21). Following the lead of Durkheim and Mauss, Dumont simply acknowledges the fact; he does not really try to question the ideological implications of such an "obligation to be free." This question, raised by Michel Foucault, has a direct bearing on our topic: to what extent did Chan followers also have to yield to that obligation, and why? Was something else at stake in their frantic search for individual salvation? For Foucault, the traditional dichotomy between society, as authority, and the individual is misleading. Individuals are never passively "subject" *to* power, for they simultaneously undergo and exercize it; they become by the same token subjects *of* power. They provide not only power's point of application but also its vehicle. Foucault argues that the individual, precisely when he believes he is resisting power, is entirely permeated by it, for he is "one of its prime effects," the element of its articulation (Foucault 1980, 98). The type of power Foucault has in mind is not simply a localized, repressive power, but the "interplay of techniques of discipline and less obvious technologies of the self" (Dreyfus and Rabinow 1983, 175), an omnipresent reality thriving on individual freedom even more certainly than on its suppression. Foucault's vision may appear rather pessimistic, and some commentators have argued that it leaves no alternative but submission to power. But judging from his own political activism, Foucault himself seems to have believed that the "individualization process," even if initiated and controlled by power, could also have "perverse" effects and produce lucid individuals able to undermine the logic of power.

Nevertheless, the fact that a few rugged "individuals" denounced this logic within Buddhism does not preclude the possibility that the Chan/Zen individualization process may by and large have served the growth of power relationships. Foucault saw in technologies for the discipline of bodies and minds the main instrument of the type of individualization that characterizes the growth of power in Western society. One main component of this technology of the self was the procedure of confession, as it developed in the Christian church and was later reinscribed in the practice of psychoanalysis. This technique arose from the compelling belief that one can, with the help of experts, discover the truth about oneself—a truth that will make one free. For Foucault, however, truth is not necessarily opposed to power, and confession, based on the exploitation of the "will to truth," participates in the process of individualization in a way similar or complementary to the technologies of discipline (see Dreyfus and Rabinow 1983, 174–175). Thus, Foucault questioned the "subjectifying" social sciences and their hermeneutic search for a deep meaning, a meaning necessarily hidden from the subject and compelling him to surrender to an external, "spiritual" authority. With the rise of the hermeneutic model, "individuality, discourse, truth, and coercion were . . . given a common location" (ibid., 180). Although the departure from this hermeneutic model in some trends of "classical" Chan implies a certain emancipation from authority, the relevance of Foucault's analysis to the development of discipline in Buddhism, and in Japanese Zen in particular, hardly needs to be stressed.

The question of the confession of sins in traditional China has been studied by Wu Pei-yi. Although his study offers many parallels with the Western case studied by Foucault, Wu does not refer to Foucault's work.[17] Concerning the many rites of repentance found in Mahāyāna, Wu points out that none includes a detailed confession of transgressions committed. There was in early Chan a strong tendency to downplay the concrete, "phenomenal" transgressions and to promote a superior form of "formless" repentance, namely, the understanding that all transgressions are fundamentally empty (see Yampolsky 1967, 144). This constitutes an important difference with Christian confession as Foucault analyzes it, a technique aimed at exacerbating culpability. Interestingly, the only Chan case of formless repentance mentioned by Wu seems to imply that repentance was considered a form of healing physical illness. A layman comes to consult the second Chan patriarch Huike and tells him: "I am suffering

[17] See Wu Pei-yi 1978; Eberhard 1967; and Alex Wayman, "Purification of Sin in Buddhism by Vision and Confession," in *Bonnō no kenkyū* (A Study of *Kleśa*), ed. Genjun Sasaki (Tokyo: Shimizu Kōbundō, 1976) 58–79.

from rheumatism. Please repent my sins for me." Huike answers: "Tell me your sins, and I shall repent them for you." After pondering for a long time, the layman says: "I looked for my sins, but could not find any."[18] According to Wu, this story suggests that "both were acquainted with a healing rite in which a patient whose affliction could not be attributed to a specific wrongdoing was required to disclose all his sins to a confessor who would expiate them and effect a cure for the penitent. Such an episode resembles Daoist faith healing rather than the Buddhist *uposatha*" (Wu 1978, 13). Wu concludes that "none of the subsequent patriarchs established his fame as a healer of physical afflictions, nor was the problem of guilt and sin a main concern to the Chan school" (ibid.). The question of repentance, however, is omnipresent in early Chan texts such as the *Dasheng wusheng fangbian men*, the *Lengqie shizi ji*, or the *Platform Sūtra*. Wu himself remarks that, in the later tradition, for at least one Chan master this was an important issue. Zhuhong (1535–1615), the man credited with the revival of the *upoṣadha* ritual and the author of an interesting *Self-Reproach*, gives a detailed list of all his failures before concluding: "Consequently, day and night I am plagued by shame, anxiety and fear: I travel, dwell, sit, and sleep as if I were always in thorns and brambles" (see *Yunqi fahui*, quoted in Wu 1978, 19). This sounds very Christian, and it may be worth recalling that Zhuhong was also the author of one of the most famous pamphlets against Christianity.

At any rate, confession was only one of several disciplinary techniques studied by Foucault, and certainly the importance of discipline in Chan cannot be overestimated. The Chan school achieved a ritualization of all the aspects of clerical life, and spontaneity itself, although highly valued as an ideal, was ritually framed in Chan dialogues. The technique of meditation can also easily be interpreted as a disciplinary *mise au pas* of recalcitrant minds and bodies or conventional selves, in the name of a greater—and forever elusive—self. Chan meditation is essentially a matter of control and discipline—part of what Jon Elster calls "the highly paradoxical goal of Buddhist character-planning" (Elster 1983, 54). Incidentally, the character used to partially transcribe the Sanskrit dhyāna and read Chan in Chinese means "submission," and the fact that this character was eventually selected to designate the school issued from Bodhidharma is perhaps not entirely insignificant. The physical painfulness of cross-legged sitting or the exacting perfection of ritual gestures inscribe Chan orthopraxy on the body of practitioners. This emphasis on the body, which finds its hyperbole in the Buddhist ideal of self-mummification, seems paradoxical in a school apparently so concerned with mind that it derives

---

[18] A variant of this story, quoted in Keizan's *Denkōroku*, involves Huike and his disciple Sengcan. According to Keizan, "The sickness plaguing [Sengcan] in his first meeting with Huike was leprosy." *Denkōroku* 31; see Cleary 1990, 130–131.

from it one of its appellations (*xin zong*, "School of the Mind"). Significantly, the two most famous mummies in the Chan tradition are those of
Huineng (638–713) and of Hanshan Deqing (1546–1623), two individuals who played important roles in the development of the autobiographical genre in China (see Wu Pei-yi 1990, 72–73, 142–159; Faure 1991).
Another important aspect of the Western technology of discipline is what
Foucault describes as the ideal of the panopticon—a penitentiary device in
which the prisoner can be constantly seen by his guardian, while never
seeing him (Foucault 1979). Although far from this ideal, life in Chan/Zen
monasteries is also panoptical in that the monk fulfils all his daily routines
under the supervision of his peers and superiors, and the ritualized meetings with the master (J. *dokusan*) reinforce this constant scrutiny—and
tend to exacerbate his feeling of guilt and his subjectivity. The elders,
however, are entitled to private quarters, and each elevation within the
hierarchy brings more autonomy.

The individualization process in Chan/Zen was also affected by changes
in literary and artistic techniques. The *Platform Sūtra*, for example, illustrates the emergence of the (fictional) autobiographical genre.[19] As noted
earlier, the interiorization of writing and the development of printing
played perhaps a significant role in the development of an inner sphere, the
reserved space of the individual. The development of the recorded sayings
(yulu) as a literary genre appears both as a cause and an effect of an
increasing consciousness of intersubjectivity. While increasing the master's
authority, the development of "personal consultations" (*dokusan*) also
permitted a more intimate relationship between master and disciple. This
feeling of intimacy is well reflected, for instance, in Dōgen's autobiographical account of his relationship with his Chinese master Rujing or in his
conversations with his disciple Ejō (see *Hōkyō ki, Zuimon ki*). Furthermore, the development of a patriarchal lineage, with its emphasis on transmission, tended to reintegrate the "orphaned" individual into a kind of
traditional kinship system and to reassert the dominance of the group.

Lewis Mumford once remarked that autobiography appeared when
man was able to fabricate good mirrors (quoted in Dumoulin 1984). We do
not know if mirrors were common in Buddhist monasteries, but they play a
conspicuous role in the *Platform Sūtra* and other early Chan texts. They
were perhaps instrumental in the development of self-portraits, which are
not uncommon in Zen art. As Heinrich Dumoulin points out, "Every self
portrait proceeds from and points back to a self-aware individual" (ibid.,
1984, 162). More generally, the stress given by the patriarchal tradition on

---

[19] In his study of the "autobiographical" passages in the *Platform Sūtra*, Wu Pei-yi overlooks the fact that these passages, like the rest of the text, are apocryphal (and hagiographical). See Wu 1990, 72–73. However, his general conclusions regarding the rise of the autobiographical genre in Chinese Buddhism remain valid.

individual transmission seems to explain in part the development of portraiture and of calligraphy in Chan after the Tang. The individuality reflected by these portraits, paintings or statues, which are said to look—and are indeed revered—as if alive, bears witness to the emergence and the belief in the survival beyond death of a new type of individual. One needs only to mention well-known portraits such as those of Dōgen, Rankei Dōryū, Musō Soseki, Daitō, Ikkyū, and Hakuin. The development of these Chan "icons," however, had more complex reasons, and it is not possible to equate too quickly the type of "diffused" individuality they reflect with Western conceptions of a self-contained self (see Faure 1991, 169–174).

SOLITAIRE/SOLIDAIRE

> Dwell making yourself an island.
> (*Mahaparinibbana-sutta*)

> No man is an island, entire of itself; every man is a piece of the continent, a part of the main.
> (John Donne, *Devotion* xvii)

Our point of entry in Chan/Zen philosophical anthropology is the paradigmatic opposition between Linji's "true man of no-rank" and Dōgen's "true man with a rank" (*T.* 82, 2582: 181c). I would like to consider some epistemological and sectarian implications of this opposition. What is the "configuration of subjectivity" in Linji's case? Although Linji's individualism reflects his personal charisma, is it not also to a certain extent the expression of a "charisma of office" deriving from his "rank" in the Chan lineage? Linji's "humanism," praised by Demiéville, is manifest in his denial of nature and gods and of the "mythical" conception of man. Like the "free thinker" Zhuangzi, however, his playfulness renders him elusive, and his contribution to a Chan "philosophical anthropology" is complex and manifold.

Linji's definition of the "man of no-rank" (*wuwei zhenren*), a term borrowed from Daoism, lends itself to an "essentialist" interpretation and was criticized on that ground.[20] Like his contemporary Zongmi, well known for a piece of "philosophical anthropology" entitled *Yuanren lun* (Searching for Man), Linji was heir to the Tathāgatagarbha tradition that found one expression in the Chan motto, "Seeing one's nature and becoming a

---

[20] Take for instance the following passage: "On your lump of red flesh is a true man without a rank who is always going in and out of the face of everyone of you" (Fuller Sasaki 1975, 3). Linji seems to be quoting from a verse by Fu Xi: "The mind[-king] resides in the body, entering and leaving through the gates of the face." *Xinwang ming*, in *T.* 51, 2076: 457a. See also Fuller Sasaki 1975, 8, 18, 29.

Buddha" (*jianxing chengfo*). This "vision of one's nature" (*jianxing*, J. *kenshō*) was already a leitmotiv of both the *Platform Sūtra* and the apocryphal *Shoulengyan jing*. Linji also shows a "subjectifying" tendency when he denies all forms of hierarchy and objectivation, beginning with that of the empirical self (ibid., 10–11). The transcendental principle itself, becoming subjective (ibid., 30–31), seems more akin to Valéry's "pure potentiality" than to a permanent entity: "Then, when I cast off everything, the student is stunned and, running about in wild confusion, cries, 'You are naked!' Then I say: 'Do you know me, the man who wears these robes?'" (ibid.; see also Demiéville 1972, 140). Linji's "essentialism" is contradicted or relativized by his famous tetralemma, in which he dialectically advocates "at times to take away man and object" (ibid., 10). Perhaps, for Linji as for Robert Musil, "subjectivity turns its back to our inner being as much as objectivity" (Musil 1956, 2: 609).

Yet, Linji's criticism of the social self as so many "robes" or "roles" is itself to a large extent socially determined and reflects the loosening of social networks and sectarian consciousness that took place toward the end of the Tang. His denial of the traditional Buddhist belief in supranormal powers (*abhijñā*) derives in part from this criticism, for these "powers" are valuable only for the empirical self and its alter egos. This denial may also have to do with the Chan epistemology of immediacy: whereas the empirical self was traditionally conceived in Buddhism as a hierarchy of powers, "sudden" Chan, with its claim of an immediate (unmediated) experience, rejected precisely that hierarchical model. Whereas the notion of an "implicated" self seems to go hand in hand with "gradualism," the emergence of the "transcendental" self (the "man without qualities") appears to overlap with the "sudden" perspective and its denial of any implication in the soteriological process or in the "will to truth." Because the "sudden" approach (or nonapproach) also leads to a critique of the act (karma) and its agent, Linji consistently rejects all practices that amount to producing karma—"Seeking Buddha and seeking Dharma is only making hell-karma" (Fuller Sasaki 1975, 18–19)—and simultaneously denies the ontological reality of karmic causality or the so-called "dependent origination" (*pratītya-samutpada*).[21] Ironically, his eminently individualistic position is made possible by the Mahāyāna reinterpretation of dependent origination, a reinterpretation that marks the transition from the soteriological individualism of early Buddhism toward a more holistic conception of salvation (the "all in one" model of Huayan). We thus find two types of pratītya-samutpada: the psychogenetic model of early Buddhism, with its twelve links leading from ignorance to birth and death, and the structural

[21] "Just make yourself master of every situation, and right away you will be true. . . . Even the impregnations of your past karma and the five sins of immediate retribution will then become the sea of deliverance." See Demiéville 1972, 71; Fuller Sasaki 1975, 12.

model of Mahāyāna, based on the notion of *śūnyatā*. As noted earlier, the structural model may also reflect a shift from a time-based to a space-based epistemology.

If the notion of *karma* is denied, then what about the correlative notion of an *agent*, which was so crucial in the Western definition of the person? It is at first glance also denied in Chan, —as it was in early Buddhism, which claimed that "there is an act but no one that acts." But such doctrinal statements can hardly be taken at face value: more likely, it is *because* the agent had emerged as a category that it could (and had to) be denied. The appearance of such a category seems related with temporality, it implies a change in the perception of time. As Jean-Pierre Vernant points out in the Greek case, the agent is the one who foresees how his action is going to take place, and this foresight denies spontaneity (Vernant 1979, 92). Therefore, Linji's advocacy of pure spontaneity—as an obedience to the "order of things" ("to shit and piss," to be "without affairs")—amounts to a denial of both agent and moral responsibility.[22] More important than Linji's contradicting statements in regard to the self, however, is his uniquely personal "style" in relation to others (and to himself), a style that puts him on a par with a Socrates or a Diogenes. After all, is not the "true man without qualities" merely a kind of "shit-wiping stick"? (Fuller Sasaki 1975, 3).

After reviewing some epistemological changes that permitted the appearance of a strong individual such as Linji, suffice it to allude to the sociohistorical factors. Linji was politically dependent on his new patrons, the military commanders who had seized power in the provinces after the breaking up of the centralized power of the Tang. Inner freedom seems to presuppose external dependence, and self-consciousness itself is socially produced or at least dialogically strengthened. Perhaps Linji was able to acquire his (relative) freedom by playing off conflicting networks of power, an achievement possible only during a limited period of sociopolitical instability—in the interstices of power, as it were.

To what extent does Foucault's analysis of the Western predicament of the self apply to Chan/Zen? Is it true that "the awakening of the self is paid for by the acknowledgement of power as principle of all relations"? (Horkheimer and Adorno 1972, 9). As in the case of Indian Buddhism, conflicting notions of the self are used here strategically, almost

---

22 An extreme example of moral ambivalence is provided by the following passage of a ninth-century Chan tract, the *Jueguan lun*: "Asked: 'Can there be any condition under which killing is made possible?' Answered: 'A field burns hills; fierce wind breaks trees; an avalanche buries beasts; and flooding water drifts worms. To the mind who works likewise killing a man will also be possible and passable. If the mind has any hesitation, if it sees life, and if it sees killing, so long as the mind therein does not exhaust itself, even an ant would keep you tied in bondage" (Tokiwa 1973, 14).

casuistically, depending on societal, political, and sectarian stakes. The notion of self becomes a component in complex and ambiguous discursive strategies that result in an increase of power (for the Chan master, the Buddhist community, or society). The "technologies of the self" described by Foucault (discipline, confession) sometimes reinforce, sometimes also weaken, these strategies.

The contrast between Linji and Dōgen on the question of the self sheds some light on the linkage between self and power in the Chan/Zen tradition. There is for instance in *Shōbōgenzō Genjō kōan* an often quoted passage on the self:

> To learn the Buddha Way is to learn one's own self.
> To learn one's self is to forget one's self.
> To forget one's self is to be confirmed by all dharmas.
> (T. 82, 2582: 23c; Waddell and Abe 1972, 134)

Dōgen attacks wrong—that is, "essentialist" or "spontaneist"— conceptions of the self, which he believes lead to the "naturalist heresy" (*jinen gedō*). Using the comparison of a man who goes off in a boat and erroneously believes that the shore is moving while the boat stands still, Dōgen denounces the phenomenological illusion that causes us to believe in the existence of a substantial self (Waddell and Abe 1972, 135) Devoid of intrinsic reality, the self changes constantly; conversely, the apparent changes in our environment mask a fundamental immobility. Dōgen elaborates on the theme of the "immutability of things," borrowed from the Chinese monk and philosopher Sengzhao, with the example of wood and ashes: for him, wood only seems to turn into ashes, while in reality wood and ashes remain ontologically distinct, perfect stages of Suchness (ibid.). Therefore, what is seen as impermanence is none other than Suchness. Everything dwells at its own Dharma rank, and nothing or no one (not even Linji) can claim to be "without a rank." In this way, Dōgen reintroduces a kind of hierarchy into the absolute, although such a hierarchy is considerably modified or displaced by the Mahāyāna notion of Emptiness.

According to Dōgen, the "naturalist" or Senika heresy originally denounced by the Buddha, but still alive in Buddhism, covers two false conceptions of the self (what Chan masters call the "pure mind" and the "ordinary mind"): one is the perception of the self as an imperishable and purely spiritual Buddha nature; the other is the understanding of the self as a spontaneous expression of an immanent Buddha nature. The expression "naturalist heresy" refers to what Indian Buddhists called *pudgalavāda*— that is, the belief in an immortal principle transmigrating from one life to another.[23] To this erroneous view, Dōgen opposes his notion of a transcen-

[23] See also Musō Soseki's *Muchū mondō* (Dialogues in a Dream), which, after describing various forms of "mind," compares the Chan "essentialist" interpretation of the motto "This

dental self anterior to any division between subject and object, a decentered self "authenticated by the myriad things." Along the same lines, he criticizes the "essentialist" conception of "mind and [Buddha] nature" found in Chinese Chan masters such as Dahui Zonggao. However, as noted earlier, Dōgen's immediate target is probably the Darumashū, which claimed descent from Dahui and took as its motto the expression: "This very mind is the Buddha" (J. *sokushin zebutsu*). One main text of this school, a document recently rediscovered in the Kanazawa Library, is significantly entitled *Kenshō jōbutsu ron* (Treatise on Seeings One's Nature and Becoming Buddha). Dōgen traced this misunderstanding from Dahui back to Linji's notion of the "true man of no-rank," and his criticism eventually extended to the *Platform Sūtra* itself, which Dōgen held as apocryphal precisely because of its essentialist advocacy of "seeing one's own nature." The sectarian aspect in Dōgen's criticism of the "true man of no-rank" has been noted by Mujaku Dōchū:

> If the non-stopping of words means that one has not yet reached the goal, one must say that Śākyamuni and Bodhidharma had not reached it. Why? The first said that all sentient beings have a Buddha nature, he did not say yet that all sentient beings lack a Buddha nature. The second spoke only of "a special transmission outside the Scriptures, no dependence on the written letter," he did not say yet that, in the teaching, everything transmits "establishing the written letter." If one scrutinizes words [to criticize them], the Buddha-patriarchs of the three periods should also be examined—as well as Dongshan and Caoshan. Therefore, one cannot select only Linji's words on the "true man of no-rank" [for criticism]. This true man of no-rank must be seen directly—this is to reach truly the goal. (Quoted in Kagamishima 1961, 245)

This sectarian and dialogical nature of Dōgen's work is usually forgotten or downplayed by Japanese and Western scholars.[24] Taking his cues from Louis Dumont, Robert Bellah points out the individualistic bias that makes us read more individualism in *Shōbōgenzō* than there actually is (Bellah 1985). The antinomianism of "sudden" Chan is precisely what Dōgen attempted to check with his notion of the "true man with a rank." Moreover, one should keep in mind that these radical statements—and a fortiori their criticism—took for granted a certain social order, the unquestioned existence of a rigid hierarchy to which they may be seen as a kind of imaginary compensation. The situation becomes quite different when

---

very mind is the Buddha" to the Samkhya notion of *Puruṣa* and to the views of Laozi and Zhuangzi. Musō 1976, 166–171.

[24] A case in point is *Dōgen Studies*, a collection of essays edited by William R. LaFleur (1985). The question of the self is treated at length by Francis Cook (1985, 147), who, addressing what he calls "Dōgen's view of authentic selfhood," reduces Dōgen's teaching to a rather insipid variant of humanism and sees in him a precursor to Nishida's *A Study of Good*.

Zen—or a religious figure like Dōgen—"gets translated into a culture which has been moving in the direction of hyperindividualism for two or three centuries at an ever accelerating tempo" (Bellah 1985, 152). Finally, it bears repeating that the content of Chan discourse on subjectivity does not necessarily coincide with its perlocutionary effects: the story told (self/no-self) is not always the story actually performed. Consequently, it becomes necessary to shift the focus from the content of the theory to the act of theorizing (terrorizing?) itself. What is denied—the empirical self in the case of Linji, the transcendental self in the case of Dōgen—has already been acknowledged, and this very denial tends to increase self-consciousness. Although Linji seems less absorbed in his discursive strategies, the performative or perlocutionary aspect is evident in Dōgen's discourse. Even though, Linji's sermons, advocating spontaneity and freedom of thought, necessarily create a double-bind for his listeners. As Jon Elster has pointed out, spontaneity can only be a by-product, and freedom cannot be commanded (Elster 1983, 56). Thus, the *Record of Linji* turns out to be yet another "consciousness creating device," another creation of karma.

Although the two paradigmatic positions represented by the "mountain monk" Linji and the aristocratic monk Dōgen seem at first glance to overlap with outworldly and indworldly individualism, they do not correspond to their actual situations because Linji was living in a crowded place while Dōgen secluded himself in the distant mountains of Echizen. These two positions are complementary and derive from the same hierarchical structure. However, they represent only two intermediary positions on a larger spectrum; these go from the radical nonconformism of men such as Linji's acolyte Puhua to the radical holism of Confucianized Zen masters such as Suzuki Shōsan, a Tokugawa Zen master who had completely espoused the hierarchical ideology of the ruling elite. As Royall Tyler points out, "in his concern for the stability of the social order, Shōsan left the individual no more room to move than any advocate of the *taigi meibun* (a fixed role for each person in an immutable social order) ideals" (Tyler 1984, 99; see also Ooms 1985, 122–143). Although a Zen master, he was closer to the Confucianist ideal of the "man-in-the-world" than to the early Chan ideal of asceticism and world-renouncing (*dhūta-guṇa*).

Homo Multiplex

The above discussion has suggested that Chan individualism is not necessarily accompanied by a theoretical affirmation of self, and conversely. Although providing a useful starting point, the two-tiered model used in the holism/individualism dichotomy or in the notion of *homo duplex* needs to be refined. While similar subjectifying/objectifying tendencies seem at work in the Buddhist case, the Chan/Zen constellation of the self is not the same as in the West. The essential duplicity of homo duplex reinscribes itself constantly, producing the Chan individual as *homo multiplex*. The opposition drawn by Dōgen between hierarchical man ("man with a rank") and its other ("man of no-rank") seems to confirm the dualistic model, but this ideological product implies a repression of multiplicity and fails to describe accurately the range of possibilities. In reality, all individuals are not equally individualized. By interpreting too readily Buddhism (or its Chan/Zen variants) as a kind of humanistic individualism, at the cost of other conceptions of the self, one forgets that the affirmation and negation of a unified, self-contained self are the two faces of a single epistemological/ideological phenomenon. Such a theoretical construction of self or nonself negates the traditional Chinese conception of man as a hierarchy of powers; it denies the notion of a multiple and diffuse self that constitutes an intermediary between Earth and Heaven—a notion at work, for instance, in funerary rituals (Faure 1991). Because the solo performance of charismatic individuals like Linji is is made possible by the accompaniment of a choir, they should not be allowed to steal the show. In this sense, subjectivity is always dialogical, intersubjective ("interobjective"), and the Chan individual constitutes a pluralistic space, subject to multiple tensions. Indeed, if, as Freud wrote in *Das Unheimliche*, "the 'immortal' soul is likely to have been the first double of the body" (Freud 1947, 247), Chan essentialism was perhaps a product of contemplative techniques grounded in the body. The Chan master, however, had a number of metonymic or metaphoric doubles (Arhats, portraits, relics, mummy, etc.). His was a diffracted, diffused, "qualified" individuality, not the well-contained individuality we take for granted in the West (see Geertz, 1983, 59). One can argue that the Chan practitioner is truly an individual to the extent that he opens himself to the multiplicities that traverse him, thus becoming a place of communication, of fusion between object and subject, and sometimes a battlefield. Ideally, he becomes a master only when he surrenders self-mastery. As his biographer wrote about Zongmi: "Master Mi was like a land discuted by different warring powers, no one being able to claim him under any banner" (*Song gaoseng zhuan*, in T. 50, 2060: 742b).

We find on the one hand the individual as an effect of technologies of self and power and on the other hand an individuality that results from awakening, in which the *solitaire* has become *solidaire*, but it is no longer the structural solidarity of the "man-in-the-world." Thus, the individual, although pervaded by power, may not always be a mere effect of power, but a place where the structure of power is, if not abolished, at least modified or subverted. What relationship—if any—is there between these two types of individuality, and how could the first ever lead to the second? This must remain an open question. At any rate, we can conclude that the changing perception of the self in Chan/Zen is related to larger epistemological changes in orality and literacy and in the perception of space and time. In all these cases, epistemology is intimately related to ideology and power, although never reducible to them.

EPILOGUE

ACCORDING TO a story told by Mujū Ichien in his *Shasekishū*, there once were four monks who, emulating Vimalakīrti's silence, vowed to observe seven days of silence. Toward the end of the first night, when the light was growing dim, one of them could not refrain from calling a servant to rekindle the lamp. The second monk remarked: "You are not supposed to talk." The third monk intervened: "You two have broken your vow." The fourth monk, self-satisfied, concluded: "I am the only one who didn't talk!" (*Shasekishū* 27; quoted in Reps 1957, 68). Attempting to bring this book to a close, I feel in the position of the fourth monk, who naively thought that his vantage point gave him an advantage on the others. Even when disguised as an "epilogue" (*épigramme?*), a conclusion is always an attempt to have the last word.

I have focused in this book on some conditions of production of a Chan/Zen discourse: its generative schemes, its areas of proliferation (sectarian boundaries, geographical and social anchoring) and of rarefaction (the *non-dit*, the limits of language), and its ideological and cultural framework (Sino-Japanese historiography, Western reception). By providing an interpretive account of Chan/Zen and discussing the epistemological groundings and ideological implications of both the Chan tradition and of its scholarly re-creation, this essay functioned on several levels simultaneously.

Whereas the first part of the book was concerned mainly with the discursive constraints that informed Chan/Zen scholarship, the second part dealt with the epistemological fault lines that run through the Chan/Zen tradition(s) and led to the closure of the canon. As Foucault argued, a tradition and the canon that represents it are the result of a process of limitation, of a rarefaction of discourse (Foucault 1972). It represents the ascent of an ideology, of an "essential" difference, through the repression of differences and dissent (its "differential essence"). As Westerners, our perception of Chan is necessarily mediated by Orientalist categories, which we saw at work even in the allegedly native (and for sure nativist) discourse of a Japanese scholar like D. T. Suzuki. The conditions of emergence of Western discourse on China and Japan, in particular the ideological choices made by Jesuit missionaries in favor of Confucianism, have shaped the field and continue to inform our understanding, long after the demise of the Society of Jesus. This Orientalist prejudice is in some ways alleviated, in others reinforced, by the methodological presuppositions of Sino-Japanese historiography. With Suzuki, however, Chan/Zen was constituted as an epistemological object theoretically independent from its sociohistorical contexts.

The radical antinomianism of sudden Chan derived from a "theoretical excess" that led this school to deny all mediations and to claim the privilege of an absolute, unlocalized, properly utopian standpoint. Perhaps this excess, in its iconoclastic simplicity, explains the seduction exerted by Chan on intellectuals and commoners alike during and after the Tang. However, it also proved costly: it transformed Chan into an elitist ideology characterized by linguistic taboos and the contradiction of theory and practice, by a "conspiracy of silence" that generated a host of controversies, and by the marginalization or repression of various sectors of the tradition. These biased interpretations were inherited and accentuated by Chan/Zen scholarship.

I have argued that the real changes that took place were not so much a matter of ideas and doctrine, but of style and perceptions. By "style" I mean that what made Chan a specific discourse was determined from the outset by certain linguistic, theoretical, and rhetorical modes. By change in "perceptions," I want to suggest that the "invention" of Chan—and its constant reinvention—was determined by certain epistemological shifts affecting categories, notions and values such as time, space, language, speech and writing, and self. Although we are still dealing with individuals—whether Chan monks, scholar-monks or lay scholars—the thought and actions of these individuals are themselves framed by the epistemological field in which they are inscribed. As Mauss once said, "Behind Moses . . . , there is Israel, and if Moses doubts, Israel does not" (Mauss 1985, 124). I have therefore examined the constitution of Chan/Zen as an epistemological object, focusing on different types of discourse, such as sectarian, historiographical, and Orientalist. The main thrust of my analysis has been to unsettle the object (Chan/Zen) by the use of alternative methods, while avoiding to dissolve this object into mere ideological discourse.

I also argued that Chan is not primarily a concrete social reality, but a complex and elusive epistemological object that never existed as a given outside representations, but was always in the making, through the classificatory decisions of people who saw themselves as members of the tradition. One may of course object, with some ground, that Chan was from the outset a school of Buddhism—that is, a supposedly well-defined social group. In actual practice, however, sectarian affiliation always rested on collective and individual representations, on a global perception of the religious field that was constantly fluctuating. To (re)present oneself as a Chan adherent was a performative choice, a strategical move that contributed to question or reinforce traditional classifications.

An epistemological critique of Chan reveals that, somewhere between doctrinal and institutional factors, schemes of perception have informed and systematized Chan discourse and scholarly discourse on Chan; they have thereby created specific configurations of insight and blindness. This epistemological level of analysis should not be taken as a deeper structural level, a last instance determination, because it interacts constantly with the ideological and phenomenological levels. The very search for a "deeper level" seems to derive from an epistemological constraint that imposes a spatial model on reality. Perhaps the words of the Zen master Shidō Bunan—"Those who seek the Dharma in the depths / Are those who leave it behind in the shallows" (Kobori 1970, 118)—apply to methodology as well. Like Bourdieu's *habitus*, or like the "intermediary world" of a tradition that denied intermediaries (see Faure 1991, 70–78), the epistemological approach taken here provides perhaps, if not a solution, at least a temporary mediation to the dichotomies created by the "theoretical excesses" of Chan.

Although this analysis reveals Zen to be an artificial construct, it stops short of dissolving it into a pure ideological discourse—a Buddhist emptiness of sorts. Chan/Zen needs to be preserved as a specific, tangible object of knowledge for two main reasons: First, ideology already is (and increasingly becomes, through social objectivation) part of the reality it distorts. Paradoxically, D. T. Suzuki was not simply distorting the tradition, he was in a strange way its true representative to the extent that the tradition itself emerged from the repeated distortion, not of some primordial straight (party) line, orthodoxy, but of previous distortions. Admittedly, this situation undermines the very notions of distortion and deviation (let alone orthodoxy). Nevertheless, inasmuch as Suzuki's Zen, like earlier attempts at defining an "orthodoxy," is an ideological construct, it constitutes an impoverishment of the tradition it claims to represent. Despite repeated attempts to make it fit the Procrustean bed of "classical" orthodoxy, Chan has always been (and will, I hope, remain) a "differential tradition." Even if, like Western esotericism according to Umberto Eco's *Foucault's Pendulum*, the esoteric Chan tradition comes to existence only as a "virtual focus," it tends, without ever succeeding, to turn the obsessive dream of its origins into an active reality.

The second reason for preserving Chan as an object is that the deconstructive or performative/rhetorical level of discourse needs a metaphysical or hermeneutical level on which to operate. Just like "differential" Chan needed a metaphysical/logocentric Chan to subvert, heterodox or paradoxical scholarship needs an orthodoxy to deconstruct. Far from being "purely" negative, this parasitism is truly constructive. Orthodoxy would never be possible without its constitutive margins, its play with the other within itself. Thus, the "theoretical excess" of "subitism" was always framed by and dependent on its practical, ritualistic, gradualist context. Significantly, Mazu Daoyi, the man who most contributed to Chan antino-mianism by claiming that "the ordinary mind is the Way," and Baizhang, the founder of the "Pure Rule" of Chan, were master and disciple. The libertarian spirit of sudden Chan is only the other face of the ritualized, institutionalized Chan school of the mid-Tang. The discrepancy between these two aspects can be read simultaneously as the results of an ideological cover-up and as the expression of a structural supplementarity. Hetero-doxy is not only a "different *doxa*," but it is also different from any *doxic* position—as that which cannot frontally contradict or confront ortho-doxy, but drives a wedge in it, fissures it, and makes it differ from itself. "Centric" Chan is always on the edge of becoming "differential," and the converse is also true. Thus, the difference that runs like a fault line through-out Chan discourse (and its scholarly replication) prevents me from hoping to restore the unity of a single tradition—let alone that of my own discourse. Indeed, the borderline between both primary and secondary discourses has become rather blurred; it constantly raises the question of transference between the scholar and its object of study.

Like theoretical thinking, early Chan appears as a form of dichotomic thinking. We have seen how two incommensurable visions were expressed in epistemological paradigms such as temporal/spatial, visual/auditory, written/oral, abstract/concrete, objective/subjective. Although these para-digms neither perfectly overlap nor seem to derive from some more "fun-damental" difference, they constitute various aspects of the differentiation process that was also expressed in the inclusive/exclusive, centric/ differential, or sudden/gradual tendencies of Chan. However, these the-oretical dichotomies do not prevail in practice, either because we have a *différend* between incommensurable approaches or because each term of the dichotomy regularly overflows into and contaminates the other, thus blurring the dichotomy (see Faure 1991, 32–52). Consequently, differen-tial and "centric" Chan never actually confronted each other (even in controversies such as the sudden/gradual debate), not only because they were ideal-types, but also because they were already in dialectical play with each other. Conflicting models were, in the end, reconciled—if not in theory, at least in the obscure economy of everyday practice.

Much of Chan discourse can be explained in terms of the emergence (followed by slow erosion and reinscription) of a new epistemological configuration marked by a certain dialectic of orality and literacy, a ho-mogenization of space and time that gives primacy to spatial and visual imagery, and a predominance of rhetoric over hermeneutic. This explana-

tion is not purely structural; it remains historical inasmuch as it acknowledges the importance of serendipity and the role of concrete events and
individuals. Even if the events that caused these changes and their protagonists cannot always be as easily circumscribed as those of the epoch-making
controversies, individuals played an important role in the crystallization of
this epistemological configuration. But, even if this remains a history with
individual actors and a narrative, the focus has shifted from the linear
narrative to a fragmented narrative and from the "leading role" of Chan/
Zen masters as founding fathers to their "part" as examples or witnesses of
a given *mentalité*, channeling complex forces and influences. The analysis
now focuses on a level intermediary between the structural (institutions)
and the conjunctural (event), that of "ideology." The polysemy of this
term—in its Dumézilian and Althusserian polarity (i.e., as a cognitive
framework or an inverted representation of reality)—allows us two readings; perhaps even a third reading results from the "play" between two
models—the epistemological and the "ideological" (Althusserian). Thus,
the structural tendency of the epistemological approach is corrected and
supplemented by the dialogical reinscription of the Chan epistemology
into specific strategies. As in the Two Truths model of the Madhyamika, the
constant tension, as well as the passage, between these two levels of interpretation is simultaneously created and mediated by the polysemic play.

We have examined some sectarian or ideological contexts in which the
Chan notions of self, language, and writing developed and some discursive
strategies they permitted. At the core of Dōgen's famous discussion of time
and of Buddha nature, for instance, we found sectarian concerns resulting
from his rivalry with the Darumashū. Thus, it becomes clear that categories of understanding and values are never divorced from power, although
not entirely reducible to power either. If I have tended to privilege two
specific moments in Chan/Zen history—represented by early Chan texts
and by Dōgen's *Shōbōgenzō*—as two different cultural and historical an-
chorings providing the sectarian/ideological background of the epistemological models, it is not only because these two periods are at the present
time the most well studied and happen to belong to my areas of specializa-
tion. But they also offer the strongest ideological statements because they
are times when Chan masters and their Japanese heirs were trying to obtain
recognition from the powers that be and when, to distinguish Chan from
traditional Chinese Buddhism, or (Sōtō) Zen from traditional Japanese
Buddhism and from some trends of "classical" Chan (in the case of Dōgen),
they had to formulate most transparently their ideology.

The fact that we are interpreting a culture, or part of it, in the terms of
another raises the problem of comparativism because we are working with
certain categories or values (space, time, individualism) that are histor-

ically and culturally determined—neither purely transcendental (as Kant believed) nor purely sociological (as Durkheim and Mauss argued). The awareness brought by this cultural and epistemological critique helps us to question traditional Western and Japanese accounts of Chan/Zen, and any other account for that matter. It thus leads us to question our own epistemological assumptions and to put into practice the Zen saying, *kyakka o miyo* (Look under your feet). This is precisely what Louis Dumont attempted to do with his Indian paradigm. Like the early Lucien Lévy-Bruhl, however, who contrasted civilized and primitive (or rather, rational and symbolical) thinking, Dumont tended to dichotomize cultures and hypostasize the gap between individualistic (Western) and holistic (Indian) thinking. Even though he retained this basic dichotomy throughout his work, he acknowledged that, like individuals, cultures and traditions are multiple and contain in themselves their own negation—represented in his account by the figure of the "renouncer." Likewise, in his posthumous *Notebooks*, Lévy-Bruhl stressed the coexistence of two types of thinking in both Western and non-Western societies; thus a transferential relationship could take place.

The issue of transference arises from the fact that I am writing about a tradition that, primarily in its *writings*, privileges speech and orality. Thus, the issue is not simply one of translation, but of successive trans-*scriptions*. One constant claim of this work has been that scholarship—even in its most "scientific" garb (philology, historiography, structuralism)—has a performative function. Consequently, it has to abandon its truth claims and remain content with simply offering yet another local (and localized) reading (or performance) of the tradition—and hoping that it will prove temporarily fruitful. The ultimate aporia, as Paul de Man pointed out, is that knowledge cannot be simply replaced by performance because, once it has revealed the performative dimension of any descriptive (scholarly) discourse, performative discourse cannot help deconstructing its own performance (de Man 1983, 130). Unfortunately, there is no return to the Eden of candid scholarship, and Chan scholarship, like the Chan tradition itself, is condemned to develop (or perhaps destined to thrive) in the dialogical oscillation between hermeneutics and rhetoric, between "objectivity" and imagination. This oscillation might look like limping, but, as Rückert said, "What cannot be reached by flying must be reached by limping" (quoted in Freud 1981, 115). Like that of philosophy, the limping of scholarship may be its virtue (Merleau-Ponty 1970, 61). *Et je m'en vais, clopin-clopant . . .*

GLOSSARY

Amaterasu　天照
An Lushan　安祿山
Anesaki Masaharu　姉崎正治
Annen　安然
anshōshi　暗証師

Bai Juyi　白居易
baihua　白話
Baizhang Huaihai　百丈懷海
balong yunzhuan mingguang
　八龍雲篆明光
Bankei　盤珪
Baolin　寶林
Baolin zhuan　寶林傳
Baotang　保唐
Baozhi　寶志
Beishan lu　北山錄
biguan　壁觀
Biyan lu　碧巖錄
buli wenzi　不立文字
busshō　佛性

Cang Jie　倉頡
Canlang shihua　滄浪詩話
Caodong (Sōtō)　漕洞
Caoqi　漕溪
Caoshan (Benji)　漕山本寂
Cen Shen　岑參
Chan　禪
chang le wo jing　常樂我淨
Changzong (Zhaojue)　常總照覺
Chanmen jing　禪門經
Chanmen shizi chengxi tu
　禪門師資承襲圖
chanshi yizhi　禪詩一致
Chen Zuolong　陳祚龍
Chengguan　澄觀
Chuan fabao ji　傳法寶紀
Congyi (Shenzhi)　神智從義

Da zhidu lun　大智度論
Daguan　達觀

Dahui Zonggao　大慧宗杲
Dainichi Nōnin　大日能忍
Daiō *kokushi*　大應國師
Daitō *kokushi*　大燈國師
Damo　達摩
Damo zong　達摩宗
Damoduoluo chan jing
　達摩多羅禪經
Daoxin　道信
Daoxuan　道宣
Daoyu　道育
Darumashū　達摩宗
Dasheng qixin lun　大乘起信論
Datong　大通
Deshan (Xuanjian)　德山宣鑑
diyi yi (daiichigi)　第一義
Dōgen (Kigen)　道元希玄
Dōjōji　道成寺
dokusan　獨參
Dongshan　東山
Dongshan (Liangjie)　洞山良价
dōtoku　道得
Du Fei　杜朏
Dunwu zhenzong yaojue
　頓悟眞宗要決

Eiheiji　永平寺
Ejō (Koun)　孤雲懷奘
Enmyō jikku Kannongyō
　延命十句觀音經
Enni Ben'en　圓爾辨圓
erru　二入
Erru sixing lun　二入四行論

Fachong　法沖
Faju jing　法句經
Faru　法如
Faxian　法顯
Faxiang　法相
Fazang　法藏
fojiao　佛敎
Fotuo　佛陀

Fozhao Deguang　佛照德光
Fu Xi　傳翕　(*Fu dashi* 傅大士)
Fujieda Akira　藤枝晃
Fuke　普化
Furuta Shōkin　古田紹欽
furyū monji　不立文字

Gabyō　画餅
Garandō　伽藍堂
genjō kōan　現成公案
Genkō shakusho　元亨釋書
genze riyaku　現世利益
gozan　五山
gozan bungaku　五山文學
Guan Di　關帝
Guan gong　關公
Guan Yu　關羽
guanbi　觀壁
Guangtong　光統
Guangxiao si　光孝寺
Guanxin lun　觀心論
guanxin shi　觀心釋
Guanyin　觀音
Guifeng (Zongmi)　圭峰宗密
Guishan Lingyou　潙山靈祐
gyōji　行持
Gyōnen　凝然

Ha-Kirishitan　破吉利支丹
Hakuin Ekaku　白隱慧鶴
Hakusan　白山
Han Ju　韓駒
Han Yu　韓愈
han-honji suijaku　反本地垂迹
Hanshan　寒山
Hanshan Deqing　憨山德清
he (katsu)　喝
heshang　和上
Hirata Atsutane　平田篤胤
Hisamatsu Shin'ichi　久松眞一
hōben　方便
Hōmon taikō　法門大綱
hongaku　本覺
Hongren　弘忍
Hongzhi Zhengjue　宏智正覺
Hongzhou　洪州

honji suijaku　本地垂迹
Hou Mochen Yan　候莫陳琰
Hu Shih　胡適
Huaguang (Kakō)　華光
Huatai　滑臺
huatou　話頭
Huayan　華嚴
Huayan jing shu　華嚴徑蔬
Huian　慧安
Huida　慧達
Huiguang　慧光
Huiguang (Dazhao)　大照慧光
Huihong (Juefan)　覺範慧洪
Huike　慧可
Huineng　慧能
Huiqi　會稽
Huiyuan　慧遠
Huiyuan (Huayan Master)　慧怨
huoju　活句
Hwaŏm　華嚴

Ikkyū Sōjun　一休宗純
Imakita Kōsen　今北洪川
Ingen Ryūki (Yinyuan Longqi)
　隱元隆琦
Iriya Yoshitaka　入矢義高
Ishii Shūdō　石井修道
Ishikawa Rikizan　石川力山

jakugo　著語
ji　機
ji (tera)　寺
jianxing (kenshō)　見性
jianxing chengfo　見性成佛
jiao　教
jiaochan yizhi　敎禪一致
jiaowai biechuan　敎外別傳
jinen gedō　自然外道
jinen hōni　自然法爾
jing　經
Jingang sanmei jing　金剛三昧經
Jingde chuandenglu　景德傳燈錄
Jingjue　淨覺
Jingzhong　淨衆
Jinnō shōtōki　神皇正統記
jisetsu innen　時節因綠

jiyuan　機緣
Jōdo shinshū　浄土眞宗
Jueguan lun　絕觀論
jūnanshin　柔軟心
Junkō　順高
junsui keiken　純粹経験

Kagamishima Genryū　鏡島元隆
Kakua　覺阿
Kamei Katsuichirō　亀井勝一郎
kanna-zen (*kanhua chan*)　看話禪
kannagara no michi　神道
Kanzan Egen　關山慧玄
karagokoro　唐心
Karatani Kōjin　柄谷行人
Kattō　葛藤
Kegon-zen　華嚴禪
Keisei sanshoku　渓声山色
Keizan Jōkin　瑩山紹瑾
kenmitsu bukkyō　顯密佛教
Kenshō jōbutsuron　見性成佛論
Kimura Taiken　木村泰賢
kirigami　切紙
Kitabatake Chikafusa　北畠親房
kōan (*gongan*)　公案
Kōjō　光定
Kokan Shiren　虎關師錬
kokutai　国体
kokuzu　黑豆
kongxu　空虛
konpon bukkyō　根本佛教
Kōsaka Masaaki　高坂正顯
kosoku　古則
kotodama　言靈
Kōyama Iwao　高山岩男
Kōzen gokoku ron　興禪護國論
kuangyan qiyu (see *kyōgen kigo*)
kuden　口傳
Kuroda Toshio　黑田俊雄
kyōge betsuden　教外別傳
kyōgen kigo　狂言綺語
kyōzen itchi　教禪一致

Laozi　老子
Lengqie shizi ji　楞伽師資記
Li Bai　李白

Li Madou　利瑪竇
Li Zhi　李贄
Li Zhiyi　李之儀
Liang Wudi　梁武帝
Lidai fabao ji　歷代法寶記
Lidai sanbao ji　歷代三寶記
liguan　理觀
ling　靈
Lingyun Zhiqin　靈雲志勤
Linji (Rinzai)　臨濟
Linji lu　臨濟錄
Linji Yixuan　臨濟義玄
liru　理入
Liu Kezhuang　劉克莊
Liu Wude　劉無得
Liu Xie　劉勰
Luoyang qielan ji　洛陽伽藍記

makyō　魔境
mana (*shinji*)　眞字
Manpukuji　萬福寺
Manzan Dōhaku　卍山道白
Mao shan　茅山
mappō shisō　末法思想
Matsumoto Bunzaburō
　松本文三郎
Matsumoto Shirō　松本史郎
Mazu Daoyi　馬祖道一
Meng Jiao　孟郊
Menzan Zuihō　面山瑞方
Miaoli yuancheng guan
　妙理圓成觀
miaowu　妙悟
mikkyō　密敎
Mile　彌勒
Mirai ki　未來記
Moheyan　摩訶衍
mokushō-zen　默照禪
mondō (*wenda*)　問答
Motoori Norinaga　本居宣長
Muchū mondō　夢中問答
Muhon Kakushin　無本覺心
mui no shinnin (*wuwei zhenren*)
　無位眞人
Mujaku Dōchū　無著道忠
mujō　無常

mujō seppō 無情說法
Mujū Ichien 無住一圓
mujunteki dōitsu 矛盾的同一
Musō Soseki 夢窓疎石
Myōe shōnin 明惠上人
myōkōnin 妙好人
Myōshinji 妙心寺

Nagai Masashi 長井正之
Nakamura Hajime 中村元
Nanhua si 南華寺
Nanjō Bun'yū 南條文雄
Nanpo Jōmyō 南浦紹明
Nanyue Huairang 南岳懷讓
Nanyue Huisi 南岳慧思
Nanzenji 南禪寺
nihonjinron 日本人論
Nishida Kitarō 西田幾多郎
Nishida tetsugaku 西田哲学
Nishitani Keiji 西谷啓治
Niutou 牛頭
Nukariya Kaiten 忽滑谷快天

Ōbaku 黃檗
Okakura Kakuzō 岡倉覺三
Ōtōkan 應燈關
Ou Yangxiu 歐陽修

panjiao 判教
Patuo 跋陀
Pozao Duo 破竈墮
Puhua 普化
Puji 普寂

qielan shen 伽藍神
Qingyuan Xingsi 青原行思
Qisong 契嵩

Rakugo 落語
Rankei Dōryū 蘭渓道隆
Ren Jiyu 任繼愈
Ryōkan 良寛

Saichō 最澄
Sakaino Kōyō 境野黃洋
Sanbyaku soku 三百則

sangoku shisō 三國思想
Sansheng 三聖
Sanshō dōei 傘松道詠
Sansui kyō 山水經
sanyuan bahui 三元八會
Sekiguchi Shindai 関口眞大
Sengcan 僧璨
Sengchou 僧稠
Sengna 僧那
Sengqie 僧伽
Sengzhao 僧肇
Senni gedō 先尼外道
Sessō 雪窓
Shaku Sōen 釋宗演
Shao Ling 少陵
Shaolin 少林
Shaseki shū 沙石集
Shen Deqian 沈德潛
Shenhui 神會
Shenqing 神清
shentong 神通
Shenxiu 神秀
Shide 拾得
shijie yinyuan (jisetsu innen)
　時節因緣
shikan taza 只管打坐
Shimaji Mokurai 島地默雷
shinbutsu bunri 神仏分離
shinjin datsuraku 心塵脱落
shinjin datsuraku 心身脱落
shinkoku 神國
shiroku benrei 四六駢儷 (驪)
shishi wu'ai 事事無礙
Shōbō genzō 正法眼藏
Shōtoku (Taishi) 聖德太子
Shoulengyan jing 首楞嚴經
Shūhō Myōchō 宗峰妙超
shushō ittō 修證一等
Sicong 思聰
siju 死句
Sikong Tu 司空圖
sokuhi 即非
sokushin jōbutsu 即心成佛
sokushin zebutsu 即心是佛
Sǒn 禪
Song gaosengzhuan 宋高僧傳

Song shan 嵩山
Su Shi 蘇軾 (Su Dongpo) 蘇東坡
Suzuki Daisetsu 鈴木大拙
Suzuki Shigetaka 鈴木成高
Suzuki Shōsan 鈴木正山

taigi meibun 大義名分
taigo zen 待悟禪
Takakusu Junjirō 高楠順次郎
talin 塔林
Tanabe Hajime 田邊元
Tanlin 曇林
Tendai 天台
Tenryūbune 天龍船
terakoya 寺子屋
tiandong 天洞
tianming 天命
Tiantai 天台
Tiantong Rujing 天童如淨
Tianzi 天子
Tōdaiji 東大寺
Tominaga Nakamoto 富永仲基
tōzen 東漸
Tsuji Zennosuke 辻善之介

Ueyama Daishun 上山大峻
Ui Hakuju 宇井伯壽
ui no shinnin (*youwei zhenren*)
　有位眞人
Ŭich'ŏn 義天
uji 有時
Umehara Takeshi 梅原猛

waka 和歌
waka soku darani 和歌即陀羅尼
Wang Chong 王充
Wanhui 萬廻
Watanabe Kaigyoku 渡辺海旭
Watsuji Tetsurō 和辻哲郎
wei wai wei 味外味
wen 文
Wenxin diaolong 文心雕龍
wenzi 文字
wenzi chan 文字禪
Wolun 臥輪
Wŏnhyo 元曉

Wu Zetian 武則天
Wugeng zhuan 五更轉
Wumen Huikai 無門慧開
Wumenguan 無門關
wunian 無念
wusheng 無生
Wusheng fangbian men
　無生方便門
wuwei 無爲
wuwei (Five Ranks) 五位
wuwei jiao 無爲敎
Wuxiang (Musang) 無相
wuxin (*mushin*) 無心
wuxing 五行
wuyi wunian mowang
　無憶無念莫忘
Wuzhu 無住

xianglong ta 降龍塔
Xiangyan Zhixian 香嚴智閑
xindi 心地
xindi famen 心地法門
Xinglu nan 行路難
xingqi 性起
xinzong 心宗
Xitan zhang 悉曇章
Xu gaosengzhuan 續高僧傳
Xuansha Shibei 玄沙師備
Xuanzang 玄奘
Xuefeng Yicun 雪峰義存
xuemo 血脈

Yabuki Keiki 矢吹慶輝
Yan You 嚴羽
Yanagida Seizan 柳田聖山
Yang Xi 楊羲
Yao dao ge 樂道歌
Yi jing 易經
Yifu 義福
yixin chuanxin 以心傳心
Yixing 一行
Yōkōji 永光寺
Yongping (Eihei) 永平
Yōsai (Eisai) 榮西
Yuangui 元珪
Yuanjue jing 圓覺經

Yuanren lun 原人論
yulu 語錄
yunji qiqian 雲笈七籤
yunshui 雲水
Yuquan shan 玉泉山

zenmitsu sōshu 禪密双修
Zenrin kushū 禪林句集
zenshū 禪宗
Zhang Shangyin 張商英
Zhanran 湛然
Zhaozhou (Congshen) 趙州從諗
Zhengfa yanzang 正法眼藏
Zhenyan (Shingon) 眞言

Zhida 智達
Zhikong 志空
Zhiyi 智顗
Zhong sheng dian ji 衆聖點記
Zhuangzi 莊子
Zhuhong (Yunqi) 雲棲袾宏
zhuoxi quan 卓錫泉
Zifang 子肪
Zōga 增賀
Zongjian 宗鑑
Zongmi (see Guifeng Zongmi)
zongtong 宗通
Zuozhuan 左傳
Zutang ji (Chodang chip) 祖堂集

BIBLIOGRAPHY

PRIMARY SOURCES

Baolin zhuan. Yanagida Seizan, ed., *Sōzō ichin Hōrinden, Dentō gyokuei shū.* Kyoto: Chūbun shuppansha, 1975.

Beishan lu, by Shenqing (fl. 8th cent.). *T.* 52, 2113.

Biyan lu. By Xuetou Chongxian (980–1052); commentary by Yuanwu Keqin (1063–1135). *T.* 48, 2003.

Chanlin sengbao zhuan, by Juefan Huihong (1071–1128). ZZ 1, 2B: 10, 3. (Taibei ed., vol. 137).

Chanmen jing. Apocryphon. Suzuki Daisetsu [D. T.], ed., *Suzuki Daisetsu zenshū,* vol. 3.

Chanmen shizi chengxi tu, by Guifeng Zongmi (780–841). ZZ 1, 2, 15. (Taibei ed., vol. 110).

Chanyuan qinggui, ZZ 1, 2, 16, 5. (Taibei ed., vol. 111). See also Kagamishima Genryū, Satō Tatsugen, and Kosaka Kiyū, eds. *Yakuchū Zen'en shingi.* Tokyo: Sōtōshū shūmuchō, 1972.

Chanyuan zhuquanji duxu, by Guifeng Zongmi. *T.* 48, 2015.

Chixiu Baizhang qinggui, by Dongyang Dehui. *T.* 48, 2025.

Chuan fabao ji, by Du Fei (n.d.). In Yanagida Seizan, ed., *Shoki no zenshi 1.* Tokyo: Chikuma shobō, 1971.

Chuanfa zhengzong ji, by Qi Song. *T.* 51, 2078.

Chuanxin fayao, by Pei Xiu (797–870). *T.* 47, 2012a.

Dahui shuwen. In *Daie sho,* ed., Araki Kengo. Tokyo: Chikuma shobō, 1969.

Damo dashi wuxing lun. Attr. to Bodhidharma. ZZ 1, 2, 15, 5. (Taibei ed., vol. 110).

Damo dashi xuemo lun. Attr. to Bodhidharma. ZZ 1, 2, 15, 5. (Taibei ed., vol. 110).

Dasheng qixin lun. Apocryphon. *T.* 32, 1666.

Dasheng wusheng fangbian men. *T.* 85, 2834.

Da Tang Zhongyue dong Xianjusi gu dade Gui heshang ji dechuang. In *Jinshi puzheng* 53: 7. Ed. *SKSLXB,* 7: 4849a–4850b.

Da zhidu lun. Attr. to Nāgārjuna. Trans. Kumārajīva. *T.* 25, 1509.

Denkōroku, by Keizan Jōkin (1268–1325). *T.* 82, 2585. In *Keizan,* ed., Tajima Hakudō. Tokyo: Kōdansha, 1978.

Dunwu rudao yaomen lun, by Dazhu Huihai (n. d.). ZZ 1, 2, 15, 5. (Taibei ed., vol. 110).

Eihei shingi, by Dōgen (1200–1253). *T.* 82, 2584.

Eihei Shōbōgenzō senbyō, by Mujaku Dōchū (1653–1744). In Kagamishima 1961.

Erru sixing lun. Attr. to Bodhidharma. In Yanagida 1969.

Fozu lidai tongzai [1344], by Meiwu Nianchang (1282–?). *T.* 49, 2036.

Fozu tongji [ca. 1258–1269], by Zhipan. *T.* 49, 2035.

Genkō shakusho [1322], by Kokan Shiren (1278–1346). *DNBZ* 62 470.

Guanxin lun [*Poxiang lun*]. Attr. to Shenxiu. *T.* 85, 2833.

Ha Kirishitan [1662], by Suzuki Shōsan. Woodblock printed ed. Kyoto: Zenke shorin ryūshiken.

Hōkyōki, by Dōgen. *SZ, Shūgen* 2, 1–12.

Hōmon taikō. Anon. In Shinagawa Kenritsu Kanazawa Bunko, ed., *Kanazawa bunko shiryō zensho: Butten I, Zensekihen*, 209–220. Yokohama: Kanazawa Bunko, 1974.

Honchō kōsōden, by Shiban (1626–1710). *DNBZ* 63, 472.

Jingang boruo bolomi jing [*Vajracchedikā*]. Trans. Kumārajīva. *T.* 8, 235.

Jingang sanmei jing. Apocryphon. *T.* 9, 273.

Jingde chuandeng lu [1004], by Daoyuan. *T.* 51, 2076.

Jiu Tang shu [compl. 945]. Attr. to Liu Xu (887–946). 16 vols. Beijing: Zhonghua shuju, 1975.

Jōtō shōgaku ron. Anon. In *Kanazawa bunko shiryō zensho: Butten I, Zensekihen*, ed. Shinagawa Kenritsu Kanazawa Bunko. Yokohama: Kanazawa Bunko, 1974.

Jueguan lun. In Suzuki Daisetsu, *Suzuki Daisetsu zenshū*, vol. 2. 1968. Tokyo: Iwanami shoten, 1980.

Keiran shūyō shū, by Kōshū (1276–1350). *T.* 76, 2410.

Keizan shingi [*Tōkoku shingi*], by Keizan Jōkin. *T.* 82, 2589.

Kōzen gokokuron, by Yōsai (1141–1215). *T.* 80, 2543.

Laozi. Ed. Sibu congkan. Shanghai: Shangwu yinshuguan, 1937–1938.

Lengqie shizi ji, by Jingjue (683–ca. 750). *T.* 85, 2837.

Liandeng huiyao [1183], by Wuming. *ZZ* 1, 2B, 9, 3–5. [Taibei ed., vol. 136]

Lidai fabao ji [ca. 774]. *T.* 51, 2075.

Lidai shenxian tongjian, comp. Xu Dao. Taibei: Guangwen, 1975.

Linji lu [*Zhenzhou Linji Huizhao chanshi yulu*], *T.* 47, 1985. See English trans., Fuller Sasaki 1975.

Lishi shenxian tidao tongjian, by Zhao Daoyi. *DZ* 139–148.

Liuzu dashi fabao tanjing. Attr. to Huineng (638–713). *T.* 48, 2008.

Mengqi bitan, by Shen Gua (1031–1095). *Mukei hitsudan*, ed. Umehara Kaoru. 3 vols. Tokyo: Heibonsha, 1978–1981.

Mohezhiguan, by Zhiyi (538–597). *T.* 46, 1911.

Muchū mondō, by Musō Soseki (1275–1351). Ed. Satō Taishun. Tokyo: Iwanami shoten, 1974 [1934].

Nanzong ding shifei lun, by Dugu Pei. *T.* 85, Annex. Also in *Shenhui heshang yiji*, ed. Hu Shi. 1930; reprint, Taibei: Hu Shi jiniankuan, 1970.

Quan Tang wen (ca. 1814). Comp. Dong Gao, et al. Taibei: Huawen shu ju, 1965.

Ru Lengqie jing [*Laṅkāvatāra-sūtra*]. *T.* 16, 671.

Shasekishū, by Mujū Ichien (1226–1312). Ed. Watanabe Tsunaya. Tokyo: Iwanami shoten, 1975 [1966].

Shenseng zhuan. *T.* 50, 2064.

Shimen zhengtong [1237], by Zongjian. *ZZ* 1, 2B, 3, 5. (Taibei ed., vol. 130).

Shiniu tu. *ZZ* 1, 2, 18.

Shōbōgenzō, by Dōgen (1200–1253). *T.* 82, 2582.

Shōbōgenzō zuimonki, by Ejō Kōun (1198–1290). Ed. Nishio Minoru. Nihon koten bungaku taikei 82. Tokyo: Iwanami shoten.

Shoulengyan jing. Apocryphon. *T.* 19, 945.

Shutsujō kōgo, by Tominaga Nakamoto (1715–1746). Kyōdo Jikō, ed. Tokyo: Ryūbunkan 1982.

Sokushin ki, by Shidō Bunan (1603–1676). In *Shidō Bunan zenji shū,* ed. Kōda Rentarō. Tokyo: Shunjūsha, 1956.

Song gaoseng zhuan, by Zanning. *T.* 50, 2061.

Songyue Gui chanshi yingtang ji, by Xu Chou. *QTW* 790, 17: 10435–10436.

Taiping guangji [978], by Li Fang (925–966) et al. Taibei: Guxin shuju, 1980.

Tang huiyao [961], by Wang Pu (932–982) et al. Ed. Yang Jialo. 3 vols. Taibei: Shijie shuju, 1974.

Tetsugen zenji kana hōgo. Ed. Akamatsu Shinmyō. Tokyo: Iwanami shoten, 1941.

Tōjō shitsunai danshi kenpi shiki [1749], by Menzan Zuihō (1683–1769). In *SZ* 15, Shitsuchū.

Weimojie jing [*Vimalakīrti-nirdeśa*]. Trans. Zhi Qian (fl. 3rd cent.). *T.* 14, 474.

Wudeng huiyuan [1252], by Huiming Daozuo. ZZ 1, 2B, 10–11. (Taibei ed., vol. 138).

Wumen guan, by Wumen Huikai (1183–1260). *T.* 48, 2005.

Wuxin lun. Attr. to Bodhidharma. *T.* 85, 2831.

Xin Tang shu. [1043–1060]. Comp. by Ouyang Xiu (1007–1072), Song Qi (998–1061), et al. 20 vols. Beijing: Zhonghua shuju, 1975.

Xinwang ming. Attr. to Fu Xi (497–569). In *T.* 51, 2076: 456–457.

Xitan zhang, T. 85, 2779.

Xiuxin yaolun [*Zuishangsheng lun*]. Attr. to Hongren (601–674). *T.* 48, 2011.

Xu gaoseng zhuan, by Daoxuan. *T.* 50, 2060.

Youyang zazu, by Duan Chengshi. Imamura Yoshio, ed., *Yuyō zasso.* 5 vols. Tokyo: Heibonsha, 1980–1981.

Yuanjue jing. Apocryphon. *T.* 17, 842.

Yuanjue jing dashu chao, by Zongmi. ZZ 1, 14, 3–5; 15, 1. (Taibei ed., vols. 14–15).

Yuanren lun, by Zongmi (780–841). *T.* 45, 1886.

Zengfa yanzang, by Dahui Zonggao (1089–1163). ZZ 1, 2, 23. (Taibei ed., vol. 118).

Zenrin shōkisen, by Mujaku Dōchū (1653–1744). In *Zenrin shōkisen; Kattō gosen jikkan; Zenrin kushū benmyō,* ed. Yanagida Seizan. Vol. 1. Kyoto: Chūbun shuppansha, 1979.

Zhao lun, by Sengzhao (384–414?). *T.* 45, 1858.

Zhengdao ge, by Yongjia. *T.* 48, 2014.

Zhenzong lun [*Dasheng kaixin xianxing dunwu zhenzong lun*]. *T.* 85, 2835.

Zhonglun [*Madhyamakakārikā*], by Nāgārjuna. *T.* 30, 1564.

Zhuangzi. Attr. to Zhuang Zhou; commentary by Guo Xiang. Ed. Sibu beiyao. Taibei: Zhonghua shuju.

Zongjing lu, by Yongming Yanshou (904–975). *T.* 48, 2016.

Zutang ji (K. *Chodang chip,* 952). In *Sōdōshū,* ed. Yanagida Seizan. Kyoto: Chūbun shuppansha, 1974.

Zuting shiyuan [1108], by Muan Shanqing. ZZ 1, 2, 18, 1. (Taibei ed., vol. 113). See also *Chanxue dacheng,* ed. Xieguan Shengti. Vol. 3. Taibei: Zhonghua fojiao wenhua guan, 1969.

SECONDARY SOURCES

Abe Masao. 1985. *Zen and Western Thought*. Honolulu: University of Hawaii Press.

Allen, N. J. 1985. "The Category of the Person: A Reading of Mauss's Last Essay." In *The Category of the Person: Anthropology, Philosophy, History*, ed. Michael Carrithers, Steven Collins, and Steven Lukes, 26–45. Cambridge: Cambridge University Press.

Almond, Philip C. 1988. *The British Discovery of Buddhism*. Cambridge: Cambridge University Press.

Althusser, Louis. 1972. *Lenin and Philosophy and Other Essays*. Trans. Ben Brewster. New York: Monthly Review Foundation.

Ames, Van Meter. 1962. *Zen and American Thought*. Honolulu: University of Hawaii Press.

Ampère, Jean-Jacques. 1832–1833. "De la Chine et des travaux d'Abel Rémusat." *Revue des deux mondes* (1833): 361–395.

Anesaki Masaharu. 1921. *Quelques pages de l'histoire religieuse du Japon: Conférences faites au Collège de France*. Annales du Musée Guimet. Paris: Bernard.

———. 1930. "Japanese Criticisms and Refutation of Christianity in the Seventeenth and Eighteenth Centuries." *Transactions of the Asiatic Society of Japan* 7: 1–15.

App, Urs. 1987. "Ch'an/Zen's Greatest Encyclopaedist Mujaku Dōchū (1653–1744)." *Cahiers d'Extrême-Asie* 3: 155–174.

Arima Tatsuo. 1969. *The Failure of Freedom: A Portrait of Modern Japanese Intellectuals*. Cambridge: Harvard University Press.

Armogathe, Jean-Robert. 1973. *Le quiétisme*. Que Sais-je? 1545. Paris: Presses Universitaires de France.

Arnold, Sir Edwin. [1879] 1884. *The Light of Asia*. New York: Crowell and Co.

Artaud, Antonin. 1976. *Selected Writings*. Ed. Susan Sontag. Trans. Helen Weaver. Berkeley: University of California Press.

Asada Akira. 1983. *Kōzō to chikara: kigōron o koete* (Structure and Power: Beyond Semiotics). Tokyo: Keisō shobō.

———. 1988. "Infantile Capitalism and Japan's Postmodernism: A Fairy Tale." *South Atlantic Review* 87, 3: 629–634.

Aubin, Françoise. 1987. "Missionnaires en Chine . . . Missionnaires sur la Chine . . ." *Archives de sciences sociales des religions* 63, 2: 177–188.

Augé, Marc. 1982a. *The Anthropological Circle: Symbol, Function, History*. Cambridge: Cambridge University Press.

———. 1982b. *Le génie du paganisme*. Paris: Gallimard.

Austin, J. L. 1962. *How to Do Things with Words*. Cambridge: Harvard University Press.

Bachelard, Gaston. 1964. *La poétique de l'espace*. Paris: Presses Universitaires de France.

Bakhtin, Mikhail. 1968. *Rabelais and his World*. Trans. H. Iswolsky. Cambridge: MIT Press.

———. 1970. *L'oeuvre de François Rabelais et la culture populaire au Moyen Age et sous la Renaissance.* Paris: Gallimard. (The French transcription of his name differs from the English).

———. 1981. *The Dialogic Imagination: Four Essays.* Austin: University of Texas Press.

———. 1986. *Speech Genres and Other Late Essays.* Trans. Vern W. McGee. Austin: University of Texas Press.

Balasooriya, Somaratna, ed. 1980. *Buddhist Studies in Honour of Walpola Rahula.* London: Gordon Fraser.

Balazs, Etienne. 1961. "L'histoire comme guide de la pratique bureaucratique (les monographies, les encyclopédies, les recueils de statuts)." In *Historians of China and Japan,* ed. W. G. Beasley and E. G. Pulleyblank. London: School of Oriental and African Studies, 78–94.

———. 1968. *La bureaucratie céleste: Recherches sur l'économie et la société de la Chine traditionnelle.* Paris: Gallimard.

Bareau, André. 1973. "La notion de personne dans le bouddhisme indien." In *Problèmes de la personne,* ed. Ignace Meyerson, 83–98. Colloque du Centre de Recherches de Psychologie Comparative. Paris: Mouton and Co.

Barrett, Timothy H. 1989. "Arthur Waley, D. T. Suzuki and Hu Shih: New Light on the 'Zen and History' Controversy." *Buddhist Studies Review* 6, 2: 116–121.

Barthélemy Saint-Hilaire, Jules. 1862. *Le Bouddha et sa religion,* Paris: Didier.

———. 1895. *The Buddha and his Religion.* London: George Routledge.

Barthes, Roland. 1982. *The Empire of Signs.* Trans. Richard Howard. New York: Hill and Wang.

———. 1983. "Introduction to the Structural Analysis of Narratives." In Roland Barthes, *Selected Writings,* 251–295. Glasgow: Fontana Paperbacks.

Bataille, George. 1973. *Oeuvres complètes.* Vol. 6. Paris: Gallimard.

Bayle, Pierre. 1697. *Dictionnaire historique et critique.* 4 vols. Rotterdam: R. Leers.

———. 1734–1738. *The Dictionary Historical and Critical of Mr. Peter Bayle.* 2d ed. London: J. J. and P. Knapton.

———. 1983. *Ecrits sur Spinoza.* Paris: L'Autre Rive.

Beal, Samuel. 1871. *A Catena of Buddhist Scriptures from the Chinese.* London: Trübner and Co.

———. 1884. *Buddhism in China.* London: S.P.C.K.

Bellah, N. Robert. 1985. "The Meaning of Dōgen Today." In *Dōgen Studies,* ed. William R. LaFleur, 150–158. Honolulu: University of Hawaii Press.

Belmont, Nicole. 1979. *Arnold van Gennep: The Creator of French Ethnography.* Trans. Derek Coltman. Chicago: University of Chicago Press.

Benveniste, Emile. 1966–1974. *Problèmes de linguistique générale.* 2 vols. Paris: Gallimard.

Benz, Ernst. 1962. *Zen in Westlicher Sicht: Zen-Buddhismus—Zen-Snobismus.* Weilheim/Oberbayern: Otto Wilhelm Barth.

Berger, Peter L., and Thomas Luckmann. 1967. *The Social Construction of Reality.* New York: Anchor Books.

Berling, Judith A. 1980. *The Syncretic Religion of Lin Chao-en.* New York: Columbia University Press.

———. 1985. "Self and Whole in Chuang Tzu." In *Individualism and Holism: Studies in Confucian and Taoist Values*, ed. Donald J. Munro, 101–120. Ann Arbor: Center for Chinese Studies, University of Michigan.

———. 1987. "Bringing the Buddha Down to Earth: Notes on the Emergence of *Yü-lu* as a Buddhist Genre." *History of Religions* 21, 1: 56–88.

Bernard [Bernard-Maître], Henri, S.J. 1933. *Aux Portes de la Chine: Les missionnaires du XVIe siècle, 1514–1588*. Tien-tsin: Hautes Etudes.

———. 1935. *Sagesse chinoise et philosophie chrétienne: Essai sur leurs relations historiques*. Tien-tsin: Hautes Etudes.

———. 1937. *Le Père Matthieu Ricci et la société chinoise de son temps (1552–1610)*. 2 vols. Tien-tsin: Hautes Etudes.

———. 1941. "Hīnāyāna indien et Mahāyāna japonais: Comment l'Occident a-t-il découvert le Bouddhisme?" *Monumenta Nipponica* 4: 284–289.

Berque, Augustin. 1986. *Le sauvage et l'artifice: Les Japonais devant la nature*. Paris: Gallimard.

Bielefeldt, Carl. 1979. "Dōgen's *Shōbōgenzō Sansuikyō*." In *The Mountain Spirit*, ed. Michael Charles Tobias and Harold Drasdo Woodstock, N.Y.: Overlook Press.

———. 1985. "Recarving the Dragon: History and Dogma in the Study of Dōgen." In *Dōgen Studies*, ed. William R. LaFleur, 21–53. Honolulu: University of Hawaii Press.

———. 1988. "Rethinking Zen Studies: The Case of Sacred History." Ms.

Billeter, Jean-François. 1979. *Li Zhi, philosophe maudit (1527–1602): Contribution à une sociologie du mandarinat chinois à la fin des Ming*. Geneva: Librairie Droz.

Blake, William. 1966. *Complete Writings*. Ed. Geoffrey Keynes. Oxford: Oxford University Press.

Bloom, Harold. 1973. *The Anxiety of Influence: A Theory of Poetry*. Oxford: Oxford University Press.

Bloss, Lowell W. 1973. "The Buddha and the Nāga: A Study in Buddhist Folk Religiosity." *History of Religions* 13, 1: 36–53.

Blyth, Richard H. 1960–1964. *Zen and Zen Classics*. 7 vols. Tokyo: Hokuseidō Press.

Bodiford, William M. 1989. "The Growth of the Sōtō Zen Tradition in Medieval Japan." Ph.D. diss., Yale University.

Boon, James A. 1982. *Other Tribes, Other Scribes: Symbolic Anthropology in the Comparative Study of Cultures, Histories, Religions and Texts*. Cambridge: Cambridge University Press.

Borges, Jorge Luis. 1964. *Labyrinths*. Ed. Donald A. Yates and James E. Irby. Trans. Donald A. Yates et al. New York: New Directions.

Bourdieu, Pierre. 1977. *Outline of a Theory of Practice*. Cambridge: Cambridge University Press.

———. 1979. *La distinction: Critique sociale du jugement*. Paris: Minuit.

———. 1980. *Le sens pratique*. Paris: Minuit.

———. 1982. *Ce que parler veut dire: L'économie des échanges linguistiques*. Paris: Fayard.

———. 1988. *L'ontologie politique de Martin Heidegger*. Paris: Minuit.

Boxer, Charles Ralph. 1951. *The Christian Century in Japan, 1549–1650.* Berkeley: University of California Press.

Brandauer, Frederick P. 1968. "The Encounter between Christianity and Chinese Buddhism from the Fourteenth Century through the Seventeenth Century." *Ching Feng* 11, 3: 30–38.

Braudel, Fernand. 1969. *Ecrits sur l'histoire.* Paris: Flammarion.

———. 1980. Trans. Sarah Matthews. *On History.* Chicago: University of Chicago Press.

Brémond, Claude. 1964. "Le message narratif." *Communications* 4: 4–32.

———. 1973. *Logique du récit.* Paris: Seuil.

Brown, C. Mackenzie. 1986. "Purāṇa as Scripture: From Sound to Image of the Holy Word in the Hindu Tradition." *History of Religions* 26, 1: 68–86.

Brown, Peter. 1981. *The Cult of the Saints: Its Rise and Function in Latin Christianity.* Chicago: University of Chicago Press.

———. 1988. *The Body and Society: Men, Women, and Sexual Renunciation in Early Christianity.* New York: Columbia University Press.

Burnouf, Eugène. 1844. *Introduction à l'histoire du Bouddhisme indien.* Paris: Imprimerie Royale.

———. [1852] 1973. *Le Lotus de la bonne loi.* 2 vols. Paris: Adrien Maisonneuve.

Buswell, Robert E., Jr. 1987. The "Short-cut" Approach of *K'an-hua* Meditation: The Evolution of a Practical Subitism in Chinese Ch'an Buddhism." In *Sudden and Gradual: Approaches to Enlightenment in Chinese Thought,* ed. Peter N. Gregory, 321–377. Honolulu: University of Hawaii Press.

———. 1988. "Ch'an Hermeneutics: A Korean View." In *Buddhist Hermeneutics,* ed. Donald S. Lopez, Jr., 231–256. Honolulu: University of Hawaii Press.

———, ed. 1989. *Chinese Buddhist Apocrypha.* Honolulu: University of Hawaii Press.

Carrithers, Michael, Steven Collins, and Steven Lukes, eds. 1985. *The Category of the Person: Anthropology, Philosophy, History.* Cambridge: Cambridge University Press.

Carroll, Lewis. 1960. *Alice's Adventures in Wonderland and Through the Looking Glass.* New York: New American Library.

de Certeau, Michel. 1975. *L'écriture de l'histoire.* Paris: Gallimard.

———. 1982. *La fable mystique: XVIe–XVIIe siècle.* Paris: Gallimard.

———. 1984. *The Practice of Everyday Life.* Berkeley: University of California Press.

———. 1986. *Heterologies: Discourse on the Other.* Trans. Brian Massumi. Minneapolis: University of Minnesota Press.

———. 1988. *The Writing of History.* Trans. Tom Conley. New York: Columbia University Press.

———. [1980] 1990. *L'invention de la vie quotidienne.* Vol. 1. *Arts de faire.* Paris: Folio. English trans. 1984.

Chappell, David W. 1988. "Hermeneutical Phases in Chinese Buddhism." In *Buddhist Hermeneutics,* ed. Donald S. Lopez, Jr., 175–205. Honolulu: University of Hawaii Press.

Charles, Michel. 1985. *L'arbre et la source.* Paris: Seuil.

Charlevoix, Pierre François Xavier de, S.J. 1828. *Histoire de l'établissement, du progrès et de la décadence du Christianisme dans l'empire du Japon*. 2 vols. Paris: Rusand.

⸻. 1836. *Histoire et Description Générale du Japon*. Vol. 5. Paris: Julien-Michel Gandouin.

Chartier, Roger. 1988. *Cultural History: Between Practices and Representations*. Trans. Lydia G. Cochrane. Ithaca: Cornell University Press.

Chavannes, Edouard. [1910] 1970. *Le T'ai Chan: Essai de monographie d'un culte chinois*. Taibei: Chengwen.

⸻. 1919. "Le jet des dragons." In *Mémoires concernant l'Asie orientale* 3: 53–220. Paris: Ernest Leroux.

Chen Yuan. 1977. *Zhongguo fojiao zhi lishi yanjiu* (Studies in the History of Chinese Buddhism). Taibei: Jiuxiang chubanshe.

Chidester, David. 1985. "Word against Light: Perception and the Conflict of Symbols." *The Journal of Religion* 65, 1: 46–62.

Childs, Margaret H. 1980. "Kyōgen-kigo: Love Stories as Buddhist Sermons." *Japanese Journal of Religious Studies* 12, 1: 91–104.

Cibot, Martial, ed. 1776–1814. *Mémoires concernant l'histoire, les sciences, les arts, les moeurs, les usages, etc. des Chinois par les missionnaires de Pékin*. 16 vols. Paris: Nyon.

Claudel, Paul. [1900] 1974. *Connaissance de l'Est: Suivi de L'oiseau noir dans le soleil levant*. Paris: Gallimard.

Cleary, Christopher [J. C.], trans. 1977. *Swampland Flowers: The Letters and Lectures of Zen master Ta Hui*. New York: Grove Press.

Cleary, Thomas, trans. 1990. *Transmission of the Light (Denkōroku: Zen in the Art of Enlightenment by Master Keizan)*. San Francisco: North Point Press.

Cleary, Thomas, and J. C. Cleary, trans. 1977. *The Blue Cliff Record*. 3 vols. Boulder: Shambala.

Clifford, James, and George E. Marcus, eds. 1986. *Writing Culture: The Poetics and Politics of Ethnography*. Berkeley: University of California Press.

Coleridge, Henry James. 1890. *The Life and Letters of Saint Francis Xavier*. 2 vols. London.

Collcutt, Martin. 1981. *Five Mountains: The Rinzai Zen Monastic Institution in Medieval Japan*. Cambridge: Harvard University Press.

⸻. 1986. "Buddhism: The Threat of Eradication." In *Japan in Transition: From Tokugawa to Meiji*, ed. Marius Jansen and Gilbert Rozman, 143–167. Princeton: Princeton University Press.

Collins, Steven. 1982. *Selfless Persons: Imagery and Thought in Theravāda Buddhism*. Cambridge: Cambridge University Press.

⸻. 1985. "Categories, Concepts or Predicaments? Remarks on Mauss's Use of Philosophical Terminology." In *The Category of the Person: Anthropology, Philosophy, History*, ed. Michael Carrithers, Steven Collins, and Steven Lukes, 46–82. Cambridge: Cambridge University Press.

Conze, Edward. 1961. "Dr. Koestler and the Wisdom of the East." *Hibbert Journal* 59: 178–181.

⸻. 1968. *Thirty Years of Buddhist Studies: Selected Essays*. Columbia: University of South Carolina Press.

Cook, Francis H. 1985. "Dōgen's View of Authentic Selfhood and its Socio-ethical Implications." In *Dōgen Studies*, ed. William R. LaFleur, 131–149. Honolulu: University of Hawaii Press.

Cooke, Gerald. 1974. "Traditional Buddhist Sects and Modernization in Japan." *Japanese Journal of Religious Studies* 1, 4: 267–330.

Couplet, Philippe. 1683. *Confucius Sinarum Philosophus: Sive, scientia sinensis latine exposita.* Paris: D. Horthemels.

Cros, Léonard Joseph-Marie, S.J. 1900. *Saint François de Xavier de la Compagnie de Jésus: Son pays, sa famille, sa vie; documents nouveaux.* 2 vols. Toulouse: E. Privat.

Culbertson, Michael S. 1857. *Darkness in the Flowery Land.* New York: Charles Scribner.

Culler, Jonathan. 1982. *On Deconstruction: Theory and Criticism after Structuralism.* Ithaca: Cornell University Press.

Davis, John F. 1857. *China: A General Description of that Empire and its Inhabitants.* 2 vols. London: John Murray.

Dawson, Raymond. 1967. *The Chinese Chameleon: An Analysis of European Conceptions of Chinese Civilization.* London: Oxford University Press.

de Bary, Brett. 1988. "Karatani Kōjin's *Origins of Modern Japanese Literature.*" *South Atlantic Quarterly* 87, 3: 591–613.

de Bary, Wm. Theodore, ed. 1970. *Self and Society in Ming Thought.* New York: Columbia University Press.

Delehaye, Hippolyte. [1905] 1962. *The Legends of the Saints.* Trans. Donald Attwater. New York: Fordham University Press.

Deleuze, Gilles, and Félix Guattari. 1983. *On the Line.* Trans. John Johnston. New York: Semiotext(e).

de Man, Paul de. 1979. *Allegories of Reading: Figural Language in Rousseau, Nietzsche, Rilke, and Proust.* New Haven: Yale University Press.

———. 1983. *Blindness and Insight: Essays in the Rhetoric of Contemporary Criticism.* Minneapolis: University of Minnesota Press.

DeMartino, Richard, Erich Fromm, and D. T. Suzuki. 1970. *Zen Buddhism and Psychoanalysis.* New York: Harper & Row.

Demiéville, Paul. 1927. "Sur la mémoire des existences antérieures." *BEFEO* 27: 283–298.

———. 1952. *Le concile de Lhasa: Une controverse sur le quiétisme entre les bouddhistes de l'Inde et de la Chine au VIIIe siècle de l'ère chrétienne.* Paris: Presses Universitaires de France.

———. 1957. "Le bouddhisme et la guerre: Post-scriptum à l'*Histoire des moines-guerriers du Japon* de G. Renondeau." *Mélanges publiés par l'Institut des Hautes Etudes Chinoises,* 347–385. Paris: Presses Universitaires de France.

———. 1961. "Deux documents de Touen-houang sur le Dhyāna chinois." In *Essays on the History of Buddhism presented to Professor Zenryū Tsukamoto,* 1–27. Kyoto: Nagai shuppansha.

———. 1962. "Langue et littérature chinoises." *Annuaire du Collège de France,* 329–336. Paris: Collège de France.

———. 1966. "Aperçu historique des études sinologiques en France." *Acta Asiatica* 11: 56–110.

———. 1967. "The First Philosophical Contacts between Europe and China." *Diogenes* 58: 75–103.

———. 1972. *Entretiens de Lin-tsi.* Paris: Fayard.

———. 1973a. *Choix d'études bouddhiques (1929–1970).* Leiden: E. J. Brill.

———. 1973b. *Choix d'études sinologiques (1929–1970).* Leiden: E. J. Brill.

———. 1978. "Appendice sur 'Damoduolo' (Dharmatrā[ta])." In Jao Tsong-yi et al., *Peintures monochromes de Tun-huang (Dunhuang baihua)*, 43–49. Paris: Ecole Française d'Extrême-Orient.

———. [1947] 1987. *The Mirror of the Mind.* In *Sudden and Gradual: Approaches to Enlightenment in Chinese Thought*, ed. Peter N. Gregory, 13–40. Honolulu: University of Hawaii Press.

Derrida, Jacques. 1967. *L'écriture et la différence.* Paris: Seuil.

———. 1970. "Structure, Sign, and Play in the Discourse of the Human Sciences." In *The Structuralist Controversy: The Languages of Criticism and the Sciences of Man*, ed. Richard Macksey and Eugenio Donato, 247–272. Baltimore: Johns Hopkins University Press.

———. 1972a. *Marges de la philosophie.* Paris: Minuit.

———. 1972b. *Positions.* Paris: Minuit.

———. [1967] 1974. *Of Grammatology.* Trans. Gayatri C. Spivak. Baltimore: Johns Hopkins University Press.

———. 1978. "The Rhetoric of Metaphor." *Enclitic* 2: 5–33.

———. 1981. *Dissemination.* Trans. Barbara Johnson. Chicago: University of Chicago Press.

———. 1986. *Memoirs.* New York: Columbia University Press.

———. 1987a. *Psyché: Inventions de l'autre.* Paris: Galilée.

———. 1987b. "Comment ne pas parler: Dénégations." In Jacques Derrida, *Psyché: Inventions de l'autre*, 535–595. Paris: Galilée.

———. 1988a. *Limited Inc.* Trans. Samuel Weber. Evanston: Northwestern University Press.

———. 1988b. *Mémoires pour Paul de Man.* Paris: Galilée.

Detienne, Marcel. 1973. "Ebauche de la personne dans la Grèce archaïque." In *Problèmes de la personne*, ed. Ignace Meyerson, 45–54. Paris: Mouton and Co.

———. 1986b. *The Creation of Mythology.* Trans. Margaret Cook. Chicago: University of Chicago Press.

Detienne, Marcel, and Jean-Pierre Vernant. 1974. *Les ruses de l'intelligence: La mètis des Grecs.* Paris: Flammarion.

———. 1978. *Cunning Intelligence in Greek Culture and Society.* Trans. Janet Lloyd. Atlantic Highlands: Humanities Press.

Dilworth, David A. 1969. "The Initial Formations of 'Pure Experience' in Nishida Kitarō and William James." *Monumenta Nipponica* 24, 1–2: 93–111.

———. 1970a. "Nishida Kitarō (1870–1945): The Development of his Thought." Ph.D. diss., Columbia University.

———. 1970b. "Nishida's Final Essay: The Logic of Place and a Religious Worldview." *Philosophy East and West* 20, 4: 355–367.

———. 1978. "Suzuki Daisetz as Regional Ontologist: Critical Remarks on Reading Suzuki's *Japanese Spirituality*." *Philosophy East and West* 28: 99–110.

Dinouart, Abbé. [1771] 1987. *L'art de se taire.* Paris: Jérome Millon.

Doré, Henri, S.J. 1914–1929. *Recherches sur les superstitions en Chine*. 15 vols. Shanghai: T'usewei Press.

———. 1914–1938. *Researches into Chinese Superstitions*. Trans. M. Kennely, S. J. 11 vols. Shanghai: T'usewei Press.

Dreyfus, Hubert L., and Paul Rabinow. 1983. *Michel Foucault: Beyond Structuralism and Hermeneutics*. Chicago: University of Chicago Press.

———. 1986. "What is Maturity? Habermas and Foucault on 'What is Enlightenment?'" In *Foucault: A Critical Reader*, ed. David Couzens Hoy, 109–122. London: Basil Blackwell.

du Halde, Jean-Baptiste. 1735. *Description géographique, historique, chronologique, politique et physique de l'Empire de la Chine et de la Tartarie chinoise*. 4 vols. Paris.

———. 1741. *The General History of China: Containing a geographical, historical, chronological, political and physical description of the Empire of China, Chinese-Tartary, Corea and Thibet*. London: J. Watts.

Du Songbo. 1976. *Chanxue yu Tang Song shixue* (Chan Studies and Studies on Tang and Song Poetry). Taibei: Liming wenhua shiye gongsi.

Duara, Prasenjit. 1988. "Superscribing Symbols: The Myth of Guandi, Chinese God of War." *Journal of Asian Studies* 47, 4: 778–795.

Dubose, Hampden C. 1886. *The Dragon, Image and Demon, or the Three Religions of China*. London: S. W. Partridge and Co.

Duby, Georges. 1974. "Histoire sociale et idéologie des sociétés." In *Faire de l'histoire*, ed. Jacques Le Goff and Pierre Nora, Vol. 1. *Nouveaux problèmes*, 203–230. Paris Gallimard.

Ducrot, Oswald, and Tzvetan Todorov. 1972. *Dictionnaire encyclopédique des sciences du langage*. Paris: Seuil.

———. 1979. *Encyclopedic Dictionary of the Sciences of Language*. Trans. Catherine Porter. Baltimore: Johns Hopkins University Press.

Dumont, Louis. [1960] 1971. "World Renounciation in Indian Religions." *Contributions to Indian Sociology* 4: 33–62. Reprint. Louis Dumont, *Religion, Politics and History in India*, 33–60. Paris: Mouton.

———. 1966. *Homo Hierarchicus: Le système des castes et ses implications*. Paris: Gallimard.

———. 1972. *Homo Hierarchicus: The Caste System and its Implications*. London: Paladin.

———. 1971. "The Individual as an Impediment to Sociological Comparison in Indian History." In *Religion, Politics and History in India*, 133–150. Paris: Mouton.

———. 1973. "Absence de l'individu dans les institutions de l'Inde." In *Problèmes de la personne*, ed. Ignace Meyerson, 99–109. Colloque du Centre de Recherches de Psychologie Comparative. Paris: Mouton.

———. 1985. "A Modified View of our Origins: The Christian Beginnings of Modern Individualism." In *The Category of the Person: Anthropology, Philosophy, History*, ed. Michael Carrithers, Steven Collins, and Steven Lukes, 93–122. Cambridge: Cambridge University Press.

Dumoulin, Heinrich, S.J. 1963. *A History of Zen Buddhism*. New York: Random House.

————. 1981. "Buddhism and Nineteenth Century German Philosophy." Trans. Julia Ching. *Journal of the History of Ideas* 42, 3: 457–470.

————. 1984. "The Person in Buddhism: Religious and Artistic Aspects." *Japanese Journal of Religious Studies* 11, 2–3: 143–167.

————. 1988–1990. *Zen Buddhism: A History*. Trans. James W. Heisig and Paul Knitter. 2 vols. New York: Macmillan Publishing Company.

Dunne, George, S.J. 1962. *Generation of Giants: The Story of the Jesuits in China in the Last Decades of the Ming Dynasty*. London: Burns and Oates.

Durkheim, Emile. [1915] 1965. *The Elementary Forms of the Religious Life: A Study in Religious Sociology*. Trans. Joseph W. Swain. New York: Free Press.

Durkheim, Emile, and Marcel Mauss. [1903] 1963. *Primitive Classification*. Trans. Rodney Needham. Chicago: University of Chicago Press.

Durt, Hubert. 1983. "Daigenshuri." In *Hōbōgirin* 6: 599–609.

————. 1987. "The Meaning of Archeology in Ancient Buddhism: Notes on the Stūpas of Aśoka and the Worship of the 'Buddhas of the Past' According to Three Stories in the *Samguk Yusa*. In *Buddhism and Science: Commemorative Volume for the 80th Anniversary of the Founding of Tongguk University*, 1223–1241. Seoul: Tongguk University.

————. 1988. "La date du Buddha en Corée et au Japon." Paper presented at the Göttingen Symposium on the Date of the Historical Buddha and the Importance of Its Determination for Historiography and World History.

Eberhard, Wolfram. 1967. *Guilt and Sin in Traditional China*. Berkeley: University of California Press.

Eco, Umberto. 1989. *Foucault's Pendulum*. Trans. William Weaver. San Diego: Harcourt Brace Jovanovich.

Edkins, Joseph. 1890. *Chinese Buddhism: A Volume of Sketches, historical, descriptive, and critical*. London: Kegan Paul, Trench, Trübner and Co.

Edkins, Joseph. 1893. *Religion in China: Containing a Brief Account of the Three Religions of the Chinese*. Revised ed. London: Kegan Paul, Trench, Trübner and Co.

Eitel, Ernest J. 1884. *Buddhism: Its Historical, Theoretical and Popular Aspects*. London: Trübner and Co.

Eliade, Mircea. 1959. *The Sacred and the Profane: The Nature of Religion*. Trans. Willard R. Trask. New York: Harcourt, Brace.

Elison, George. 1973. *Deus Destroyed: The Image of Christianity in Early Modern Japan*. Cambridge: Harvard University Press.

Elster, Jon. 1983. *Sour Grapes: Studies in the Subversion of Rationality*. Cambridge: Cambridge University Press.

Elvin, Mark. 1985. "Between the Earth and Heaven: Conceptions of the Self in China." In *The Category of the Person: Anthropology, Philosophy, History*, ed. Michael Carrithers, Steven Collins, and Steven Lukes, 156–189. Cambridge: Cambridge University Press.

Escayrac de Lauture. 1865. *Mémoires sur la Chine*. Paris: Librairie du Magasin Pittoresque.

Etiemble, René. 1964. *Connaissons-nous la Chine?* Paris: Gallimard.

————. 1988–1989. *L'Europe chinoise*. 2 vols. Paris: Gallimard.

Fabian, Johannes. 1983. *Time and the Other: How Anthropology Makes its Object*. New York: Columbia University Press.

Fader, Larry A. 1976. "The Philosophically Significant Western Understandings of D. T. Suzuki's Interpretation of Zen and Their Influence on Occidental Culture Examined Critically in Relation to Suzuki's Thought as Contained in His English-Language Writings." Ph.D. diss., Temple University.

———. 1980. "Arthur Koestler's Criticism of D. T. Suzuki's Interpretation of Zen." *The Eastern Buddhist* 13, 2: 46–72.

———. 1982. "Zen in the West: Historical and Philosophical Implications of the 1893 Chicago World's Parliament of Religions." *The Eastern Buddhist* 15, 1: 122–145.

———. 1986. "D. T. Suzuki's Contribution to the West." In *A Zen Life: D. T. Suzuki Remembered*, ed. Abe Masao, 95–108. New York: Weatherhill.

Faure, Bernard. 1983. "Shen-hsiu et l'*Avataṃsaka*." *Zinbun* 19: 1–15.

———. 1986a. *Le Traité de Bodhidharma: Première anthologie du bouddhisme Chan*. Paris: Le Mail.

———. 1986b. "Bodhidharma as Textual and Religious Paradigm." *History of Religions* 25, 3: 187–198.

———. 1986c. "Le maître de dhyāna Chih-ta et le 'subitisme' de l'école du Nord." *Cahiers d'Extrême-Asie* 2: 123–132.

———. 1987a. *La vision immédiate: Nature, éveil et tradition selon le Shōbō-genzō*. Paris: Le Mail.

———. 1987b. "The Daruma-shū, Dōgen and Sōtō Zen." *Monumenta Nipponica* 42, 1: 25–55.

———. 1987c. "Space and Place in Chinese Religious Traditions." *History of Religions* 26, 4: 337–356.

———. 1988. *La volonté d'orthodoxie dans le bouddhisme chinois*. Paris: Editions du C.N.R.S.

———. 1989. *Le bouddhisme Ch'an en mal d'histoire: Genèse d'une tradition religieuse dans la Chine des T'ang*. Paris: Ecole Française d'Extrême-Orient.

———. 1991. *The Rhetoric of Immediacy: A Cultural Critique of Ch'an/Zen Buddhism*. Princeton: Princeton University Press.

Favret-Saada, Jeanne. 1977. *Les mots, la mort, les sorts: La sorcellerie dans le Bocage*. Paris: Gallimard.

———. 1980. *Deadly Words: Witchcraft in the Bocage*. Cambridge: Cambridge University Press.

Flaubert, Gustave. 1976. *Bouvard and Pécuchet: With the Dictionary of Received Ideas*. Trans. A. J. Krailsheimer. London: Penguin Books.

———. 1980. *The Temptation of St. Antony*. Trans. Kitty Mrosovsky. London: Penguin Books.

Foard, James. 1980. "In Search of a Lost Reformation: A Reconsideration of Kamakura Buddhism." *Japanese Journal of Religious Studies* 7, 4: 261–291.

Foucault, Michel. 1963. *Naissance de la clinique*. Paris: Presses Universitaires de France.

———. 1972. *The Archeology of Knowledge and The Discourse on Language*. Trans. Sheridan Smith. New York: Pantheon.

———. 1973. *The Order of Things: An Archeology of the Human Sciences*. New York: Vintage/Random House.

———. 1977. *Language, Counter-memory, Practice: Selected Essays and Interviews*. Ithaca: Cornell University Press.

———. 1979. *Discipline and Punish*. Trans. Alan Sheridan. New York: Vintage/Random House.

———. 1980. *Power/Knowledge: Selected Interviews and Other Writings, 1972–1977*. New York: Pantheon Books.

———. 1984. "What Is Enlightenment?" In *The Foucault Reader*, ed. Paul Rabinow, 32–50. New York: Pantheon.

———. 1986a. *The Care of the Self: History of Sexuality 3*. Trans. Robert Hurley. New York: Vintage Books.

———. 1986b. "Of Other Spaces." *Diacritics* 16, 1: 22–27.

Foulk, Theodore Griffith. 1987. "The 'Ch'an School' and its Place in the Buddhist Monastic Institution." Ph.D. diss., University of Michigan.

Franck, Frederick, ed. 1982. *The Buddha Eye: An Anthology of the Kyōto School*. New York: Crossroad.

Freedman, Maurice. 1974. "On the Sociological Study of Chinese Religion." In *Religion and Ritual in Chinese Society*, ed. Arthur Wolf, 19–41. Stanford: Stanford University Press.

Freud, Sigmund. 1947. *Das Unheimliche*. In *Gesammelte Werke* 12: 229–268. Francfort: S. Fischer.

———. 1953. *The Complete Psychological Works of Sigmund Freud*. Standard ed. Trans. James Strachey. London: Hogarth Press.

———. 1976. *Jokes and Their Relation to the Unconscious*. Ed. Angela Richards. Trans. James Strachey. Pelican Library, vol. 6. London: Penguin Books.

———. 1981. *Essais de psychanalyse*. Paris: Payot.

Frois, Louis [Froës, Loys] S.J. [1585] 1955. *Kulturegegensätze Europa-Japan*. Ed. Josef Franz Schütte. *Monumenta Nipponica Monographs* 15. Tokyo: Sophia University Press.

Fromm, Erich, D. T. Suzuki, and Richard De Martino. 1960. *Zen Buddhism and Psychoanalysis*. New York: Harper and Brothers.

Fuller Sasaki, Ruth, trans. 1975. *The Recorded Sayings of Ch'an Master Lin-chi Hui-chao of Chen Prefecture*. Kyoto: Institute for Zen Studies.

Fuller Sasaki, Ruth, Yoshitaka Iriya and Dana R. Fraser, trans. 1971. *A Man of Zen: The Recorded Sayings of Layman P'ang*. Kyoto: Institute for Zen Studies.

Funaoka, Makoto. 1987. *Nihon Zenshū no seiritsu* (The Constitution of the Japanese Zen Sect). Tokyo: Yoshikawa Kōbunkan.

Furuta Shōkin. 1965. "Kyōge betsuden to iu koto no rekishiteki haikei" (The Historical Background of the so-called Special Transmission Outside the Scriptures). *Tōhō shūkyō* 25: 24–36.

Furuta Shōkin. 1967a. "Shaku Sōen: The Footsteps of a Modern Zen Master." *Philosophical Studies of Japan* 8: 67–91.

———. 1967b. "Daisetz Suzuki." In "Memoriam Daisetsu Teitaro Suzuki, 1870–1966." *The Eastern Buddhist* 2, 1: 116–123.

Gadamer, Hans-Georg. 1982. *Truth and Method*. New York: Crossroad.

Gaillard, Louis. 1987. *Croix et Svastika en Chine*. Milan: Archè.

Gallagher, Louis J., S.J., trans. 1953. *China in the 16th Century: The Journals of Matthew Ricci, 1583–1610*. New York: Random House.

Gauchet, Marcel. 1985. *Le désenchantement du monde*. Paris: Gallimard.

Geertz, Clifford. 1973. *The Interpretation of Cultures*. New York: Basic Books.

———. 1983. *Local Knowledge: Further Essays in Interpretive Anthropology.* New York: Basic Books.

Geil, William Edgar. 1926. *The Sacred Five of China.* Boston: Houghton Mifflin Company.

Genette, Gérard. 1966. *Figures I.* Paris: Seuil.

———. 1976. *Mimologiques: Voyages en Cratylie.* Collection Poétique. Paris: Seuil.

———. 1979. *Narrative Discourse.* Trans. J. Lewis. Ithaca: Cornell University Press.

———. 1982. *Figures of Literary Discourse.* Trans. Alan Sheridan. New York: Columbia University Press.

Gernet, Jacques. 1949. *Les entretiens du maître de dhyāna Chen-houei du Ho-tsö.* Paris: Adrien Maisonneuve.

———. 1956. *Les aspects économiques du bouddhisme dans la société chinoise du Ve au Xe siècle.* Paris: Ecole Française d'Extrême-Orient.

———. 1959. "Ecrit et histoire en Chine." *Journal de Psychologie normale et pathologique* 1: 31–40.

———. 1963. "La Chine: Aspects et fonctions psychologiques de l'écriture." In *L'écriture et la psychologie des peuples,* ed. M. Cohen, 29–49. Paris: Armand Colin.

———. 1973. "La politique de Matteo Ricci en Chine." *Archives de sciences sociales des religions* 36: 71–89.

———. 1982. *Chine et Christianisme: Action et réaction.* Paris: Gallimard. Trans. Janet Lloyd.

———. 1985a. *China and the Christian Impact: A Conflict of Cultures.* Cambridge: Cambridge University Press.

———. 1985b. "A Missionary among the Ming." *Times Literary Supplement,* 27 September, 1059–1060.

———. 1987. "Sur le corps et l'esprit chez les Chinois." In *Poikilia. Etudes offertes à Jean-Pierre Vernant,* 369–377. Paris: Ecole des Hautes Etudes en Sciences Sociales.

Gimello, Robert M. 1976. "Apophatic and Kataphatic Discourse in Mahāyāna: A Chinese View." *Philosophy East and West* 26, 2: 116–136.

Girard, René. 1965. *Desire, Deceit, and the Novel: The Self and Other in Literary Structure.* Trans. Yvonne Freccero. Baltimore: Johns Hopkins University Press.

———. 1979. *Violence and the Sacred.* Trans. Patrick Gregory. Baltimore: Johns Hopkins University Press.

Girardot, Norman J. 1979. "Chinese Religion and Western Scholarship." In *China and Christianity: Historical and Future Encounters,* ed. James D. Whitehead, Yu-ming Shaw, and Norman J. Girardot, 83–111. Notre Dame: University of Notre Dame Press.

Glüer, Winfried. 1968. "The Encounter between Christianity and Chinese Buddhism during the Nineteenth Century and the First Half of the Twentieth Century." *Ching Feng* 11, 3: 39–57.

Goethe, Johann Wofgang. 1949. *Conversations de Goethe avec Eckermann.* Trans. Jean Chuzeville. Paris: Gallimard.

Gokhale, B. G. 1965. "The Therevāda-Buddhist View of History." *JAOS* 85, 3: 354–360.

Gómez, Luis O. 1986. "D. T. Suzuki's Contribution to Modern Buddhist Scholarship." In *A Zen Life: D. T. Suzuki Rembered*, ed. Abe Masao, 90–94. New York: Weatherhill.

Goody, Jack, ed. 1977. *The Domestication of the Savage Mind*. Cambridge: Cambridge University Press.

———. 1986. *The Logic of Writing and the Organization of Society*. Cambridge: Cambridge University Press.

Gourevitch, Aaron J. [1972] 1985. *Categories of Medieval Culture*. Trans. G. L. Campbell. London: Routledge and Kegan Paul.

Granet, Marcel. 1927. *La religion des chinois*. Paris: Gauthier-Villars.

———. 1968. *La pensée chinoise*. Paris: Albin Michel.

Grapard, Allan G. 1982. "Flying Mountains and Walkers of Emptiness: Toward a Definition of Sacred Space in Japanese Religion." *History of Religions* 21, 3: 195–221.

———. 1985. "Voltaire and East Asia: A Few Reflections on the Nature of Humanism." *Cahiers d'Extrême-Asie* 1: 59–70.

———. 1987. "Linguistic Cubism: A Singularity of Pluralism in the Sannō Cult." *Japanese Journal of Religious Studies* 14, 2–3: 211–233.

Grenier, Jean. 1957. *L'esprit du Tao*. Paris: Flammarion.

Groethuysen, Bernard. 1927. *Origines de l'esprit bourgeois en France*. Paris: Gallimard.

———. 1953. *Anthropologie philosophique*. Paris: Gallimard.

———. 1968. *The Bourgeois: Catholicism versus Capitalism in Eighteenth Century France*. New York: Holt, Rinehardt and Winston.

de Groot, Jan Jakob Maria. 1892–1910. *The Religious System of China*. 6 vols. Leyden: E. J. Brill.

———. [1903–1904] 1974. *Sectarianism and Religious Persecution in China*. 2 vols. New York: Barnes and Noble.

Guignes, Joseph de. 1759. "Recherches sur les philosophes appelés samanéens." *Mémoires de littérature tirés de l'inscription des Belles-Lettres* 26: 770–804.

Guy, Basil. 1963. *The French Image of China: Before and After Voltaire*. Geneva.

Habermas, Jürgen. 1986. "Taking Aim at the Heart of the Present." In *Foucault: A Critical Reader*, ed. David Couzens Hoy, 103–108. London: Basil Blackwell.

———. 1987. *The Philosophical Discourse of Modernity*. Cambridge: Harvard University Press.

Hakamaya Noriaki. 1987. "Bukkyō to shingi: Han-Nihongakuteki kōsatsu" (Buddhism and Japanese Gods: Anti-Japanist Reflexions). *Nihon bukkyō gakkai nenpō* 52: 99–118.

Halbfass, Wilhelm. 1985. "Hegel on Meditation and Yoga." *Zen Buddhism Today: Annual Report of the Kyōto Zen Symposium* 3: 72.

———. 1988. *India and Europe: An Essay in Understanding*. Albany: State University of New York Press.

du Halde, Jean-Baptiste. 1735. *Description géographique, historique, chronologique, politique et physique de l'Empire de la Chine et de la Tartarie chinoise*. 4 vols. Paris.

———. 1741. English trans. *The General History of China: Containing a geo-*

graphical, historical, chronological, political and physical description of the Empire of China, Chinese-Tartary, Corea and Thibet. London: J. Watts.

Hansen, Valerie. 1990. *Changing Gods in Medieval China, 1127–1276*. Princeton: Princeton University Press.

Harootunian, H. D. 1988a. *Things Seen and Unseen: Discourse and Ideology in Tokugawa Nativism*. Chicago: University of Chicago Press.

———. 1988b. "Visible Discourses/Invisible Ideologies." *South Atlantic Quarterly* 87, 3: 445–474.

Harris, George. 1966. "The Mission of Matteo Ricci, S.J.: A Case Study of an Effort at Guided Cultural Change in the Sixteenth Century." *Monumenta Serica* 25: 1–168.

Hegel, G.W.F. 1953. *Reason in History: A General Introduction to the Philosophy of History*. Trans. Robert S. Hartman. New York: Macmillan.

Heidegger, Martin. 1962. *Being and Time*. Trans. John Macquarrie and Edward Robinson. New York: Harper & Row.

———. 1971. *On the Way to Language*. Trans. Peter D. Hertz. New York: Harper & Row.

Herrigel, Eugen. 1953. *Zen and the Art of Archery*. Trans. R.F.C. Hull. Foreword by D. T. Suzuki. London: Routledge and Kegan Paul.

Hisamatsu Shin'ichi. 1960. "The Characteristics of Oriental Nothingness." Trans. Richard DeMartino. *Philosophical Studies of Japan* 2: 65–97.

Hōbōgirin: Dictionnaire encyclopédique du bouddhisme d'après les sources chinoises et japonaises. 1927–1983. Vols. 1–6. Paris: Adrien Maisonneuve.

Hoffmann, Helmut. 1971. "Zen und später indischer Buddhismus." In *Asien Tradition und Fortschritt: Festschrift für Horst Hammitzsch*, ed. Lydia Brüll and Ulrich Kemper, 207–216. Wiesbaden: Harrassowitz.

Horkheimer, Max and Theodor W. Adorno. 1972. *Dialectic of Enlightenment*. Trans. John Cumming. New York: Seabury Press.

Hoy, David C., ed. 1986. *Foucault: A Critical Reader*. New York: Basil Blackwell.

Hsü, Sung-peng. 1979. *A Buddhist Leader in Ming China: The Life and Thought of Han-shan Te-ch'ing, 1546–1623*. University Park: Pennsylvania State University Press.

Hu Shih. [1930] 1970. *Shenhui heshang yiji* (The Collected Works of Master Shenhui). Taibei: Hu Shi jinian guan.

———. 1931. "What I Believe." *Forum* 85, 2: 114–122.

———. 1932. "The Development of Zen Buddhism in China." *The Chinese and Political Science Review* 15, 4: 475–505.

———. 1953. "Ch'an (Zen) Buddhism in China: Its History and Method: Is Ch'an (Zen) Beyond Understanding?" *Philosophy East and West* 3, 1: 3–24.

———. 1962. "John Dewey in China." In *Philosophy and Culture East and West: East-West Philosophy in Practical Perspective*, ed. A. Moore, 762–769. Honolulu: University of Hawaii Press.

———. 1963. "Ko Teki shi hakushi no tegami (A Letter from Dr. Hu Shih, dated 15 January 1961). *Zengaku kenkyū* 53: 162–172.

———. 1975. *Ko Teki Zengakuan* (The Writings of Hu Shih on Chan). Kyoto: Chūbun shuppansha.

Hubert, Henri, and Marcel Mauss. 1909. "Etude sommaire de la représentation du temps dans la religion et la magie." In *Mélanges d'histoire des religions*, 189–229. Paris: Félix Alcan.

———. 1964. *Sacrifice: Its Nature and Function*. London: Cohen and West.

Huc, Evariste-Régis. 1928. *Travels in Tartary, Thybet and China, 1844–1849*. 2 vols. London: Routledge and Sons.

Hunt, Lynn, ed. 1989. *The New Cultural History*. Berkeley: University of California Press.

Ichikawa Hakugen, Iriya Yoshitaka, and Yanagida Seizan, eds. 1972. *Chūsei zenke no shisō* (The Thought of Medieval Zen). Tokyo: Iwanami shoten.

Imamura, Yoshio, ed. 1980. *Yuyō zasso* (*Youyang zazu*). 4 vols. Tokyo: Heibonsha.

Inoue, Ichii. 1941. "Kan U shibyō no yurai narabini hensen (The Origin and Development of Temples Dedicated to Guan Yu). *Shirin* 26: 41–51, 242–283.

Iriya Yoshitaka. 1973. "Chinese Poetry and Zen." *The Eastern Buddhist* 6, 1: 54–67.

Isambert, François-André. 1982. *Le sens du sacré: Fête et religion populaire*. Paris: Editions de Minuit.

Ishii Shūdō. 1987. *Sōdai zenshūshi no kenkyū* (Researches on the History of the Chan School during the Song). Tokyo: Daitō shuppansha.

Jakobson, Roman. 1963. *Essais de linguistique générale: Les fondations du langage*. Paris: Minuit.

James, William. [1902] 1961. *The Varieties of Religious Experience: A Study in Human Nature*. New York: Collier Books.

Jameson, Fredric. 1972. *The Prison-House of Language: A Critical Account of Structuralism and Russian Formalism*. Princeton: Princeton University Press.

———. 1981. *The Political Unconscious: Narrative as a Socially Symbolic Act*. Ithaca: Cornell University Press.

———. 1985. "The Realist Floor-plan." In *On Signs*, ed. Marshall Blonski, 373–383. Baltimore: Johns Hopkins University Press.

Jan Yün-hua. 1964. "Buddhist Historiography in Sung China." *Zeitschrift der deutschen morgenländischen Gesellschaft* 114, 2: 360–381.

———. 1966. *A Chronicle of Buddhism in China (580–960 A.D.): Translations of the Monk Chih-p'an's Fo-tsu t'ung-chi*. Santiniketan: Visva-Bharati.

———. 1972. "Tsung-mi: His Analysis of Ch'an Buddhism." *T'oung Pao* 58: 1–54.

———. 1983. "Seng-ch'ou's Method of Dhyāna." In *Early Ch'an in China and Tibet*, ed. Whalen C. Lai and Lewis R. Lancaster, 51–63. Berkeley: Asian Humanities Press.

Jankélévitch, Vladimir. 1977. *La mort*. Paris: Flammarion.

Jay, Martin. 1986. "In the Empire of the Gaze: Foucault and the Denigration of the Gaze in Twentieth-century French Thought." In *Foucault: A Critical Reader*, ed. David Couzens Hoy, 175–204. New York: Basil Blackwell.

———. 1989. "The Rise of Hermeneutics and the Crisis of Ocularcentrism." In *The Rhetoric of Interpretation and the Interpretation of Rhetoric*, ed. Paul Hernadi, 55–74. Durham: Duke University Press.

Johnson, Barbara. 1980. *The Critical Difference: Essays in the Contemporary Rhetoric of Reading*. Baltimore: Johns Hopkins University Press.

Johnston, Reginald Fleming. 1913. *Buddhist China*. London: John Murray.

de Jong, J. W. 1974. "A Brief History of Buddhist Studies in Europe and America." *The Eastern Buddhist* 7, 1: 55–56; 7, 2: 49–82.

———. 1987. "Lamotte and the Doctrine of Non-Self." *Cahiers d'Extrême-Asie* 3: 151–153.

Jousse, Marcel. 1974–1978. *L'anthropologie du geste*. 3 vols. Paris: Gallimard.

Jullien, François. 1982a. "L'absence d'inspiration: Représentations chinoises de l'incitation poétique." *EOEO* 1: 31–71.

———. 1982b. "Le plaisir du texte: L'expérience chinoise de la saveur littéraire." *EOEO* 1: 73–119.

———. 1984. "L'oeuvre et l'univers: Imitation ou déploiement (Limites à une conception mimétique de la création littéraire dans la tradition chinoise)." *EOEO* 3: 37–88.

———. 1985. *La valeur allusive: Des catégories originales de l'interprétation poétique dans la tradition chinoise (Contribution à une réflexion sur l'altérité culturelle)*. Paris: Ecole Française d'Extrême-Orient.

———. 1986. "Naissance de l''imagination': Essai de problématique au travers de la réflexion littéraire de la Chine et de l'Occident." *EOEO* 7: 23–81.

———. 1989. *Procès ou création: Une introduction à la pensée des lettrés chinois*. Paris: Seuil.

Kaempfer, Engelbert. 1732. *Histoire naturelle, civile et ecclésiastique de l'Empire du Japon*. 3 vols. The Hague: P. Gosse and J. Neaulme.

Kagamishima Genryū. 1961. *Dōgen zenji to sono monryū* (Dōgen and His Disciples). Tokyo: Seishin shobō.

———. 1965. *Dōgen zenji to in'yō kyōten goroku no kenkyū* (A Study of the Classics and Recorded Sayings Quoted by Dōgen). Tokyo: Mokujisha.

Kalupahana, David J. 1976. *Buddhist Philosophy: A Historical Analysis*. Honolulu: University Press of Hawaii.

Kamata Shigeo and Tanaka Hisao, eds. 1971. *Kamakura kyū-bukkyō* (Ancient Buddhism during Kamakura). Tokyo: Iwanami shoten.

Karatani Kōjin. 1988. "One Spirit, Two Nineteen Centuries." *South Atlantic Review* 87, 3: 615–628.

Kasulis, Thomas P. 1978. "The Zen-Philosopher: A Review-article on Dōgen Scholarship." *Philosophy East and West* 28: 353–373.

———. 1982. "The Kyōto School and the West: Review and Evaluation." *The Eastern Buddhist* 15, 2: 125–145.

———. 1985. "The Incomparable Philosopher: Dōgen on How to Read the *Shōbōgenzō*." In *Dōgen Studies*, ed. William LaFleur, 83–98. Honolulu: University of Hawaii Press.

Katō, Shūichi. 1967a. "Tominaga Nakamoto, 1715–1746: A Tokugawa Iconoclast." *Monumenta Nipponica* 22, 1–2: 177–193.

———, trans. 1967b. "*Okina no fumi*: The Writings of an Old Man by Tominaga Nakamoto." *Monumenta Nipponica* 22, 1–2: 194–210.

Katz, Steven T. 1978. "Language, Epistemology, and Mysticism." In *Mysticism and Philosophical Analysis*, ed. Katz, 22–74. New York: Oxford University Press.

Kelsey, W. Michael. 1981. "Salvation of the Snake, the Snake of Salvation:

Buddhist-Shintō Conflict and Resolution." *Japanese Journal of Religious Studies* 8, 1–2: 83–113.

Kern, Iso. 1984–1985. "Matteo Riccis Verhältnis zum Buddhismus." *Monumenta Serica* 36: 65–126.

Ketelaar, James Edward. 1990. *Of Heretics and Martyrs in Meiji Japan: Buddhism and Its Persecution*. Princeton: Princeton University Press.

King, Winston. 1970. "A Comparison of Theravāda and Zen Buddhist Methods of Meditation and Goals." *History of Religions* 9, 4: 304–315.

Knauth, Lothar. 1965. "Life is Tragic: The Diary of Nishida Kitarō." *Monumenta Nipponica* 20, 3–4: 335–358.

Kobori Sohaku, trans. 1970–1971. "*Sokushin-ki*, by Shidō Munan Zenji." *The Eastern Buddhist* 3, 2: 89–118; 4, 1: 116–123; 4, 2: 119–127.

Kodera, Takashi James. 1980. *Dōgen's Formative Years in China: An Historical Study and Annotated Translation of the Hōkyōki*. London: Routledge and Kegan Paul.

Koestler, Arthur. 1960a. "The Lotus and the Robot." *Encounter* 15: 13–32.

———. 1960b. "Neither Lotus nor Robot." *Encounter* 16: 58–59.

———. 1961. *The Lotus and the Robot*. New York: MacMillan.

Kōsaka Masaaki, Nishitani Keiji, Kōyama Iwao, and Suzuki Shigetaka. 1942. "Sekaiteki tachiba to Nihon" (The Viewpoint of the World and Japan). Tokyo: Chūōkōronsha.

Kōun Chisan, ed. 1937. *Jōsai daishi zenshū* (The Collected Works of the Great Master Jōsai, a.k.a. Keizan). Yokohama: Daihonzan Sōjiji.

Koyré, Alexandre. 1965. *Newtonian Studies*. Cambridge: Harvard University Press.

Kracht, Klaus. 1984. "Nishida Kitarō (1870–1945) as a Philosopher of the State." In *Europe Interprets Japan*, ed. Gordon Daniels, 198–203. Tenterden, Kent: Paul Norbury.

Kuroda Toshio. 1981. "Shintō in the History of Japanese Religion." Trans. James C. Dobbins and Suzanne Gay. *Journal of Japanese Studies* 7, 1: 1–21.

LaCapra, Dominick. 1983. *Rethinking Intellectual History: Texts, Contexts, Language*. Ithaca: Cornell University Press.

———. 1985. *History and Criticism*. Ithaca: Cornell University Press.

———. 1988. "A Review of a Review." *Journal of the History of Ideas* 49, 4: 677–687.

———. 1989. *Soundings in Critical Theory*. Ithaca: Cornell University Press.

LaCapra, Dominick, and Steven L. Kaplan, eds. 1982. *Modern European History: Reappraisals and New Perspectives*. Ithaca: Cornell University Press.

Lach, Donald. 1965. *Asia in the Making of Europe*. Vol. 1, book 2. *The Century of Discovery*. Chicago: University of Chicago Press.

Lacoue-Labarthe, Philippe. 1987. *La fiction du politique: Heidegger, l'art et la politique*. Paris: Christian Bourgeois.

La Croze [Lacroze], M. V. 1724. *Histoire du Christianisme des Indes*. The Hague: Vaillant and N. Prevost.

LaFleur, William R. 1983. *The Karma of Words: Buddhism and the Literary Arts in Medieval Japan*. Berkeley: University of California Press.

———, ed. 1985. *Dōgen Studies*. Honolulu: University of Hawaii Press.

———. 1990. "A Turning in Taishō: Asian and Europe in the Early Writings of Watsuji Tetsurō." In *Japanese Intellectuals During the Interwar Years*, ed. J. Thomas Rimer, 234–256. Princeton: Princeton University Press.

Lagerwey, John. 1985. "The Oral and the Written in Chinese and Western Religion." In *Religion und Philosophie in Ostasien: Festschrift für Hans Steininger*, ed. Gert Naundorf, Karl–Heinz Pohl, and Hans–Hermann Schmidt, 301–322. Würzburg: Königshausen and Neumann.

Lai, Whalen W. 1983. "Sinitic Mandalas: The *Wu-wei t'u* of Ts'ao-shan." In *Early Ch'an in China and Tibet*, ed. Whalen W. Lai and Lewis R. Lancaster, 229–257. Berkeley: Asian Humanities Press.

Lamairesse, E. 1893. *L'Empire chinois: Le Bouddhisme en Chine et au Tibet*. Paris: Georges Carré.

Lamotte, Etienne. 1944–1980. *Traité de la Grande Vertu de Sagesse*. Vols. 1–5. Louvain: Institut Orientaliste.

———. 1962. *L'enseignement de Vimalakīrti*. Louvain: Institut Orientaliste.

Lancashire, Douglas. 1968–1969. "Buddhist Reaction to Christianity in late Ming China." *Journal of the Oriental Society of Australia* 6, 1–2: 82–103.

———. 1969. "Anti-Christian Polemics in Seventeenth Century China." *Church History* 38: 218–241.

Lau, D. C., trans. 1963. *Lao Tzu: Tao Te Ching*. Harmondsworth: Penguin Books.

Le Comte [Lecomte], Louis Daniel. [1696] 1990. *Un Jésuite à Paris: Nouveaux mémoires sur l'état présent de la Chine 1687–1692*. Paris: Phébus.

———. 1697. *Memoirs and Observations Topographical, Physical, Mathematical, Mechanical, Natural, Civil, Ecclesiastical, Made in a late Journey Through the Empire of China*. London: Benjamin Tooke.

Le Gobien, Charles, S.J., ed. 1717–1776. *Lettres édifiantes et curieuses, écrites des missions étrangères, par quelques missionnaires de la Compagnie de Jésus*. 34 vols. Paris: N. Le Clerc.

Le Goff, Jacques. 1977. *Pour un autre Moyen Age: Temps, travail et culture en Occident: 18 essais*. Paris: Gallimard.

———. 1980. *Time, Work and Culture in the Middle Ages*. Trans. Arthur Goldhammer. Chicago: University of Chicago Press.

———. 1985. *L'imaginaire médiéval: Essais*. Paris: Gallimard.

———. 1988. *The Medieval Imagination*. Trans. Arthur Goldhammer. Chicago: University of Chicago Press.

Lévi, Jean. 1986. "Les fonctionnaires et le divin." *Cahiers d'Extrême-Asie* 2: 81–110.

———. 1987. "Les fonctions religieuses de la bureaucratie céleste." *L'homme* 101: 35–57.

Lévi, Sylvain, and Edouard Chavannes. 1916. "Les seize Arhat protecteurs de la Loi." *Journal Asiatique* 8: 5–48, 189–304.

Lévi-Strauss, Claude. [1950] 1966b. "Introduction à l'oeuvre de Marcel Mauss." In *Sociologie et anthropologie*, ed. Marcel Mauss, xi–lii.

———. [1955] 1965. *Tristes tropiques*. Trans. John Russell. New York: Atheneum.

———. [1958] 1963. *Structural Anthropology*. Trans. Claire Jacobson and Brooke Grundfest Schoepf. New York: Basic Books.

———. [1962] 1966a. *The Savage Mind*. Chicago: University of Chicago Press.

———. [1964] 1969. *The Raw and the Cooked*. New York: Harper & Row.

———. [1973] 1974. *Structural Anthropology, Volume Two*. Chicago: University of Chicago Press.

———. 1979. "Claude Lévi-Strauss Reconsiders: Interview with Jean-Marie Benoist." *Encounter*.

———. 1985. *La potière jalouse*. Paris: Plon.

———. 1987. *Introduction to the Work of Marcel Mauss*. Trans. Felicity Baker. London: Routledge and Kegan Paul.

———. 1988. *The Jealous Potter*. Trans. Bénédicte Chorier. Chicago: University of Chicago Press.

Lévy-Bruhl, Lucien. [1895] 1910. *How Natives Think*. Princeton: Princeton University Press.

———. [1949] 1975. *The Notebooks on Primitive Mentality*. Trans. Peter Rivière. Oxford: Oxford University Press.

Li Chi. 1974. *The Travel Diaries of Hsü Hsia-k'o*. Hong Kong: Chinese University of Hong Kong.

Liebenthal, Walter. [1948] 1968. *Chao-lun: The Treatises of Seng-chao*. Hong Kong: Hong Kong University Press.

Liu, James J. Y. 1975. *Chinese Theories of Literature*. Chicago: University of Chicago Press.

Longobardo [Longobardi], Nichola. 1701. *Traité sur quelques points de la religion des Chinois*. Paris: J. Josse.

Lopez, Donald S., Jr., ed. 1988. *Buddhist Hermeneutics*. Honolulu: University of Hawaii Press.

———. 1990. "Inscribing the Bodhisattva's Speech: On the *Heart Sūtra*'s Mantra." *History of Religions* 29, 4: 351–372.

Loubère, Simon de la. 1693. *A New Historical Relation of the Kingdom of Siam*. London: n.p.

Lubac, Henri de. 1952. *La rencontre du bouddhisme et de l'Occident*. Paris: Aubier.

Luk, Charles (Lu K'uan-yü). 1966. *The Śūrangama Sūtra (Leng Yen Ching)*. London: Rider.

Lynn, Richard John. 1987. "The Sudden and the Gradual in Chinese Poetry Criticism: An Examination of the Ch'an-Poetry Analogy." In *Sudden and Gradual: Approaches to Enlightenment in Chinese Thought*, ed. Peter N. Gregory, 381–427. Honolulu: University of Hawaii Press.

———. 1992. "Sung Dynasty Poetry Theory." In *Sources of Neo-Confucianism*, ed. Irene Bloom, W. Theodore De Bary, and Wing-tsit Ch'an. New York: Columbia University Press.

Lyotard, Jean-François. 1985. "Histoire universelle et différences culturelles." In "La traversée de l'Atlantique." *Critique* 456: 558–568.

———. 1988. *The Differend: Phrases in Dispute*. Trans. Georges van Abbeele. Minneapolis: University of Minnesota Press.

Lyotard, Jean-François, and Jean-Loup Thébaud. 1985. *Just Gaming*. Trans. Wlad Godzich. Minneapolis: University of Minnesota Press.

Magaillans [Magalhaes], Gabriel de. 1688a. *Nouvelle relation de la Chine, contenant la description des particularités les plus considérables de ce grand empire*. Paris: Claude Barbin.

————. 1688b. *A new history of China containing a description of the most considerable particulars of that vast empire*. Trans. John Quilby. London.

Magliola, Robert. 1984. *Derrida on the Mend*. West Lafayette: Purdue University Press.

Mair, Victor. 1986. "Oral and Written Aspects of Chinese Sūtra Lectures (*chiang-ching wen*)." *Chinese Studies* 4, 2: 311–334.

Mallarmé, Stéphane. 1945. *Oeuvres complètes*. Ed. Henri Mondor and G. Jean-Aubry. Bibliothèque de la Pléiade. Paris: Gallimard.

Manuel, Frank E. 1959. *The Eighteenth Century Confronts the Gods*. Cambridge: Harvard University Press.

Maraldo, John C. 1986a. "Is There Historical Consciousness within Ch'an?" *Japanese Journal of Religious Studies* 12, 2–3: 141–172.

————. 1986b. "Hermeneutics and Historicity in the Study of Buddhism." *The Eastern Buddhist* 19, 1: 17–43.

————. 1989. "Translating Nishida." *Philosophy East and West* 39, 4: 465–496.

March, Andrew L. 1966. "Self and Landscape in Su Shih." *JAOS* 86, 4: 377–396.

Maspero, Henri. 1981. *Taoism and Chinese Religion*. Amherst: University of Massachusetts Press.

Mather, Richard B. 1976. *Shih-shuo Hsin-yü: A New Account of Tales of the World*. Minneapolis: University of Minnesota Press.

Matignon, J.-J. 1936. *La Chine hermétique: Superstition, crime et misère*. Paris: Paul Geuthner.

Matsumoto Bunzaburō. 1911. *Daruma* (Bodhidharma). 2 vols. Tokyo: Tosho kankōkai.

Matsumoto Shirō. 1987. "Bukkyō to shingi: Han-Nihonshūgi kōsatsu" (Buddhism and Japanese Gods: Anti-Japanist Reflexions). *Nihon bukkyō gakkai nenpō* 52: 119–142.

Mauss, Marcel. [1950] 1985. *Sociologie et anthropologie*. Paris: Presses Universitaires de France.

————. 1968–1969. *Oeuvres*. Paris: Minuit. 3 vols.

McRae, John R. 1986. *The Northern School and the Formation of Early Ch'an Buddhism*. Honolulu: University of Hawaii Press.

————. 1988. "Religion as Revolution in Chinese Historiography: Hu Shih (1891–1962) on Shen-hui (684–758)." Ms.

————. 1990. "Sudden Enlightenment and the Southern School: The Role of Ho-tse Shen-hui (684–758) in Ch'an Buddhism and Chinese History." Ms.

Merleau-Ponty, Maurice. 1953. *Eloge de la philosophie*. Paris: Gallimard.

————. [1963] 1970. *In Praise of Philosophy and Other Essays*. Trans. John Wild, James Edie, and John O'Neill. Evanston: Northwestern University Press.

————. 1964a. *The Primacy of Perception and Other Essays on Phenomenological Psychology, the Philosophy of Art, History and Politics*. Ed. James M. Edie. Evanston: Northwestern University Press.

————. 1964b. *Signs*. Trans. Richard McCleary. Evanston: Northwestern University Press.

————. 1964c. *L'oeil et l'esprit*. Paris: Gallimard.

————. 1968. *The Visible and the Invisible*. Trans. Alphonso Lingis. Evanston: Northwestern University Press.

Merton, Thomas. 1967. *Mystics and Zen Masters*. New York: Delta.

———. 1968. *Zen and the Birds of Appetite*. New York: New Directions Books.

Miura, Isshu, and Ruth Fuller Sasaki. 1966. *Zen Dust: The History of the Kōan and Kōan Study in Rinzai (Lin-chi) Zen*. New York: Harcourt, Brace, and World.

Miyakawa Hisayuki. 1979. "Local Cults around Mount Lu at the Time of Sun En's Rebellion." In *Facets of Taoism*, ed. Holmes Welch and Anna Seidel, 83–102.

Molinos, Miguel. 1970. *Le guide spirituel*. Paris: Fayard.

Morioka, Heinz, and Miyoko Sasaki. 1990. *Rakugo: The Popular Narrative Art of Japan*. Cambridge: Harvard University Press.

Morrell, Robert, trans. 1985. *Sand and Pebbles (Shasekishū): The Tales of Mujū Ichien, A Voice for Pluralism in Kamakura Buddhism*. Albany: State University of New York Press.

Mungello, David E. 1985. *Curious Land: Jesuit Accommodation and the Origins of Sinology*. Honolulu: University of Hawaii Press.

Munro, Donald J., ed. 1985. *Individualism and Holism: Studies in Confucian and Taoist Values*. Ann Arbor: Center for Chinese Studies, University of Michigan.

Mus, Paul. [1935] 1978. *Barabuḍur: Esquisse d'une histoire du bouddhisme fondée sur la critique archéologique des textes*. 2 vols. New York: Arno Press. [1990, Paris: Arma Artis.]

Musil, Robert. 1956. *L'homme sans qualités*, trans. Philippe Jaccottet. 2 vols. Paris: Editions Seuil.

Musō [Soseki]. 1974. *Dialogues dans le rêve*. Trans. M. and M. Shibata. Paris: Maisonneuve et Larose.

Nagashima Takayuki. 1978. *Truths and fabrications in Religion: An Investigation from the Documents of the Zen (Ch'an) Sect*. Probsthain Oriental Series 29. London: Probsthain.

Needham, Joseph, ed. 1954–. *Science and Civilization in China*. 15 vols. Cambridge: Cambridge University Press.

———. 1977. *La science chinoise et l'Occident: Le grand titrage*. Paris: Seuil.

Neufeldt, Ronald W. 1983. "Western Perceptions of Asia: The Romantic Vision of Max Müller." In *Traditions in Contact and Change*, ed. P. Slater and D. Wiebe, 593–606. Waterloo, Ontario: Wilfrid Laurier University Press.

Nietzsche, Friedrich. 1957. *The Use and Abuse of History*. Trans. Adrian Collins. Indianapolis: Bobbs-Merril Company.

———. [1873] 1974. "On Truth and Falsity in their Ultramoral Sense." In *The Complete Works of Frederick Nietzsche*, ed. Oscar Levy. Trans. Maximilian A. Magge. New York: Gordon.

Nishida Kitarō. 1953. "Nihon bunka no mondai" (The Problem of Japanese Culture). In *Nishida Kitarō zenshū*, supplementary volume [*bekkan*] 6. Tokyo: Iwanami shoten.

———. 1960. *A Study of Good*. Trans. V. H. Viglielmo. Tokyo: Ministry of Education.

———. 1965. *Nishida Kitarō zenshū* (The Complete Works of Nishida Kitarō). 19 volumes. Tokyo: Iwanami shoten.

———. 1987. *Last Writings: Nothingness and the Religious Worldview*. Trans. David A. Dilworth. Honolulu: University of Hawaii Press.

———. 1990. *An Inquiry into the Good.* Trans. Abe Masao and Christopher Ives. New Haven: Yale University Press.

———. 1991. *La culture japonaise en question.* Trans. Pierre Lavelle. Paris: Publications Orientalistes de France.

Nishitani Keiji. *Religion and Nothingness.* Trans. Jan Van Bragt, Berkeley: University of California Press.

Noda Matao. 1955. "East-West Synthesis in Kitaro Nishida." *Philosophy East and West* 4: 345–359.

Nukariya Kaiten. 1923–1925. *Zengaku shisōshi* (A History of Zen Thought). 2 vols. Tokyo: Genkōsha.

———. 1930. *Chōsen zenkyōshi* (A History of Korean Zen Doctrine). Tokyo: Shunjūsha.

Obry, Jean Baptiste François. 1863. *Du Nirvāṇa bouddhique en réponse à M. Barthélémy Saint-Hilaire.* Paris: Auguste Durand.

Ogawa Tadashi. 1978. "The Kyōto School of Philosophy and Phenomenology." In *Japanese Phenomenology: Phenomenology as the Trans-cultural Philosophical Approach*, ed. Nitta Yoshihiro and Tatematsu Hirotaka, 207–221. Analecta Husserliana 8. Dortrecht: D. Reidel.

Okakura Kakuzō. 1903. *The Ideals of the East: With Special Reference to the Art of Japan.* London: J. Murray.

———. 1964. *The Book of Tea.* Ed. Everett F. Bleiler. New York: Dover Publications.

Ong, Walter J. 1982. *Orality and Literacy: The Technologizing of the Word.* London: Methuen.

Ooms, Hermann. 1985. *Tokugawa Ideology: Early Constructs, 1570–1680.* Princeton: Princeton University Press.

Otto, Rudolf. 1924. "Professor Rudolf Otto on Zen Buddhism." *The Eastern Buddhist* 3: 117–125.

———. 1950. *Mysticism East and West.* New York: Macmillan.

Overmyer, Daniel L. 1976. *Folk Buddhist Religion: Dissenting Sects in Late Traditional China.* Cambridge: Harvard University Press.

———. 1980. "Dualism and Conflict in Chinese Popular Religion." In *Transitions and Transformations in the History of Religions: Essays in Honor of Joseph M. Kitagawa*, ed. Frank Reynolds and Theodore M. Ludwig, 153–184. Leiden: E. J. Brill.

Pachow, W. 1965. "A Study of the Dotted Record." *JAOS* 85, 3: 342–349.

Panofsky, Erwin. 1975. *La perspective comme forme symbolique et autres essais.* Paris: Minuit.

Pascal, Blaise. 1966. *Pensées.* Trans. A. J. Krailsheimer. London: Penguin Books.

———. 1967. *The Provincial Letters.* Trans. A. J. Krailsheimer. London: Penguin Books.

Paul-Lévy, Françoise, and Marion Segaud. 1983. *Anthropologie de l'espace.* Paris: Centre Georges Pompidou.

Pelliot, Paul. 1923. "Notes sur quelques artistes des Six Dynasties et des T'ang." *T'oung Pao* 22: 215–291.

Perera, Simon Gregory, trans. 1930. *The Temporal and Spiritual Conquest of Ceylon: By Father Faernaõ de Queyroz.* Colombo: A. C. Richards.

Pfister, Aloys [Louis], S.J. 1932–1934. *Notices biographiques et bibliographiques sur les Jésuites de l'ancienne mission de Chine, 1552–1773.* 2 vols. Variétés Sinologiques 59. Shanghai: T'usewei Press.

Philosinensis. 1834. "Remarks on Buddhism; Together with Brief Notices on the Island of Poo-to and of the Numerous Priests Who Inhabit It." *The Chinese Repository* 2: 214–225.

Pinot, Virgile. 1932. *La Chine et la formation de l'esprit philosophique en France.* Paris: Paul Geuthner.

Piovesana, Gino K. 1968. *Recent Japanese Philosophical Thought, 1862–1962: A Survey.* Rev. ed. *Monumenta Nipponica* Monographs 29. Tokyo: Sophia University.

Plutschow, Herbert E. 1978. "Is Poetry a Sin? *Honjisuijaku* and Buddhism versus Poetry." *Oriens Extremus* 25: 206–218.

Pollack, David. 1986. *The Fracture of Meaning: Japan's Synthesis of China from the Eighth through the Eighteenth Centuries.* Princeton: Princeton University Press.

Pomian, Krzysztof. 1984. *L'ordre du temps.* Paris: Gallimard.

Powell, William. 1986. *The Record of Tung-shan.* Honolulu: University of Hawaii Press.

Prip-Møller, J. [1937] 1982. *Chinese Buddhist Monasteries: Their Plan and its Function as Setting for Buddhist Monastic Life.* Hong Kong: Hong Kong University Press.

Propp, Vladimir. 1968. *Morphology of the Folktale.* Austin: University of Texas Press.

Pye, Michael. 1983. "The Significance of the Japanese Intellectual Tradition for the History of Religions." In *Traditions in Contact and Change,* ed. Peter Slater and Donald Wiebe. Waterloo, Canada: Wilfrid Laurier University Press.

———. 1984. "Tominaga Nakamoto (1715–1746) and Religious Pluralism." In *Europe Interprets Japan,* ed. Gordon Daniels, 191–197. Tenterden, Kent: Paul Norbury.

Rabelais, François. 1970. *The Histories of Gargantua and Pantagruel.* Trans. J. M. Cohen. London: Penguin Books.

Rabinow, Paul, ed. 1984. *The Foucault Reader.* New York: Pantheon Books.

———. 1986. "Representations are Social Facts: Modernity and Post-Modernity in Anthropology." In *Writing Culture,* ed. James Clifford and George E. Marcus, 234–261. Berkeley: University of California Press.

Rahula, Walpola. 1959. *What the Buddha Taught.* New York: Grove Press.

von Ranke, Leopold. 1983. *The Theory and Practice of History.* Trans. Wilma Iggers. Manchester, N.H.: Irvington.

Ratnayaka, Shanta. 1980. "Zen Is the Theravāda Branch of Buddhism in Mahāyāna Countries." In *Buddhist Studies in Honour of Walpola Rahula,* ed. Somaratna Balasooriya et al. 223–233. London: Gordon Fraser.

Rawlinson, Andrew. 1986. "Nāgas and the Magical Cosmology of Buddhism." *History of Religions* 16, 2:135–153.

Reichelt, Karl L. 1934. *Truth and Tradition in Chinese Buddhism: A Study of Chinese Mahāyāna.* Trans. Kathrina van Wagenen Bugge. Shanghai: Commercial Press.

Reichwein, Adolf. 1925. *China and Europe: Intellectual and Artistic Contacts in the Eighteenth Century.* New York: A. A. Knopf.

Rémusat, Jean-Pierre Abel. 1825–1826. *Mélanges Asiatiques ou Choix de morceaux critiques et de mémoires relatifs aux religions, aux sciences, aux coutumes, à l'histoire et à la géographie des Nations orientales*. 2 vols. Paris: Librairie orientale de Dondry-Dupré.

———. 1829. *Nouveaux Mélanges Asiatiques*. 2 vols. Paris: Librairie orientale de Dondry-Dupré.

———. 1843. *Mélanges posthumes d'histoire et de littérature orientales*. Paris: Imprimerie royale.

Ren Jiyu. 1963. *Han Tang fojiao sixiang lunji* (Collected Essays on Buddhist Thought during the Han and the Tang). Beijing: Renmin chubanshe.

———. 1984a. "A Brief Discussion of the Philosophical Thought of the Chan Sect." *Chinese Studies in Philosophy* 15, 4: 3–69.

———. 1984b. "On Hu Shih's Mistakes in his Study of the History of the Chan Sect." *Chinese Studies in Philosophy* 15, 4: 70–98.

Reps, Paul, comp. 1957. *Zen Flesh, Zen Bones*. London: Penguin Books.

Ricci, Matteo, S.J. 1911–1913. *Opere Storiche*. Ed. Pietro Tacchi-Venturi, S.J. 2 vols. Macerata: Giorgetti.

———. 1942–1949. *Fonti Ricciane: Storia dell' Introduzione del Christianesimo in China scritta da Matteo Ricci*. Ed. Pasquale M. d'Elia, S.J. 3 vols. Rome: Libreria dello stato.

Ricci, Matteo, S.J. , et al. 1965. *Bianxue yidu* (Letters on Buddhism and Christianity). In *Tianxue chuhan*, ed. Li Zhizao, 2: 637–687.

Ricoeur, Paul. 1974. *The Conflict of Interpretations: Essays in Hermeneutics*. Ed. Don Ihde. Evanston: Northwestern University Press.

———. 1977. *The Rule of Metaphor: Multidisciplinary Studies in the Creation of Meaning in Language*. Trans. Robert Czerny. Buffalo: University of Toronto Press.

———. 1981. *Hermeneutics and the Human Sciences*. Ed. and trans. John B. Thompson. Cambridge: Cambridge University Press.

———. 1984–1988. *Time and Narrative*. 3 vols. Trans. Kathleen McLaughlin and David Pellauer (vols. 1 and 2); Karen Blamey and David Pellauer (vol. 3). Chicago: University of Chicago Press.

Riffaterre, Michael. 1972. "Système d'un genre descriptif." *Poétique* 9: 15–30.

———. 1983. *Text Production*. Trans. Térèse Lyons. New York: Columbia University Press.

———. 1984. *Semiotics of Poetry*. Bloomington: Indiana University Press.

Rimer, Thomas J. , ed. 1990. *Culture and Identity: Japanese Intellectuals During the Interwar Years*. Princeton: Princeton University Press.

Robert, Jean-Noël. 1980–1981. "Conférence." In *Annuaire de l'Ecole Pratique des Hautes Etudes: Résumé des conférences et travaux* 89: 209–214.

Robinet, Isabelle. 1979. *Méditation taoïste*. Paris: Dervy-Livres.

Rule, Paul A. 1968. "Jesuit and Confucian? Chinese Religion in the Journals of Matteo Ricci." *Journal of Religious History* 5: 105–124.

Said, Edward. 1979. *Orientalism*. New York: Vintage Books.

———. 1985. "Orientalism Reconsidered." *Cultural Critique* 1: 89–108.

Sakai, Naoki. 1988. "Modernity and its Critique: The Problem of Universalism and Particularism." *South Atlantic Quarterly* 87, 3: 475–504.

Sakaino, Kōyō. 1907. *Shina bukkyōshi kō* (An Outline of the History of Chinese Buddhism). Tokyo: n.p.

————. [Satoru]. 1927. *Shina bukkyōshi kōwa* (Conferences on the History of Chinese Buddhism). Tokyo: Kyōritsusha.

————. 1930. *Shina bukkyōshi no kenkyū* (Researches on the History of Chinese Buddhism). Tokyo: Kyōritsusha.

Sakamoto Hiroshi. 1977. "D. T. Suzuki and Mysticism." *The Eastern Buddhist* 10, 1: 54–67.

————, trans. and comm. 1983. "Voicing of the Way: Dōgen's *Shōbōgenzō Dōtoku.*" *The Eastern Buddhist* 16, 1: 90–105.

Sanford, James H. 1977. "Shakuhachi Zen: The Fukeshū and Komusō." *Monumenta Nipponica* 32, 4: 411–440.

Sangren, P. Steven. 1984. "Great Traditions and Little Traditions Reconsidered: The Question of Cultural Integration in China." *Journal of Chinese Studies* 1: 1–24.

————. 1987. *History and Magical Power in a Chinese Community.* Stanford: Stanford University Press.

————. 1988. "Rhetoric and the Authority of Ethnography: 'Postmodernism' and the Social Reproduction of Texts." *Current Anthropology* 29, 3: 405–435.

Sargent, Galen Eugene. 1957. "Tchou Hi contre le bouddhisme." In *Mélanges publiés par l'Institut des Hautes Etudes Chinoises,* 1–157. Paris: presses Universitaires de France.

Saussure, Ferdinand de. 1982. *Cours de linguistique générale.* Paris: Payot.

Schipper, Kristofer M. 1976. "The Written Memorial in Taoist Ceremonies." In *Religion and Ritual in Chinese Society,* ed. Arthur P. Wolf, 309–324. Stanford: Stanford University Press.

————. 1982. "The Taoist Body." *History of Religions* 17: 355–386.

————. 1983. *Le corps taoïste.* Paris: Fayard.

Schmidt, J. D. 1974. "Ch'an, Illusion, and Sudden Enlightenment in the Poetry of Yang Wang-li." *T'oung Pao* 60, 4–5: 230–281.

Schurhammer, Georg, S.J. 1929. "Die Disputationen des P. Cosme de Torres S.J. mit den Buddhisten in Yamaguchi im Jahre 1551." *Mitteilungen der Deutschen Gesellschaft für Natur-und Völkerkunde Ostasiens* 21, 1. Tokyo: Gesellschaft für Natur-und Völkerkunde Ostasiens.

————. 1982. *Francis Xavier: His Life, His Times.* Vol. 4: *Japan and China, 1549–1552.* Rome: Jesuit Historical Institute.

Schütte, Josef Franz, S.J. 1980. *Valignano's Mission Principles for Japan.* Trans. John J. Coyne, S.J. 2 vols. St. Louis: Institute of Jesuit Sources.

Schwab, Raymond. 1950. *La renaissance orientale.* Paris: Payot.

————. 1984. *The Oriental Renaissance: Europe's Rediscovery of India and the East, 1680–1880.* Trans. Gene Patterson-Black and Victor Reinking. New York: Columbia University Press.

Seidel, Anna. 1981. "*Kokuhō*: Note à propos du terme 'Trésor national' en Chine et au Japon." *BEFEO* 69: 229–261.

————. 1983. "Imperial Treasures and Taoist Sacraments: Taoist Roots in the Apocrypha." In *Tantric and Taoist Studies in Honour of R. A. Stein,* ed. Michel Strickmann, 2: 291–371. Brussels: Institut Belge des Hautes Etudes Chinoises.

Sekiguchi Shindai. (1957) 1969. *Daruma daishi no kenkyū* (Researches on the Great Master Bodhidharma). Tokyo: Shunjūsha.

———. 1967. *Daruma no kenkyū* (Researches on Bodhidharma). Tokyo: Iwanami shoten.

Shibata Masumi. 1981. "The Diary of a Zen Layman: The Philosopher Nishida Kitarō." *The Eastern Buddhist* 14, 2: 121–131.

Shinagawa Kenritsu Kanazawa Bunko, ed. 1974. *Kanazawa bunko shiryō zensho: Butten, zensekihen I* (Documents of the Kanazawa Library: Buddhist Scriptures, Section on Zen Texts, vol. 1). Yokohama: Shinagawa Kenritsu Kanazawa Bunko.

Smith, Jonathan Z. 1978. *Map is Not Territory: Studies in the History of Religions.* Leiden: E. J. Brill.

———. 1982. *Imagining Religion: From Babylon to Jonestown.* Chicago: University of Chicago Press.

Somers, Robert M. 1986. "Time, Space, and Structure in the Consolidation of the T'ang Dynasty (A.D. 617–700)." *Journal of Asian Studies* 45, 5: 971–994.

Soothill, William Edward. [1923] 1973. *The Three Religions of China: Lectures Delivered at Oxford.* Westport, Conn.: Hyperion Press.

Soper, A. C. No date. "Literary Evidence for Early Buddhist Art in China." *Artibus Asiae,* suppl. 19. Ascona, Switzerland: Artibus Asiae Publishers.

Soyen Shaku. 1971. *Sermons of a Buddhist Abbot.* Trans. D. T. Suzuki. New York: Samuel Weiser.

Soymié, Michel. 1956. "Le Lo-feou chan: Etude de géographie religieuse." *BEFEO* 48: 1–132.

———. 1961. "Sources et sourciers en Chine." *Bulletin de la Maison Franco-Japonaise* (n.s.) 7, 1: 1–56.

Spence, Jonathan D. 1984. *The Memory Palace of Matteo Ricci.* New York: Penguin Books.

Spiro, Melford E. 1982. *Buddhism and Society: A Great Tradition and its Burmese Vicissitudes.* Berkeley: University of California Press.

Staal, Frits. 1985. "Substitutions de paradigmes et religions d'Asie." *Cahiers d'Extrême-Asie* 1: 21–57.

Staggs, Kathleen. 1983. " 'Defend the Nation and Love the Truth': Inoue Enryō and the Revival of Meiji Buddhism." *Monumenta Nipponica* 38, 3: 251–281.

Stambaugh, Joan. 1976. "Time-being: East and West." *The Eastern Buddhist* 9, 2: 107–114.

Starobinski, Jean. 1971. *Les mots sous les mots: Les anagrammes de Ferdinand de Saussure.* Paris: Gallimard.

———. 1979. *Words upon Words: The Anagrams of Ferdinand de Saussure.* Trans. Olivia Emmet. New Haven: Yale University Press.

Staten, Henry. 1984. *Wittgenstein and Derrida.* Lincoln: University of Nebraska Press.

Stein, Sir Aurel. 1964. *On Ancient Central-Asian Tracks: Brief Narrative of Three Expeditions in Innermost Asia and Northwestern China.* Chicago: University of Chicago Press.

Stewart, James Livingstone. 1926. *Chinese Culture and Christianity: A Review of China's Religions and Related Systems from the Christian Standpoint.* New York: Fleming H. Revell Company.

Stock, Bryan. 1983. *The Implications of Literacy: Written Language and Models of*

Interpretation in the Eleventh and Twelfth Centuries. Princeton: Princeton University Press.

Stone, Jackie. 1990. "A Vast and Grave Task: Interwar Buddhist Studies as an Expression of Japan's Envisioned Global Role." In *Japanese Intellectuals During the Interwar Years,* ed. J. Thomas Rimer, 217–233. Princeton: Princeton University Press.

Strauss, Leo. 1979. "The Mutual Influence of Theology and Philosophy." *The Independent Journal of Philosophy* 3: 111–118.

Strickmann, Michel. 1980. "History, Anthropology, and Chinese Religions." *HJAS* 40: 201–248.

———. 1981. *Le taoïsme du Mao chan: Chronique d'une révélation.* Paris: Presses Universitaires de France.

———. 1990. "Chinese Poetry and Prophecy: The Written Oracle in Eastern Asia." Forthcoming in *Mélanges chinois et bouddhiques.*

Stroumsa, Gedaliahu G. 1990. "*Caro salutis cardo*: Shaping the Person in Early Christian Thought." *History of Religions* 30, 1: 25–50.

Sugimoto Shunryū. [1938] 1982. *Zōtei Tōjō shitsunai kirigami narabini sanwa no kenkyū* (Researches on the Esoteric *Kirigami* and *Sanwa* of the Sōtō Sect). Tokyo: Sōtōshū Shūmuchō.

Sullivan, Lawrence E. 1986. "Sound and Senses: Toward a Hermeneutics of Performance." *History of Religions* 26, 1: 1–33.

Suzuki, Daisetsu (D. T.) [1930] 1977. *Studies in the Lankavatara Sutra.* Taibei: Southern Materials Center.

———. 1936. *Kokan Shōshitsu issho oyobi kaisetsu furoku: Daruma no zenpō to shisō oyobi sono ta* (A Critical Edition of the *Lost Writings of Shaoshi,* with an Explanation). 2 vols. Osaka: Ataka bukkyō bunko.

———. 1949. *The Zen Doctrine of No Mind: The Significance of the Sūtra of Huineng Wei-lang.* London: Rider and Company.

———. 1949–1953. *Essays in Zen Buddhism.* 3 vols. London: Rider and Company.

———. 1953. "Zen: A Reply to Hu Shih." *Philosophy East and West* 3, 1: 25–46.

———. [1957] 1969. *Mysticism: Christian and Buddhist.* New York: MacMillan.

———. [1959] 1970. *Zen and Japanese Culture.* Princeton: Princeton University Press.

———. 1960. "How to Read Nishida." In *A Study of Good,* ed. Nishida Kitarō, iii–iv. Trans. V. H. Viglielmo. Tokyo: Ministry of Education.

———. 1961. "A Reply from D. T. Suzuki." *Encounter* 17: 55–58.

———. 1968–1971. *Suzuki Daisetsu Zenshū* (The Complete Works of Suzuki Daisetsu). Ed. Hisamatsu Shin'ichi, Yamaguchi Susumu, and Furuta Shōkin. Tokyo: Iwanami shoten.

———. 1972. *Japanese Spirituality.* Trans. Norman Waddell. Comp. Japanese Commission for UNESCO. Tokyo: Japanese Society for the Promotion of Science.

———. 1976. "Dōgen, Hakuin, Bankei: Three Types of Thought in Japanese Buddhism." *The Eastern Buddhist* 9, 1: 1–17; 9, 2: 1–20.

Suzuki Kakuzen, Sakurai Shūyū, Sakai Tokugen, and Ishikawa Rikisan, eds. 1989. *Dōgen zenji zenshū* (The Complete Works of Dōgen). Vol. 5. Tokyo: Shunjūsha.

Tada, Michitaro. 1981. "Sacred and Profane: The Division of a Japanese Space." *Zinbun* 17: 17–38.

Tambiah, Stanley J. 1968. "The Magical Power of Words." *Man* (n. s.) 3: 175–208.

———. 1981. "A Performative Approach to Ritual." In *Proceedings of the British Academy* 65: 113–169. New York: Oxford University Press.

———. 1984. *The Buddhist Saints of the Forest and the Cult of Amulets*. Cambridge: Cambridge University Press.

Tanaka Ryōshō. 1981. "Relations between the Buddhist Sects in the T'ang Dynasty through the Ms. P. 3913." *Journal Asiatique* 269: 163–169.

Taylor, Mark C. 1984. *Erring: A Postmodern A/theology*. Chicago. University of Chicago Press.

Tedlock, Dennis. 1983. *The Spoken Word and the Work of Interpretation*. Philadelphia: University of Pennsylvania Press.

Teiser, Stephen F. 1988. *The Ghost Festival in Medieval China*. Princeton: Princeton University Press.

Terada Tōru. 1974. *Dōgen no gengo uchū* (The Linguistic Universe of Dōgen). Tokyo: Iwanami shoten.

Terada Tōru, and Mizuno Yaeko, eds. 1975. *Dōgen*. 2 vols. Tokyo: Iwanami shoten.

Thelle, Notto R. 1984. "'The Flower Blooms at the Cliff's Edge': Profile of Nishitani Keiji, a Thinker between East and West." *Journal of American Religion* 13, 3: 47–56.

Tillich, Paul, and Hisamatsu Shin'ichi. 1971–1973. "Dialogues, East and West: Conversations between Dr. Paul Tillich and Dr. Hisamatsu Shin'ichi." *The Eastern Buddhist* 4, 2: 89–107; 5, 2: 107–128; 6, 2: 87–114.

Todorov, Tzvetan. 1978. *Symbolisme et interprétation*. Paris: Seuil.

———. 1984a. *Critique de la critique: Un roman d'apprentissage*. Paris: Seuil.

———. 1984b. *Mikhail Bakhtin: The Dialogical Principle*. Trans. Wlad Godzich. Minneapolis: University of Minnesota Press.

———. 1987. *Literature and Its Theorists: A Personal View of Twentieth-Century Criticism*. Trans. Catherine Porter. Ithaca: Cornell University Press.

Tokiwa Gishin, trans. 1973. *A Dialogue on the Contemplation-Extinguished: Translated from the Chüeh-kuan lun, an Early Chineze Zen Text from Tunhuang*. Kyoto: Institute for Zen Studies.

Tominaga Nakamoto. 1982. *Shutsujō kōgo*. Ed. Kyōdō Jikō. Tokyo: Ryōbunkan.

———. 1990. *Emerging from Meditation*. Trans. Michael Pye. Honolulu: University of Hawaii Press.

Tracy, David. 1981. *The Analogical Imagination: Christian Theology and the Culture of Pluralism*. New York: Crossroad.

———. 1987. *Plurality and Ambiguity: Hermeneutics, Religion, Hope*. San Francisco: Harper & Row.

Trigault, Nicholas, S.J. , trans. 1615. *De Christiana expeditione apud Sinas suscepta ab societate Jesu ex P. Matthaei Ricci ejusdem societatis commentarius*. Agustae Vindekorum: C. Mangium. (See Gallagher 1953).

Trungpa, Chogyam, and Rechung Rinpoche. 1988. *Myth of Freedom: And the Way of Meditation*. Ed. John Baker and Marvin Casper. Berkeley: Shambala.

Tsuji Zennosuke. 1944–1955. *Nihon bukkyōshi* (A History of Japanese Buddhism). 10 vols. Tokyo: Iwanami shoten.

Tsukamoto Zenryū, Shibuyama Zenkei, and Nishitani Keiji. 1975. "Dialogue: Chinese Zen." *The Eastern Buddhist* 8, 2: 66–93.

Tsunoda Ryusaku, Wm. Theodore de Bary, and Donald Keene, eds. 1964. *Sources of Japanese Tradition.* 2 vols. New York: Columbia University Press.

Tuan, Yi-fu. 1977. *Space and Place: The Perspective of Experience.* Minneapolis: University of Minnesota Press.

Turner, Terence. 1977. "Narrative Structure and Mythopoesis: A Critique and Reformulation of Structuralist Concepts of Myth, Narrative and Poetics." *Arethusa* 10, 1: 103–163.

Turner, Victor. 1969. *The Ritual Process: Structure and Anti-structure.* Chicago: University of Chicago Press.

———. 1974. *Dramas, Fields, and Metaphors: Symbolic Action in Human Society.* Ithaca: Cornell University Press.

Tyler, Royall. 1984. "The Tokugawa Peace and Popular Religion: Suzuki Shōsan, Kakugyō Tōbutsu, and Jikigyō Miroku." In *Confucianism and Tokugawa Culture,* ed. Peter Nosco, 92–119. Princeton: Princeton University Press.

Ueda Shizuteru. 1983. "Ascent and Descent: Zen Buddhism in Comparison with Meister Eckhart." *The Eastern Buddhist* 16, 1: 52–73; 2: 72–91.

Ui Hakuju. [1935–1943] 1966. *Zenshūshi kenkyū* (Researches on the History of the Chan School). 3 vols. Tokyo: Iwanami shoten.

Valéry, Paul. 1970. *Analects.* Trans. Stuart Gilbert. Bollingen Series XLV–14. Princeton: Princeton University Press.

———. 1973–1974. *Cahiers.* 2 vols. Bibliothèque de la Pléiade. Paris: Gallimard.

Valignano, Alexandro, S.J. [1583] 1954. *Sumario de las Cosas de Japón.* Ed. José Luis Alvarez-Taladriz. *Monumenta Nipponica* Monographs 9. Tokyo: Sophia University.

———. 1990. *Les Jésuites au Japon: Relation missionnaire (1583).* Trans. J. Bésineau, S.J. Collection Christus 72. Paris: Desclée de Brouwer.

Vandermeersch, Léon. 1974. "De la tortue à l'achillée." In *Divination et rationalité,* ed. Jean-Pierre Vernant et al. , 29–51. Paris: Seuil.

van Gulik, Robert. 1956. *Siddham: An Essay on the History of Sanskrit Studies in China and Japan.* Nagpur: Arya Bharati Mudranalaya.

Venturi, Pietro Tacchi, S.J. , ed. 1913. *Opere Storiche,* vol. 2, *Le Lettere dalla China.* Macerata.

Vernant, Jean-Pierre. 1965. *Mythe et pensée chez les Grecs: Etudes de psychologie historique.* Paris: Maspero. 2 vols.

———. 1979. *Religions, histoires, raisons.* Paris: Maspero.

Vernant, Jean-Pierre, et al. , eds. 1974. *Divination et rationalité.* Paris: Seuil.

Veyne, Paul. 1984. *Writing History.* Trans. Mina Moore-Rinvolucri. Middletown: Wesleyan University Press.

———. 1988. *Did the Greeks Believe in their Myths? An Essay on the Constitutive Imagination.* Chicago: University of Chicago Press.

de Visser, M. W. 1913. *The Dragon in China and Japan.* Amsterdam: Johannes Müller.

Vissière, Isabelle, and Jean-Louis Vissière, eds. 1979. *Lettres édifiantes et curieuses de Chine.* Paris: Garnier.

Vogel, Jean Philippe. 1926. *Indian Serpent-Lore or the Nāgas in Hindu Legend and Art.* London: Arthur Probsthain.

Voltaire. [1764] 1962. *Philosophical Dictionary*. Trans. Peter Gay. New York: Basic Books.

de Voragine, Jacobus. 1900. *The Golden Legend: Or, Lives of the Saints*. Englished [*sic*] by William Caxton. The Temple Classics. London: J. M. Dent and Co.

Waddell, Norman, trans. 1977. "Dōgen's *Hōkyō-ki*." *The Eastern Buddhist* 10, 2: 102–139; 11, 1: 66–84.

———. 1979. "Being Time: Dōgen's *Shōbōgenzō Uji*." *The Eastern Buddhist* 12, 1: 114–129.

Waddell, Norman, and Masao Abe, trans. 1971a. "Dōgen's *Bendōwa*." *The Eastern Buddhist* 4, 1: 88–115.

———. 1971b. " 'One Bright Pearl': Dōgen's *Shōbōgenzō Ikka Myōju*." *The Eastern Buddhist* 4, 2: 108–118.

———. 1972. "*Genjōkōan*." *The Eastern Buddhist* 5, 2: 129–140.

Waldenfels, Hans. 1966. "Absolute Nothingness: Preliminary Considerations on a Central Notion in the Philosophy of Nishida Kitarō and the Kyōto School." *Monumenta Nipponica* 21, 3–4: 354–391.

———. 1980. *Absolute Nothingness: Foundations of a Buddhist-Christian Dialogue*. New York: Paulist Press.

Waley, Arthur. 1949. *The Life and Times of Po Chü-i, 772–846 A.D.* New York: Macmillan.

———. 1955. "History and Religion." *Philosophy East and West* 5: 75–78.

Wargo, Robert J. J. 1972. "The Logic of Bashō and the Concept of Nothingness in the Philosophy of Nishida Kitarō." Ann Arbor: University Microfilms International.

Watson, Burton, trans. 1968. *The Complete Works of Chuang Tzu*. New York: Columbia University Press.

———. 1988. "Zen Poetry." In *Zen Tradition and Transformation: A Sourcebook by Contemporary Zen Masters and Scholars*, ed. Kenneth Kraft. New York: Grove Press.

Weber, Max. 1951. *The Religion of China: Confucianism and Taoism*. Trans. H. H. Gerth. Glencoe, Ill.: Free Press.

———. 1964. *The Sociology of Religion*. Boston: Beacon Press.

Welbon, Richard. 1968. *The Buddhist Nirvāṇa and its Western Interpreters*. Chicago: University of Chicago Press.

Welch, Holmes H. 1968. *The Buddhist Revival in China*. Cambridge: Harvard University Press.

Welch, Holmes, and Anna Seidel, eds. 1979. *Facets of Taoism: Essays in Chinese Religion*. New Haven: Yale University Press.

Werblowsky, R. J. Zwi. 1986. "The Western Image of Chinese Religion from Leibniz to De Groot." *Diogenes* 133: 113–121.

White, Hayden. 1973. *Metahistory: The Historical Imagination in Nineteenth-Century Europe*. Baltimore: Johns Hopkins University Press.

———. 1978. *Tropics of Discourse: Essays in Cultural Criticism*. Baltimore: Johns Hopkins University Press.

———. 1987. *The Content of the Form: Narrative Discourse and Historical Representation*. Baltimore: Johns Hopkins University Press.

Whitehead, James D. , Yu-ming Shaw, and Norman J. Girardot, eds. 1979. *China and Christianity: Historical and Future Encounters*. Notre Dame: University of Notre Dame Press.

Wieger, Léon. [1927] 1969. *A History of the Religious Beliefs and Philosophical Opinions in China from the Beginning to the present Time*. Trans. Edward Chalmers Werner. New York: Paragon Book Reprint Corp.

Wittgenstein, Ludwig. 1958. *Philosophical Investigations: The English Text of the Third Edition*. New York: MacMillan.

Wolf, Arthur, ed. 1974. *Religion and Ritual in Chinese Society*. Stanford: Stanford University Press.

Wright, Dale S. 1992. "Historical Understanding: The Ch'an Buddhist Transmission Narratives and Modern Historiography." *History and Theory* 31, 1: 37–46.

Wu, Pei-yi. 1975. "The Spiritual Autobiography of Te-ch'ing." In *The Unfolding of Neo-Confucianism*, ed. Wm. Theodore de Bary, 67–92. New York: Columbia University Press.

———. 1978. "Self-examination and Confession of Sins in Traditional China." *HJAS* 39, 1: 5–38.

———. 1990. *The Confucian's Progress: Autobiographical Writings in Traditional China*. Princeton: Princeton University Press.

Xavier, St. Francis. 1944–1945. *Epistolae S. Francisci Xaverii aliaque euis scripta*. Ed. George Schurhammer and Joseph Wicki. 2 vols. Rome: Historical Institute of the Society of Jesus.

Xu Guolin. 1937. *Dunhuang shishi xiejing tiji yu Dunhuang zalu* (A List of Titles of Dunhuang Manuscripts and Varia from Dunhuang). 2 vols. Shanghai: Shangwu yinshuguan.

Xu Yun. 1988. *Empty Cloud: The Autobiography of the Chinese Zen Master Xu Yun*. Trans. Charles Luk. Longmead: Element Books.

Yabuki Keiki. 1930. *Meisha yoin* (Echoes from Mingsha). Tokyo: Iwanami shoten.

———. 1933. *Meisha yoin kaisetsu* (An Explanation of *Meisha yoin*). Tokyo: Iwanami shoten.

Yamaguchi Sakae. 1973. "Ko Teki no chūgoku zenshūshi ni tsuite" (Concerning Hu Shih's History of the Chan School in China). *Junsei tanki daigaku kenkyū kiyō* 3: 63–76.

Yampolsky, Philip B. 1967. *The Platform Sūtra of the Sixth Patriarch*. New York: Columbia University Press.

Yanagida Seizan. 1961. "*Zenmonkyō* ni tsuite" (On the *Chanmen jing*). In *Tsukamoto hakase shōju kinen: Bukkyō shigaku ronshū*, 869–882. Tokyo: Tsukamoto hakase shōju kinenkai.

———. 1963. "*Den hōbōki* to sono sakusha" (The *Chuan fabao ji* and its Author). *Zengaku kenkyū* 53: 45–71.

———. 1967. *Shoki zenshū shisho no kenkyū* (Researches on the Historiographical Works of the Early Chan School). Kyoto: Hōzōkan.

———. 1969. *Daruma no goroku* (The Recorded Sayings of Bodhidharma). Tokyo: Chikuma shobō.

———. 1971. *Shoki no zenshi 1: Ryōgashijiki; Den hōbō ki* (The History of Early Chan I: *Lengqie shizi ji; Chuan fabao ji*). Tokyo: Chikuma shobō.

———. 1974. "Hokushū zen no shisō" (The Thought of Northern Chan). *Zen bunka kenkyūsho kiyō* 6: 67–104.

———. 1976. *Shoki no zenshi 2: Rekidai hōbōki* (The History of Early Chan II: *Lidai fabao ji*). Tokyo: Chikuma shobō.

———. 1978. "Shinzoku tōshi no keifu: Jo (1)" (The Lineage of the "Histories of the Lamp). *Zengaku kenkyū* 59: 1–39.

———. 1982. "Kūbyō no mondai" (The Problem of *Śūnyata* Sickness"). In *Bukkyō shisō*, ed. Bukkyō Shisō Kenkyūkai, 7: 755–798. Kyoto: Heirakuji shoten.

———. 1983a. "The *Li-tai fa-pao chi* and the Ch'an Doctrine of Sudden Awakening." Trans. Carl Bielefeldt. In *Early Ch'an in China and Tibet*, ed. Whalen Lai and Lewis R. Lancaster, 13–49. Berkeley: Asian Humanities Press.

———. 1983b. "The 'Recorded Sayings' Texts of Chinese Ch'an Buddhism." Trans. John R. McRae. In *Early Ch'an in China and Tibet*, ed. Whalen Lai and Lewis R. Lancaster, 185–205. Berkeley: Asian Humanities Press.

———. 1984a. "Zen bukkyō no jikanron" (The Zen Discourse on Time). In *Kōza Nihon shisō*, 4: 79–131. Tokyo: Tōdai shuppankai.

———. 1984b. "Dōgen to Chūgoku bukkyō" (Dōgen and Chinese Buddhism). *Zen bunka kenkyūsho kiyo* 13: 3–128.

———. 1985. "Goroku no rekishi: Zen bunken no seiritsu shiteki kenkyū" (A History of the "Recorded Sayings" Genre). *Tōhō gakuhō* 57: 211–663.

Yang Hsüan-chih. 1984. *A Record of Buddhist Monasteries in Lo-yang*. Trans. Wang Yi-t'ung. Princeton: Princeton University Press.

Yates, Frances. 1966. *The Art of Memory*. Chicago: University of Chicago Press.

Yokoi, Yuho. 1976. *Zen Master Dōgen: An Introduction with Selected Writings*. New York: Weatherhill.

Yusa Michiko. 1986–1987. "The Logic of *Topos* and the Religious Worldview." *The Eastern Buddhist* (n.s.) 19, 2: 1–29; 20, 1: 81–119.

Yusa, Michiko. 1991. "Nishida and the Question of Nationalism." *Monumenta Nipponica* 46, 2: 203–209.

Yu, Antony, trans. 1977–1983. *The Journey to the West*. 4 vols. Chicago: University of Chicago Press.

Yü, Chün-fang. 1981. *The Renewal of Buddhism in China: Chu-hung and the Late Ming Synthesis*. New York: Columbia University Press.

———. 1982. "Chung-feng Ming-pen and Ch'an Buddhism in the Yüan." In *Yüan Thought: Chinese Thought and Religion Under the Mongols*, ed. Hok-lam Chan and Wm. Theodore de Bary, 419–477. New York: Columbia University Press.

Zhang Longxi. 1985. "The *Tao* and the *Logos*: Notes on Derrida's Critique of Logocentrism." *Critical Inquiry* 11: 385–398.

Zürcher, Erik. 1985. "The Lord of Heaven and the Demons: Strange Stories from a late Ming Christian Manuscript." In *Religion und Philosophie in Ostasien: Festschrift für Hans Steininger*, ed. Gert Naundorf, Karl-Heinz Pohl, and Hans-Hermann Schmidt, 359–375. Würzburg: Königshausen and Neumann.

INDEX

agent: in Buddhism, 263; in Western culture, 248, 263
Althusser, Louis, 3
Ampère, Jean-Jacques, 21
anátman theory, 251–254
Anesaki Masaharu, 52–53
Annen, 179
apocrypha (in Chan), 238–239
Arima Tatsuo, 77, 80
Augé, Marc, 9, 146
Austin, J. L., 213, 232–233
author, 128, 139
autobiography, 260
Avataṃsaka-sūtra, 116

Bai Juyi, 205
Baizhang Huaihai: and the fox, 176; and the Pure Rule of Chan, 272
Bakhtin, Mikhail, 8, 112, 163
Baozhi, 132
Barthélémy Saint-Hilaire, Jules, 36–39
Barthes, Roland, 197, 198; on *kōan,* 215; on meaning, 143; on realistic effect, 111
Bayle, Pierre, 32–33
Bellah, Robert, 265–266
Benjamin, Walter, 141
Benveniste, Emile, 197–198, 201, 248
Berling, Judith, 255–256
Bernard-Maître, Henri: on Chan Vedantism, 43; on Jesuits, 21
Bloch, Ernst, 175
Bodhidharma, 181; and the Apostle Thomas, 45–49; biography of, 126–129; and Bodhiruci, 132–133; Daoxuan on, 127; de Groot on, 48; and Fu Xi, 132; and Huike, 172; Johnston on, 49–50; Kokan Shiren on, 188; and Liang Wudi, 199; poisoning of, 141–142; prediction of, 183; Sekiguchi on, 107; and Sengchou, 130–131; Tominaga Nakamoto on, 49, 101; and wall-contemplation, 59, 127, 172; Wieger on, 41–42
Bodhidharma's legend, structural analysis of, 129–135
Bodhiruci, 122–133, 141–142

Boon, James, 112
Borges, Jorge Luis, 128, 194
Bourdieu, Pierre, 4–5, 59, 88, 161; on objectivism, 111
Braudel, Fernand, 122
Buddhism: Barthélémy Saint-Hilaire on, 36–38; Bayle on, 32–33; Burnouf on, 39; du Halde on, 29, 30–31; Edkins on, 41; Flaubert on, 39; Hegel on, 35; as humanism, 99; La Croze on, 32; as nihilism, 36–38; as quietism, 29–34; Rémusat on, 40; Ricci on, 20–21, 24–29; Taishō revival of, 100
Burnouf, Eugène, 39

Caoxi, 172, 173
Certeau, Michel de, 170; on hagiography, 129; on objectivism, 111–112
Chan: antinomianism, 58, 265, 270, 272; dialogues, 211–214, 239; foundational, 147; hermeneutics of, 238; humanism in, 72–73; identity of, with poetry, 208–209; individualism in, 267–268; as Jainism, 43–44; literature in, 210–211; logocentrism of, 220–225; mysticism in, 40–41, 44, 61–63, 81; Northern, 157, 171; orality in, 226–233; patriarchal lineage of, 47, 101, 130; rhetoric of, 237–238; and Theravāda, 44–45; tradition in, 118–121; as Vedantism, 41–43; writing in, 233–234
Chan/Zen meditation: Frois on, 18; Kaempfer on, 33
Changzong Zhaojue, 204
Chanmen jing, 117, 238
Charles, Michel, 237
Chinese Rites controversy, 26
Chuan fabao ji, 180
Claudel, Paul, 25, 50–51
Collins, Stevens, 251, 252
comparativism, 10–11, 61, 62, 273–274
confession: in Chan, 258–259; in Christianity, 258
Confucianism: criticism of Buddhism, 31; on writing, 222–223
Couplet, Philippe (Jesuit missionary), 31